CHRISTIANITY AND CHINESE CULTURE

This book is due for return on or before the last date shown below.

Christianity and Chinese Culture

Edited by

Miikka Ruokanen and Paulos Huang

West Malvern Road
West Malvern
Worcestershire
WR14 4AY
Tel: 0845 302 6758
Fax: 0845 302 6759

WILLIAM B. EERDMANS PUBLISHING COMPANY
GRAND RAPIDS, MICHIGAN / CAMBRIDGE, U.K.

Published 2010 by
Wm. B. Eerdmans Publishing Co.
2140 Oak Industrial Drive N.E., Grand Rapids, Michigan 49505 /
P.O. Box 163, Cambridge CB3 9PU U.K.

Printed in the United States of America

16 15 14 13 12 11 10   7 6 5 4 3 2 1

Library of Congress Cataloging-in-Publication Data

Christianity and Chinese Culture: a Sino-Nordic Conference
on Chinese Contextual Theology (2003 : Lapland, Finland)
    [Jidu zong jiao yu Zhongguo wen hua. English]
    Christianity and Chinese culture / edited by Miikka Ruokanen and Paulos Huang.
        p.   cm.
    In English, translated from Chinese, some of which was translated from other languages.
    Includes bibliographical references.
    ISBN 978-0-8028-6556-4 (pbk.: alk. paper)
    1. Christianity and culture — China — Congresses.
    I. Ruokanen, Miikka.   II. Huang, Paulos Zhanzhu.   III. Title.

BR1285.C57313   2003
261.0951 — dc22
                                                        2010037792

www.eerdmans.com

Contents

PREFACE   ix

CONTRIBUTORS   xviii

I. CHRISTIANITY IN RELATION TO THE CHINESE RELIGIOUS TRADITION

1. The Goodness of Human Nature and Original Sin:
   A Point of Convergence in Chinese and Western Cultures   3
   Zhao Dunhua

   Response   12
   Miikka Ruokanen

2. Sin and Evil in Christian and Confucian Perspectives   22
   Zhang Qingxiong

   Response   37
   Diane B. Obenchain

   Response   51
   Svein Rise

Contents

3. The Compatibility of Christianity with the Traditional
   Chinese Religions in Their Theories of the Divinity   56

   He Guanghu

   Response   70

   Paulos Huang

4. Reasons for an Easy Access of Christianity into Chinese Culture:
   Cultural Relativity between Religion and Morality on the Basis
   of the Method of Matteo Ricci's Missionary Work in China   85

   Wan Junren

5. *Ren* as a Fundamental Motif and the Promise and Problem
   of a Contextual Theology of an *Agape-Ren* Synthesis:
   A Dialogue with Anders Nygren   102

   Lo Ping-cheung

   Response   120

   You Bin

6. Dialogue between Christianity and Taoism:
   The Case of Lin Yutang   124

   He Jianming

7. Reflections on the History of Buddhist-Christian
   Encounter in Modern China   145

   Lai Pan-chiu

   Response   160

   Jorgen Skov Sorensen

   Response   166

   Jyri Komulainen

8. The Impact of Contemporary Chinese Folk Religions
   on Christianity   170

   Gao Shining

II. CHRISTIANITY IN THE CONTEXT OF MODERN CHINA

9. Comprehensive Theology: An Attempt to Combine
   Christianity with Chinese Culture   185
   Zhuo Xinping

   Response   193
   Notto R. Thelle

10. The Contextualization of Chinese Christian Theology
    and Its Main Concerns   197
    Yang Huilin

    Response   205
    Thor Strandenaes

11. How Do Social and Psychological Needs Impact the
    Existence and Growth of Christianity in Modern China?   211
    Li Pingye

    Response   228
    Vladimir Fedorov

12. Eliminating Five Misunderstandings about Christianity
    in Chinese Academic Circles   234
    Wang Xiaochao

    Response   254
    Choong Chee Pang

13. The Faith of Chinese Urban Christians: A Case Study of Beijing   259
    Gao Shining

    Response   273
    Zhang Minghui

14. The Position of Religion in Chinese Society   276
    Li Qiuling

    Response   287
    Fredrik Fällman

    Response   291
    Birger Nygaard

Contents

III. CHALLENGES TO THE CONTEMPORARY
CHINESE PROTESTANT CHURCH

15. The Basis for the Reconstruction of Chinese
Theological Thinking   297
   Deng Fucun
Response   309
   Chen Xun
Response   312
   Gerald H. Anderson

16. Call for Dialogue and Cooperation:
Reflections on the *Jianshe* or the Reconstruction
of Theological Thinking   319
   Zhu Xiaohong
Response   336
   Sun Yi

17. Christ and Culture: A Reflection by a Chinese Christian   339
   Chen Yongtao

18. A Chinese Christian's Reading of Two Ethical
Themes of *Zhuangzi*   355
   Lin Manhong

19. A Flourishing Discipline: Reflections on the Study
of Christianity in Academic Institutions in China Today   367
   Wu Xiaoxin

Preface

The book at hand contains papers that were given in a very special theological conference, "Christianity and Chinese Culture: A Sino-Nordic Conference on Chinese Contextual Theology," held in Lapland, Finland, August 13-17, 2003.[1] This was the first time that a widely representative group of Chinese university scholars and theologians of the Protestant Church of China had joined around the same table to discuss how Protestant Christianity is reacting to the challenges arising from traditional Chinese culture and from the present historical and cultural situation.

The aim of the conference was to promote academic and theological reflection on the formation of Protestant Christianity in the context of traditional Chinese culture, and in the context of modern Chinese culture and society. Our purpose was also to foster theological discussion between Chinese academic specialists of Christianity and theologians from the Chinese Protestant Church, in critical discussion together with theologians from northern Europe and from other countries. All of the conference papers were given by Chinese scholars and theologians. Nordic and other scholars

1. The conference was organized by the North European NIME research organization (Nordic Institute for Missionary and Ecumenical Research) in cooperation with the Department of Systematic Theology, Faculty of Theology, University of Helsinki, and the Union for Christian Culture of Finland. NIME includes members from all the Nordic theological faculties. The conference was financed by the Academy of Finland. Financial help was also received from Areopagos, the Finnish Evangelical-Lutheran Mission, and the Finnish Bible Society. The Chinese version of the conference book was published under the title *Jidu zongjiao yu Zhongguo wenhua* by China Social Sciences Press, Beijing, 2004.

acted as respondents to their papers. After the conference we invited additional papers from Chinese scholars and theologians to fill some gaps in the field of topics.[2]

We are very happy that leading scholars of the Christian religion from Chinese academic circles as well as a number of leading theologians of the Chinese Protestant Church made their contributions to this conference and to the book at hand. For a long time there has been a feeling on both sides that this kind of encounter between *akademia* and *ekklesia* is very much needed.

Toward a New Cultural System

Every day we hear news about how China, the country with the largest population in the world, is experiencing unforeseen economic growth, and many social, cultural, and other changes are taking place there at an accelerating speed. According to analysts of various fields, this changing China will have an increasingly influential role in the world. The future belongs to China and to the Chinese.

The great changes taking place in Chinese society are accompanied by "a transformation of a new cultural system" in modern China, as was pointed out in the Sino-Nordic conference. The system of beliefs, ethics, and values among the Chinese is in the process of formation. The socialist value and moral system is on the losing side, whereas traditional Chinese beliefs and morals, as well as many new ideas, are gradually filling the vacuum.

Confucian ethics, linked with some religious ideas, is the classical backbone of Chinese morals. Today Confucianism as a moral system is experienc-

---

2. Most of the papers of the present volume were given at the 2003 conference. The papers added afterward are:
- "Dialogue between Christianity and Taoism: The Case of Lin Yutang" by He Jianming
- "The Impact of Contemporary Chinese Folk Religions on Christianity" by Gao Shining
- "Christ and Culture: A Reflection by a Chinese Christian" by Chen Yongtao
- "A Chinese Christian's Reading of Two Ethical Themes of *Zhuangzi*" by Lin Manhong
- "A Flourishing Discipline: Reflections on the Study of Christianity in Academic Institutions in China Today" by Wu Xiaoxin.

All the papers presented at the conference received two responses from international experts. A selection of these responses is published in this volume. Please note: the responses refer to the original text of the main papers as they were given in the conference; the actual wording may differ slightly from the published version, which has undergone some editing and elaboration.

ing a renaissance in China. Buddhism, the religion with the largest number of followers, is thriving in China. The complex phenomenon of Chinese folk or popular religion, often linked with elements of traditional Taoism, is becoming more and more influential, especially among rural people.[3] All the religions in China are winning new followers in increasing numbers, Protestant Christianity being the fastest-growing among them. According to some scholars, Christianity has already become an important factor in reshaping Chinese values and morals. Christianity is more influential in China than ever before.

In February 2007 the East China Normal University published figures on Protestant Christianity in China: there are some 20 million believers in the registered congregations and another 20 million in the nonregistered or so-called house churches. Out of the total population of China, about 3 percent are Protestant Christians.[4] In total, some two million adults receive Christian baptism each year. According to the same source, 31 percent of the Chinese over sixteen years of age say they are religious. This figure is about three times bigger than the official government figure on religion.

Many Chinese intellectuals are worried about how the hard values of the market economy are penetrating modern China, leaving the masses of the poor without attention and care. Growing concentration on money and individualism increases indifference to the well-being of society's weakest. To counterbalance the bad effects of the market economy, modern Confucian-oriented intellectuals are trying to revive the Chinese people's soul by recovering the spirit of Chinese culture, the original spirit of Confucianism.

Others believe that China should develop herself as an open and pluralistic culture that can combine elements from various intellectual traditions: Confucianism, Taoism, Buddhism, Marxism, and Christianity. Seeking a common ground of humanity and morality can contribute to social justice and social harmony. The consensus is that religion is the very root of human

---

3. We decided to write *Taoism,* not *Daoism,* when naming this ancient Chinese philosophy/religion. This is the normal expression in the English language. The most important Taoist concept, however, will be spelled *Dao,* following the *pinyin* spelling system of modern Chinese. The present volume employs *pinyin* whenever possible; some names and expressions commonly used outside of mainland China may use another spelling system.

4. According to scholars of religion in China, there are some 12 million Catholics, half of whom belong to the public "patriotic" church and the other half to the more-or-less underground church. Around 1 percent of the Chinese are Catholic. For the sake of simplicity, the present book concentrates on the relationship between the Protestant version of Christianity and Chinese culture. In China, Catholicism (*Tianzhu jiao,* "religion of the Heavenly Lord") and Protestantism (*Jidu jiao,* "religion of Christ") are seen as different religions.

culture; therefore, any cultural renewal should be combined with religious and spiritual dimensions.

A Need for a Spiritual Culture

Many Chinese scholars believe that both Confucianism and Christianity might have an important role in the moral reconstruction of modern China. In the field of ethics, Confucianism and Christianity have a lot in common; they ask similar moral questions. The "moral ethics of benevolence" in Confucianism and the "religious ethics of love" in Christianity are not far from each other. Confucianism and Christianity both also emphasize the intrinsic goodness of all created nature — though their conception of the extent to which evil has spoiled this nature may differ greatly.

Implied in the conference papers at hand is the notion that some kind of cooperation of these two thinking systems could benefit both. On the one hand, human-oriented Confucianism needs the religious vitalism of Christianity; Confucianism alone cannot meet the deep religious needs of people, such as answering to the questions about the ultimate reality, the meaning of existence, our final destiny, or the absolute value of life. On the other hand, Christianity can never become a really significant religion in China unless it is inculturated into the overall Confucian context of Chinese culture. In order to become deeply contextualized, Chinese Christianity needs to respect traditional Chinese culture, its way of thinking, its folk customs, and its concept of political authority.

One of the leading themes in the Sino-Nordic conference was the question about the need for a "spiritual culture" in modern China. It seems that any moral or ethical system, in order to be objective, binding, and motivating, needs some kind of link to a religious or spiritual realm, or to the idea of "the holy." History has shown that any sort of materialism or atheism works poorly as a basis for morality. An ethical system linked with transcendence increases the universal and obligatory nature of that system, and an ideal of an absolute transcendent goodness offers the basis for the progress of morality. The true validation of a system of ethics cannot be just an agreement among human beings; it requires a connection with the concept of some suprahuman value and goodness or with the concept of the ultimate value of life. In other words, there is a strong link between secular values and holy values.

And even more important, the religious or spiritual link is necessary for the practical implementation of morality. It is obvious that the human being exists in such a condition of weakness that often he does not follow the rational moral principles he knows to be true — he needs some other type of motivation and energizing to do the good and the right. It seems that all moral systems — whether secular or religious — face a similar problem: how to make moral life a reality, or "how to keep the Heavenly degrees."[5] This perennial question is an urgent problem in modern China as well.

The Church Encounters an Old Culture and a Modern Society

The Chinese Protestant Church, being one of the fastest-growing Christian churches in history, is faced by several challenges. First, how to adapt her message and life into the still strongly influential traditional Chinese cultural ways of thinking and ways of life. Second, how to adapt herself to modern Chinese society, which is a mixture of political socialism and market economy capitalism. Third, how to overcome the syncretistic influences of rising folk religions; in many places Christianity and traditional popular beliefs and practices are mixed. Fourth, how does Chinese Christianity encounter and enter into dialogue with the other lively world religions in China — Buddhism, Taoism, and Islam?

As the content of the book at hand illustrates, many traditional Chinese cultural, religious, and spiritual concepts and practices are a reality in the lives of Chinese Christian believers. The encounter between the two great spiritual heritages is taking place anyway, even within the church herself — consciously or unconsciously.

In the Sino-Nordic conference we paid little attention to the reasons for the phenomenal growth of the church — the vacuum of beliefs and values is certainly one of them. Our focus was on the question of both inculturation and contextualization: how to adapt Christian teaching to both the cultural tradition and the modern social, political, and economic context of China. At present, the Chinese Protestant Church is tackling these problems in the process of a "Reconstruction of Theological Thinking," which started in the late 1990s. The book at hand offers varied insights into this process.

So far the process of reconstructing Chinese theological thinking has dealt mainly with questions of how Christians should understand themselves as loyal members of their socialist society or as patriotic Chinese. We

5. In the book at hand, the Chinese concept of Heaven (divine transcendence) is written with a capital letter, whereas the Christian concept of heaven (God's "dwelling place") is written with a small letter.

could assume that in the future there might be more emphasis on analyzing the relationship between Christianity and the 5,000-year heritage of Chinese culture. This, combined with an analysis of the encounter of the Christian faith with global modernity, influential in today's China, is of vital importance for the development of Christianity in China.

Another aim of the program of the Reconstruction of Theological Thinking is to expand the traditionally rather narrow scope of Chinese Protestant theology. Most of the traditional theology and spirituality in the Chinese Protestant Church is still following the trail of old missionary theology, with a strong emphasis on the salvation of individuals. Chinese theologians are now looking for an authentically Chinese way of biblical interpretation. Rightfully, the new program is widening the theological spectrum into the directions of Trinitarian theology, the theology of creation, theological anthropology, theological ethics, Christians' responsibility in this world, etc. There is an emphasis on the goodness of God's creation. A similar enrichment of theological views, including many other themes, is typical also in many other Protestant churches elsewhere in the world.

Furthermore, the Chinese Protestant Church is now paying more attention to the role of women in theology and church. This is a just evolution in a church where the majority of believers are women. The same could be said in regard to the poor. In many places in the Chinese countryside, the poor masses are flooding into churches. What might be the theology or spirituality of a poor Chinese woman?

As we learn from the book at hand, the program of the Reconstruction of Theological Thinking is not aiming at altering the truths of the Christian faith. Biblical faith, expressed in the ecumenical creeds, is still the basis of all healthy Christian theology. The foundation of the faith is unchangeable, but theological thinking can and must be adjusted in a contextually sensitive and relevant way. In China this happens in sensitivity to the still relevant elements of classical Chinese culture and in solidarity with progressive modern Chinese culture. Discussion on inculturation and contextualization is a hot topic of theology everywhere in the modern world, where Christianity is becoming increasingly a non-Western religion.

Christianity Meeting Other Chinese Religions

The so-called theology of religions is one of the new trends in global theological research and thinking. The theology of religions means an analysis and understanding of other religious traditions and phenomena from the point of view of Christianity. Dialogue is the method employed in the theology of religions. Dialogue aims at two things: first, at a better and deeper mutual understanding of each other's true religious and spiritual convictions; second, at discussion on common interests of ethical issues and at attempting to put them into practice together.

Surely, the chances of mutual understanding are much more promising in the sphere of ethics than in the sphere of religion proper, where, even at best, an agreement can always be only partial. In any case, dialogue will enhance peaceful coexistence of various religious groups at all levels of society. Eventually, it is hoped, such dialogue will foster world peace and the development of the global human community.

In the present book, there are articles that attempt to discover constructive ways of dialogue between Protestant Christianity and non-Christian religions in the context of China. But it must be admitted that this kind of activity is just in its very beginning. Hopefully the further development of Chinese theology will also bring about new resources for dialogue and the theology of religions. It is of vital importance too because other religions, especially folk or popular religion in the countryside, are in any case exercising an influence on the formation of Chinese Christianity. In fact, in some places folk religion, with its charismatic self-designated leaders and emphasis on miracles, dreams, visions, etc., has already infiltrated church life.

Growing Needs for Religious and Theological Education

We also touched the topic of religious education in China. New programs of research and teaching in the field of religious studies have been launched in leading Chinese universities during recent years. It seems that an academic interest in the study of religion is spreading in China, but still there is practically no information on religions available at the lower or middle levels of the educational system. It was suggested that some amount of religious knowledge at all levels of education would be beneficial in helping young people to make a distinction between an established religion and sheer superstition, religious manipulation, or cult.

As to theological education, we learned that the fast-growing Protestant Church of China is lacking pastors. In some townships there can be tens of thousands of believers with no trained ministers. Competent teaching and leadership are needed to nourish and guide the spiritually hungry flocks;

otherwise irrational heresies and harmful schisms may plague the church and the society.

There is an urgent need for both the quantitative increase and the qualitative improvement of theological training in the Chinese church. The quantitative need is most felt in the countryside, where an increasing number of the poor are joining the church; the qualitative need — especially raising the quality of preaching — is imperative in the big cities, where the well-doers are getting more interested in the Christian faith.

An earnest hope was echoed in the Sino-Nordic conference: Could there be more cooperation between theological seminaries and secular universities in order to foster theological education? Could there in the future be an academically qualified faculty of theology, jointly run by the church and by some universities?

The Chinese authorities have gradually accepted the fact that religions are not harmful to society; on the contrary, they are an enormous moral power and hold potential for educating people for the good and the right. In their own way, Christians are fostering the unity and healthy development of the nation. From the point of view of ethics and religion, China is certainly the most interesting place in the world: one billion people without a religion are looking for a new orientation to understand the value and meaning of their lives.

*   *   *

We would like to express our deep gratitude to Dr. Rhea Menzel Whitehead and Professor emeritus Dr. Samuel C. Pearson for helping us polish the English of the present work. The biblical quotations are from the New Revised Standard Version of the Holy Bible.

We would also like to state that the various opinions expressed in this volume do not necessarily reflect the views of the editors.

Miikka Ruokanen (Chinese name: Luo Mingjia, 罗明嘉)
Ph.D., Professor of Dogmatics (Systematic Theology), University of Helsinki
Guest Professor, Renmin (People's) University of China, Beijing
Head of the Deparment of Systematic Theology, University of Helsinki
Advisory Professor, Fudan University, Shanghai
Visiting Professor, Nanjing Union Theological Seminary

Ruokanen's latest publication related to Christianity in the Chinese context is: "K. H. Ting's Contribution to the Contextualization of Christianity in China," *Modern Theology* (Jan. 2009): 107-22.

Paulos Huang (Chinese name: Huang Baoluo, 黄保罗)
Ph.D., Th.D., Adjunct Professor, Department of World Cultures, University
  of Helsinki
Kuang Yaming Chair Professor, Jilin University, China
  Guest Professor, Institute of Sino-Christian Studies, Hong Kong

Huang's latest publication related to Christianity in the Chinese context
is: *Confronting Confucian Understandings of the Christian Doctrine of Salvation: A Systematic-Theological Analysis of the Basic Problems in the Confucian-Christian Dialogue,* Studies in Systematic Theology (Leiden:
E. J. Brill, 2010).

Addresses for communication:

Prof. Miikka Ruokanen
Faculty of Theology
Box 33
00014 University of Helsinki
Finland
Email: miikka.ruokanen@helsinki.fi
Tel.: +358-40-572 4411
Fax: +358-9-191 23033
Tel. in China: +86-13611 302090

Dr. Paulos Huang
Department of Comparative Religion
Box 59
00014 University of Helsinki
Finland
Email: pauloshuang@yahoo.com
Tel.: +358-40-8360793

Contributors

PROF. DR. ZHAO DUNHUA is Director of the Department of Philosophy and Religion, Beijing University (zhaodh@phil.pku.edu.cn).

PROF. DR. ZHANG QINGXIONG is Director of the Center for Christian Studies in the Department of Philosophy, Fudan University, Shanghai (qxzhang@fudan.edu.cn).

PROF. DR. DIANE B. OBENCHAIN is Professor of Religious Studies in the Department of Religion, Calvin College, and Visiting Professor in the Department of Philosophy and Religion, Beijing University (db05@calvin.edu).

PROF. DR. SVEIN RISE is Professor of Theology at the School of Religion and Education (Norsk Laererakademi) in Bergen, Norway (sr@vh.nla.no).

PROF. DR. HE GUANGHU is Professor in the Department of Philosophy and Religious Studies at Renmin (People's) University of China, Beijing (heguanghu@china.com).

PROF. DR. WAN JUNREN is Head of the Department of Philosophy at Tsinghua University, Beijing (wan_jr@263.net).

PROF. DR. LO PING-CHEUNG is Associate Dean of Faculty of Arts, Director of the Centre for Applied Ethics, Professor of Religion and Philosophy, Hong Kong Baptist University (pclo@hkbu.edu.hk).

PROF. DR. YOU BIN is Professor in the Department of Philosophy and Religion, Central University for Nationalities in Beijing (youbin99@sohu.com).

PROF. DR. HE JIANMING is Professor in the Department of Philosophy, Renmin University of China, Beijing (jianmhe@ruc.edu.cn).

PROF. DR. LAI PAN-CHIU is Head of the Department of Religion, Chinese University of Hong Kong (pclai@cuhk.edu.hk).

DR. JORGEN SKOV SORENSEN works in the Centre for Multireligious Studies, Faculty of Theology, University of Aarhus, Denmark (jskov@teologi.au.dk).

DR. JYRI KOMULAINEN is Adjunct Professor of Dogmatics, Faculty of Theology, and University Lecturer in Religious Education, Faculty of Education, University of Helsinki (jyri.komulainen@helsinki.fi).

PROF. GAO SHINING is Professor in the Institute of World Religions, Chinese Academy of Social Sciences, Beijing (gaosn@cass.org.cn).

PROF. DR. ZHUO XINPING is Director of the Institute of World Religions, Chinese Academy of Social Sciences, Beijing (zhuoxp@cass.org.cn).

PROF. DR. NOTTO R. THELLE is Professor emeritus of Systematic Theology in the Faculty of Theology, University of Oslo, Norway (n.r.thelle@teologi.uio.no).

PROF. DR. YANG HUILIN is Vice-President of Renmin University of China, Beijing, and Professor and Head of the Chinese Department (huilin@public.bta.net.cn).

PROF. DR. THOR STRANDENAES is Professor of Mission in the School of Mission and Theology, Stavanger, Norway (thor.strandenaes@mhs.no).

DR. LI PINGYE is Vice General Secretary of the Chinese Friendship Association, United Front of China (pylchina@msn.com).

ARCHPRIEST, PROF. DR. VLADIMIR FEDOROV is Director of the Orthodox Institute of Missiology and Ecumenism, St. Petersburg, Russia (vffedorov@yahoo.com).

PROF. DR. WANG XIAOCHAO is Professor and Vice-Head of the

Department of Philosophy, Tsinghua University, Beijing (xiaochao@tsinghua.edu.cn).

PROF. DR. CHOONG CHEE PANG is Visiting Professor of Beijing University and of the Chinese University of Hong Kong, and Senior Research Fellow of the University of London (choongcp@singnet.com.sg).

Ms. ZHANG MINGHUI is Master of Theology of the University of Helsinki, Finland (minghui_zhan@hotmail.com).

PROF. DR. LI QIULING is Professor in the Department of Philosophy, Renmin University of China, Beijing (lql57@sina.com).

DR. FREDRIK FÄLLMAN is Lecturer in the Chinese Department, University of Stockholm, Sweden, and Researcher at the Academy of Sciences, Sweden (fallman@mac.com).

MR. BIRGER NYGAARD is Director of Areopagos, Denmark, Norway, and Hong Kong (birger.nygaard@areopagos.org).

REV. DENG FUCUN is Vice-President of the Three-Self Patriotic Movement of the Chinese Christian Church (tspmdengfc@online.sh.cn).

DR. CHEN XUN is Teacher at the Yanjing Theological Seminary, Beijing (xunrongru@hotmail.com).

DR. GERALD H. ANDERSON is Director emeritus, Overseas Ministries Study Center, New Haven, Connecticut, USA (anderson_gh@hotmail.com).

PROF. DR. ZHU XIAOHONG is Professor in the Department of Philosophy, Fudan University, Shanghai (rachelbs1@hotmail.com).

PROF. DR. SUN YI is Professor in the Department of Philosophy, Renmin University of China, Beijing (sunyi7@yahoo.com).

REV. CHEN YONGTAO is Teacher of the Nanjing Union Theological Seminary and Ph.D. student at the Faculty of Theology, University of Helsinki (yongtao.chen.nj@gmail.com).

DR. LIN MANHONG is Teacher and Interim Dean of the Nanjing Union Theological Seminary (mhmlin.njuts@gmail.com).

DR. WU XIAOXIN is Director of the Ricci Institute for Chinese-Western Cultural History, University of San Francisco (wu@usfca.edu).

PART I

Christianity in Relation to the Chinese Religious Tradition

1 The Goodness of Human Nature and Original Sin: A Point of Convergence in Chinese and Western Cultures

Zhao Dunhua

Someone once objected to me that the Christian dogma of original sin was given through the revelation in the Bible, whereas the Confucian theory of the goodness of human nature was founded upon human reason. The two, therefore, cannot be compared since there is no connection between divine revelation and human reason. To this I replied that the comparison is not my innovation. Quite a few Western scholars have drawn particular attention to a comparison of this kind, for example, in such works as *The Sixth Volume of the True Meaning of Heavenly Doctrines (Tianxue Shiyi)* by Matteo Ricci, the *Prolegomena of Mencius's Work* by James Legge, *Chinese Religion* by Max Weber, and, most recently, *China and the Christian Impact: A Conflict of Culture* by Jacques Gernet.

All of these writers, except for Ricci, emphasized the irreconcilable conflict between the doctrine of original sin and the theory of the goodness of human nature. It is worthwhile noting that there has been a contrary trend among Western scholars, especially among the thinkers of the Enlightenment in the eighteenth century, who to a certain extent adapted the Confucian idea of the goodness of human nature when rethinking the Christian notion of original sin. In spite of the differences in standpoint and orientation, both parties generally agreed on the divergence of the Christian and Confucian views on human nature. This paper will express a disagreement with this prevalent assumption, pointing out, as its subtitle suggests, the convergence of these two different views on human nature.

From the very beginning, I would like to acknowledge that I do not deny the divergence in question. If it is true that nothing but the reflection of different nations on their own nature can show most clearly the cultural difference between them, then the Confucian and Christian viewpoints on human nature certainly manifest, in a concentrated manner, the divergence between Chinese and Western cultures. The key point is, however, that this divergence has appeared to many scholars as a diametrical opposition and total incompatibility.

For example, Max Weber wrote: "Completely absent in Confucian ethics was any tension between nature and deity, between ethical demand and human short-coming, consciousness of sin and need for salvation, conduct on earth and compensation in the beyond, religious duty and socio-political reality."[1]

James Legge wrote: "Mencius' doctrine of human nature was defective in as much as even his ideal does not cover the whole field of duty. . . . That he never indicates any wish to penetrate futurity, and ascertain what comes after death, that he never indicates any consciousness of human weakness, nor moves his mind God-ward, longing for more light: these are things which exhibit strongly the contrast between the mind of the East and the West. His self-sufficiency is his great fault. To know oneself is commonly supposed to be an important step to humility, but it is not so with him."[2]

It seems to me that both these conclusions are a little hasty. I often feel that assertions of this kind have perhaps been derived from overgeneralized and superficial impressions and have led to popular yet naïve opinions. The philosophical ideas and argumentation involved in this question have constantly been ignored or underestimated. If we compare the distinctions and clarifications, arguments and inferences, explanations and interpretations made by Chinese and Western philosophers concerning these two views of human nature, we can reveal the similarity in mentality and moral consciousness beneath the appearance of Chinese and Western cultural divergence. On the basis of this line of reasoning, I shall attempt to demonstrate that the doctrine of original sin and the theory of the goodness of human nature are (1) logically noncontradictory, (2) theoretically complementary, and (3) in practice, playing a similar moral role.

---

1. Max Weber, *The Religion of China*, trans. H. H. Gerth (Glencoe: Free Press, 1951), p. 214.

2. James Legge, *Prolegomena of Mencius' Work*, in *Chinese Classics*, vol. 2 (Oxford: Clarendon Press, 1895), p. 26.

Logically Noncontradictory

Logically, the theory of the goodness of human nature contradicts the theory of the evil of human nature. This contradiction was given expression in the historical controversy between Mencius and Xunzi. However, when Mencius spoke of human nature he was not referring to the same notion that Xunzi discussed. The former refers to the moral essence of human beings, that is to say, the four origins of humanity and rightness:[3] namely, the feeling of commiseration as the origin of humanity, the feeling of shame and dislike as that of rightness, the feeling of reverence and respect as that of propriety, and the feeling of right and wrong as that of wisdom.[4]

Xunzi thought of human nature as natural instincts, that is, the sensuous desires originating in the organs of the body.[5] Mencius did not deny these instincts and desires, but made a further distinction between nature and fate. Sensuous instincts and desires are people's fate, in the sense that they are always present, determined, and unavoidable. Moral essence, on the other hand, is what is natural to people in the sense that it awaits realization. Their failure to realize it would result in its absence or even complete loss. Mencius, who was concerned with the realization of human moral nature, comments that a gentleman attributes instincts to fate but not to human nature, and moral essence to human nature but not to fate.[6] Mencius's distinction between fate and nature is decisive in resolving the apparent contradiction between his theory of the goodness of human nature and Xunzi's theory of the evil of human nature.

Some traditional Chinese philosophers disagreed with the theory of the goodness of human nature either individually or collectively. Yang Xiong (53-18 BCE), from the perspective of the individual, spoke of the mixture of good and evil in human nature. Dong Zhongshu (179-104 BCE) and Han Yu (768-824 CE), from the perspective of the collective, spoke of the three degrees of human nature, that is to say, the high degree of pure good, the middle degree of the mixture of good with evil, and the low degree of complete evil. Generally speaking, the mainstream of Confucianism endorses Mencius's theory of the goodness of human nature but incorporates in it the

---

3. The word *yi* was translated as "righteousness." I prefer to translate it as "rightness."

4. Mencius, *Books,* 6A:6.

5. Hsun Tzu, "On Nature," in *A Source Book in Chinese Philosophy,* trans. Wing-Tsit Chan (Princeton: Princeton University Press, 1963), p. 116.

6. Mencius, *Books,* 7B:24.

above views of Yang Xiong and Dong Zhongshu, even compromising it with the above-mentioned view of Xunzi on the evil nature.

Most Confucians believed that good and evil are not opposed at the same level. Good, they argued, is fundamentally metaphysical. This is the level to which human moral nature belongs. Evil, on the other hand, is related to the corporeal and as such, physical or physiological. This is the level to which human sensuous elements belong. For example, Li Ao (772-841) differentiated between nature and feeling, saying that "nothing in nature is not good," and "feeling is illusionary and wicked."[7] The Confucian rationalist Zhu Xi (1130-1200), like his predecessors, distinguished between Heavenly nature and material nature. According to his interpretation, the good nature that Mencius spoke of refers to original nature which can be equated with Heavenly Reason, while material nature is derivative due to the fact that any human characteristic is formed together with something corporeal, yet still made out of Heavenly reason. The mixed or hierarchical nature of good and evil as proposed by other Confucians is thus assigned to the derivative position of characteristic nature.[8] His teacher, Hu Hong (1106-61), put it clearly: "good" is the lofty term for praise, to which no evil can be opposed.

I conclude from the above that no theory of human nature in traditional Chinese thought, in the final analysis, is really in conflict with Mencius's theory of the goodness of human nature. I will now look at the doctrine of original sin. This doctrine can by no means be reduced to the simplistic assertion that people are by nature evil, especially, morally evil. On the level of moral metaphysics, Christian theologians shared with Confucians the view that all nature, insofar as it is created by God, is fundamentally good. Human nature in particular is good since people were made according to the image of God. Augustine explained moral evil in terms of aversion (or, more precisely, perversion) of true nature. Evil is not, properly speaking, a nature, and consequently has no real existence; it is only the privation of existence. He thus denied the evil of human nature in the ontological sense of the term.[9]

According to some theologians, even after the Fall, when human nature had become corrupted it had not completely lost the goodness that God created in human beings. In philosophical and theological terms, the un-

---

7. Li Ao, "The Recovery of the Nature," in *A Source Book in Chinese Philosophy*, pp. 456-58.

8. *The Complete Works of Chu Shi*, 62-66, in *A Source Book in Chinese Philosophy*, pp. 623-25.

9. Augustine, *On Free Will*, ii, 19.

changeable goodness of human nature consists either in freedom of will, and/or in the truthfulness of reason (ratio), and/or in the innocence of conscience (synderesis). Thomas Aquinas, for example, wrote, "what is natural to man was neither taken away nor added to him by sins" and "since human nature is not so completely corrupted by sin as to be totally lacking in natural goodness, it is possible for him in the state of corrupted nature to do some particular good things by virtue of his nature."[10]

Admittedly, almost all theologians have insisted that the goodness of human nature is so weak in its corrupted state that human beings are incapable of saving themselves; hence, they need grace. Generally speaking, the Christian view on human nature holds that it is a mixture of good and evil (as did the Confucian Yang Xiong). Nevertheless, Christian theologians did not spend as much time, as Confucians did, on clarifying the level, distinction, and interrelationship between good and evil in human nature. The doctrine of original sin often appears ambiguous on the question whether human nature is good or evil. This is probably a partial reason why the struggle of the Catholic Church with Pelagianism on the issue of freedom of will in the Middle Ages became so entangled that even the orthodox position could not extricate itself from the accusation of semi-Pelagianism by Martin Luther. Even so, the ambiguous view on the mixture of good and evil implied in the notion of original sin, in the final analysis, in no way contradicts the clear view on the level and distinction of good and evil in the theory of the goodness of human nature.

Theoretically Complementary

The precondition of sin is free will. This should be judged as one of the most important contributions of Christianity to ethics. One of the general principles of ethics is that a person is responsible only for what he or she freely chooses. Thus, if there were no free choice there would be no moral responsibility.

The Christian doctrine of original sin speaks about will in terms of capacity to make free choices, but it also stresses that the will is not equally free to choose between good and evil. Otherwise, the will would be as perplexed as Buridan's ass, which was unable to decide to which haystack it should turn to eat. There is a tendency inherent in free choice to choose good over evil.

---

10. Thomas Aquinas, *Summa Theologiae* I, i, 98, 2.

According to Augustine, the hierarchy of nature was created in such a way that the lower should obey the higher. Since desire is a faculty lower than reason, the will naturally tends to choose reason, to which desire subordinates itself. Yet, in the dispute with Pelagianism, he stressed that human beings have lost free will and are in need of grace to recover it.

Anselm of Canterbury amended this with his own doctrine of free choice. He insisted that the capacity for free choice can never be lost, no matter what the condition. What was lost after the Fall was the actual tendency toward good.[11] Thomas Aquinas accepted the Aristotelian notion of prudent reason as the deliberative decision in the procedure of choosing good ends and means. He defined will as "rational volition."[12] Later, Martin Luther attacked the Scholastic doctrine of freedom of will, but he did not, as he is unjustly accused of, give up the notion of the freedom of the individual. He declared in a well-known statement, "A Christian is a perfectly free lord of all, subject to none; a Christian is a perfectly dutiful servant of all, subject to all."[13]

In summary, the doctrine of original sin does not content itself with the natural tendency toward good, but emphasizes the difficulty of choosing good and avoiding evil in the state of human corruption. In this way, it intensifies the Christian duty before God, and cultivates the personal consciousness of moral responsibility. Basically, Christianity provides both exterior and interior incentives to morality. The exterior factor is the divine imperative. The interior factor is freedom of will in choosing between good and evil.

Confucian ethics, on the other hand, regards moral prescripts and actions as the autonomous realization of a human nature that is intrinsically good. Confucius said, "seek for humanity and then gain it" and "I wish humanity, and then it reaches to me."[14] Mencius's theory of the goodness of human nature, as has been seen, aims at the a priori origin of morality. All of these entail the notion of the autonomy of morality. Confucians always insisted that ethical norms flow from the heart of people and follow the principle of Heaven. As such, they are based on autonomous self-restraint and not determined by heteronomous imperatives.

Confucians assigned to sages the status of lawgivers. Sages formulated

---

11. "Freedom of Choice" I, in *Anselm of Canterbury*, vol. 2, ed. J. Hopkins and H. Richardson (Toronto: Edwin Mellen Press, 1976), pp. 105-6.

12. *Summa Theologiae* I, ii, 6, 2.

13. Luther, *Werke* (Weimarer Ausgabe), 7:21.1ff.

14. *Analects*, 7:14, 29.

moral rules in accordance with the Heavenly principle. Confucius and Mencius seemed to stress natural inclination rather than artificial formulation. Confucius said, "Establish what I want for myself, then establish it for man. Achieve what I want for myself, then achieve it for man. To be able to judge of others in analogy to what is close to me, this can be said as the rightness of humanity."[15] Mencius said, "The ancient who did not make big mistakes is good at extending what he did for himself."[16] More important, the universal validity and applicability of the moral law were explained by the common good nature shared by sages and ordinary people. In Mencius's words, "sages and I belong to the same species." "Emperor Shun is a man, I am a man, too," and hence, "Everybody can become Emperor Yao and Emperor Shun."[17]

From what has been stated above, it follows that the theory of the goodness of human nature is the foundation of the Confucian idea of the autonomy of morality. This idea was weakened, even ignored, in history in circumstances in which Confucian ethics was used by political rulers as a set of coercive codes and rules. The doctrine of the heart, as presented by Lu Jouyuan (1139-93) and Wang Yangming (1472-1528), made a great effort to revive the Confucian notion of autonomy.

Its ideas include the original heart of humanity and justice, the moral practice as reaching one's own conscience, the natural flowing of original heart, against sophisticated rites and contrived decorum. The historical significance of those ideas can be evaluated on the basis of the relation of the theory of the goodness of human nature to the autonomy of morality. The above analysis reveals the possibility that Confucianism and Christianity can complement each other. The God of Christianity is an absolute lawgiver. His transcendence and the unbridgeable gap between God and humans make it difficult for Christian prescripts to be autonomous. Some theologians, for example, Thomas Aquinas, often appealed to the Stoic notion of natural law to defend moral autonomy. Nevertheless, the autonomous acceptance of natural law can hardly avoid the negative effect of original sin within the framework of religious faith. The Christian theory of natural law is not as successful as that of the Stoics, nor is it as coherent as that of Confucians.

The Confucian theory of the goodness of human nature, on the other hand, attributed the failure to realize the good nature to the unnatural or

---

15. *Analects*, 6:28.
16. Mencius, *Books*, 1A:7.
17. Mencius, *Books*, 6A:7, 6B:2.

A Response to Professor Zhao Dunhua:
An Agapistic View of the Theology of Creation and Theological Ethics

Miikka Ruokanen

I thank Professor Zhao Dunhua for his excellent scholarly essay. In a subtle and accurate way he exposes the Christian theological concept of the goodness of the good God's creation, and shows how ethics is based on this concept of goodness. He skillfully compares the Christian view with the Confucian notion of humanity and morality. I am grateful to learn his persuasive argumentation for the similarity of the ideas of the goodness of human nature and morality in traditional Chinese thinking and in Christianity.

Being still just an elementary student of Chinese philosophy and religion, I will limit my comments basically to Professor Zhao's analysis of Christianity. At the same time, however, I will try to suggest what resources the Christian faith might offer for solving some of the problems common to both Confucianism and Christianity.

My main argument runs thus: Christianity emphasizes the goodness of creation. On this basis, it underlines the common morality of humankind based on the natural moral law. Men are rational beings who have a conscience. This is expressed by stating that man was created in the "image of God." Therefore, human beings know what is right and what is wrong, what is good and what is bad. And at least to some extent, they also are able to put into practice what they know to be good and right.

But the peculiarity of the Christian view is in its emphasis on the limits of the realization of the natural moral law. First, because sin weakens the naturally good potential of man, human beings need divine revelation to "remind" them what is the content of morality. Second, for the same reason, they also need the help of God's grace to fulfill better the requirements of the natural moral law.

Quite different from these issues is the religious question about original sin and the salvation of the sinner. In Christianity, ethics and soteriology are not mixed with each other; they must be clearly distinguished. Mixing the concept of original sin with ethics is confusing.

Professor Zhao clearly implies that the concept of original sin has caused ambiguity in how to understand Christian ethics. The Christian view of human nature as a mixture of good and evil is perplexing. Professor Zhao is right when stating: "Christian theologians did not spend as much time, as Confucians did, on clarifying the level, distinction, and interrelationship between good and evil in human nature. The doctrine of original sin often appears ambiguous on the question whether human nature is good or evil." I hope to throw some light on this problem.

Natural Moral Law: Both Divine and Natural

"Nature is good" *(natura est bona)* is one of the axioms of Augustine's theology. God is the only Maker and Creator of all the universe — no one else created anything that exists. God the Creator is absolutely good; consequently all creation and all the created beings are ontologically good. Similarly Thomas Aquinas follows Augustine's basic line of thought by stating: "Being is good" *(esse est bonum)*. Because all existence is God's gift, by definition all existence is good.

Professor Zhao points out correctly the Augustinian view of sin: sin is not an ontological reality, because it is not created; on the contrary, sin is a privation of existence and a perversion of true nature. As is commonly known, Augustine, the great Christian thinker of Western antiquity, is "a theologian of love." Augustine specified his understanding of sin by defining it as "the perversion of love" *(perversio amoris)*. As a creature, the human being was supposed to love his Creator as his ultimate good *(summum bonum)* above everything else. But instead, his love was perverted so that he began to love created things as his highest good — himself, this world, dominion and power over others, earthly and sensual pleasures, money, etc. Instead of the Creator, this world and man himself became his god. According to Augustine, original sin is exactly this permanent tendency of all human beings toward pride *(superbia)* and self-love *(amor sui)*.[1]

---

1. Here I refer to my own study on Augustine: *Theology of Social Life in Augustine's* De civitate Dei (Göttingen: Vandenhoeck & Ruprecht, 1993), especially see ch. 3. The work was published in Chinese in Beijing by China Social Sciences Press in 2008.

13

The theology of creation is the basis of Christian ethics. The good Creator engraved his will, his law of life and love, on every rational being's rational conscience *(synderesis)*. Augustine says that God's law is written on every human heart "like a seal on a ring that passes onto wax, without leaving the ring."[2] Professor Zhao offered some excellent quotations from Thomas Aquinas. Let me add one more: "The natural law is nothing other than the light of understanding placed in us by God; through it we know what we must do and what we must avoid. God has given this light or law at the creation."[3] Man is called "God's image" *(imago Dei)* because he is able to hear God's will in his conscience, which advises him to live in a relationship of love and harmony with his Creator and with his fellow human beings.

Also the modern *Catechism of the Catholic Church* (promulgated by Pope John Paul II in October 1992) emphasizes the natural moral law: "The natural law is a participation in God's wisdom and goodness by man formed in the image of his Creator. It expresses the dignity of the human person and forms the basis of his fundamental rights and duties."[4] This law is at the same time both "divine and natural" because it is God-given, but it is naturally known to all rational beings. The Catholic Catechism emphasizes that this law is both universal, similarly binding on all human beings, and immutable — permanent throughout the variations of history. "It subsists under the flux of ideas and customs and supports their progress. Even when it is rejected in its very principles, it cannot be destroyed or removed from the heart of man."[5] Here the standard Catholic view of Christian ethics is in harmony with Professor Zhao's interpretation of Confucianism: "I am convinced that Confucian ethics was characterized by a combination of secular and holy values."

The Limits of the Natural Moral Law

According to the standard Christian view, the good natural moral law, which at the same time is the divine law of the Creator, was weakened — but not lost! — because of sin. This weakening has two aspects: first, sin makes the understanding of the principles dimmer, and second, sin — at least to some extent — incapacitates human beings from doing what they know is right.

---

2. *De Trinitate* 14.15.21; Patrologia Latina 42, 1052.

3. *Dec. praec.* I, cited from *Catechism of the Catholic Church* (New York: Doubleday, 1995), § 1955.

4. *Catechism of the Catholic Church,* § 1978.

5. *Catechism of the Catholic Church,* §§ 1956, 1958.

The Catholic Catechism is once again helpful here when explaining the weakened cognitive capacity of man to know what is right: "The precepts of natural law are not perceived by everyone clearly and immediately. In the present situation sinful man needs grace and revelation, so moral and religious truths may be known by everyone with facility with firm certainty and with no admixture of error."[6] Consequently, people must be taught over and over again the content of the Ten Commandments, the Golden Rule, and the Double Commandment of Love to remind them about the will of their Creator, i.e., the natural moral law which is already engraved on their consciences.

The same Catechism illustrates the contradiction between the knowledge of the right and the incapacity to fulfill the law: "Like a tutor the Law shows what must be done, but does not of itself give the strength, the grace of the Spirit, to fulfill it. Because of sin, which it cannot remove, it remains a law of bondage."[7] The Catechism goes on to quote from the famous passage of the apostle Paul in Romans 7. Professor Zhao refers to the same text: "I can will what is right, but I cannot do it. For I do not do the good I want, but the evil I do not want is what I do. . . . When I want to do what is good, evil lies close at hand. For I delight in the law of God in my inmost self, but I see in my members another law at war with the law of my mind, making me captive to the law of sin that dwells in my members. Wretched man that I am!"[8]

Professor Zhao points exactly to the same problem of human weakness as he leads us to understand that the biggest problem is the practical realization of moral ideals. According to both Confucianism and Christianity, people generally know in their conscience the basic common human moral principles, but yet there seems to prevail such a weakness in the human race that people are not often able to put the moral principles fully into practice. Human beings seem to be crucially powerless in the sense that they know what is right, but they lack the capacity to accomplish it. They are inclined to underscore their human and ethical ideals, partly willingly, partly against their own will.

The concept of original sin is one way of expressing this human tragedy. Quite to the point, Professor Zhao says that "the doctrine of original sin does not content itself with the natural tendency toward good, but emphasizes the difficulty of choosing good and avoiding evil in the state of human

---

6. *Catechism of the Catholic Church*, § 1960.

7. *Catechism of the Catholic Church*, § 1963.

8. Romans 7:18-24. Here the quotation is a bit longer than in the *Catechism*. Professor Zhao quotes v. 25, which is not included here.

corruption." So, the knowledge of good is basically there, but the ability of accomplishing it is vitiated.

Distinction between Morality and Religion

For the correct understanding of the Christian faith and ethics, it is crucially important to make a healthy distinction between what is commonly human and what is properly religious. Since the days of Thomas Aquinas, Catholic theology uses the pair of concepts such as nature-supernature or nature-grace to make this distinction. These two aspects are related yet distinguished from each other; "grace does not negate nature, put perfects it" (gratia non tollit naturam, sed perficit), states the famous axiom of Thomism. God's grace purifies and strengthens that good which was already given in creation but spoiled by sin.

Here, however, I refer to Martin Luther's foundational distinction between what is "below oneself" (se inferior) and what is "above oneself" (se superior). Luther follows the basic intentions of Augustine when introducing this idea in his famous magnum opus The Bondage of the Will (De servo arbitrio, 1525).[9] As the title of his work tells, he developed his view when analyzing the limits of human freedom.

Luther teaches that the human being exists in two realms at the same time; he is "a citizen of two kingdoms." First, he lives "in front of the world" (coram mundo) where he is a naturally free agent to make moral decisions, do his daily business, form human relationships, take part in social affairs as a citizen, etc. These are the things that are "below oneself"; human will (voluntas) is free,[10] yet somewhat harmed by sin. People know what is right and may voluntarily act either in harmony with the moral law or against their knowledge of the law. Human life in this "earthly kingdom" is organized on the basis of natural moral law, which is also expressed in the commandments of the Bible. Here God is ruling and regulating human life through his law.

Luther emphasizes that people should actively use their rational reflection to find out what is right in each actual concrete situation and how to

9. Here I follow the analysis of my own yet-unpublished monographic work The Pneumatological Concept of Grace in Luther's De servo arbitrio.

10. In The Bondage of the Will Luther employs the Latin word voluntas when speaking about the naturally free will man uses in earthly matters, and the word arbitrium when he describes man's non-free relationship with the transcendental powers of God and the devil.

implement the principle of the Golden Rule in each case. The revelation offers only the basic principles; in reality human beings need to put their moral consideration into active practice.

The other realm where the human being exists is "in front of God" (*coram Deo*); one's existence is determined by what is "above oneself." Here the human being has no free will! He is enslaved by original sin — here is exactly the place where the concept of original sin belongs. The human being is at the mercy of transcendental powers, the power of evil, sin, Satan, and death on the one hand, and the power of the triune God's saving grace, his forgiveness and mercy, on the other hand. In the state of integrity before the Fall, the human being had the freedom of choosing the basic orientation of his life; he had the free decision or will (*liberum arbitrium*) to love or not to love his Creator.

But after the Fall, the human being lost this freedom and now has a "captivated free will" (*liberum arbitrium captivatum*); he is the slave of sin, lacking faith and love in God. The very kernel of original sin is not a moral reality; it is unbelief, lack of faith, a crime against the First Commandment and against the first part of the Double Commandment of Love. After the Fall, man does not love his Creator above everything else, "with all his heart and with all his soul and with all his mind."[11]

The human being cannot stop his unfaithfulness to God by his free choice, he cannot convert himself from unfaith to faith by his own psychic powers, and he cannot connect himself with God's saving grace by his own free decision. Augustine says that by his own natural powers, man "cannot but sin" (*non posse non peccare*; literally: man is "not able not to sin"). Luther describes the natural man as "a log, a stone, or a piece of ice," a person "twisted around himself"; the natural man is in a permanent rebellion against God. In fact, the above-quoted passage from Romans 7 belongs also to this context: it is not so much a description of man's moral inadequacy as a profound confession of man's absolute incapacity to please God, to establish a proper relationship of love between the fallen creature and his Creator.

The initiative and the power for the change of mind must come from outside: God's Holy Spirit must be active first; he must convert the resisting human mind. This is the famous Augustinian concept of "prevenient grace"

---

11. Jesus teaches the Double Commandment of Love: "'You shall love the Lord your God with all your heart, and with all your soul, and with all your mind.' This is the greatest and first commandment. And a second is like it: 'You shall love your neighbor as yourself'" (Matt. 22:37-39).

(gratia praeveniens). When God's Spirit moves the mind, creates faith, and connects the sinner with God's saving grace, the human person becomes somewhat liberated: Augustine employed the concept "liberated free will" *(liberum arbitrium liberatum)*. Luther says that the converted human being becomes a citizen of God's kingdom, where God is ruling through the liberating gospel of Jesus Christ.

As Professor Zhao also points out in his essay, Luther was not as optimistic about the notion of the freedom of will as the Scholastics, but "he did not give up the notion of the freedom of the individual." This is exactly true. Luther is totally pessimistic about the freedom of will in regard to man's relation to the transcendental reality, but he is positive about the duty of every human being — whether a Christian or a non-Christian — to follow the Creator's natural moral law in our common human social life, in matters that are in the control of our free will.

I fully agree with Professor Zhao when he criticizes some scholars of the European Enlightenment for a wrong comparison of Christianity and Confucianism, making their moral systems incompatible. The kernel of the problem is, as Zhao says: "All of these writers, except for Ricci, emphasized the irreconcilable conflict between the doctrine of original sin and the theory of the goodness of human nature."

I see that the basic reason for this misunderstanding was that those scholars did not make a proper distinction between religion/soteriology (what is "above oneself") and ethics (what is "below oneself"). They mixed religion and ethics, and consequently, mixed the concept of original sin with that of morality. The concept of original sin belongs to the realm "above oneself" and the concept of morality to the realm "below oneself," but the enlightened critics did not realize that. Their starting point was mixing "the two kingdoms," confusing the negative idea of original sin with moral questions, not the positive doctrine of creation. Consequently, they could not pay proper attention to the positive existence of the natural moral law in Christianity.

The existence of original sin does not annul the existence of the goodness of creation and of the universal natural moral law, which is the Law of Love. Even in spite of original sin, rational beings are able both to know and to practice what is good and what is right. They are able to recognize and to follow the precepts of the natural law engraved on their rational conscience, although sin has somewhat weakened their ability to act in accordance with this law.

I am inclined to agree with Professor Zhao as he states that the doctrine of original sin and the theory of the goodness of human nature — both properly understood, without mixing the religious and the ethical concepts — are "logically noncontradictory, theoretically complementary, and in practice playing a similar moral role."

Where to Find Resources for Moral Improvement

Our common empirical everyday experience proves that in no culture and in no religion is morality practiced up to the ideal standard. In every culture people underscore those ethical criteria they know to be right. Referring to Professor Zhao's wording, we have the problem: From where does the power come for transformation, for purifying one's mind, and for perfecting human nature? In relation to Confucianism, Zhao expresses the problem by saying: "The Confucian theory on the goodness of human nature, on the other hand, attributed the failure to realize the good nature to the unnatural or pervasive conditions and accidental ignorance. This often resulted in decrease in moral enthusiasm and a reduction in a sense of responsibility . . . and often failed to provide sufficient incentive for good to overcome evil."

Professor Zhao rightly points out that "Christianity provides both exterior and interior incentives to morality." I agree that Christianity can offer some help in both of these aspects. First, by teaching the Ten Commandments, the Golden Rule, the Double Commandment of Love, and other explicit contents of the revealed law, Christianity can be helpful or provide exterior incentives to morality, educating people "to remember" what is the content of the natural moral law common to all human beings, to remind them what is already written in their rational conscience. To put it as short as possible, the main content of the moral code is the Law of Love: love your neighbor as yourself.

Second, the specifically Christian answer to how to empower people to do what they naturally know to be right is to refer to the sanctifying power of the Holy Spirit who dwells in every believer. This reference to the metaphysical power or the influence coming from "above oneself" is how Christianity can provide interior incentives to human morality. The Catholic Catechism says about the life of Christians: "The New Law is called a law of love because it makes us act out of the love infused by the Holy Spirit. . . . Sanctifying grace is infused by the Holy Spirit into the soul to heal it of sin."[12]

12. *Catechism of the Catholic Church*, §§ 1972, 2023.

God is love *(agape)*, and especially the Holy Spirit is the "bond of love" between the Father and the Son, as Augustine teaches. God is seen as the communitarian reality of the Holy Trinity, in which the divine persons exist in a communion of love. Thus, love is the essence of the Trinitarian life. This same divine "substance of love" is poured into the heart of every Christian and can empower the believer gradually to grow in the capacity of loving God and neighbor. Augustine's favorite quotation from Paul runs: "God's love has been poured into our hearts through the Holy Spirit which has been given to us."[13]

Thus the believer, in a real ontic way, participates in the divine *agape*, God's own substance, being at the same time both the object of God's love and the subject of it, enabled by God's Spirit to love the Creator and to extend his love to all people. According to the classical Christian understanding, sanctification is a lifelong process of growth in love. A Christian is never ready-made, but by God's grace and through the believer's cooperation, the believer's ability to love will gradually increase.

Sanctification is not a demand but a gift of the triune God. God's grace and Spirit initiate the growth in love, and the believer cooperates in this "healing process" that will gradually capacitate the human being to improve, to some extent, his moral quality, i.e., his ability to love. Augustine prays: "Lord, ask me to do anything you want, but give me that what you want." Christian ethics can be called agapistic ethics for two reasons: first, because its exterior factor is God's Law of Love; second, because its interior factor is the energization to love through participation in the triune God's own *agape*.

In his essay, Professor Zhao comes to the conclusion that "the difference between Confucianism and Puritanism [Protestant Christianity] lies in the aspect of transformation and not, as Weber assumed, in the attitude toward this world." I understand this concluding statement as indicating that Confucianism and Christianity share the same optimistic view about the goodness of our existence, but their means of attaining the goals of goodness are different. I think that perhaps Confucianism needs some reemphasis on the metaphysical links of human existence, the emphasis on the Heavenly mandate and the holy values as the basis of human morality in order to make ethics more binding. But saying this, I do not think that in those countries where Christianity is a dominant religion, moral ideals are better practiced than in China!

13. Romans 5:5.

I like the way Immanuel Kant connects ethics with metaphysics or religion; I mean his definition of ethics, not of religion. I believe that he partly adopted his view from Protestant Christianity, but his conception seems to have some universally valid value. According to Kant, first, we need the idea of a suprahuman lawgiver in order to make morality universal, common to all human beings. Second, the idea of divine lawgiver is also needed in order to make morality obligatory and binding; man needs the sense of being responsible to someone who is above him. Ethics is not just agreements and contracts between human beings. And third, we need the idea of a morally perfect being in order to make progress in morality; otherwise morality could flatten down to the level of human compromises. In Kant's moral system, God is the universal legislator, the judge, and the absolute good.

According to my understanding, Confucian scholars and Christian theologians could continue fruitful dialogue and cooperation in two fields. First, they could reflect together on the metaphysical foundation of ethics. It seems evident that a purely atheistic ethics or a purely humanistic ethics does not work out well. A moral system needs a suprahuman validation in order to be workable. Second, there is the continual practical task of understanding and expressing rationally the concrete contents of the universal natural moral law common to the human race. This is vitally important for the peace and the development of each nation and of the whole world. The most important is that this promising dialogue will continue.

2 Sin and Evil in Christian and Confucian Perspectives

Zhang Qingxiong

Early Christian missionaries in China noticed some similarities between the biblical concept of God and the notions of *Tian* (Heaven) or *Di* (Sovereign) in the Book of History *(Shangshu)*. This was the reason why the Catholics translated *God* into "Master of Heaven" *(Tianzhu)* and Protestants translated the same name into "Sovereign on High" *(Shangdi)*. In addition to the notion of God, there are other similarities between Christianity and Confucianism, such as the notions of sin, evil, and salvation. Of course, there are also obvious differences in understanding these concepts in the two systems of thinking.

From the Book of History and the Old Testament we can find similarities between the ancient Israelites and the Chinese concerning two issues. One is how God protected righteous people in Israel and those rulers of China who followed *Dao*. Another is how God punished evil people in both contexts. In regard to the New Testament and the *Analects (Lunyu)*, we can find more differences between Paul's interpretation of original sin and of the salvation provided by Christ on the one hand, and Confucius's new understanding of the mandate of Heaven and his definition of who is a gentleman, on the other hand. To a certain extent, these similarities and differences show the special features of Christianity and Confucianism. The present article attempts to make a comparison between Christian and Confucian perspectives on the notions of sin and evil in the light of Paul's and Confucius's teaching.

All the dates in the article are added by the translator for the convenience of Western readers.

In Christian theology, "sin" does not refer only to a kind of wrong action, but to the situation of alienation between man and God. "Evil" includes moral and natural evils. The former means evil caused by displaced human will and action; the latter refers to the disorders of nature, such as earthquakes, storms, or pestilences, which bring about calamities to human beings. What has made sin an important theological theme is that sin is closely related to the idea of salvation, so central in the Bible and the Christian faith. This is to say that since human beings have fallen into the state of sin, they cannot save themselves. They need the salvation coming from God, and this emphasizes the central role of Jesus Christ.

The Question of Theodicy

The problem of theodicy has made evil a theological theme: it is so difficult to answer how any evil can exist in the world created by the omnipotent God who is understood to be universal love. The question of sin is closely related with that of evil, and evil can be considered as both the cause and the effect of sin. Theologians try to show that the calamities of the human race are caused by the fact of sin; sin, on its part, is based on the fact of the overwhelming power of evil.

Although sin and evil are important theological concepts, there are disputes concerning them. If the power of evil caused by the transcendent evil being Satan is emphasized too much, it may result in a dualistic view of good and evil: God versus Satan, light versus darkness. On the other hand, if the free will of human beings is emphasized too much, the need of salvation given through Christ will be diminished. Christian theologians try to find a middle way. On the one hand, they insist on the belief that the world and human beings were created good by the good God who is omniscient, omnipotent, righteous, and loving. On the other hand, they do not deny either the existence of evil and sin or the need of salvation offered from outside of fallen humanity by Christ.

In the Christian tradition, the classical doctrine of sin and evil must be seen in the light of the writings of Paul. During his mission, Paul wrote many letters to various churches in order to explain the meaning of salvation brought about by Christ. What Paul says about sin and evil is closely related to that idea of salvation. The epistle to the Romans is one of the most important of his letters. Therein he employs the doctrine of salvation in Christ to solve the problem of the Fall in the story of Adam in the book of Genesis. Paul explains the meaning of Jesus' atonement on the cross and the reconciliation between God and human beings from the viewpoint of original sin.

Augustine too played an important role in defending the Christian view of sin and evil. In his time, the dualism of Manicheanism and the moralism of Pelagianism attacked the traditional Christian doctrine of sin and evil from different perspectives. Manicheanism taught the duality of good and evil by referring to the duality between the divinity of light and the divinity of darkness. The Manicheans placed Jesus together with such figures as Buddha, Zoroaster, and Mani; consequently, they denied the status of Jesus Christ as the Son of God, the second person of the Holy Trinity. Pelagius and his followers emphasized human free will to the extent that they denied the reality of original sin and the absolute necessity of grace.

Originally Augustine himself was a Manichean before his conversion to Christianity. Using especially Paul's epistle to the Romans, Augustine developed his own theology of sin and evil, criticizing both Manicheanism and Pelagianism. Eventually, Augustine's position was widely accepted and became what could be called the classical Western Christian view.

When trying to make a summary of the Christian concepts of sin and evil, our main evidences are the story of the Fall of Adam and Eve in Genesis, Paul's interpretation of that story in Romans, and Augustine's systematic discussion on the same topic.

1. Human beings exist in the state of original sin. According to Genesis, God created Adam and Eve, the ancestors of the human race, to live in the Garden of Eden. Initially, they both obeyed God's will and had a very happy life there. Later, they were tempted by the evil one to disobey God's order, and eventually ate the forbidden fruit. As a consequence, God punished them and forced them to leave the Garden. Since then, human beings have experienced the harshness of sinful life. In regard to the relationship between God and man, this act of disobedience is called sin; in regard to the actual condition of human life, it is called evil.

2. The sin of Adam and Eve should not be seen only as the Fall of two individuals, but as a symbolic and representative act common to all members of the human race. But there is also the aspect of heritage: the early ancestors committed a sin that would bear consequences for all of their descendants. Accordingly, Paul says that Adam "is a type of the one who was to come" (Rom. 5:14). "For just as by the one man's disobedience the many were made sinners, so by the one man's obedience the many will be made righteous" (Rom. 5:19).

3. One of the evil results of original sin is death. There is a conversation between the woman and serpent in Genesis:

> He [the serpent] said to the woman, "Did God say, 'You shall not eat from any tree in the garden'?" The woman said to the serpent, "We may eat of the fruit of the trees in the garden; but God said, 'You shall not eat of the fruit from the tree that is in the middle of the garden, nor shall you touch it, or you shall die.'" But the serpent said to the woman, "You will not die; for God knows that when you eat of it your eyes will be opened, and you will be like God, knowing good and evil." (Gen. 3:1-5)

Since Adam did not listen to God and ate the forbidden fruit, death became the lot of human beings. The result of death is very influential: "death exercised dominion from Adam to Moses, even over those whose sins were not like the transgression of Adam" (Rom. 5:14). "Therefore, just as sin came into the world through one man, and death came through sin, and so death spread to all because all have sinned" (Rom. 5:12).

4. Why did Adam and Eve dare to disobey God's order even though they knew the risk of death? According to the Genesis story, they hoped to acquire God's wisdom; they wished to "be like God, knowing good and evil." In fact, this means that human beings hope to become gods themselves. This attitude meant a transition from a God-centered life to a self-centered one. This transformation became the origin of sin. Since human beings no longer obediently surrender themselves to God, they believed themselves to be as omniscient and omnipotent as God himself, and they relied on themselves in building happy lives. However, the pride and weakness of human beings made them more easily tempted by evil; thus, they started committing more and more sins.

5. Human beings do not only exist in the state of original sin; they also commit personal sins. The latter refers to their disobedience of God's commandments. The first four of the Ten Commandments concern human beings' relationship with God: believing in Yahweh as the only God, not worshiping idols, not taking God's name in vain, and observing the Sabbath in remembrance of God's creation of the world. In Christianity, disbelief in God is the foundational sin, since denying God's love and considering his faithfulness as not worth trusting in are the origin of all sorts of sins.

The other six commandments concern moral issues among human beings: respecting parents, not killing, not committing adultery, not stealing, not bearing false witness against neighbors, not coveting a neighbor's wife and belongings. Disobeying the moral orders given by the Creator, as well as failing to do the good one knows should be done, is all called sin in Scripture.

6. Sin refers to the alienation and disharmony between God and man. As Paul says, "all have sinned and fall short of the glory of God" (Rom. 3:23). And the result of sin is to be "alienated from the life of God" (Eph. 4:18). Thus, human beings lost their freedom and safety; they have to live under the punishment and curse of God, and they experience suffering, calamities, and death.

7. Human beings have fallen into sin, and their hearts have been polluted. Therefore, they cannot be liberated from the slavery of sin by their own efforts. Like a leopard that cannot change its spots, the human being used to sin cannot change his mind from pride and selfishness to pure goodness. The Christian solution to the sin of man is God's grace: God sent his Son Jesus Christ, who is without sin, into the world to die on the cross in order to atone for human beings with his own body and blood. Forgiveness is a free gift from God, and it cannot be obtained by trying to do good, through merits, self-cultivation, or sacrifices. As Paul says, "In him we have redemption through his blood, the forgiveness of our trespasses, according to the riches of his grace" (Eph. 1:7). Christianity teaches that only through Jesus Christ can the problem of sin be solved, since Jesus Christ is the only Savior for human beings.

8. Since Jesus Christ redeemed human beings from the slavery of sin, he brought about reconciliation between God and humanity, and between different human groups; therefore, the sinful human race again has hope to become a new people. The apostle Paul says, "For he is our peace; . . . He has abolished the law with its commandments and ordinances, that he might create in himself one new humanity . . . " (Eph. 2:14-15).

9. Christianity does not employ the good-evil duality to explain the origin of evil. The whole universe was created by God, and is therefore good by definition. Evil does not belong ontologically to the origin of the universe; originally the world was not composed of both good and evil powers. Evil did not exist from the beginning of the world; in fact, it appeared within the good world. The story of Adam tells the anthropological beginning of evil in this world; after the humans committed sin, evil began to appear in the visible world and to spread into God's good creation.

10. Adam and Eve had freedom to choose whether to obey God's order or not; they failed to obey him. In the light of this possibility of choice, neither sin nor evil were inevitable; rather, they were accidental, caused by a wrong decision. This choice was not made only in a moment of weakness,

but was essentially related to permanent human desires such as their wish to be omniscient and omnipotent like God. These desires were in conflict with the fact of the finitude of human nature, thus causing all kinds of suffering and unhappiness. Here the serpent symbolizes the human situation, vulnerable to temptation. The serpent cannot force people to eat the forbidden fruit; all it can do is tempt them to eat the fruit. On the one hand, this indicates that evil is not inevitable; human beings should be regarded as responsible for their own fall. On the other hand, the story indicates the weakness of human nature; the pitfalls of life show that human beings are unable to get rid of difficulties.

The Problem of Evil in Chinese Culture

In the following space, I attempt to introduce some of the main features of the concept of sin and evil in the context of Chinese traditional culture, making a comparison between the Christian and the traditional Chinese approaches to these questions.

Confucian understanding of sin and evil can be found in *Yao yue*, the twentieth of Confucius's *Analects*. There are three chapters in this section. In the first chapter Confucius quoted the discussions of Yao, Shun, Yu, Tang of Shang, and King Wu of Zhou; then he himself made his own brief remarks. Both Heavenly Revenue *(Tianlu)* and sin were discussed here. In the second chapter, Confucius answered Zizhang concerning how to conduct government; also the Five Excellences and the Four Evils were discussed. In the third chapter, Confucius united the Heavenly Mandate and Human Action, and this chapter seems to be the summary of the first and second chapters. It is meaningful to look at the three chapters together.

> (20:1:1) Yao said, "Oh! you, Shun, the Heaven-determined order of succession now rests on your person. Sincerely hold fast the Due Mean. If there shall be distress and want within the four seasons, your Heavenly revenue will come to a perpetual end." Shun also used the same language in giving charge to Yu.
>
> Tang said, "I, the child Lu, presume to use a dark-colored victim, and presume to announce to Thee, O most great sovereign Heaven, that the sinner I dare not pardon, and thy ministers, O Heaven, I do not keep in obscurity. The examination of them is by thy mind, O Heaven. If, in my person, I commit offenses, they are not to be attributed to the people of

the myriad regions. If you in the myriad regions commit offenses, these offenses must rest on my person."

Zhou conferred great gifts, and the good were enriched. "Although he has his near relatives, they are not equal to my virtuous men. The people are throwing blame upon me, the one man." He carefully attended to the weights and measures, examined the body of laws, reinstated the discharged officers, and the good government of the empire took its course. He revived states that had been extinguished, restored families whose line of succession had been broken, and called to office those who had retired into obscurity, so that throughout the empire the hearts of the people turned towards him. He attached chief importance to the food of the people, the duties of mourning, and sacrifices. By his generosity, he won all. By his sincerity, he made the people repose trust in him. By his earnest activity, his achievements were great. By his justice, all were delighted.

(20.2) Zizhang asked Confucius, saying, "In what way should a person in authority act in order that he may conduct government properly?" The Master replied, "Let him honor the five excellent, and banish away the four bad things; . . . then may he conduct government properly."

Zizhang said, "What are meant by the five excellent things?" The Master said, "When the person in authority is beneficent without great expenditure; when he lays tasks on the people without their repining; when he pursues what he desires without being covetous; when he maintains a dignified ease without being proud; when he is majestic without being fierce."

Zizhang said, "What is meant by being beneficent without great expenditure?" The Master replied, "When the person in authority makes more beneficial to the people the things from which they naturally derive benefit; . . . is not this being beneficent without great expenditure? When he chooses the labors which are proper, and makes them labor on them, who will repine? When his desires are set on benevolent government, and he realizes it, who will accuse him of covetousness? Whether he has to do with many people or few, or with things great or small, he does not dare to indicate any disrespect; . . . is not this to maintain a dignified ease without any pride? He adjusts his clothes and cap, and throws a dignity into his looks, so that, thus dignified, he is looked at with awe; . . . is not this to be majestic without being fierce?"

Zizhang then asked, "What are meant by the four bad things?" The Master said: "To put the people to death without having instructed them; . . . this is called cruelty. . . . To require from them, suddenly, the full tale of work, without having given them warning: . . . this is called oppression. To issue orders as if without urgency, at first, and, when time comes, to insist on them with severity; . . . this is called injury. And, generally speaking, to give pay or rewards to men, and yet to do it in a stingy way; . . . this is called acting the part of a mere official."

(20.3) The Master said, "Without recognizing the ordinances of Heaven, it is impossible to be a superior man. Without an acquaintance with the rules of Propriety, it is impossible for the character to be established. Without knowing the force of words, it is impossible to know men."[1]

From the above three chapters of Confucius's text we can find important differences and similarities between Confucianism and Christianity on the notions of sin and evil.

In the *Shangshu* it was obvious that the authority of a ruler was endowed by Heaven. The duration of a dynasty and the wealth of a ruler were all arranged by the Sovereign on High and decided by Heaven. As long as Heaven did not stop such an endowment a dynasty could continue to exist. Once Heaven withdrew her support, the dynasty would face its end. In the latter situation, Heaven would raise a "revolution," i.e., the dynasty would be changed. *Yijing, Tuanzhuan* mentioned "revolution" in the interpretation of the symbol of Ge by saying: "Heaven and earth undergo their changes, and the four seas complete their functions. Tang changed the appointment [of the line of Xia to the throne], and Wu [that of the line of Shang], in accordance with [the will of] Heaven, and in response to [the wishes of] men." This indicates that the mandate of Heaven can change, and it is not an easy thing to receive and conduct the mandate of Heaven.

The same idea has been expressed in the *Shijing, Daya, Wenwang* as saying, "Heaven's decree may change," and "It is hard to keep decree." How can the decree be kept? This is the question that good rulers should think about. The first sentence in the *Yao yue* of the *Analects* is Yao's summary on the experience of keeping the decree of Heaven. This experience was employed by Yao to teach his successor Shun and by Shun to teach his successor Yu. The main idea of this passage is: the Heaven-determined order of succession now rests on Shun. Thus, Shun should sincerely hold fast the Due Mean. If there is distress and want within the four seas, Shun's Heavenly revenue will come to a perpetual end. Shun also used the same language in giving charge to Yu.

---

1. This translation is cited from James Legge's translation in *Sishu* (Changsha: Hunan chubanshe, 1992), pp. 255-57.

Hereby, the correct conduct of government is closely related to the distress or want in the country. Whether the Heavenly decree of a ruler can be kept or not is also closely related to the situation of the lives of the masses. The ruler, who has received the Heavenly decree, should bear the responsibility to enable the masses to live happily and well. If the masses live in poverty, they will rise and make a revolution, since it is the thing that fits the will of both Heaven and the masses.

In his commentary to the second part of *Yao yue* (20:1), Zhu Xi (1130-1200) says that the speech of Tang was made when Tang returned to Shang's capital Hao after he won Jie of the Xia dynasty. And this speech was part of a declaration to the subjects who came to respect Tang. This declaration explained the reason that Tang attacked Jie, but it also told Tang's new principle of conducting government. Thus, by "the sinner I dare not pardon," Tang means that he does not dare to pardon Jie, since he has committed sins against Heaven; when saying "thy ministers, O Heaven, I do not keep in obscurity," Tang means that he does not keep the ministers in obscurity, since they are the ministers of Heaven.[2]

For two reasons, I do not think that this interpretation by Zhu Xi is entirely correct. First, Zhu Xi added two key words, "Jie" (the ruler of Xia dynasty) and "I," in order to offer his interpretation. Second, there is a clear similarity between the ideas of *Yao yue* and *Shangshu, Shanggao*. The version that Zhu Xi saw was a later edition of the Jin dynasty (265-420 CE), and scholars of the Qing dynasty (1644-1911) have proven that this version was a collection of quotations of *Shangshu* from various pre-Qin (before 220 BCE) classics; thus, its authenticity is problematic. According to Mozi and the *Lushi, Chunqiu,* the speech of Tang in the *Yao yue* was made when Tang prays for rain from Heaven after his victory over Jie. I consider this a correct interpretation. In the following I will emphasize Tang's prayer to Heaven, and will interpret this speech from the viewpoint of Tang's attitude to Heaven. In his speech, Tang presumes to employ the figure of a dark-colored victim, and announces to the great sovereign Heaven that he will not pardon the sinner and will not keep the ministers in obscurity. Heaven will examine the rightness of their actions. If Tang commits offenses, they should not be attributed to the people of the myriad regions. If the myriad regions commit offenses, these offenses must rest on Tang.

The term "commit offenses" here means the sin by which human beings

---

2. See Zhu Xi's *Lunyu jizhu*, p. 83; Sheng Cheng's *Shujing jizhuan*, pp. 45-46. The two passages can be found in Sishu wujing (shangce), *Shijie shuju*, 1936.

have offended God. God knows their sins and punishes the people involved by sending disasters. This concept is similar to the idea of "sin" in Christianity. Since Jie of Xia brought about many bad things to his people, God sent disasters to indicate his sin. Since Tang destroyed Xia, the Heavenly decree rested on the rulers of Shang; the drought that started in the time of Xia had not yet stopped. Therefore, Tang prays to Heaven for rain.

Tang prays to Heaven with the status of himself being the Son of Heaven, "Lu." In his prayer he said, should he commit offenses, they should not be attributed to the people of the myriad regions. If the people of the myriad regions commit offenses, the consequences of these offenses should rest on him, Tang. This proves that Tang would like to bear the responsibility for the masses' faults in order to save them from disasters. To a certain extent, this can be compared with the death of Jesus Christ on the cross for the sake of the sins of human beings. Of course, there are important differences between these two figures.

First, because of the lack of the concept of "original sin" in Chinese Confucianism, there is no query about the source of the unhappiness of all human beings. Second, Tang considers himself as the Son of Heaven because he has received the Heavenly decree; Jesus too considers himself the Son of God, but the reason is that he is part of the Holy Trinity. Third, when saying that if he commits offenses the punishment should not be attributed to the people, or if the people commit offenses the punishment should be put on him, Tang expresses his feeling of responsibility rather than an idea of atonement. Tang realizes that the masses should not be charged for the crimes of their rulers, and the crimes of the masses are caused by the disordered behavior of the rulers. Now, as he himself is holding authority to govern the whole country, his responsibility is great, and he has to do his utmost to fulfill this responsibility. His attitude indicates that he fully realizes his own duty and responsibility; he should be strict toward himself and tolerant toward others.

Confucius continues to explain why King Wu of Zhou captured the ruling power from the Shang dynasty and why King Wu received the decree of Heaven in order to establish the new dynasty of Zhou (1111-249 BCE) favored by the masses. First, King Wu of Zhou employed ministers properly, and he had a clear principle for how to reward and punish. "Zhou conferred great gifts, and the good were enriched" means that King Wu of Zhou rewarded good people, made them rich to motivate them toward further contributions to the government. "Although he has his near relatives, they are not equal to my virtuous men" means that King Wu of Zhou employed ministers based on their virtues rather than their relations to the king. That was a mistake made by King Zou of Shang. Consequently, King Wu of Zhou succeeded better than King Zou of Shang. Second, like Tang of the Shang dynasty, King Wu of Zhou realized the importance of receiving the decree of Heaven. Thus, King Wu of Zhou believed that "if the myriad regions commit offenses, these offenses must rest on him."

Third, King Wu of Zhou carefully conducted a series of reforms in economical, legal, and political regulations, employing many means to comfort the masses. He paid careful attention to weights and measures, examined the body of laws, and reinstated the discharged officers. In this way, good government of the empire took its course. He also revived states that had been extinguished, restored families whose line of succession had been broken, and called to office those who had waned into obscurity. For example, King Wu of Zhou employed the descendants of the Yellow Emperor, Yao, Shun, Xia, and Shang. Furthermore, he offered freedom to Qizi, who had been jailed; he also restored the position of Shangrong. Throughout the empire, the hearts of the people turned toward him.

Confucius further concludes that the most important achievement of King Wu of Zhou was to provide food for the people and to establish the duties of mourning and sacrifices. This indicates how the ancient Chinese rulers realized that the people are the root of a country, food is the life of people, and rituals — such as funerals and sacrifices — can make people return to simple and kindly virtues. In this way, the state will have peace and the people will have safety. The above expressions can also be found in *Shangshu*.

The last paragraph of Confucius's speech is a summary about the way of governing conducted by Yao, Shu, Tang, and Wu. Being generous, they could win anything. Being sincere, they gained the people's trust. Through their earnest activity, their achievements were great. By their justice, all were delighted. Confucius considered generosity, sincerity, earnest activity, and justice as the four main virtues, because they are the key elements that influenced the success and failures in politics during ancient Chinese history.

In 20:1 Confucius summarizes the experience of the ancient rulers' methods of government. In 20:2 Confucius discusses how gentlemen should conduct government. This issue is expressed through a conversation between Zizhang and Confucius. Compared to the previous part, this part is much clearer. Hereby both good and bad things are being discussed; the discussion does not focus on natural goodness and evil but on moral and political goodness and evil. Appreciating the "Five Good Things" means that gentlemen should follow these five good rules and virtues: (1) the person in authority should be beneficial without great expenditure; (2) he should lay tasks on the people without stirring their resentment; (3) he should pursue what he desires without being covetous; (4) he should maintain a dignified ease without being proud; and (5) he should be majestic without being fierce.

Confucius further explains to Zizhang how these Five Good Things can be fulfilled: When the person in authority makes people benefit from things that are natural for them, is this not being beneficent without great expenditure? When he chooses proper laborers to do labor appropriate to them, who will resent it? When he makes a benevolent government to become a reality, who will accuse him of covetousness? Whether he is dealing with many people or just a few, or with things great or small, he does not indicate any disrespect; is not this maintaining a dignified ease without pride? When he adjusts his clothes and cap, and gives his appearance dignity, he is looked at with awe; is not this being majestic without being fierce?

Finally, Confucius explains to Zizhang what the four bad things are: (1) putting people to death without having instructed them: this is called cruelty; (2) requiring from them suddenly the full account of their work, without having given them warning: this is called oppression; (3) issuing orders, first as if without urgency, and, when the time comes, insisting on them with severity: this is called injury; and (4) paying rewards to men, and yet doing it in a stingy way: this is acting in the role of a mere official.

Confucius's Interpretation of the Causes of Evil

The above is an expression of Confucius's view of politics. In fact, Confucius has a famous sentence that "Tyranny is fiercer than a tiger." A question arises, whether Confucius also realized the bad things in nature. I believe that he noted this, but if compared with the harshness that a natural disaster brings to people, tyranny is fiercer. In *Shangshu* we have seen that ancient people considered natural disasters as God's punishment for human crimes. This is not much different from the God of the Old Testament, who burned the cities and destroyed the countries of unrighteous people. Confucius must have noticed that natural disasters happened even in the good times, when virtuous rulers were in authority.

We may imagine the following situation: When Tang of the Shang dynasty attacked Jie of the Xia dynasty, there was a drought in Xia. Therefore, Tang declared that this drought was a disaster sent by God in order to expose the crimes of Xia. In this way Tang justified his rebellion and got the support of the people. However, after Tang's victory over Xia, drought still continued, and became even worse; therefore, Tang started fervently praying to Heaven for rain. After seeing such a phenomenon Confucius became careful in his estimations about the relationship between natural disasters and the sins of human beings. Thus, it was recorded that "The master does not talk about strange powers, disasters, and gods." Similar problems were considered by Job in the Old Testament. The issue puzzling Job was why righteous people should suffer; he did not find a clear answer to his question. In the New Testament, especially in Paul's epistles, there is an explanation that relates human suffering to original sin, since "by the one man's disobedience the many were made sinners" (Rom. 5:19). Only in the salvation provided by God through Jesus Christ can evil be overcome.

In Chinese Confucianism, there is no similar soteriological solution. Confucianism neither employs the notion of original sin to explain why benevolent and good people suffer, nor uses the idea of the immorality of soul and of an eschatological judgment to solve the problem of justice. Evil includes both natural and human-made calamities. There is no unified opinion concerning whether natural disasters are the warning and punishment of Heaven to human beings: Confucius doubts, Xunzi opposes, and Dong Zhongshu agrees with that idea. Based on the evidence in *Shangshu* and other ancient classics, Dong Zhongshu's opinion is closer to the ancient tradition; both Confucius and Xunzi have gone in different directions from what the ancient Chinese believed. Concerning human-made calamities, there are no greatly varying opinions among the Confucians. They all believe that human-made calamities have their root in political evil, the result of the disorder caused by bad rulers.

There is a question as to whether in *Shangshu* the relationship between Heaven and man is seen as similar to the relationship between God and man in the Bible. It seems clear that, if compared with the ideas of Confucius, the view of *Shangshu* is more closely related to the biblical understanding. In *Shangshu*, the terms *Tian* (Heaven), *Di* (Sovereign), *Shangdi* (Sovereign on High), and *Tiandi* (Sovereign of Heaven) can be freely exchanged with each other. Thus, the relationship between Heaven and man is in fact that between God and man. Through the teaching of Confucius, the notion of Heavenly decree has been kept, but concerning the existence of a personal God, Confucius is silent. Confucius emphasized the question of how the riddle of evil can be solved by human beings — this happens by means of moral cultivation and good politics rather than by turning to Heaven. Does this mean that Confucius has changed the religious thought in *Shangshu* into a secular moral and political philosophy?

In order to answer this question, we should be clear about how to understand the notion of "religion." In fact, behind the moral and political philosophy of Confucius, there is a metaphysical basis requiring belief. Support for this view can be found in the last part of *Yao yue* 20:3. Confucius said: "Without recognizing the ordinances of Heaven, it is impossible to be a superior man. Without an acquaintance with the rules of Propriety, it is impossible for the character to be established. Without knowing the force of words, it is impossible to know men." "Without an acquaintance with the rules of Propriety" means that if one does not know how to behave with people, one is ignorant of the rules of relationships. "Without knowing the force of words" means that one will know neither the good or evil of a person nor the ability of a person, if one does not understand the person's words. These two points show how one should behave in a secular world. But human beings need a transcendental belief in Heavenly decrees for establishing proper behavior in the secular world.

Zhu Xi quoted from Cheng Hao (1032-85) and Cheng Yi (1033-1107) in order to answer the question of why "one cannot become a gentleman if he does not know the decrees." Cheng says: "The one who knows the decrees, knows the existence of the decrees and believes in them. If one does not know the decrees, he will certainly avoid them once he meets calamity and will certainly seek them once he meets benefits. How can such a person become a gentleman?"[3] Cheng mentions about the Heavenly decrees that "it is called a decree in Heaven, it is called a principle of righteousness, and it is called a natural disposition in human beings. The subject of this decree is the heart in the human body. In fact, these different terms are names of one and the same decree."[4] Through these discussions we may find, from Confucius to neo-Confucianism in the Song (960-1279) and Ming (1368-1644) dynasties, that "to know the decrees of Heaven" was closely related to the issues of self-cultivation, educating human nature, improving the state government, and making peace in the world. Therefore, we may say that secular Confucian philosophy takes the transcendental decrees of Heaven as its basis, and to a certain extent, it can be said that Confucianism is based on a religious spirit.

Some people insist that philosophy should take wisdom as its object of investigation, whereas religion should take spirits, gods, life, and death as its object of study. So thinking, Confucianism should have nothing to do with religion. Confucius holds a doubtful attitude to issues such as the existence

3. Zhu Xi's *Lunyu jizhu*, p. 83 in Sishu wujing (shangce), *Shijie shuju*, 1936.
4. Cheng Hao and Cheng Yi, *Yishu*, vol. 18.

of spirits and gods, and life after death. As is well known, he said: "While not yet to be able to serve people, how can one serve spirits?" and "While not knowing life yet, how can one know death?" In my opinion, Confucius still has a perspective on the questions of life and death, since he also talked about "respecting Heavenly decrees" and "holding firm until death in perfecting the excellence of the *Dao*." This can be seen as a kind of Chinese religion. Confucius mentioned many times that gentlemen should die for the *Dao*. For example, he said: "If one hears the *Dao* in the morning, he will be satisfied to die in the evening" *(Lunyu, Liren)*.

Master Zeng said: "The scholar may not be without breadth of mind and vigorous endurance. His burden is heavy and his course is long. Perfect virtue is the burden he considers it is his to sustain; . . . is it not heavy? Only with death does his course stop; . . . is it not long?" *(Lunyu, Taibo)*. Confucius said: "With sincere faith the gentleman unites the love of learning; holding firm to death, he is perfecting the excellence of his course" *(Lunyu, Taibo)*. The viscount of Wei withdrew from the court; the viscount of Ji became a slave of Zhou; Bi Gan remonstrated with him and died. Confucius commented: "The Yin dynasty possessed these men of virtue" *(Lunyu, Weizi)*.

Confucian perspectives on sin and evil can be summarized as follows: kings and rulers as the Sons of Heaven receive their decrees from Heaven; their duties are to conduct government well so as to make people happy and safe. If kings and rulers do not follow the *Dao* and thus cause people to fall into trouble and poverty, this is the sin by which they offend Heaven. Consequently, the mandate given them by Heaven will face an end, and a change of dynasty will occur.

Only those people who know the Heavenly decrees can become gentlemen. The duty of the gentleman is to hold firm until death in perfecting an excellence of conduct. Gentlemen should assist rulers to govern even if they have to give their lives for the rulers' sake. Evil results mainly from tyranny, and it depends upon human efforts to get rid of such an evil. But such efforts are also based on the feeling of the divine duty, "knowing the decree and believing in it." Here lies an important difference between Christianity and Confucianism: in overcoming the power of original sin and evil Christianity relies on the reconciliation brought about by Jesus Christ, the Son of God, whereas the improvement of humanity in Confucianism is based on the facts of our present world, which can be changed by human efforts. Confucian philosophy of morality and politics is based on the idea of the unity of Heaven and man — this expresses the special Chinese religious spirit.

A Response to Professor Zhang Qingxiong: Deepening the Dialogue

Diane B. Obenchain

Professor Zhang Qingxiong has written a reflective paper exploring Christian and *Ru* (Confucian) perspectives on sin and evil and the human role, if any, in causing and/or alleviating sin and evil. Zhang's astute discernment requires careful reply. In responding, I do so as (1) a comparative historian of religion, who has focused for thirty-five years on the Chinese *Ru,* Taoist, Buddhist, and folk traditions, (2) a Westerner, who has taught (in Chinese) for fifteen years in religious studies at Peking University, Fudan University, and Zhejiang University, and (3) one who engages phenomenological comparison in order to encourage better interpersonal discussion and sharing of what we know to be true.[1]

My response begins with a summary of Zhang's analyses of Christian and *Ru* approaches to sin and evil. Then, to further Zhang's line of inquiry, I suggest that greater engagement with (1) historical-critical use of sources, (2) contextual hermeneutics, (3) the practice of inner moral cultivation, and (4) the Chinese classical discernment of *ti yong* (substance-function), will deepen and add yet greater clarity to conversation across traditions.

Zhang begins by confirming similarities between "God" in the Old Testament and *"Tian"* (Heaven) and *"Di"* or *"Shangdi"* (Lord-on-High)[2] in the

---

1. See Max L. Stackhouse and Diane B. Obenchain, *God and Globalization: Theological Ethics in a Pluralistic World,* vol. 3, *Christ and the Dominions of Civilization* (Harrisburg: Trinity Press International, 2002).

2. During the Western Zhou dynasty (c. 1025-722 BCE), the name *Tian* (Heaven) referred to the cyclical order of sun, stars, seasons, and so forth. The names *Di* (Lord) and *Shangdi* (Lord-on-High) referred to a powerful divine presence perhaps linked with the ancestors of the Shang king, and therefore, the Shang people.

Shu (Book of History).[3] What draws Zhang's attention are similarities between the Judeo-Christian understanding of God and the ancient Chinese understanding of *Tian*, especially in regard to (1) praise and protection of righteous leaders and (2) condemnation and punishment of leaders who depart from God's will or *"Tian ming"* (Heaven's mandate or Heaven's order). Turning to the New Testament and to the *Lunyu* (*Analects*), Zhang focuses on the apostle Paul's explanations of "original sin" and of "salvation in Christ" and on Kongzi's (Confucius's) explanations of *Tian ming* and of *"junzi"* (one of noble birth; benevolent leader). It is here, affirms Zhang, that important differences between the Christian and *Ru* traditions emerge. To these differences we now turn our attention.

Zhang Qingxiong's Summary of the Christian Approach to Sin and Evil

Drawing from Paul's epistle to the Romans and Augustine's interpretations, Zhang summarizes what he discerns as the Christian approach to sin and evil. First, by going against God's command, Adam and Eve "sinned"; the fruit of their sinful actions is a harsh life of pain and suffering, "evil." One of the evil results of Adam and Eve's original sin is death. Hence, a life of suffering that ends in death is the inherited human condition resulting from Adam and Eve's sinful action. In choosing, against God's command, to eat from the tree of knowledge of good and evil, Adam and Eve desired to be like God. But their sinful action resulted only in exchanging a "life centered on God" for a "life centered on oneself." Rather than trust God, heed his commands, and receive life in abundance, Adam and Eve chose not to trust God, not to heed his commands, to put trust in themselves, and to rely on their own efforts to pursue an abundant life. But their sinful action resulted in being thrown out of the Garden and having to toil night and day for a living, once again exchanging good for evil. Second, in addition to original sin, an individual human being sins against God by breaking one of the Ten Commandments. Here again, one suffers the consequences for sin by exchanging good for evil.

3. The *Shu* (Book of History) compiles pronouncements and documents purportedly of the Xia, Shang, and Zhou dynasties; it is one of five extant "normative books" (classics) attributed to Kongzi (Confucius). As such, the *Shu* is a repository of classical political wisdom, with exemplary models of leadership. While Kongzi is credited with collecting, editing, and commenting on the *Shu*, modern scholars date those efforts to the mid to late Zhou dynasty.

The effect of sin is that humans are separated and out of harmony with God and with each other. Both human nature and the human heart are harmed as human beings lose freedom and peace. Moreover, relying on human effort alone, human beings are not able to heal, to restore, or to save themselves from the fruits of their sin, which are suffering, calamity, and death. Yet, for followers of Jesus there is hope. Although himself sinless, Jesus Christ chooses to take upon himself the consequences (separation from God and loss of freedom and peace) for all of humanity's sinful actions. Instead of humanity or individual human beings paying the price (consequences) for sin, Jesus Christ steps into the breach between God and humanity and pays the price for sin in humanity's place. By the passion and death of Jesus Christ, the harmonious relationship between God and human beings is restored and renewed. In addition, out of separated individuals there emerges one new people in Christ, with both hope and a guarantee.

In Zhang's understanding, evil has no ontological origin, that is, no ontological place in God's creation. Evil did not exist before the created world. Evil occurs in the "good world" after the world is created. This means that evil has an anthropological origin: because human beings sinned, there is evil. Importantly, "freedom to choose" does not require the existence of sin and evil. Rather, sin and evil result from a moment's shortcoming in human thinking and choosing, influenced by an uncontrollable human desire to be like God. So understood, in the Adam and Eve story, the serpent symbolizes humanity's being easily tempted; human beings alone are responsible for sin and evil which are avoidable; weak and stumbling human nature gives rise to living with constant difficulty. In Zhang's discernment, all is predetermined by God — from limited human nature in contradiction with uncontrollable desire, to separation from God due to original and personal sin, to human return to God through salvation in Christ.

Zhang Qingxiong's Analysis of the *Ru* (Confucian) Approach to Sin and Evil

Turning to the *Ru* perspective on sin and evil, Zhang's analysis is based on chapter 20, the *"Yao yue"* (King Yao said), of the *Lunyu (Analects)* of Kongzi.[4]

4. The *Lunyu (Analects)*, attributed to Kongzi (Confucius), c. 551-479 BCE, is a collection of discussions and instructions remembered, recorded, and transmitted by his followers and their followers. Scholars have long debated dates of composition for the chapters. It is generally agreed that chapters 6 through 9 are the earliest. Chapters 11-15 address concerns

Zhang relies upon Zhu Xi's (1130-1200) commentary to exposit the "*Yao yue.*" Then, Zhang uses this chapter as well as the *Shu* (Book of History) as a basis for comparing Christian and *Ru* perspectives.

Drawing mainly from Zhang's analysis and incorporating a few high-lights from my own work,[5] I offer this summary of Zhang's discernment of the *Ru* perspective on sin and evil. First, from the *Shu* it is clear that the authority of the *wang* (king) is mandated by *Tian*. Second, *Tian ming* (Heaven's mandate) is discerned as supporting both life and social harmony. Third, the king's role is to provide for the people in accordance with *Tian ming*; therefore, reception of and keeping *Tian ming* to lead the people is contingent upon how well the king leads. The hearts of the people are the sign of *Tian's* judgment.[6] If people are poor and in distress, they will revolt. If people are fed, clothed, sheltered, and educated, they will act rightly.

Fourth, by example, King Tang of the Shang dynasty (c. 1751-1025 BCE) recognized that the king (not *Tian* or the people) is responsible for all suffering on the part of the people. Here Zhang interprets the king's "offense" as being against *Tian* (and the people); similarly, "sin" is against God (and the people) in the Christian tradition. Just as God punishes human beings for sin, so also *Tian*[7] punishes (warns) the king with disasters in his kingdom. Unfortunately, it is the people who suffer in the process. Fifth, King Tang, admitting his offense, prays to Tian for rain. In so doing, he asks *Tian* not to punish the people, but rather to punish himself (Tang) for his offenses in not providing well for the people. Here Zhang notes that King Tang's offering of himself to be punished is like Jesus' offering himself on the cross to bear punishment for sin on the part of humanity.

---

of the mid to late Warring States period (fourth and third centuries BCE). Chapters 16-20, including the passage that Zhang cites here, differ considerably in content and style from the first fifteen chapters and are considered to have been added to the corpus perhaps during the late third century BCE. Even so, it is possible that material in any of the chapters may be genuinely from Kongzi himself.

5. This summary of the *Ru* (Confucian) perspective on sin and evil is largely from Zhang Qingxiong's essay. However, I do try to highlight and to clarify Zhang's points with themes from my "Ministers of the Moral Order: Innovations of the Early Chou [Zhou] Kings, the Duke of Chou [Zhou], Chungni [Zhongni], and Ju [Ru]" (unpublished Ph.D. dissertation, Harvard University, 1984), pp. 31-47.

6. Obenchain, "Ministers of the Moral Order," pp. 93-148.

7. For simplicity, I have substituted *Tian* for *Shangdi* here. During the Western Zhou period, when the *Shu* began to be compiled, these two names to denote transcendental power over everything in the world were often amalgamated and sometimes interchangeable. See my "Ministers of the Moral Order," pp. 31-47.

Yet Zhang notes three differences. (a) There is no "original" sin in *Ru* thought. (b) King Tang considers himself to be "son of *Tian*" in receiving *Tian*'s mandate to lead the people. Jesus is "son of God," mandated to lead the people in the kingdom of God. However, in the Christian tradition, God is discerned as one substance in three persons. Thus, Jesus as "son of God" is one of the three persons of God. (c) King Tang wanted *Tian* to be strict with himself and lenient toward the people; so also Jesus wanted God to be strict with Jesus and lenient toward the people. King Tang, however, wanted to assume responsibility for what he himself had done, but Jesus took responsibility for what the people have done.

Sixth, by the second example, in *Lunyu* 20, the *"Yao yue,"* Kongzi discusses King Wu, who founded the Zhou dynasty (c. 1025-249 BCE). Kongzi affirms that it was King Wu's appointing ministers on the basis of their moral character, not due to their blood relation with the king, that brought success.[8] Seventh, taking personal responsibility for disasters and not blaming others, King Wu also took positive political action: (a) in the sphere of weights and measures, (b) in penal law, (c) in restoring to leadership those in proper succession, and (d) in attending to food for the people, to proper rituals in mourning the dead, and to sacrificial offerings to the ancestors. Eighth, moreover, by his inward cultivation of *kuan* (generosity) he won the people, of *xin* (sincerity) he enabled the people to entrust him to lead, of *min* (sensitivity in leadership) he won the people's hard work, and of *gong* (justice) he persuaded the people and settled their disputes. Ninth, so instructing his student, Zizhang, Kongzi affirms it is the leader's cruelty, oppression, injury, and stinginess that bring evil to the people: suffering, calamity, and natural disasters.

Tenth, Kongzi concludes tersely: "Without knowledge of *Tian ming* (Heaven's mandate), one is without that by which to become a *junzi* (benevolent leader); without knowledge of *li* (ritual), one is without that by which to establish moral character; without knowledge of *yan* (words . . . including the principles of the inner heart expressed in words [the cumulative collection of oral-written records of the way of the ancient sage-kings], one is without that by which to know others."[9] In summary, by attending to proper outward actions to govern the people well and by attending to inner moral cultivation, King Wu eased the burden of the people, won their hearts, and thereby won *Tian ming* to lead, founding the Zhou dynasty.

---

8. See also my "Ministers of the Moral Order," especially pp. 204-96.

9. My translation is based on James Legge's *The Chinese Classics*, vol. 1 (Oxford: Clarendon Press, 1893), pp. 350-54.

Suffering and Human Effort in the Christian and *Ru* Traditions

Relying on the apostle Paul and Augustine on the Christian side and on Kongzi and the Song dynasty commentator, Zhuxi (1130-1200) on the *Ru* side, Zhang laments that in both traditions good people suffer. The New Testament explains that, because of original sin, good people suffer and that original sin is atoned for by the sacrifice and death of Jesus Christ. The *Ru* tradition teaches that good people suffer because of poor leadership. Moreover, in Zhang's discernment, the people's suffering (which is evil) is resolved not by *Tian* but by human beings who, with inner moral cultivation and proper political methods, provide better leadership of the people. Then, peace and harmony in the kingdom prevail. Nonetheless, Zhang also wants to argue that although *Ru* teachings urge profound reliance on human effort to rid the world of evil disasters, there is still some kind of "religious" or "spiritual" discernment of *Tian ming*, with which a leader must align to know how to provide well for the people and avoid disasters (evil).

Putting together both *Tian ming* and human effort, Zhang concludes that in *Ru* thinking, as evidenced in Kongzi, Xunzi (c. 298-238 BCE), and Dong Zhongshu (c. 179-104 BCE), evil calamities are both human-made and *Tian*-made. Moreover, there is an intimate connection between these two causes. Evil calamities are human-made by a ruler's cruelty, oppression, injury, and stinginess. Evil calamities are *Tian*-made as natural warnings to a ruler that he is not aligning with *Tian ming* and thereby causing the people to suffer. This is why in *Lunyu* 20, Kongzi instructs that the solution to human-made and *Tian*-made calamities is not prayer to *Tian*, as with King Tang of the Shang dynasty, but with human inner cultivation of generosity, sincerity, sensitivity, and justice outwardly manifested in appropriate political action.

Suffering, Human Effort, and Religious Spirituality in the *Ru* Tradition

Zhang asks whether Kongzi's emphasis on human efforts to solve calamity and evil represents a shift from the religious thinking of the *Shu* that depicts King Tang praying to *Tian* for rain. In other words, do inner moral cultivation and political action depart from the "religious" or "spiritual" dimension of the early Shang? Zhang says "no" and insists that Kongzi explicitly states that discernment of *Tian ming* is necessary both to inner moral cultivation and to political action. While Kongzi put at a distance all strange powers and spirits, Kongzi, like the former sage-kings, did acknowledge *Tian ming*, which sustains the livelihood of the people and the natural order. It is the responsibility of the leader to align himself with *Tian ming* in order to "channel" *Tian's* life-supporting power to the people.

Zhang further draws from Zhu Xi, who cites the two Cheng brothers, Cheng Yi (1033-1107) and Cheng Hao (1032-85), to affirm (a) that which resides in *Tian* is *ming* (order); (b) that which resides in righteousness is *li* (principle); (c) that which resides in humanity is *xing* (nature); d) that which is master in human beings is the *xin* (heart-mind). Order, principle, nature, and heart-mind are all one and the same, says Zhang. Thus, inner moral cultivation of the heart-mind aligns one with *Tian ming*. Perfected in inner moral cultivation, a leader, or a minister who assists a leader, relies on his own human effort to rid the world of evil.

Thus, *Tian* and human beings both have a role in ridding the world of evil. This close connection between *Tian ming* and the human heart-mind, in Zhang's assessment, is the special contribution that Chinese culture has to make to the human "religious" spirit. Zhang concludes that Kongzi and the *Ru* tradition do, in fact, continue the religious spirit of both the Shang and the Zhou dynasties. Moreover, the *Ru* solution to evil in the world, relying both on *Tian* and on human efforts, is different from the Christian solution to evil. According to Zhang's interpretation of the Christian view above, all is predetermined by God and depends on what Jesus Christ does. (Not all Christians would agree with Zhang's interpretation of Christian teaching, as it greatly diminishes the Christian understanding of humanity made in the image of God.) Thus, in Zhang's view, the *Ru* and Christian traditions are "religious" in different ways.

Deepening the Dialogue between Christian and *Ru* Approaches to Sin and Evil

With Zhang's assessments of the Christian and *Ru* perspectives on sin and evil in mind, I suggest that there are four ways by which we can bring these two perspectives into yet deeper interconnection on these issues. While interconnecting these two traditions is not Zhang's purpose, my interest, as one seeking to understand better God's purposes in the global era, is to explore how the unique gifts of each of these perspectives support each other.[10]

10. On globalization and interaction of revelations/gifts, see my "The Study of Religion

1. *Historical-Critical Methods*

First, it is important to detail the cumulative layers of textual sources for both the *Ru* and Christian traditions. On the *Ru* side, Zhang draws from (1) the purported Western Zhou (1025-722 BCE) classic of the *Shu*,[11] (2) the mid-Zhou (550-350 BCE) *Lunyu* attributed to Kongzi[12] with some commentary on the *Shu*, and (3) Zhu Xi's (1130-1200 CE) commentary on the *Lunyu* (*Lunyu jizhu*),[13] along with a few other commentaries. On the Christian side, Zhang draws from (1) Genesis of the Old Testament (compiled probably from the tenth through fourth centuries BCE),[14] (2) Paul's epistle to the Romans (written c. 55 or 56 CE),[15] in which Paul discusses topics from the Genesis account of Jewish history, including the Fall of Adam and the covenant of Abraham, and (3) Augustine's (354-430 CE) comments on Paul's epistle to the Romans.[16]

In order to compare in some depth the *Ru* and Christian views on sin and evil, choosing specific layers of text from these two cumulative traditions requires careful investigation. For example, recent research suggests that only twelve of the twenty-eight documents of the modern text, which is but one of the extant versions of the *Shu*, can be used as reliable source material for the Western Zhou.[17] Also chapter 20, the *"Yao yue,"* of the *Lunyu*, upon which Zhang relies in his analysis of the views of Kongzi and the *Ru*

---

and the Coming Global Generation," in Stackhouse and Obenchain, *God and Globalization*, pp. 96-109.

11. On the *Shu*, see Ch'en Meng-chia, *Shang Shu T'ung-lun* (A General Discussion of the Documents) (Shanghai: Commercial Press, 1957).

12. On the *Lunyu (Analects)*, see note 9 above.

13. On the *Lunyu Jizhu* of Zhu Xi, see Ch'en Jung-chieh (Wing-tsit Chan), *Chu-hsüeh lun-chi* (Collected Works of Zhu Xi) (Taipei: Student Book Co., 1982).

14. Modern scholars generally concur that Genesis is a composite work of the "Yahwist" school (J) with additions of the "Elohist" school (E), probably compiled during the "Solomonic renaissance" (c. 900-875 BCE), and the "Priestly" school (P), probably compiled during the neo-Babylonian period (538-323 BCE) when temple worship was restored. See John Barton, *The Cambridge Companion to Biblical Interpretation* (Cambridge: Cambridge University Press, 1998), pp. 181-97.

15. On Paul's letter to the Romans, see, for example, Paul W. Meyer, "Romans," in *The HarperCollins Bible Commentary* (San Francisco: HarperCollins, 2000), pp. 1038-73.

16. The draft of Zhang Qingxiong's paper with which I am working does not provide detail for the sources of Augustine that Zhang is using. One may consult Augustine's *Epistles*, *The Literal Interpretation of Genesis*, and *On the Grace of Christ and Original Sin*.

17. See H. G. Creel, *The Origins of Statecraft in China*, Appendix A (Chicago: University of Chicago Press, 1970), pp. 447-63.

tradition, was probably composed in the late Warring States period of the dying Eastern Zhou (c. 350-250 BCE). During this time, the monarchic, de-centralized leadership of the Zhou was greatly diminished and a new state system of centralized authority took shape. The family hierarchy of blood relatives was being replaced by a kind of skilled bureaucracy, with the Zhou king as titular head. As large states absorbed smaller states through a period of constant warfare, chronologies of different clan groups became interwoven, with combined lists of former kings extending back into time. The earlier one's ancestral forebear was, the greater the position of power one ought to have now.

It was during the mid to late Warring States period that the chronology of the *wang dao* (Kingly Way) was advanced by followers of Kongzi and the *Ru* school, which sought to preserve the Zhou legacy of morality as the basis of leadership. The chronology of ancient kings Yao, Shun, Yü, T'ang, and Wu that we find in the *"Yao yue"* chapter of the *Lunyu* is precisely this kind of chronology. Moreover, while argument is made for ministers of inner moral cultivation, rather than of blood relation, emphasis is also put on methods useful to centralizing power (weights and measures, laws and statutes, rewards and punishments), a combination typical of the *Ru* school in the late Warring States and Han periods. Thus, the *"Yao yue"* chapter probably tells us more about late fourth- and third-century *Ru* teachings than the teachings of Kongzi in the late fifth and early fourth centuries, which focused primarily on inner moral cultivation through study.[18] To Kongzi, kings Yao, Shun, and Yü, as examples of illustrious *de* (inner moral virtue), by which they benefited the people and possessed all under *Tian*, are far more exemplary than the militaristic kings T'ang and Wu, who are mentioned only in the *Lunyu*'s chapters 19 and 20, considered to be of the late Warring States period. Knowing the dates of composition for layers of texts in a tradition enables more precise interconnection on specific issues.

2. *Contextual Hermeneutics*

Since tradition is always cumulative, deeper interconnection among traditions requires attention to contextual hermeneutics. A sacred "text" is the "at

---

18. For the teachings of Kongzi and the teachings of his followers in the *Ru* school, see my "Ministers of the Moral Order," particularly the section titled "Model Kings of Yore," pp. 180-203.

first oral and later written" record of some revelation which, when recognized by a group of persons, enables them to bond, to become members of a group. "Context" refers to collective and individual responses, in all spheres of life, of persons who find meaning in a sacred text. As persons attach their experiences to a sacred text, they are illumined and life becomes meaningful in shared ways. Yet, meanings that group members find in a sacred text are often somewhat diverse. Moreover, different meanings find yet further diversity of expression in intentions, feelings, thoughts, and actions of particular persons, each with his or her own situational concerns.

Thus, contextual hermeneutics, the analysis of specific communities' responses, layer upon layer in a cumulative tradition, to shared sacred texts, is important to comparing traditions. For example, using historical methods to determine layers and probable dates of composition of the *Shu* and of Genesis, and drawing upon textual material that can be reliably dated, it is exciting to compare the early Western Zhou kings Wen and Wu (eleventh and tenth centuries BCE) and their reception of *Tian ming* to lead the people with kings David and Solomon (eleventh and tenth centuries BCE) called by God to lead the people of Israel. Both sets of leaders held hegemonic power in their respective domains. In both cases, the link between *Tian* or God and the leader is vitally close.

In both cases, a leader is called "son" of *Tian* or God, but a son who is "adopted" on the basis of what he has accomplished for the people, not a son on the basis of bloodline relation. In both cases, the king is under "order" from *Tian* or God to provide for the people. If he does, blessings from *Tian* or God will flow. If he does not, inevitably some curse comes upon and through the people to the king. Hence, what the king does in relation to *Tian* or God is extremely important. In both cases, *Tian* or God is on the side of the people, and so the early Zhou or early Israelite king does not need to "think up" or "create" a "human, artificially made" order to provide for the people. Rather, in both cases, the king has only to discern *Tian*'s or God's order, align himself with it, and *Tian*'s or God's blessings flow through the king to the people.[19]

19. On ancient Chinese concepts of *wang* (king), see Ch'en Meng-chia, *Yin-hsu pu-tz'u tsung-shu* (Beijing, 1956); Hsu Cho-yun, *Ancient Chinese in Transition* (Stanford: Stanford University Press, 1965); Homer H. Dubs, "Archaic Royal Jou Religion," *T'oung Pao* 46 (1959): 217-59; David N. Keightley, "The Religious Commitment: Shang Theology and the Genesis of Chinese Political Culture," *History of Religions* 17 (1978): 211-25; Benjamin I. Schwartz, "Transcendence in Ancient China," *Daedalus* (Summer 1975): 57-68. On monarchy in ancient Israel, see Moshe Weinfeld, "The Covenant of Grant in the Old Testament and in the

When *Tian*'s or God's power bestowed upon a king is not used on behalf of the people, but rather used to augment the power of a king, then the peace, harmony, and prosperity of the people are lost as they and the king become victims of great suffering due to famine, flood, and war. Very clearly, in both *Ru* and Judeo-Christian traditions, what Zhang calls the "evil results" of offense or sin against *Tian* or God are, in Zhang's terms, both "human-made and *Tian*/God-made." What can explain the king's misuse of power? Is there something about human nature that is the problem? While the answer from a specific historical context on the *Ru* side may differ greatly from an answer from a specific historical context on the Christian side, nonetheless, when these two traditions are studied cumulatively and historically, surface differences fade away to reveal remarkable similarities.

The main *Ru* view that human beings are good and have some kind of direct link with *Tian*, which ensures that human beings in some significant way resemble *Tian*, is quite similar to the Judeo-Christian view of humanity "made in the image of God." Moreover, for both, despite the *Tian*-given or God-given capacity for good in human beings, there is also an uncertain something that leads in the direction of what is not-good, that is, what is not beneficial to oneself or to the community. Moreover, for both, the teaching is that sin and evil arise from human beings' using power to augment themselves rather than using power to provide for others.

3. Ru *Inner Moral Cultivation and Christian Sanctification*

Where *Ru* and Christian traditions seem on the surface do have considerable difference, as Zhang points out, is on the issue of (1) what is to be done to prevent sin from happening in the first place, and (2) if there is sin, what is to be done to recover from what Zhang calls its "evil" results. On the *Ru* side, on both counts, what is to be done is to cultivate one's inner moral character. As Zhang points out, in traditional Chinese discernment, *Tian ming* (Heaven's order), *li* (right principle), *xing* (human nature), and *xin* (the heart-mind of humanity) are one and the same. Nonetheless, throughout

Ancient Near East," *Journal of the American Oriental Society* (1970): 184-203; Martin Noth, "Jerusalem and the Israelite Tradition," in his *The Laws in the Pentateuch and Other Studies*; G. Von Rad, *Old Testament Theology* I (Edinburgh and London: Oliver & Boyd, 1962); J. M. Miller and J. Hayes, *A History of Ancient Israel and Judah* (London: SCM Press, 1992); W. Brueggemann, *First and Second Samuel* (Louisville: Westminster John Knox Press, 1990).

the *Ru* legacy, there is recognition that the source of that which is not-good in the world is the human mind-heart that has lost *Tian ming*. Song *Daoxue* (neo-Confucian) scholars explain that *ren xin* (the human-made heart-mind) is at variance from *Tian xin* (*Tian*-made heart-mind). How does one get rid of the "human-made" and return to the "*Tian*-made"?

The *Ru* solution was to study *(xue)*, "to study in order to emulate" the ancient sage-kings who, following the way of *Tian*, provided for the people as good parents. To express in all one's feelings, thoughts, words, and deeds the *Tian*-endowed heart-mind of care and concern for the people, constant practice to put aside self-interest is necessary. This kind of study-practice requires will and vigilance. Such study is not to gain information, but to put into practice what the *Tian*-endowed heart-mind knows to be true. The *Lunyu* and later commentaries are all manuals for cultivating *ren* and *yi* (benevolence and appropriate right action). If *ren* and *yi* are not put into practice, neither are they known in the heart-mind.

Ru cultivation of inner moral character is remarkably similar to Christian "sanctification" (to make holy and more like God). Throughout Christian history, whether in Roman Catholic, Protestant, or Orthodox contexts, there are different views on "sanctification." What is at issue is what role God has and what role humans have in "making humans holy and more like God" in providing life-giving support to others. In fact, for *Ru* and Christian traditions, *Tian*/God and humanity both have roles in moral cultivation and sanctification, respectively. On the *Ru* side, there is innate close connection between *Tian* and humanity's *Tian*-endowed heart-mind; greed brings separation. On the Christian side, human beings are made in the image of God; again, greed brings separation. On the *Ru* side, what overcomes separation between *Tian* and humanity is human effort to cultivate benevolence and righteousness.

On the Christian side, what overcomes separation between God and humanity is, in the first place, the "justifying" sacrifice of Jesus Christ that cleanses humanity of sin so that human beings are "just as though they had never sinned." This justification puts humans back into right relationship with God. Moreover, the transforming grace of the resurrected Christ continues to hold those forgiven of sin and raised to new life in restored right relationship. Second, based on the first, human effort puts into practice faith, hope, love, and charity toward others and thereby demonstrates that God has already overcome all that separates humanity from God and from one another. While Christian Catholics, Orthodox, and Protestants may disagree on the role of human effort in "justification," all agree that human effort is, to some extent, "sanctifying" as one expresses God's love here in the world (cf. Phil. 2:12-13).[20] Thus, both *Ru* and Christian traditions affirm that recovery from sin and resultant evil here in this world involve both *Tian*/God and human effort.[21] The great difference is that in the Christian tradition, after sin and evil have taken hold, the input from God includes not only humanity's being made in the image of God, but also God's *restoring humanity* to that image even as sin yet occurs in this world.

4. Ti *(substance) and* Yong *(function): Treasure in a Clay Jar*

The Chinese philosophical distinction between *ti* (substance) and *yong* (function)[21] may provide one other way to bring the *Ru* and Christian traditions into deeper interconnection. Here I do not intend Zhang Zhidong's (1837-1909) approach to reform that puts Chinese learning as *ti* and Western learning as *yong*. Nor do I advocate that Christian faith is *ti* and all other religion is *yong*. Instead, I suggest that inner moral cultivation rather than religion is what is shared in common across cumulative traditions.[23] *Tian*/God/ more-in-life-than-meets-the-eye is enabling human persons to be like and to cooperate with *Tian*/God/more-in-life-than-meets-the-eye in providing peaceful, harmonious, abundant life here in the world. Different revelations disclose provisions from *Tian*/God/more-in-life-than-meets-the-eye. Although not the same, these provisions are not in competition with each other. Possibly, one may receive and benefit from more than one provision as one practices inner moral cultivation.

That which is provided — whether *Tian ming* (Heaven's order), the grace of the crucified Christ, or the one heart-mind — is treasure that has power. Cumulative tradition as a way of living is an outer clay jar that ex-

---

20. See *Practicing Theology: Beliefs and Practices in Christian Life,* ed. Miroslav Volf and Dorothy C. Bass (Grand Rapids: Eerdmans, 2002).

21. See the epistle to Titus on God and human cultivation (sanctification) in overcoming evil in the world.

22. *Ti-yong* (substance-function), *nei-wai* (inner-outer), and *ben-mo* (root-branch) are all concepts indigenous to China and central to Chinese metaphysics. See Daniel Kwok, *The Chinese Tradition,* University of Hawaii, Center for Chinese Studies, Occasional Papers, no. 3 (1989), pp. 18-19, and Fung Yu-lan, *The History of Chinese Philosophy,* vol. 2, trans. Derk Bodde (Princeton: Princeton University Press, 1953).

23. See my essay, "Inner Moral Cultivation: Interconnecting the Gifts," *International Conference on the Dialogue between Buddhism and Christianity, Xian, China* (Nov. 21-24, 2003).

presses and protects the inner treasure.[24] That which is within and has power is *ti* (substance); we have only begun to fathom it. Outer, materially expressed, cumulative tradition is *yong* (function).[25] *Ti* is revealed in *yong*, and *yong* is ever rectified by *ti*. In this global era of extraordinary interaction and interconnection, *ti* is breaking through the clay of our traditionally separate clay jars and fashioning one new, multicolored, multipatterned clay jar *(yong)* from the shards.[26]

24. 2 Corinthians 2:17; 3:1-5; 4:6-7. An ancient Near Eastern custom was to store a great treasure in a clay jar.

25. For Chinese *yong* here, I have in mind Karl Barth's notion of "plenitude." On Barth's distinguishing between God encountering humanity and humanity responding to God, see Karl Barth, *The Humanity of God* (Richmond: John Knox Press, 1960), ch. 2, "The Humanity of God."

26. One interactive, mutually transforming history of traditions of faith is an important theme in the work of Wilfred C. Smith, *Towards a World Theology* (Philadelphia: Westminster Press, 1981), pp. 18, 20, 38-44, 53, 113-15, 117, 164-68, 173-75, 178, 194.

A Response to Professor Zhang Qingxiong

Svein Rise

I appreciate very much the opportunity to comment on Professor Zhang Qingxiong's interesting analysis of "Sin and Evil in Christian and Confucian Perspectives."

There can be no doubt that sin and evil are two of the most important issues discussed in theology throughout the centuries. Quite naturally the theme has been discussed partly in light of the Christian idea of God, partly in light of different philosophical concepts of God. Theology has, however, a tradition of interpreting the subject from the angle of the history of religion. I therefore welcome the present paper as a valuable starting point for a discussion of comparative systematic theologies.

What I intend to do in this comment is to highlight a very important similarity, an aspect regarding the sin that seems a striking feature in both Christianity and Confucianism: namely tyranny. Tyranny is the will to power; the will to oppress or to rule, whether in the field of politics, society, or the smaller community. Zhang refers to Confucius's statement that "tyranny is fiercer than a tiger." He states in conclusion that "evil has resulted mainly from tyranny, and it is dependent upon human efforts to get rid of the evil." I will focus on tyranny by relating it to God, and finally to the Trinitarian concept of God.

According to Emil Brunner, there is a connection between the image of God and the image of man, or between the belief in God and the belief in humanity. He states: "In every culture, in every epoch of history it can be said: Tell me which God you believe in, and I will tell you who you as human beings are."[1]

---

1. See Emil Brunner, *Der Mensch im Widerspruch* (Berlin: Furche-Verlag, 1937), pp. 38-39 (my own translation).

With this quotation in mind I will now look closer at the concept of sin and humanity. My interpretation will be made in the light of Irenaeus's theology. Later, I will return to the idea of God.

Irenaeus emphasizes that man being God's image does not mean that he is a divine being.[2] The Divinity is able to model and to create man. Humanity means to be modeled and created by God. Against this background we can understand that the fundamental fallacy in human life is to conceive of oneself as divine. To regard oneself as a divine being is to be in rebellion against the Creator, who continually creates and sustains life. But at the same time, rebellion against the Creator is also rebellion against life itself. The ultimate consequence of this is death. To the extent that the human person has broken the natural link with life, he has become a captive of death. To have broken the natural link with the Creator — the stream of life — is to be shut in the house of death, against nature, and also against that person's own nature.

All of nature is in a certain sense filled with death and transience. Death is not to be understood here as the specific *day* of death, but as a power that threatens and harms life in general. In addition comes the fact that death attacks human security and confidence, reducing the ability and will to survive. Accordingly, humans have to secure their own life, and in doing so, they grasp benefits at the expense of others. This harsh situation causes competition for the resources of the earth and the good things in life. No human can avoid being a threat toward his or her fellow human beings.

In the light of this it is understandable that Irenaeus should regard the consequences of sin as ethical. Describing the fundamental damage that makes human life inhuman, Irenaeus utilizes a terminology — a language — that makes it possible for everyone to recognize the nature of sin: sin is to place oneself above one's fellow human beings, and at the same time fail to do good. In this situation the sinner reveals a lack of ability to manifest that which had been intended at the very beginning: being God's image. There is only one path that can lead the human being out of this mess: to be drawn into God's redeeming work through the life, death, and resurrection of the one human being — Jesus Christ. Through salvation the human person quite simply comes into being. This, in rough outline, is Irenaeus's under-

---

2. Cf. Irenaeus's main work, *Adversus haereses,* ed. A. Roberts and J. Donaldson, *The Ante-Nicene Fathers,* vol. 1 (Grand Rapids: Eerdmans, 1977), pp. 315-567. See also G. Wingren, *Människa och kristen* (Lund: Verbum, 1983). The interpretation of Irenaeus that Wingren gives here is based largely on his doctoral dissertation *Människa och inkarnationen* (1947). Cf. S. Rise, *The Christology of Wolfhart Pannenberg: Identity and Relevance* (Lewiston, NY: Edwin Mellen Press, 1997), pp. 35-41.

standing of the nature of sin and of the human being's possibility of escaping the captivity of death.

So far I have focused on the nature of sin and on a person's option for escaping the captivity of death. What then of the idea of God? The problem I want to deal with here is what impact the concept one has of God can have on one's perception of human nature, in particular the character of sin. Moving from Irenaeus to modern theology, scholars would, I suppose, agree with the statement of Brunner: "In every culture, in every epoch of history, it can be said: Tell me which God you believe in, and I will tell you who you are as human beings."

One of the most important books recently published on the concept of the Trinity is that by Gisbert Greshake.[3] He holds that at the moment the Trinitarian doctrine of God came to an end, the power of belief that sustains Christian life died. Allow me to mention just one of the reasons given by Greshake: As God in modern times was increasingly conceived of as an absolute, singular subject, without communion and communication, the human being also was seen as a "unitarian" and autonomous being, continually circling around its own self. This person can be characterized as a self-positing and self-constituting essence.

The final step in this historical process was that the human being found himself without his natural link to God the Creator — since man "proclaimed" himself "god." Will-to-power replaced solidarity; egoism, distrust, and lack of confidence replaced compassion and sympathy. In short, the human person echoed "the modern God," lacking interrelationship and communion. The last step in this historical process was the first step to tyranny.

It is worth considering against this background the significance that a Trinitarian concept of God has as a counterweight against sin's reality, egoism, and tyranny. In God — that is to say, in the Trinity — there is a unifying love that flows from the divine persons' identities as divine beings. We have to think the power of love in God as God's divine nature. In the light of the mutual love and dependence that characterize the divine persons, we could describe the Holy Trinity as a paradigm for our lives. Looking back to Irenaeus, we can therefore interpret his teaching of God by stating that the only way to realize true humanity in this life is to be drawn into the divine relationship of love. The reason is that by ourselves we are unable to get away from the captivity of death, to escape the ultimate consequence of tyranny.

---

3. Gisbert Greshake, *Der dreieinige Gott: Eine trinitarische Theologie* (Freiburg im Breisgau: Herder, 1998).

With this analysis made, it is possible to identify a parallel with the Confucian religion. The most representative statement in Zhang's paper that I will deal with here is the following: "In fact, behind the moral and political philosophy of Confucius, there is a metaphysical basis requiring belief." In addition comes the remark that "human beings need a transcendental belief in Heavenly decrees for establishing proper behavior in the secular world." These are in my opinion very significant observations. The "metaphysical basis requiring belief" and "transcendental belief in Heavenly decrees" can in this context be conceived of namely as an "authority" outside the moral subject, or as a "moral other."

I would also apply some terminology from Emmanuel Levinas: he too talks about the "Thou" in relation to "Myself," even though both Levinas and Confucius are silent concerning the existence of a personal God.[4] The point here is that the "moral other" beyond the subject can bring the self-constituting "I," the singular and autonomous "self," to an end. One should not, however, suppose that the "I" disintegrates in Zhang's interpretation of Confucianism. The moral capacity remains, as Zhang indicates in his paper, emphasizing that a human is capable of "moral cultivation and good politics." It should also be noted here, according to Zhang, that "to get rid of evil" depends "upon human efforts."

The parallel referred to above would lose its credibility if we do not identify God in the Christian religion as Trinitarian. The relationship between God and the human being in the Christian religion can be thought of as a parallel to the relationship between the human person and the metaphysical "other" in Confucianism, but only if God himself in Christianity is identified as a relational reality. The human being is created in the image of God, and thus the human being is like God in his relational character. To the extent that God is thought of as a subject, lacking communion and communication, God is not thought of as the Christian God. Lacking communion and communication, God is nothing but a "product" of man's thinking. As a singular subject, God is an image of one's own "Myself," of a magnified "Myself." This God is thereby a delusion, since mankind simply cannot exist in the singular. A human being has to be in communion to truly be human.

Now, some final remarks. In both Confucianism and Christianity the human being has an "authority" beyond himself that can be thought of as a "power" that causes the self-constituted "Myself" to come to an end. This

---

4. On Levinas, see *Time and the Other*, trans. R. A. Cohen (Pittsburgh: Duquesne University Press, 1987).

"power" occurs in Confucianism as a "metaphysical basis behind the moral and political philosophy" and as a "transcendental belief in Heavenly decrees." We can say this in Confucianism without mentioning the concept of a personal God. This makes us understand why the "metaphysical other" in Confucianism cannot have the power to overcome sin.

Nevertheless, we are dealing with a notable similarity between Christianity and Confucianism, inasmuch as we are able to identify in both systems of thinking a "power" apart from the human being. Moreover, the "power" outside man in both systems can be conceived of as a counterweight to the self-seeking "I": that egoism which is the first step to tyranny. The aspect that indeed lies behind the difference between the two religions is what makes that power outside man different: God's Trinitarian nature. God is different because the Father, the Son, and the Holy Spirit are different divine persons. This is the reason why God is a living God, worthy of our prayers and praise. And not to forget: This is the reason why God can help us overcome sin.

3 The Compatibility of Christianity with the Traditional Chinese Religions in Their Theories of the Divinity

He Guanghu

In various positive religions, the philosophical ontology concerning the origin of the world is based on the idea of the divine as the object of faith. In this paper I will discuss the theory of the Divinity from the perspective of religious philosophy; the concept "the divine" or "God" used in the paper should not be understood as being limited to any particular religious doctrine. Rather, it should be considered as the general name or a common designation of the object of religious faith, or in Rudolf Otto's words, *Das Heilige*.[1]

In fact, the difference in theories concerning the attributes of God or Divinity among certain religions is much smaller than among some others; in the previous case, the possibility that the theories could be compatible with each other is much greater. The theories of the Divinity of Christianity and of the traditional Chinese religions — Confucianism, Buddhism, and Taoism — belong to this category.

Transcendence

In philosophical language, the question about the origin of the world or Being itself is closely related to the question about the human being or the rec-

1. See Rudolf Otto, *The Idea of the Holy* (Oxford: University of Oxford Press, 1936), Chinese translation by Cheng Qiong et al. (Chengdu: Sichuan People's Publishing House, 1995). As for the reason for a broad and a narrow usage of the concept "religion," see the first chapter of my book *The Pluralized Idea of God* (Guiyang: Guizhou People's Publishing House, 1991).

ognizing subject. Similarly, in religious language, the concept of the Divinity is also closely related with that of humanity and enters human consciousness in such a relation. Thus, all the theories about the Divinity are more descriptions of religious experience than descriptions of God's objective attributes. Of course, since the experience of God or of the Divinity constitutes the core or center of religious experience, it also constitutes the basis for all the theories of the Divinity in various religions.

What we are concerned about here are the compatible elements or common aspects in the theories of the Divinity of Christianity and of Chinese religions. Among those elements or aspects, the most important and basic is the idea of the transcendence of the world's origin, or God. The objects of sacrifice in Confucian rituals included Heaven, Earth, ancestors, and various gods. Among them, Heaven, as the supreme Being or the highest God, has had a basically suprahuman or transcendental nature since it became the object of sacrifice and divination, being named as *Shangdi* (Sovereign on High) and *Tiandi* (Sovereign in Heaven). It was believed that all human activities and their success or failure depended upon the Heavenly will or Providence.[2]

The ideas of the collective unconscious and the archetype of the ancient Chinese often appear on a conscious level even today, as we can see in the common Chinese saying, "Moushi zai ren, chengshi zai Tian" ("Man proposes, God disposes"). Furthermore, although the idea of the "Earth" could be interpreted as belonging to the natural world in a modern philosophical sense, in Confucian rituals the Earth was understood as divine. There were the gods of the "Five Mountains" and "Four Rivers." They were believed to have supernatural and superhuman powers over climate, drought, geologic changes, and other natural phenomena. As for other "various gods," including the Sun, the Moon, the Land, the Grain, the Wind, the Rain, Thunder, and Lightning, they were all believed to have mysterious and superhuman powers over human life, hence some kind of transcendence.

Likewise, the gods in the Taoist pantheon have attributes similar to those in Confucianism. Not to mention that the highest triad of Yuqing Yuanshi Tianzun, Shangqing Lingbao Tianzun, and Taiqing Daode Tianzun, as the personal *Dao*, have a transcendental nature beyond any human reach. Even the gods from Yuhuang Dadi to Chenghuang Tudi in the popular system of gods, which sees gods quite anthropomorphically, have some kinds of powers and attributes far beyond the human world. For example, the god of thunder, "Lei Gong," one of the lowest gods in the system, could also "give

---

2. *The Book of History,* "Grand Norm."

blessing and curses from above, keep the judgment of things, control the material and the human, and administer life and death."[3]

In Buddhism, the objects of worship among the believing masses compose a very complex system of gods. The first of them is the Buddha, whose supernatural and superhuman nature is understood in such a way that it can be properly called a kind of transcendence. And all other Buddhas who are believed to exist in any time and in any place also have the same nature. Even the Bodhisattvas represented by Avalokitesvara, the innumerable Arhats, and other lower gods also have the attributes far beyond those that natural and human beings could have. Among such qualities are, for instance, being out of the life-death cycle and being in Nirvana.

For Christians, God has not only created the world and human beings, but also has infinite power in controlling everything in the world, including the authority of rewarding and punishing. God's transcendence is immeasurable, as we can read in the prophet Isaiah:

> To whom then will you liken God,
> or what likeness compare with him? . . .
> It is he who sits above the circle of the earth,
> and its inhabitants are like grasshoppers; . . .
> who brings princes to naught,
> and makes the rulers of the earth as nothing. . . .
> Lift up your eyes on high and see:
> Who created these?[4]

It must be noted that many Chinese scholars often take the personality of God as the most peculiar feature of the Christian concept of the Divinity, paying too little attention to the Christian idea of God's transcendence. In fact, we can read some other famous lines in the same Isaiah:

> For my thoughts are not your thoughts,
> nor are your ways my ways, says the Lord.
> For as the heavens are higher than the earth,
> so are my ways higher than your ways
> and my thoughts than your thoughts.[5]

---

3. Wushang Jiuxiao Yuqing Gufan Ziwei Xuandu Leifing Yujing.
4. Isaiah 40:18-26.
5. Isaiah 55:8-9.

The Christian God is so far beyond human beings that he can be addressed as "the Wholly Other" to show the enormous distance between God and man, indicating that the difference is not in quantity but in quality. As the Creator, Sustainer, and Perfecter of the world, he is not only above human beings, but also above everything else in the world. Based on this kind of understanding of the object of faith, we can discern a compatibility of the theories of the Divinity in Confucianism, Buddhism, Taoism, and Christianity.

Comprehensiveness

In religious experience, it would be impossible or unimaginable for believers to communicate with any "god" who has no personhood. So, an entity without any hint of personhood could not be worshiped as a god in any true religion. And respectively, any "god" who has no superhuman nature could never become an object of worship in any true religion. A religion would become a quasi-religion or pseudo-religion, if it respected as its object of worship something having merely human personality. Hence a question: What is the relationship between the human and the superhuman in Divinity?

If we recall that God or Divinity is the name of the origin of the world in philosophy, we could say that such a relationship must be a comprehensive relationship; the divine is related to everything in the universe. As the whole world with everything in it, including human beings, owes existence to its superhuman origin, the divine does indeed transcend and completely comprehend or cover the whole world and the entire human race.

As far as the Confucian Heaven is concerned, it comprehends everything justly. Before the period of Spring and Autumn (479 BCE) when the origin of the world could be designated as *Tian* as well as *Shangdi*, the object of religious worship was obviously a comprehensive one, as we can read in *The Book of Odes*:

> Heaven sees over the below,
> gathers all that He wills.[6]

and:

> O! Sovereign on High is great and glorious!
> He presents to the below with majesty.

6. *The Book of Odes*, Daya, Daming.

He surveys all the lands,
seeking for the people's peace.[7]

And after the period of Spring and Autumn, when the origin of the world could be designated as *Tian* and *Di* (the Earth), *Tian* still had the greatest comprehensiveness. For, as Zuo's *Chronicles* said, "Tian has the six Qi (energies),"[8] which means the *Yin*, the *Yang*, the wind, the rain, the darkness, and the brightness; and "Tian creates the five materials,"[9] which means metal, wood, water, fire, and soil — all the elements that compose the concrete phenomena in the world.

Tian Dao (Heavenly Way) is another term for the Divinity in Confucianism. And Zuo's *Chronicles* also declare that "Tian Dao is full, broad, and level,"[10] and "just as rivers and lakes contain dirt, mountains give dens to the wicked, and the sovereigns use jade to hide their disgrace, so is the Heavenly Way."[11] This reminds us of the Divinity revealed in Jesus Christ who comprehends everything, including suffering, and accepts everyone, including sinners.

In the doctrine of Taoism, *Dao* is the origin of the world and the object of religious faith; sometimes it is named as *Tian Dao* or *Tian Di*. Laozi says:

Tao is invisible and empty, but its usefulness cannot
be exhausted. It is so fathomless, like the ancestor of all things.[12]

and:

Isn't between Heaven and Earth like a bellow?
While vacuous, it is not inexhaustible;
the more it is drawn off, the more air it sends forth.[13]

Of course, such a *Dao* is infinite, eternal, and all-embracing:

Dao, as the abyss where all things are hidden,
is effective and precious to good men, and also
must be preserved by bad men. . . .

---

7. *The Book of Odes*, Daya, Huangyi.
8. *Zuo's Chronicles*, The Year 1 of the Duke Zhaogong.
9. *Zuo's Chronicles*, The Year 27 of the Duke Xianggong.
10. *Zuo's Chronicles*, The Year 4 of the Duke Zhuanggong.
11. *Zuo's Chronicles*, The Year 15 of the Duke Xuangong.
12. *The Book of Laozi*, 4.
13. *The Book of Laozi*, 5.

Why is Dao so much valued from the old days on?
Can it not be said that (with it) one can get what
he seeks for and be forgiven his sin?
Thus it is valued by all under heaven.[14]

So, the persons who attained *Dao* were called "sages":

The sage has no fixed personal will,
he regards the people's will as his own:
To those who are good, I am good;
and to those who are not good, I am also good.[15]

Such an interpretation seems very similar to Christian theology; as Jesus said, the Father in Heaven "makes his sun rise on the evil and on the good, and sends rain on the righteous and on the unrighteous."[16]

According to another representative of Taoism, Zhuangzi, who called the origin of the world as *Tian Di* (the Heaven and the Earth), "Tian covers all things, and Di supports all things." He holds that everything has the same value in the light of *Tao*, because "Tao does not exhaust itself in what is greatest, nor is it ever absent from what is least; and therefore it is to be found complete and diffused in all things."[17]

In comparison, we can recall some words on God from Augustine:

You are the most hidden from us and yet the most present amongst us. . . . You are ever active, yet always at rest. You gather all things to yourself, though you suffer no need. You support, you fill, and you protect all things. You create them, nourish them, and bring them to perfection. You seek to make them your own, though you lack for nothing. . . . You are never in need yet are glad to gain, never covetous yet you exact a return for your gifts.[18]

Following the words we mentioned above, Jesus said: "Be perfect, therefore, as your heavenly Father is perfect."[19] The perfection of God is what we

---

14. *The Book of Laozi*, 62.
15. *The Book of Laozi*, 49.
16. Matthew 5:45.
17. *The Book of Zhuangzi*, Tiandao, section 9.
18. Augustine, *Confessions*, trans. R. S. Pine-Coffin (London: Penguin Books, 1973), book I, ch. 4.
19. Matthew 5:48.

call "the comprehensiveness of the Divinity." However, this kind of comprehensiveness is not partial but perfect, not temporal but eternal, not conditional but unconditional; in other words, it is not relative but absolute. In this aspect, the theory of the Divinity in Christianity is also compatible with traditional Chinese religions.

Absoluteness

At the end of the last section we mentioned another important aspect of the Divinity — absoluteness. The so-called "absoluteness" does not only cover all the positive or affirmative attributes that people can imagine, but also stresses that all the attributes are infinite, eternal, unconditional, supreme, etc. For example, when we speak of the absolute justice of God, what we mean is not that he acts always according to some principle of justice, but that he himself is the source of the principle of justice, or even that he is the very justice itself. Human justice is finite, temporal, and conditional — in a word, relative. The ultimate, transcendental, and comprehensive origin of the world is the ultimate resource of justice on which humankind can rely and refer to.

In the Chinese classics we find such teaching as "Heaven provides us with the institutions and constitutions. . . . Heaven ordered us with rituals and proprieties" in *The Book of History*;[20] "neither know nor understand, just follow the principle of the Sovereign on High" in the *Zuo's Chronicles*;[21] "only Tian is great, so it is what Yao[22] kept on following" in Confucius's *Analects*;[23] and "man follows the Earth, the Earth follows the Heaven, the Heaven follows the Dao, the Dao follows the way of itself" in *The Book of Laozi*.[24] *Dao* is the way or the principle as it is.

In the Bible we can read in the book of Job: "Of a truth, God will not do wickedly, and the Almighty will not pervert justice. Who gave him charge over the earth and who laid on him the whole world?"[25] Any human words describing divine attributes are just images trying to grasp something that is beyond the reach of human words. These images are used for describing the

20. *The Book of History,* Declaration of Gaotao.
21. *Zuo's Chronicles,* The Year 9 of the Duke Xigong.
22. The name of the first of ancient sages whom Confucius admired highly.
23. *Analects,* Taibo.
24. *The Book of Laozi,* 25.
25. Job 34:12-13.

being itself or the origin of the world. We can use religious language only in an analogical or symbolic sense. The basic reason for this is that the object of religious language is something that is absolute. However, as relative beings, we have to attempt to use relative language to express our own experience of the Absolute. These kinds of attempts are similar in Christianity and Chinese religions.

May I give two examples of this similarity? From the Chinese side, my example comes from *The Book of Huai Nan Zi*, whose authors were canonized as Taoist Immortals. From the Christian side my example is the *Confessions* of Augustine, who was canonized as a Christian saint. Both of them have to employ much artistic language to express the human experience of the Absolute.

The Book of Huai Nan Zi reads: "Tao is the highest with nothing higher, the deepest with nothing deeper, more level than any leveler, more straight than any ruler, more round than any compasses, squarer than any squares; it covers the cosmos, without any outside and inside, carries all things, without any obstacles."[26] As the absolutely high and the absolutely deep, *Dao* is the standard of standards, the principle of principles, reminding us of Thomas Aquinas's argument for God as the absolutely true, the absolutely good, and the absolutely beautiful.

And *The Book of Huai Nan Zi* continues: *Dao*, it says,

> covers the Heaven and the earth, contains and grants in formless ways, explodes like a spring but flows slowly . . . being in itself but also being able to extend, secret in darkness but being able to be manifest, weak but being able to be strong, soft but being able to be hard. It stretches out to the four dimensions and includes the *Yin* and the *Yang*, orders time and space, and directs the sun, the moon, and the stars. . . . Just owing to it, the mountains can be high, the waters can be deep, the beasts can run, the birds can fly.[27]

It is made clear here that *Dao* is understood as the Absolute, which is the origin of all the relative abilities and possibilities and positive attributes we see in the world. Let us turn to the *Confessions*. Augustine began this Christian classic with a quotation from the Bible: "Can any praise be worthy of the Lord's majesty? How magnificent his strength! How inscrutable his wisdom!"[28]

---

26. *Moucheng Xun.*
27. *Yuandao Xun.*
28. *Confessions*, book I, ch. 1; see also Psalm 145:3.

Such a power can be understood as the origin of all powers, and such wisdom as the source of all the wisdom in the world.[29] Augustine continued to declare that God is the origin of all things: "For I should not be there at all unless, in this way, you were already present within me. . . . So, then I should be null and void and could not exist at all, if you, my God, were not in me."[30]

Then Augustine gave us a description of the Divinity of God who "made" heaven and earth: "O Thou, the greatest and the best, mightiest, almighty, most merciful and most just, utterly hidden and utterly present, most beautiful and most strong, abiding yet mysterious, suffering no change and changing all things: never new, never old, making all things new."[31]

It is amazing how similar Augustine's thought of the Divinity here is to that of the Taoist *Dao* and the Confucian *Tian!* And according to the more philosophical description of Thomas Aquinas, the divine being is the purely actual, the utterly infinite, and the impassibly eternal,[32] "the highest and the primary truth"[33] — in a word, the infinite and the ultimate Absolute.

Holiness

All the divine attributes of the Divinities described in the above sections have a common characteristic: the element of mystery or numinousness, because the "origin" or the "ultimate" is beyond human understanding. Of course, different theologians, philosophers, and readers in various religions may, according to their religious experience, add some other attributes to the Divinities, or some other specifications in the attributes we have given in the last sections. However, no matter how many divine attributes may be listed, we eventually end up with the idea of holiness based on that of numinousness. Once again, referring to Otto: above all, the Divinity is the Holy One, *Das Heilige.*

The concept of holiness refers to the nature of God being an object of the utmost reverence of humankind. This holiness transcends all the positive spheres of human life, such as morality, purity, perfection, etc. When we use the concept "holiness" in contrast with that of "numinousness," it is in

29. See John Macquarrie, *Principles of Christian Theology* (London: SCM Press, 1979), p. 205.

30. *Confessions,* book I, ch. 2; see also Romans 10:13-14.

31. *Confessions,* book I, ch. 4.

32. *Summa Theologiae,* I, 9, 10.

33. *Summa Theologiae,* I, 16, 5.

relation to the human experience of the Numinous touching human life. While experiencing it as some overwhelming demand or pressure, people express its nature with "justice" or "righteousness"; while experiencing it as some powerful support or help, people describe its nature with "graciousness" or "love." These attributes can be experienced and understood by people in their life experience; therefore, the holiness composed by these positive attributes, as Otto observed, refers to the rational aspect of grasping the Divinity. In other words, it indicates the shift of the experience of the Divinity from irrationality to rationality.[34]

Holiness is a combination of positiveness and loftiness in the concept of the Divinity. As to the positiveness, it refers to the true, good, beautiful, just, righteous, benevolent, and loving qualities of the Divinity. As to the loftiness, it indicates that the Divinity is immeasurably beyond human existence. In some sense, the holiness includes the transcendence, the comprehensiveness, and the absoluteness, but at the same time it stresses the positive or affirmative aspect of all attributes of the Divinities. The idea of holiness is constitutive for any religious experience of the Divine. For instance, only combining the quality of justice with that of holiness can bring about such a complex experience as "awe."

We can see such a combination in Confucian theory. For example, the *Interpretations* in *The Book of Changes* begins with the words: "The Heaven is lofty and honored and the Earth is low and subservient, Qin and Kun or the world is accordingly settled."[35] The same passage continues: "The successive movement of the inactive and active (*Yin* and *Yang*) operations constitute what is called Dao. That which ensures the result is goodness; that which shows it in its completeness is the natures (of men and things)." It is manifested in the benevolence (of its operations), and (then again) it conceals and stores up its resources. It gives stimuli to all things, without having the same anxieties that possess the sage. "It is complete in the abundance of virtue and in the greatness of its stores!"[36] The loftiest is also the most honorable. The goodness of the origin of the world gives the same good charter to all created things, and "benevolence" refers to its nature as giving birth to myriad things.

In *The Book of Changes* there is also the following passage ascribed to Confucius himself: "Its wisdom is lofty and its ritual is low. The loftiness is af-

---

34. Cf. Otto, *The Idea of the Holy.*
35. *The Book of Changes,* Interpretations 1.
36. *The Book of Changes,* Interpretations 1.

ter the pattern of the Heaven, and the lowliness after the pattern of the Earth. It completes the nature of all things and preserves the being of all things, so it is the gate from which come forth morality and righteousness."[37]

Furthermore, we can discover an obvious shift from irrationality to rationality in the Chinese idea of God, in the development of the concept *Tian* or *Di* (the Heavenly Sovereign). During the Shang dynasty (1711-1066 BCE) what was dominant in the idea of *Di* or *Shangdi* (God) was its mysterious or numinous nature. Except for the ancestors of Shang rulers, no human beings could have contact with God. There were even no sacrifices or prayers presented to God, who was believed to be the cause of all the good and all the bad in the world. But during the Zhou dynasty (1066-256 BCE) the concept of *Di* was gradually replaced with that of *Tian*, and, at the same time, the element of rationality increased in the understanding of the Divinity, *Tian*.

The most obvious evidence of this shift is the so-called "fitting in Heaven with virtue" principle: Heaven was more and more seen as the source of the good, not as the cause of the evil; the most important divine attribute is virtue. Such a theory was initiated by the famous ruler and sage Duke Zhougong, and the movement of this new thought renewed the idea of God throughout the history of China. *Tian* possesses various positive qualities and has much to do with human rationality. Therefore, what it arouses in man is not only fear, but also "awe," which is a complex idea including the elements of both reverence and love.[38] There are so many examples of this in the Confucian scriptures that I hope to be excused from further quotation.

Besides virtue or morality, the rational element of the new idea of the Divinity involves some kind of insistence on a moral order. In this understanding, the reward and punishment from Heaven was no longer an arbitrary and mysterious act. We can see many examples of such an idea throughout *The Book of History*, such as "a disaster is not caused by the cruelty of Tian, but is a direct result from the wrongdoing of the people themselves,"[39] and "Tian Dao gives happiness to the good, and disaster to the wicked."[40]

This idea is very close to the interpretation of the idea of wrath by the Christian theologian C. H. Dodd. Dodd pointed out that the apostle Paul never spoke of God's anger, and the concept of wrath only referred to the di-

---

37. *The Book of Changes*, Interpretations 1.

38. According to Robert R. Marett, we must admit "wonder, admiration, interest, respect, even love perhaps, to be, no less than fear, essential constituents of the elemental mood of awe." *The Threshold of Religion* (London: Methuen, 1909), pp. xxiii-xxviii.

39. *The Book of History*, Jiugao.

40. *The Book of History*, Tanggao.

vine moral order's reaction to wrongdoing and evil acts. There is a certain moral structure in human life, and the violation of this structure will necessarily bring about disaster — this is the logic of wrath.[41] This interpretation considered the divine nature as a rational rule of justice. This is a very important reason for calling God the Holy One.

In the Taoist classics, we also find plenty of support and evidence showing that the divine element in *Dao* is closely linked with the idea of a loftiness that is capable of arousing awe among humans. *The Book of Huai Nan Zi* said: "Tao has systematic and insistent norms and orders, and, as the only one root, it connects all the myriad of branches and leaves. With it, therefore, the noble have something to obey, the mean have something to stand on and enjoy, the poor have something to keep on living, and people in difficulties have something to deal with and resolve their problems."[42] In the passage, we find that, in addition to the positive and ultimate attributes, *Dao* also has a strong quality of rationality or *logos*.

Furthermore, "the supreme Dao created all things, but does not possess them as its properties; Dao perfected all phenomena, but does not rule over them as its slaves."[43] And we can continue with a further quotation: "Tian . . . lets its creatures act in the daylight and rest at night, makes them dry with wind, gives them drink with rain. It raises up the creatures in such a way that we cannot see its feeding; it sweeps out the creatures in such a way that we cannot see its killing. This is what we call Divine Wisdom."[44] Such an idea is consistent with the Western idea of the Divinity; it does not surprise us to find the following description of *Dao* so similar to the Christian understanding of God: "The Heavenly Dao has nothing for itself, nothing to go with, nothing to leave. The one who is good at it will have more than he needs; the one who is not good at it will be in lack. The one who follows it will become prosperous; the one who is against will be destroyed."[45]

In the West, the idea of the Divinity was also combined with that of rationality. This was directly grounded on the basic faith that the Holy One is the origin of the world, the Creator, and the Sustainer and the Perfecter of the world as well. This faith is most clearly expressed in the following quotation from the book of Isaiah:

---

41. Quoted from John Hick, *Philosophy of Religion* (Englewood Cliffs, NJ: Prentice-Hall, 1963). Chinese translation by He Guanghu (Beijing, 1988), p. 32.

42. *The Book of Huai Nan Zi*, Chuzhen Xun.

43. *The Book of Huai Nan Zi*, Yuandao Xun.

44. *The Book of Huai Nan Zi*, Daizu Xun.

45. *The Book of Huai Nan Zi*, Lanmin Xun.

It is he who sits above the circle of the earth,
and its inhabitants are like grasshoppers;
Who stretches out the heavens like a curtain,
and spreads them like a tent to live in;
who brings princes to naught,
and makes the rulers of the earth as nothing. . . .
To whom then will you compare me,
or who is my equal? says the Holy One.
Lift up your eyes on high and see:
Who created these?[46]

The following quotations from Isaiah can be compared with the above quotation from *The Book of Huai Nan Zi*:

[The Lord] does not faint or grow weary;
his understanding is unsearchable.
He gives power to the faint,
and strengthens the powerless.[47]
For thus says the high and lofty one
who inhabits eternity, whose name is Holy.[48]

In the West, the concept of *logos* has a lot to do with the concept of rationality, but also the mysterious dimension of *logos* has been recognized in Christianity. This is most obviously expressed in the beginning of the Gospel of John, which is the basic text for any Christian ontology: "In the beginning was the Word *(logos),* and the Word was with God, and the Word was God. He was in the beginning with God. All things came into being through him, and without him not one thing came into being. What has come into being in him was life, and the life was the light of all people. The light shines in the darkness, and the darkness did not overcome it."[49]

This passage indicates that the holiness of Jesus Christ primarily consists in his unity with God. This unity is expressed in how the Father created the world through the Son. For this reason, John Macquarrie, having clarified the meaning of the concept the "Holy Being," explained the Father as "primordial Being," the Son as "expressing Being," and the Holy Spirit as

---

46. Isaiah 40:22-23, 25-26.
47. Isaiah 40:28-29.
48. Isaiah 57:15.
49. John 1:1-5.

"uniting Being." All three persons can be said to be three different movements of the one Holy Being.[50]

In fact, in various great religions, holiness has become the essential element of the Divinity. But in religious experience, there still remains a numinous or irrational element connected with the idea of the Holy. Yet, the concept of holiness has undergone the rationalization of the mysterious element and the transformation of *mysterium tremendum et fascinans* into the object of "awe." The highest expression of the Divinity as the Holy One is to understand him as the origin of the world. He is the foundation of the creation, the sustenance and unity of the world — of the basic facts of existence beyond human understanding. Our analysis here has found support for this claim from the sources and theories of Christianity and the Chinese religions. For this reason, I think that John Macquarrie's definition of God as the "Holy Being," with its combination of fact with value and subjectivity with objectivity, describes the object of worship in all true religions.

50. Macquarrie, *Principles of Christian Theology,* pp. 103-22.

A Response to Professor He Guanghu:
Different Reactions to the Similarities between Christianity and the Traditional Chinese Religions

Paulos Huang

After reading the essay of Professor He Guanghu on the compatibility of Christianity with traditional Chinese religions in regard to their theories of the Divinity, I would like to respond to it by analyzing different reactions to the relationship[1] between Christianity and Chinese traditional religions so as to identify, among these different reactions, those reflecting the position found in He Guanghu's research. Since Professor He focused his essay on the issue of the Divinity, I will limit my response to the conception of God, which is larger than the conception of the "Divinity" but includes it.

Concerning the relationship between Confucian and Christian conceptions of God, there are two contrary arguments. Some people argue that the Christian God and Confucian Heaven (Sovereign on High) are homogeneous. Thus, Christian missionary work is, in fact, to help the Chinese people rediscover their own God whom they have forgotten. Jesuit missionaries such as Matteo Ricci referred to the similarities between the Chinese classics and the Bible in order to preach such a message to Chinese Confucians in the sixteenth century.[2] This approach has been challenged by increasing numbers of people, since it is difficult to imagine that the Christian God and

---

1. The concept of "relationship" is seen here as flexible; it may cover many elements, such as "difference," "similarity," or "compatibility."

2. Matteo Ricci, *The True Meaning of the Lord of Heaven*, trans. Douglas Lancashire and Peter Hu Kuo-chen (St. Louis: Institute of Jesuit Sources, 1985), ch. 1, "A discussion on the creation of heaven, earth, and all things by the Lord of Heaven, and on the way He exercises authority (over them) and sustains them"; ch. 2, "An explanation of mistaken views concerning the Lord of Heaven current among them."

Confucian Heaven (Sovereign on High) are the same, and Confucians may also respond to missionaries that if the Christian God is the same as the Confucian Heaven, there is no need to introduce the Christian God.

Other people argue that the Christian God and Confucian Heaven (Sovereign on High) are heterogeneous. For example, some modern scholars such as Gernet[3] and Cummins[4] argue that Christian missionaries deliberately concealed the truth about Christ and strategically compromised with Confucianism and deceived their interlocutors, as they realized that the heterogeneity of different cultural traditions cannot be synthesized. However, Criveller has rejected the above argument, and says that the anti-Christian opposition was not generated by the late discovery of an alleged Jesuit fraud, since no traditional neo-Confucian has been found who first accepted Christianity and then refused it. On the contrary, the opposition from some Confucians was there right from the beginning. At the same time, right from the beginning, some traditional neo-Confucians (a small minority) accepted Christianity, fully conscious of the significance and the implications of such an anti-conformist choice.[5]

In the present paper I will make an analysis in order to find why there are different reactions to the Christian God from the Chinese side. Are the Christian God and Chinese Heaven (Sovereign on High) heterogeneous or homogeneous? If they are heterogeneous, is a dialogue still possible between them? What are the contact points that can help people create a dialogue between the Christian God and Chinese Heaven (Sovereign)?

The Reaction of Traditional Neo-Confucians

The first group of Confucians who reacted to Christianity will be called "traditional neo-Confucians" in the present work. This refers to those Chinese neo-Confucians in the time of Matteo Ricci in the sixteenth and seventeenth centuries.[6] Christianity was highly appreciated by most of the neo-

---

3. Jacques Gernet, *China and the Christian Impact: A Conflict of Cultures*, trans. Janet Lloyd (London and New York: Cambridge University Press, 1985), pp. 40-47, 57.

4. J. S. Cummins, *A Question of Rites: Friar Domingo Navarrete and the Jesuits in China* (Aldershot, UK: Scholars Press, 1993), pp. 54-59 (on Ricci), pp. 76-77, 111-12 (on Aleni), p. 100 (on the converts), pp. 140-41 (on Schall).

5. Gianni Criveller, *Preaching Christ in Late Ming China: The Jesuits' Presentation of Christ from Matteo Ricci to Giulio Aleni* (Taipei: Taipei Ricci Institute, 1997), pp. 402-3.

6. Neo-Confucian reactions to Christianity in the eighteenth and nineteenth centuries

Confucians at that time; some of them were even converted by missionaries. But Christianity was also criticized by Buddhists and other neo-Confucians, especially after Ricci's death. Thus, there are different groups among the traditional neo-Confucians; some are Christian converts, some are sympathetic to Christianity but are not Christians, and some are against Christianity. Their positions should be indicated when each of them is analyzed. Later, because of the Rites Controversy,[7] anti-Christian movements occurred, and finally the Qing emperor Yongzheng forbade Christianity in 1724.

For over one hundred years, these traditional neo-Confucians had been acting as the main dialogue partners to Christians, and this situation did not change until the first half of the twentieth century. Among this group of traditional neo-Confucians both negative and affirmative reactions to Christianity can be found, and we call both of them "traditional neo-Confucians." Different neo-Confucians usually took different primary Confucian scriptures as their primary sources for interpreting Confucianism in their reactions to Christianity.

For example, those neo-Confucians who reacted affirmatively to Matteo Ricci's argument of God's existence usually referred to primary Confucian scriptures such as *Shujing* and *Shijing;* but other neo-Confucians who reacted negatively to the existence of God usually referred to secondary Confucian scriptures such as the writings of Zhu Xi. For many of this kind of neo-Confucian, the secondary scriptures of the Song and Ming neo-Confucians became primary scriptures, and they did not doubt the tenability of these interpretations. Therefore, although both types of neo-Confucians claim that they represent Confucianism, in fact, they speak different things. Although both of them react to Christianity in the name of Confucianism, they have, however, different presuppositions. Thus, it is necessary to discover the different presuppositions behind various Confucian reactions to different Christian conceptions if one hopes to answer the question of whether China can really accept Christianity.

---

will not be studied in the present work, since they were basically similar to those of traditional neo-Confucianism. Patriotism and nationalism occupied the dominant role.

7. Tu (Du) Weiming, "Confucianism," in *Our Religions,* ed. Arvind Sharma (New York: Harper, 1995), pp. 167-80.

The Reaction of Cultural Nationalist Neo-Confucians

The second group of Confucians who reacted to Christianity are the first (1921-49) and second (1950-79) generations of neo-Confucians, as discussed by Bresciani;[8] in the present work we will call them "cultural nationalist neo-Confucians." They are the people who have followed both neo-Confucianism and rationalism of the Enlightenment tradition since the beginning of the twentieth century. One of the main features of this group's reactions to Christianity is nationalism. Since the nineteenth century, Christianity has been associated with Western imperialism in the minds of Chinese people, because both Catholics and Protestants came to China together with Western imperialists. Although Christianity is not identical with Western imperialism, in the memories of the Chinese they were very closely related. Thus, the encounter between Christianity and Chinese culture became a struggle between nationalism (and patriotism) and imperialism.

Beginning in the 1910s, China witnessed repeated anti-Confucian and anti-Christian campaigns, especially focused in the May Fourth Movement of 1919.[9] As Chinese intellectuals saw their land endure one humiliation after another at the hands of foreigners in the nineteenth and early twentieth centuries, they came to consider Christianity as the representative of Western cultural imperialism, and they came also to believe that Chinese civilization itself had broken down and failed its own people. Since Confucianism was so closely identified with the central values of the civilization, Confucianism came under severe attacks as the chief villain responsible for all the ills of Chinese life, including political despotism, social disintegration, economic backwardness, poverty, disease, starvation, and even foot-binding and opium addiction.[10]

While both Chinese Confucianism and Western Christianity were attacked, the dominant ideologies of that time were nationalism and modernism, which included scientism, democracy, etc. The Communist Party preferred Marxist dialectical materialism, and the then-ruling Guomindang

---

8. Umberto Bresciani, *Reinventing Confucianism: The New Confucian Movement* (Taipei: Taipei Ricci Institute, 2001).

9. This movement was started on May 4, 1919. Its main features were directed against Western imperialism and Chinese feudalism. Confucianism was criticized as a negative feudalist heritage. Religions, including Christianity, were criticized as irrational. Science and democracy were appreciated, and the Enlightenment tradition of rationalism was emphasized.

10. Tu Weiming, *Our Religions*, p. 214.

Party preferred Dr. Sun Yat-sen's Three People's Principles (Nationalism, Democracy, and the People's Livelihood). The two parties agreed in advocating that China should learn Western science and technology so as to overcome Western imperialism.

During this period, cultural nationalist neo-Confucians did not occupy the dominant position as a conversation partner with Christianity because Confucianism itself was also under attack. However, a group of cultural nationalist neo-Confucians had also begun to reinterpret Confucianism so as to face the challenges posed by the modernism of scientism and technology and from the rationalism of the Enlightenment tradition. In this process Christianity was generally treated negatively. Liang Shuming, Feng Youlan, Xiong Shili, Tang Junyi, Xu Fuguan, Fang Dongmei, and Mou Zongsan were the primary representatives of these cultural nationalist neo-Confucians.[11] They tried to correct what they regarded as the mistakes of the May Fourth Movement's approach of criticizing Confucianism, and they reaffirmed Confucianism. In 1958 some of them published a "Manifesto for the Reappraisal of Sinology and Reconstruction of Chinese Culture" in Hong Kong. In this manifesto, the signatories emphasized the harmony between the "way of Heaven" *(Tiandao)* and the "way of man" *(rendao)* as the central legacy of Confucianism.[12] The reactions of these cultural nationalist neo-Confucians to Christianity were negative, with a strong nationalist sense. They were "not always completely fair."[13]

As far as its reaction to Christianity is concerned, the feature of this "cultural nationalist neo-Confucianism" can be described as follows. On the one hand, it has absorbed certain Western elements (such as rationalism) so as to reconstruct Confucianism; on the other hand, it has a strong nationalistic sensitivity and seeks to protect Confucianism from the influence of Western religions. Thus, its attitude to Christianity was not always objective and often had a defensive feature. In their reaction to Christianity, these cultural nationalist neo-Confucians usually follow the Mencian tradition. As to the secondary scriptures, some Confucians appreciate the tradition of Zhu Xi's Learning of Principle and others prefer the tradition of Wang Yang-

11. Different scholars have given various names to these figures, and in the present work they are called "cultural nationalist neo-Confucians."

12. MRSRCC (A Manifesto for the Reappraisal of Sinology and Reconstruction of Chinese Culture, 1958), published in Carsun Chang (Zhang), *The Development of Neo-Confucian Thought*, vol. 2, Appendix (New York, 1963).

13. Hans Küng and Julia Ching, *Christianity and Chinese Religions* (London: SCM Press, 1993), p. 98.

ming's Learning of Heart-mind. When the secondary scriptures become their preference, they face the danger of losing their intention or ability to criticize these secondary scriptures.

Cheng Zhongying (1935-), a "modern Confucian," has summarized the dialogue between Chinese and Westerners in the twentieth century as moving in two directions. One is the rejection of tradition in the name of complete Westernization; another is the effort by the cultural nationalist neo-Confucians to Sinicize Western philosophy based on an assumption of the superiority of Chinese culture.[14] Of the great leaders of cultural nationalist neo-Confucianism, Cheng Zhongying is both a critic and an admirer. For instance, Cheng is not sympathetic to Liang Shuming and Xiong Shili, who criticize Western philosophy without having a direct knowledge of it. Cheng finds that Tang Junyi, Mou Zongsan, and Xu Fuguan have a better knowledge of Western thought, but they are apologists of the traditional type and do not engage in debate or dialogue with Western philosophy. According to Cheng, even Mou Zongsan, although he had acquired a deep understanding of Kant, did not attain an overall comprehension of Western philosophy.[15] This weakness has influenced their reactions to Christianity.

The Reaction of Modern Confucians

The third group of Confucians who have been reacting to Christianity are mostly members of the third generation of neo-Confucians (1980-) as discussed by Bresciani; but they are called "modern Confucians" in the present work. Some figures not mentioned by Bresciani are also included in this group here. Their reactions to Christianity date from the beginning of the 1980s. The self-defending feature of the above two groups has gradually been replaced by syncretistic and academic characteristics.[16] We divide these scholars into the following two subgroups:

The first subgroup of modern Confucian reactions to the Christian concept of God includes individuals of the Mencian tradition, which emphasizes

14. See Bresciani, *Reinventing Confucianism,* p. 404.

15. Cheng Zhongying, *Zhongguo zhexue de xiandaihua yu shijiehua* (The Modernization and Globalization of Chinese Philosophy) (Taipei: Jinglian chubanshe, 1994). Cf. Bresciani, *Reinventing Confucianism,* pp. 402-9.

16. See John Berthrong, "Boshidun ruxue" (Boston Confucianism), in *Xin rujia pinglun* (Discussions on Neo-Confucianism), vol. 2, ed. Zheng Jiadong et al. (Beijing: Zhongguo guangbo dianshi chubanshe, 1995), pp. 30-50.

the tradition of Zisi, Mencius, Lu Jiuyuan, Zhu Xi, Wang Yangming, and Mou Zongsan, but exhibits no strong nationalist sense as the cultural nationalist neo-Confucians do. Liu Shuxian (1934-) and Du Weiming (1940-) are representatives. These scholars have brought Confucianism, Christianity, and the Enlightenment way of thinking, e.g., rationalism and scientism, to the same agenda for discussion, and the Western Enlightenment tradition has become an important element in the discussion. Although both the anti-Confucian and anti-Christian approaches since the May Fourth Movement of 1919 have been criticized, the Confucianism that holds the Five Classics and Four Books as its primary scriptures has not been rejected. However, for the modern Confucians of the Mencian tradition, neo-Confucianism from the Song dynasty to the 1970s is not regarded as a complete, perfect system.

Modern Confucians of the Mencian tradition have suggested learning things such as the concept of transcendence from Christianity in order to modernize Confucianism.[17] These modern Confucians know both Western and Chinese cultures quite well and usually hold a much more objective attitude toward both Western and Chinese traditional cultures. Du said that the three dominant ideologies in the tradition of the May Fourth Movement are materialism, scientism, and utilitarianism. The only aspect of Western thought that Chinese intellectuals of that time were interested in was technological development; Christianity was ignored or totally rejected. Now, nearly a century later, Du suggests that China should learn the concepts of "Transcendent God" and "Original Sin" from Christianity.[18] Liu identifies the Christian God as external transcendence, a concept that neo-Confucians should learn about.[19] Thus, they both react to the Christian God affirma-

---

17. Liu Shuxian, "Some Reflections on What Contemporary Neo-Confucian Philosophy May Learn from Christianity," in *Confucian-Christian Encounter in Historical and Contemporary Perspective* (Lewiston: Edwin Mellen Press, 1991), pp. 61-68. See also Liu Shuxian, "Modernization of Confucianism and Christianity," *Pacific Theological Review* (1993): 67-70.

18. The suggestion of Liu Shuxian has also been supported and elaborated by Du Weiming; see "Wenhua Zhongguo jiangshen ziyuan de kaifa yu chuanjian," presented by Du in South New England High Technology Exchange Conference on November 11, 1994. See also Du's "Zui yu shan: Ren xingxing de tantao," in *Dao zhu guanghui: Zhongguo wenhua yu Jidu jiao xinyang duihua yantaohui* (1994), later published also in *Wenhua Zhongguo* (March 1995): 6-16.

19. Liu Shuxian, "Dangdai xin rujia keyi xiang jidujiao xue xie shenme" (What Contemporary Neo-Confucians Can Learn from Christianity), in *Dalu yu haiwai: Chuantong de fanxing yu zhuanghua* (Mainland and Overseas: The Rethinking and Transformation of the Tradition) (Taipei: Yunchen chubanshe, 1989), pp. 259-71.

tively, and their attitude is not only different from that of traditional neo-Confucians who were against Matteo Ricci during the Ming dynasty, but is also different from that of the cultural nationalist neo-Confucians such as Liang Shuming, Feng Youlan, Xiong Shili, and their followers. Therefore, in the present, in order to develop Confucianism, the following three challenges should be met and resolved: the transcendence and immanence of Christian thought, economic development and modernization, and Freudian conceptions of human nature.

These modern Confucians of the Mencian tradition seek to preserve Confucianism, but they are also open to Western science, democracy, and capitalism. In mainland China, scholars of the Chinese Cultural Institute-school (Zhongguo wenhua shuyuan pai), e.g., Tang Yijie and Li Zehou, are the representatives of this approach, and it seems they have been permitted by the Communist government. There is, however, a difference between scholars of the modern Confucian Mencian tradition and them, since the former group (e.g., Liu Shuxian and Du Weiming) have accepted what they regard as too much of the neo-Confucian interpretations of the Song and Ming dynasties, which are themselves overly dependent on metaphysical assumptions drawn from Buddhism.

Contemporary mainland Chinese intellectuals do not have this feature, and they have been mostly influenced by the Enlightenment tradition. Du Weiming, Liu Shuxian, and Tang Yijie are not Christians, although they have stressed that much can be learned from Christianity. Both Du and Liu are considered the primary representatives of modern Confucianism. Tang Yijie and his colleagues are not official representatives of modern Confucianism, but Confucianism of the Mencian tradition is an important part of their cultural identity. The presuppositions of their reactions to Christianity are taken from Confucianism of the Mencian tradition, the secondary scriptures of Confucianism, and the rationalism of the Enlightenment; but few of them have taken the Five Classics of Confucianism as the direct basis for their presuppositions.

Another subgroup of modern Confucian reactions to the Christian God is the Xunzi tradition, and many members of this group are Christians, theologians, and scholars of religious studies. Qian Mu (1895-1990) and his disciple Yu Yingshi (1930-) oppose the *daotong* (tradition of Orthodoxy, philosophical tradition), which considers a Mencian interpretation as the only correct understanding of Confucianism.[20] Cheng Zhongying has also

---

20. This is quoted in Yu Yingshi, *Youji fengchui shuishang ling: Qian mu yu xiandai Zhongguo xueshu* (Taipei: Sanmin shuju, 1991), p. 56. This tradition was begun during the

rejected as prejudiced the neo-Confucian position that considers Mencius the orthodox heir to Confucius, and Xunzi a deviant sideline. Cheng sets himself above these kinds of historical divisions (he stresses that both Mencius and Xunzi are deviant!), and avows his support for Confucianism in general, and even for Taoism, since he often mentions both, and professes that both of them together represent more completely the Chinese philosophical tradition. Cheng's aim is to establish a new global world philosophy which he terms "onto-hermeneutics," the purpose of which is to ascertain and define the relationship between being and method.[21]

The Confucianism of the Xunzi tradition has been especially stressed by Boston University's Robert Neville[22] and John Berthrong,[23] who emphasize the tradition of ritual propriety. Both of these scholars are Christians, but they accept Confucianism. Neville is dean and professor of philosophy, religion, and theology in the School of Theology at Boston University. Berthrong is associate dean for academic and administrative affairs and director of the Institute for Dialogue among Religious Traditions at Boston University.[24] Neville and his school call for the recovery and uniquely American development of the ancient emphasis on *li* as ritual propriety. The heart of the program is the defense of the thesis that American pragmatism offers a Western philosophical language for expressing the relevance of Confucian ritual theory for the modern world. The book *Xunzi* has been considered a primary scripture of Confucianism by this tradition.[25]

Modern Confucianism of the Xunzi tradition has four features:

1. Stressing original sin. They have not made a choice between original goodness and original sin, between the doctrine of Mencius and that of

---

Song and Ming dynasties of the tenth century by Cheng-Zhu and Wang Yangming; later it was followed by Xiong Shili and his three disciples Tang Junyi, Xu Fuguan, and Mou Zongsan.

21. See Cheng Zhongying, *Zhongguo zhexue de xiandaihua yu shijiehua*. Cf. also Bresciani, *Reinventing Confucianism*, pp. 402-9.

22. Neville published a book titled *Boston Confucianism* in 2000; he says, "I am a serious practicing Christian, indeed, the dean of a Christian theological school, as well as a Confucian." See his *Boston Confucianism: Portable Tradition in the Late-Modern World* (Albany: State University of New York Press, 2000), Preface.

23. John Berthrong is a bureaucrat and a thinker with integrity (he worked as a bureaucrat for the United Church of Canada for a decade); see Neville, *Boston Confucianism*, Preface, p. xxxiv. In 1995 Berthrong published an article in Chinese titled "Boston Confucianism."

24. Neville, *Boston Confucianism*, pp. 1-2.

25. Neville, *Boston Confucianism*, pp. 3, 6.

Christianity, but have included both of them in one whole via the doctrine of Xunzi. This is to say, original nature is good or is neither good nor evil, but in reality and in their social lives human beings exhibit evil and sinful features.

2. Stressing external ritual propriety. This resembles the Jewish-Christian tradition of God's commandments and laws. This is complementary to the Confucian Mencian tradition, which emphasizes self-cultivation. In translating the Confucian notion of ritual/etiquette into Western ideas, Neville relies on Fingarette's study, *Confucius: The Secular as Sacred.* Herein a much wider concept of ritual is adopted, referring to all the "signs" in our relationships: signs of friendship, love, commitment. It goes beyond courtesy to a definition of roles in relationships, although these can be very flexible.[26]

3. Stressing rationality (*jujing qiongli*). They oppose premature intuition. This is in accordance with Western rationalism.

4. Stressing inner transcendence.

As a Christian, Neville tries to reconcile Confucianism and Christianity, and to do this he looks for some form of transcendence (an absolute beyond the perceptible phenomena) in Confucianism to match the transcendent Christian God. Hall and Ames have shown that such transcendence does not exist in early Confucianism, and Neville has criticized this rejection of transcendence.[27] Neville does point to the neo-Confucian conception of "principle," which is transcendental since it structures all things and man. This could therefore be a bridge toward Christianity. Thus, people can be Western Confucians. Some Christians, theologians and scholars of religious studies, have also been considered close to this group of the Xunzi tradition. The presuppositions of these reactions to Christianity consist of Confucianism of the Xunzi tradition and rationalism of the Enlightenment tradition. Some members of this group have also taken the Five Classics of Confucianism as their presupposition to react to Christianity.

All three of these groups are different from ancient Confucians. The main feature of Confucian reactions to Christianity is that Confucians un-

26. Herbert Fingarette, *Confucius: The Secular as Sacred* (Long Grove, IL: Waveland Press, 1998).

27. David L. Hall and Roger T. Ames, *Thinking Through Confucius* (Albany: State University of New York Press, 1987). See also the section "Roger T. Ames and David L. Hall," in Neville, *Boston Confucianism*, pp. 47-50, and "Motifs of Transcendence," in Neville, *Boston Confucianism*, pp. 147-65.

derstand Christianity in the light of Confucianism. In reacting to the Christian conception of God, some Confucians have based their arguments on Confucian primary sources such as the Five Classics and the Four Books, and others have based them on secondary scriptures of Confucianism such as the works of Zhu Xi, Lu Jiuyuan, and Wang Yangming. This difference has often been ignored when these Confucians criticize others, as they cannot agree with one another. Among different Confucian primary scriptures, different interpretations have been made, with different points emphasized by different schools, some elements suppressed, and others exaggerated; the interpretations of primary scriptures can be plainly contradictory to one another, and it is always important to recognize that the role primary scriptures play in one school or another is as much a function of the school as of the scriptures themselves.[28]

Thus, in the encounter between Confucianism and Christianity, various reactions to Christianity have appeared. For example, facing the Christian conception of God, some Confucians refer to the conception of Heaven and Sovereign on High in the *Shujing* and *Shijing,* some refer to the *Analects,* and again some others have referred to the secondary scriptures of later neo-Confucians such as the writings of Zhu Xi, Wang Yangming, and others. All of the Confucians claim that they react to Christianity in the light of orthodox Confucianism, but their understandings of Confucianism are different; and their Confucian primary sources, upon which they build their interpretations of Confucianism, are also different. Thus one Confucian reaction to Christianity is sometimes contradictory with another, and both of them claim they are correct and the authentic representative of Confucian orthodoxy. In order to investigate the real Confucian reactions to Christianity and the reasons behind them, it is necessary to discover the presuppositions of Confucian reactions to Christianity.

Therefore, when Confucianism and Confucians are mentioned, we must distinguish many different terms from one another. "Ancient Confucianism" refers to the tradition based on the Five Books. Confucianism refers to the ideology and worldview based on the Five Classics and the Four Books. "Neo-Confucianism" refers to developments during the Tang, Song, Ming, and Qing dynasties from the tenth to the nineteenth century. "Traditional neo-Confucianism" refers to neo-Confucians of the Ming dynasty in the sixteenth and seventeenth centuries, and they include Christian converts, Christianity sympathizers, and anti-Christian traditional neo-Confucians.

28. Neville, *Boston Confucianism,* p. 4.

"Cultural nationalist neo-Confucianism" refers to some of the first (1921-49) and second (1950-79) generations of neo-Confucians. "Modern Confucianism" refers to the third generation (since 1980) of neo-Confucians and includes both modern Confucians of the Mencian tradition and modern Christian Confucians of the Xunzi tradition.

The Reactions of Chinese Christians Who Take Confucianism as Part of Their Identity

Many conservative Christians propose to regenerate Chinese culture with Christianity, and this policy of evangelization has decided their basic attitude to the relationship between Christianity and Chinese culture. Zhuang Zukun, a contemporary Chinese Christian pastor in the USA, made an investigation in 1994 in North America concerning the "crisis feeling" in China (both mainland and Taiwan). He obtained the following results: more than 80 percent of mainland Chinese intellectuals who live in North America think that there is a crisis of faith in mainland China.[29] Eighty-six percent of mainland Chinese intellectual Christians and 61 percent of non-Christians think that there is danger of moral collapse in mainland China.[30] Concerning the solution of the crisis, 64 percent of non-Christians say, "do not know" or "there is no solution," 6 percent of non-Christians say that Confucianism is the solution, and 26 percent of non-Christians say that Christianity is the solution. Less than 2 percent say that either Buddhism or Communism can be the solution.[31] Eighty-four percent of Christians from mainland China say that Christianity is the solution to China's crisis. It should be noted also that 92 percent of Taiwanese Christians and 77 percent of non-Christians think that there is a danger of moral collapse in Taiwan.[32] Zhuang proposes a cultural regeneration in China through Christianity.

Liu Xiaofeng criticizes traditional Chinese culture and suggests importation of Christianity into China. Liu is one of the representatives of Cultural Christians *(wenhua jidutu)* in mainland China, a group that ap-

29. Zhuang [Chuang] Zukun, *Ripening Harvest: Mission Strategy for Mainland Chinese Intellectuals in North America* (Paradise: Ambassadors for Christ, 1995), p. 75.

30. Zhuang Zukun, *Ripening Harvest*, p. 77.

31. Zhuang Zukun, *Ripening Harvest*, pp. 78-79.

32. Zhuang Zukun, *Qihe yu zhuanhua: Jidujiao yu Zhongguo wenhua gengxin zhi lu* (Agreement and Transformation: The Way of Chinese Cultural Regeneration) (Taipei: Yage chubanshe, 1998), p. 134.

proaches Christianity through philosophy and literature. However, the main emphasis of this school has been focused on the translation of Western theological works into Chinese, and little reaction to Christianity in the light of Confucianism has been produced.[33] Liang Yancheng, a Lutheran theologian who has an inclusive approach to Confucianism, has tried to integrate Christianity and Confucianism.[34] He Shiming (1911-96), a modern Confucian Christian in Hong Kong, has made a detailed study comparing Christianity and Confucianism.[35] Wang Cisheng (born at the beginning of the twentieth century) and Xu Songshi (born at the beginning of the twentieth century) have also written books on the relationship between Christianity and Confucianism.[36] All four of these Christians hold that there are similarities between Christianity and Confucianism although there are also many differences. Yuan Zhiming and Ethel Nelson are radical evangelical representatives who argue that the Christian God has already revealed himself in the Chinese classics, history, and writing system.[37]

33. Concerning Cultural Christians, see Liu Xiaofeng, *Zhenghiu yu xiaoyao* and *Xiaoyao yu zhengjiu* (Taipei: Fengyun shidai chubanshe, 1990). See also the papers of Li Qiuling, Li Jingxiong, Ceng Zuoren, Liu Zongkun, and Zeng Qingbao (Chin Ken-pa) in *Wenhua jidutu: Xianxiang yu zhenglun* (Hong Kong: Hanyu jidujiao wenhua yanjiusuo, 1997). Many of these papers were responses to Luo Bingxiang's article on the cultural Christians.

34. See Cai Renhou, Zhou Lianhua, and Liang Yancheng, *Huitong yu zhuanhua: Jidujiao yu xin rujia de duihua* (Syncretism and Transformation: Dialogue between Christianity and Neo-Confucianism) (Taipei: Yuzhouguang chubanshe, 1985).

35. He Shiming has written five books concerning Christianity and Confucianism, which were republished by Zongjiaowenhua chubanshe in Beijing in 1999. The books are *Jidujiao yu ruxue duitan, Jidujiao ruxue sijiang, Zhongguo wenhua zhong zhi youshenlun yu wushenlun, Cong jidujiao kan Zhongguo xiaodao,* and *Rongguan shenxue yu rujiao sixiang*.

36. Xu Songshi, *Jidujiao yu Zhongguo wenhua* (Christianity and Chinese Culture) (Hong Kong: Jinxinhui chubanshe, 1991); Wang Cisheng, *Zhongguo wenhua yu shengjing zonghe yanjiu* (Dallas: Philman Publishing, 1997).

37. See Yuan Zhiming, *Laozi vs. Shengjing* (Laozi vs. the Bible) (Taipei: Yuzhongguang chubanshe, 1997) and *Shenzhou chanhui lu: Shangdi yu wuqian nian Zhongguo* (The Record of China's Confession: God and the Five Thousand Years of China) (Taipei: Xiaoyuan shufang chubanshe, 1998). For a criticism of Yuan, see Paulos Huang, *The Dao of Laozi and Christian God: Yuan Zhiming's Theology on the Encounter Between Christianity and Chinese Culture* (Helsinki: Department of Systematic Theology, 2002), p. 156. See also *JZWGY* (Jidujiao yu Zhongguo wenhua gengxin yantaohui huibao), ed. Chen Huiwen (Argyle: Great Commission Center International, 2000); Ethel R. Nelson and Richard E. Broadberry, *Kongzi wei jiekai de mi* (Mysteries Confucius Couldn't Solve) (Taipei: Ganlan jijinhui, 1997).

The Reaction of Chinese Academic Intellectuals

In his article "Chinese Intellectuals and Christianity," Zhuo Xinping, a contemporary mainland Chinese scholar, has analyzed the relationship between Chinese intellectuals and Christianity and the attitudes of Chinese intellectuals toward Christianity as moving from criticism to resistance, from compatibility to combination, and from identification to conversion. He points out that the understanding of Christianity by Chinese intellectuals is based first on interest in the whole nation's social, cultural, and spiritual development, and second on the impact of the personality of Christian believers. Finally, he raises the question of the form and meaning of Christian existence in China and shows clearly that the relationship between Chinese intellectuals and Christianity depends upon life testimony and efforts from both sides.[38]

There are many affirmative reactions from many mainland and overseas modern Confucians to Christianity. The best-known representatives of contemporary Chinese theologians and scholars of religious studies are Zhuo Xinping (Institute of World Religions at the Chinese Academy of Social Sciences in Beijing), Zhao Dunhua (Department of Philosophy and Religion at the University of Peking), Yang Huilin, He Guanghu, Li Qiuling (Renmin University), Zhang Qingxiong (Department of Philosophy and Religion at Fudan University), and Wang Xiaochao and Wan Junren at Tsinghua University, plus several other scholars from various Chinese universities and academies.

The main feature of these scholars is their attempt at objectivity. They usually hold a sympathetic attitude to Christianity and suggest that China may learn something from Christianity, but they are not Christians. Zhuang Zukun has considered many of these scholars as representatives of Cultural Regeneration in his work: *Qihe yu zhuanhua* (Agreement and Transformation) and *Jidujiao yu Zhongguo wenhua gengxin zhi lu* (The Way of Chinese Cultural Regeneration).[39] The common feature of these intellectuals is that they consider themselves academic rational scholars rather than neo-Confucians. They are, however, different from those intellectuals of the May Fourth Movement tradition since they have, on the one hand, realized the limits of rationalism and of the Enlightenment tradition and, on the other hand, expressed respect for both Christianity and Confucianism.

38. Zhuo Xinping, "Zhongguo zhishi fenzi yu jidujiao" (Chinese Intellectuals and Christianity), *Jindao xuekan* 7 (Hong Kong, 1997).
39. Zhuang Zukun, *Ripening Harvest.*

The presentation of Professor He Guanghu can also be considered as belonging with the work of this group of academic intellectuals, since he has discussed the concept of the Divinity from a perspective of religious philosophy. Thus, the conception of "God" in the doctrine of God should not be understood as limited by any particular religious doctrine, and it should be considered as the general name of the object of various religious faiths.

Professor He has also referred to Rudolf Otto's concept of the holy, and has considered "the holy," abbreviated as "God," as the essence of religions. Based on such an orientation, Professor He has put forward the four features of transcendence, comprehensiveness, absoluteness, and holiness as the points of compatibility between Christianity and traditional Chinese religions with regard to their theories of the Divinity. Although I agree with Professor He in most cases, I want to point out that these features of God's nature held in common between the two traditions are only contact points in the encounter. For example, there are many similarities between Christianity and Chinese traditional religions in terms of "transcendence"; however, there are also many differences between them on this issue. Such a contact point offers us a possibility of exploring the relationship between the two traditions rather than proving that the two traditions are same.

In my own research I have distinguished "transcendence" into five types: (1) transcendence as a principle of explanation, (2) transcendence as defining the self, (3) transcendence as place or perspective beyond borders, (4) transcendence as change or growth beyond limits, and (5) transcendence as the capacity of consciousness to objectify itself and step back to look at itself. Therefore, we should not jump to the conclusion that the Chinese God (or Heaven or Sovereign on High) and the Christian God are the same merely because they both have the feature of transcendence, since their understandings of transcendence differ in many other respects. However, it is also true that a contact point such as transcendence can help us methodologically to build a bridge to exchange between the two traditions. The important thing is to correctly establish the position and function of various contact points; otherwise people may be misled by the appearance of similarities and ignore the essential differences.

4 Reasons for an Easy Access of Christianity into Chinese Culture: Cultural Relativity between Religion and Morality on the Basis of the Method of Matteo Ricci's Missionary Work in China

Wan Junren

The Question and the Aim

It is obvious that the theme of this essay hints at a basic cultural judgment according to which, in an open encounter between Chinese and foreign cultures (including religions), Western Christianity as a religious culture more easily enters Chinese culture than do other religious cultures. So Christianity can easily become an organic part of Confucian-dominated Chinese culture and produce a corresponding cultural influence on the spiritual world of Chinese society. This is to say, in the history of the meeting, conflict, exchange, and dialogue between traditional Chinese and foreign cultures, the dialogue between Christianity and Chinese Confucianism can give people more faith and expectation in the encounter and dialogue between different cultures and religions than the encounter between Confucianism[1] and other foreign religions.

I am well aware that there is a considerable risk in making such a judg-

---

1. There are different understandings and translations for the term "Confucianism," which can refer to a philosophy (*ruxue* or *rujia*) or a religion *(rujiao)*. In the present work this term will be used in a general sense to cover all of the above-mentioned meanings.

The writing of this article has benefited from the book *Jidujiao yu Mingmo ruxue* (Christianity and Confucianism in the Late Ming Dynasty) (Beijing: Dongfang chubanshe, 1994) written by Sun Shangyang, my good friend and former colleague in the Department of Philosophy at Beijing University. Some important historical materials are drawn from this important work.

85

ment, not only in the sense of cultural politics but also in the sense of theoretic academics, since in order to prove the tenability of this judgment I require many preconditions and evidences. In this essay I will not be able to complete the task of proving this judgment true, and I probably cannot even establish some basic theoretic proof. However, I still would like to put forward this judgment, in which I have strong faith. The subtitle of this essay indicates that I will choose Matteo Ricci's missionary work in China as a special case in order to focus on the cultural relation between religion and morality. Through an analysis of Christianity and Confucianism, which share the same goal of making morality secular by different routes, I hope to find theoretic evidence for my judgment. I know this evidence cannot warrant the above judgment, but I hope to motivate other scholars' further studies through a preliminary attempt.

First, I will employ an approach of contrast to defend my cultural judgment — one of my purposes in writing the present article. A more ambitious aim is to reject Professor Alasdair MacIntyre's cultural pessimism about the heterogeneity of different cultural traditions that cannot be harmonized. I hope to show that, insofar as certain necessary environments and preconditions of dialogue are offered, or insofar as certain proper methods of exchange are offered, it is possible for two heterogeneous cultural traditions to understand and accept each other to a certain extent or even in the sense of inner value and spirit.[2]

In the modern world, which is in the process of globalization, it is more important than ever before for the different heterogeneous cultural and especially religious traditions to engage in dialogue, to understand each other, and to accept each other. The terrorist tragedy of September 11, 2001, should certainly not be thought of as a mere violent political event; there is hidden behind it a conflict of the politics of cultures, and it is evidence of the spiri-

---

2. I am grateful for Professor Alasdair MacIntyre's reminder to me. In his response to my article "The Parallax between Confucian Virtue Ethics and Aristotelianism of A. MacIntyre," he mentioned the possibility of dialogue between different cultural and religious traditions including Confucius and Aristotle. His suggestion has reminded me to have more faith in the dialogue and exchange between different religions and moral/cultural traditions. His responding article, "Once More on Confucian and Aristotelian Conceptions of Virtues: A Response to Professor Junren Wan," was first published in Chinese in *China Scholarship* 3, no. 1 (2002). My article was published in the same journal, no. 2 (2001). The English versions of the two articles were collected in *Philosophy in Contemporary China: New Opportunities for East-West Dialogue,* ed. Robin (Rongrong) Wang (Albany: State University of New York Press, 2003).

tual cultural war between different religions and beliefs. Nor should the present conflict in Iraq be regarded simply as a righteous war against terrorism. There is insufficient justification for the United States to adopt a preemptive strategy, since this approach enables it to extend the war against terrorism into a war without limits between different nations. The direct aim of such a war is not only to attack terrorism but also to change the nature of another country's authority. In addition, the method of such a war is itself a form of terrorism, i.e., the so-called strategy of terrorizing and frightening with military forces. For the common people of Iraq and the world in general, this strategy is as terrorizing as terrorism itself.

I need to introduce another precondition of cultural comparison and a modern theoretic background. When I claim that Christianity may relatively easily enter Chinese culture, my presupposition is, in fact, that among the foreign religions that have been transmitted into China, Christianity has gained easier access into Chinese culture. Such a precondition is based on the analysis of the transmission and ways of influence of these different religions. For example, this can be indicated by comparing Christianity with Buddhism and Islam, which have also been transmitted into China. In the present article I will not be able to describe the concrete situations of these foreign religions' coming to China in detail, since such a work is too large to be included in the present article. Thus, I will only analyze certain aspects of these religions' transmission and ways of influence in China. Such an analysis is necessary since, on the one hand it is related to the aim of the present article, and on the other hand this issue itself has become an important question in modern cultural discussion.

In the summer of 1993, Professor Samuel P. Huntington, a well-known expert in international politics at Harvard University, published his controversial article "The Clash of Civilizations?" in the journal *Foreign Affairs.* Fortunately I was then a visiting scholar at Harvard and had the opportunity to listen to his lectures. Consequently, I have had a strong feeling concerning his opinion about the conflict of civilizations. Huntington thinks that, after the Cold War ended, the world's military conflicts will gradually be replaced by conflicts of different regional civilizations or different cultural traditions. He especially mentioned the possibility that Eastern Confucianism and Islam might unite to challenge Western civilization or culture. This is to say, East Asian and Chinese Confucianism may more easily unite with Arabic Islam, since the difference between them is much less than that between these two and Christianity. This means that the possibility of combination between Confucianism and Islam is much greater than that between them and Christianity.[3]

Many scholars inside and outside China have criticized Huntington's claim.[4] I personally agree with Huntington that certain differences exist between different cultural traditions and civilizations, and I may even agree with him that there is a possible clash between different cultures; but I do *not* agree with him either that Confucianism may be united with Islam or that the possibility of combination between Confucianism and Islam is greater than that between Confucianism and Christianity. For me, Professor Huntington's claim is an arbitrary decision that lacks reasonable logical evidence, since it seems that he has not studied well those cultural traditions he has been talking about. I prefer to consider his claim as a political guess in foreign affairs rather than a strict academic argument. Of course, Huntington later modified his claim a little bit,[5] but these corrections have not changed the arbitrary feature of his judgment regarding the clash of civilizations. In the present article I will present my arguments for rejecting Huntington's claim about a clash of civilizations. I shall now answer the question regarding why Christianity may more easily enter Chinese culture.

The Way of Cultural Transmission and the Wisdom Tradition of Confucian China

I need to explain my claim that Christianity may more easily enter Chinese culture, since it is mentioned mainly in the light of culture. This is to say, I do not mainly rely on the number of converts Christianity has gained in China; this is a task that cannot be fulfilled in the present article, because it needs not only much material evidence but also examination of the different elements that decide the character and nature of the Chinese people.[6] Thus,

3. Cf. Samuel P. Huntington, "The Clash of Civilizations?" *Foreign Affairs* (Summer 1993).

4. Such critics are too numerous to be mentioned — for example, Harald Müller, *Das Zusammenleben der Kulturen: Ein Gegenentwurf zu Huntington* (Frankfurt am Main: Fischer Verlag, 1998). There are also many critics among Chinese scholars, but they are not yet very systematic.

5. Cf. Lawrence E. Hamison and Samuel P. Huntington, *Culture Matters* (London: Basic Books, 2000).

6. According to exact records, the number of Christians in China is not great. Even if the estimate is based on "Cultural China," a conception of Prof. Du Weiming at Harvard

I will emphasize Chinese intellectuals' reactions to foreign religions, especially the influence of foreign religions on Chinese intellectuals. I will take
"Chinese culture" rather than "Chinese society" as the context of Christianity entering China. My aim is to explore the ways of encounter and extent of
acceptance of different cultural traditions in the spirit of knowledge and
value.

According to historians' investigation,[7] the entrance of Christianity into
China can be traced to 635 CE. It was transmitted from Persia into China by
the Nestorian Bishop Alopen, who traveled to Changan (today's Xi'an), then
the capital of China, where his teaching was welcomed by Emperor Taizong
of the Tang dynasty. Christianity then developed in China, for it received
protection from six generations of emperors. In 845 CE, when Emperor
Wuzong rejected Buddhism, Nestorianism was also banned, and it disappeared almost totally until 1000 CE. After 1300, when the Mongolians in-
vaded Europe, Nestorianism again came to China, and it developed in
northwestern and southeastern areas of China.

However, Christianity did not become established in China until the
middle and late sixteenth century. Christianity entered China later than
Buddhism even though we take the year 635 as the starting point, and it has
been a long and difficult process for Christianity to gain real access to China.
Missionaries Michael P. Ruggieri (1543-1607) and Matteo Ricci (1552-1610)
were the two main figures who helped Christianity enter China. It was Ricci
who understood the ethos of Chinese culture that was to be the dialogue
partner of Christianity, and thereby found an effective way of enabling
Christianity to enter China.

Michael P. Ruggieri came to China before Ricci, arriving at Zhaoqing in
Guangdong Province. However, Ruggieri did not succeed in his missionary
work, since he misunderstood Chinese culture and employed a purely reli-

---

University, which refers to all those people who consider Chinese culture as part of their
identity even if they are not citizens of the People's Republic of China, there are fewer Chinese Christians than Chinese Buddhists. For example, in 1949 there were around two million
Catholic Christians and one million Protestant Christians in mainland China, and the total
of both was still less than that of Chinese Buddhists. Of course, the times and scopes of the
two religions' missions in China are different; but even without these reasons, Christians do
not outnumber Buddhists. One of the reasons is that Christian missionary work in China
had more a cultural and intellectual sense. Thus, I will limit my study in the present article
to the scope of culture.

7. See Chen Linshu and Zhu Senbo, *Shijie qi da zongjiao* (Chongqing: Chongqing
chubanshe, 1986), pp. 30-33.

gious way of doing missionary work. For him Buddhism was the officially recognized religion in China; he therefore decided to make Christianity follow the model of Buddhism in order to gain recognition in China. Consequently he clothed himself as a Buddhist monk once he entered China.[8] It is obvious that Ruggieri hoped to choose a direct approach to preach the Christian message through close cooperation with the Chinese government and the Chinese religion of Buddhism. History proved this to be an unsuccessful approach. Buddhism, which Ruggieri emphasized, was not Chinese by origin; it was a foreign religion.

In fact, even if Ruggieri had received recognition from the Chinese government, he could not have succeeded in his Christian missionary work. One of the main reasons is that missionary work is a matter of culture rather than politics. Whether Christian missionary work can succeed or not is not dependent on the order of the emperor but on the reactions of the Chinese spiritual cultural world. Of course, official authority is also an effective means for doing missionary work. For example, in the early stages of Buddhist development, it was the Chinese emperor of the Tang dynasty rather than Indian monks who started to spread Buddhism in China. That is to say, Buddhism was not sent by foreigners to China, but was sought by the Chinese government.[9] However, the approach of doing missionary work by relying on the royal court is exceptional rather than normal. Thus, it cannot be a general feature of missionary work.

In distinction from Ruggieri, Matteo Ricci chose a different approach, to do missionary work through Chinese intellectuals, since intellectuals have the power to influence the areas of knowledge, culture, and politics. In this manner, Ricci understood the ethos of Chinese culture so as to find a way for Christianity to enter China. His was a rational and indirect way, which

8. Sun Shangyang, *Jidujiao yu Mingmo ruxue*, p. 15.

9. Buddhism entered China around 200 BCE (the first year of Emperor Ai in the Western Han dynasty). In the period of Western Han, Buddhism existed only in the royal court. During the reign of Emperor Ming of Eastern Han, after the emperor had seen a dream, he inquired of his subject Fu Yi about this dream, and the latter told him the dream was a revelation from Buddha to predict the prosperity of the country. Thus, the emperor was happy and sent several subjects to India to learn Buddhism and then to introduce it to China. This can be considered the first introduction of foreign culture. Later the Tang dynasty's monk Xuanzang was sent by the emperor to get the Buddhist canon from India, which was the second event of introducing foreign culture. I think these two events are interesting topics that deserve to be studied in more detail in the light of cultural philosophy or comparative religion. The records concerning these events can be found in Chen Linshu and Zhu Senbo, *Shijie qi da zongjiao*, pp. 133-34.

aimed to approach local Chinese culture and its deep spirit. History has shown that Ricci was more successful than Ruggieri. What is the reason for this? It is not easy to find an answer. In addition to the elements such as chance, historical atmosphere, and certain conditions, I think there are two essential reasons.

On the one hand, the two missionaries had different understandings of Chinese politics. On the other hand, they had different understandings of how to do missionary work. Ricci's success was possible because he had a more correct judgment and choice than Ruggieri had in both points. The situation was probably as follows: for Ruggieri, in fact, for many modern Westerners even today, China was a kingdom in which the emperor had authority over everything, thus no social events, including religion, could be separated from politics. Any movement that aims to enter China should get permission from the government. Therefore, to rely directly on the government and on official religion would be the only approach for a foreign religion seeking to enter China. This does not seem wrong, and the history of Buddhism seems also to have offered support for such a judgment.

It is true that the royal court had authority over everything in the kingdom of China, which had a hereditary system. Official permission was necessary for any legal and normal communication of cultures. However, this was not the essence of Chinese traditional culture. The family hereditary and dynastic politics were the basic features of Chinese politics, but they were not the root of the Chinese feudal system. In the history of China it was not inevitable which family or person would rule the country as emperor; in fact, it was often accidental. Since before the Qin dynasty (220 BCE), "to fit Heaven with virtue" had become the basic ideology and ideal of Chinese politics. For the ancient Confucians who lived before Qin dynasty, the concept "virtue" was the value achievement of a politician that had been gained in practical life and could be judged by empirical standards. Therefore, human virtue was not something that Heaven had given to a certain person, family, or group.

Since the unification of wisdom and virtue and of knowledge and action became an ethical model of good virtue in ancient Confucianism, seeking virtue and seeking knowledge complemented each other, and they became a process of reaching official positions. This means that Chinese intellectuals, who should consider seeking knowledge as their natural duty, are given the cultural privilege to influence politics and become candidates for political leadership. Although intellectuals have had different destinies in different historical stages in China, this cultural privilege has always existed.

This tradition became an important basis for the establishment of the imperial examination system in China. The imperial examination system aimed to choose political leaders for the country, and it could also be considered the cultural basis of Chinese traditional politics. On such an understanding we may say that Chinese intellectuals have been the political administrators. Matteo Ricci noticed this feature of Chinese intellectuals and chose Confucians to be his discussion partners when introducing Christian theology, since Confucians had a special position in Chinese society. On the one hand, they were respected by the masses, and on the other hand, they were trusted by the royal court.

The close contact with Confucians led Christians to understand Confucianism, and it also provided an approach for their entering Confucian China. This approach was cultural, spiritual, or moral-ethical rather than political. Matteo Ricci understood the essence of Chinese culture: if he wanted to fulfill his holy mission to preach Christianity to the Chinese people, he had to first enter the Chinese cultural world, which was dominated by Confucianism. Thus, to build contacts with Confucians became essential.

Therefore, in distinction from Ruggieri, Matteo Ricci clothed himself as a Confucian and showed his appreciation and acceptance of Confucianism. As some scholars pointed out, Ricci's action also showed his religious sincerity;[10] in other words, he preferred to accept a secular culture (e.g., Confucianism) rather than a pagan religion (e.g., Buddhism). But the real reason for his action was his choice of the manner in which to do missionary work among the Chinese people. The fact that Ruggieri clothed himself as a Buddhist monk did not mean that he had rejected his Christian belief; what he had done was for the sake of doing Christian missionary work. It was the same with Ricci. The difference was that Ruggieri did not find the correct way to do missionary work among the Chinese people, and Ricci did.

Ricci was good not only at finding the essential feature of Chinese culture but also at understanding his holy mission correctly. In the sixteenth century, Western missionaries came to China to preach Christianity, but they differed as to how to do the missionary work. The failure of Ruggieri was related to his understanding of missionary work. Ricci's success was also related to his understanding of missionary work, since he had taken an open cultural attitude and considered missionary work as a cultural event. In fact, any religious missionary work will face such a challenge: religion and religious faith are exclusive; to transmit a certain religion into another society

10. Sun Shangyang, *Jidujiao yu Mingmo ruxue*, p. 16.

and cultural tradition will mean asking people to reject and even to replace one religion with another. There is no transcendental God in Chinese culture, and Christian missionary work may not raise conflict with Chinese culture on this issue, but there are certainly contradictions between Christianity and Chinese culture in many other respects.

In fact, Confucianism itself has features of a secular religion, and Taoism and Chinese Ch'an (Zen)-Buddhist religions are also important parts of Chinese culture. In such a situation, in order to enter China, Christianity should gain acceptance from the Chinese cultural world rather than from a certain religious group. Since Chinese culture is dominated by Confucianism, it is natural for Christians to earn sympathy and acceptance from Chinese Confucians. Ricci did this, and this had much to do with his success. He employed a cultural approach to do his holy mission.

The history of Christian missions in China has shown that the destiny of Christianity in China is closely related to its cooperation with the Chinese cultural world, especially Confucianism. On the one hand, this was determined by the characteristics of Chinese culture; on the other hand, it was also the only way for Western Christianity to enter China, an Eastern, nonreligious or super-religious secular cultural kingdom. Thus, to do missionary work through concordance with Confucianism (*furu*) was not only the secret of Ricci's success; in fact, concordance with Confucianism (*furu*) is the essential approach for any foreign culture or religion seeking to enter China.[11]

The Ultimate Concern and Confucian Ethics

If the mission of Ricci were only a concordance with Confucianism (*furu*) in terms of cultural policy, it would be questionable whether Christianity could establish itself in China. Concordance with Confucianism means Christianity can accept or share at least certain elements of cultural values with Confucianism; only in this way may Christianity enter Chinese culture and be-

---

11. I will not elaborate on such a claim in the present article, since it is not my topic. In order to offer a little explanation, I present two examples. One is the saying of modern Chinese leader Sun Yat-sen concerning Western Christianity, modern liberal ideology, and Chinese Confucian moral ethics. Another is the dialogue of contemporary neo-Confucianism with the religious features of Confucianism, Christianity, Confucian ethics, and Western liberalism. Both themes are interesting topics, and I am hereby employing them to support my claim that Confucianism is important for any foreign culture and religion seeking to enter China.

come a part of Chinese culture. When two divergent cultural traditions encounter one another, their ability to have effective dialogue is the primary element deciding the process and result of the encounter. In other words, the theses of the two sides are the basic conditions that decide the way and result of the encounter.

It is generally known that Confucianism is essentially an ethic of morality concerned with society and human ethics. This is why Chinese intellectuals have always sought unification between knowledge and action and have sought to take social responsibility with morality and knowledge. This is the element that shapes Chinese intellectual political culture. Famous Sinologist Joseph Levenson has said that Chinese Confucians in the Ming dynasty had the amateur style of Max Weber, and what they were doing was sanctifying this amateur style of culture.[12] In fact, not only the intellectuals of the Ming dynasty had such an amateur style of culture, but all the traditional Chinese Confucians also had such a cultural characteristic. This feature was, in fact, an indication that Confucians looked down on "tool rationality" and "professional skill and ability," since they emphasized values and spiritual ethics. Therefore, Confucian unification between knowledge and action was not the fulfillment of tool rationality but the social politics of humanity and ethical morality. This is the main feature of all Chinese traditional culture. Therefore, getting to know and share Confucian basic ideas indicates understanding and accepting the Confucian ethics of morality.

Matteo Ricci realized this. However, the difficulty he faced was how to approach Confucianism and how to accept Chinese Confucian ethics to a certain extent while maintaining the independence of Christianity. To maintain the independence of Christianity was the precondition for these Western missionaries; otherwise their work would change the essence of Christianity rather than Christianize the mission. To approach and to accept Confucian ethics and morality was another precondition for these missionaries; otherwise their work would be impossible for the Chinese people to accept. As mentioned earlier, missionary work is a cross-cultural phenomenon that includes cultural dialogue and spiritual exchange. Facing such a difficulty, Matteo Ricci showed wisdom, since he employed a tolerant religious ethical way. Through a humanist connection between religion and culture, he started a dialogue between the Chinese Confucian ethics of morality and the Western Christian religion of God.

12. Joseph Levenson, *Confucian China and Its Modern Fate*, vol. 1: *The Problem of Intellectual Continuity* (Berkeley: University of California Press, 1958), p. 16.

First, Matteo Ricci realized the religious feature of Chinese Confucianism, since in ancient Confucianism and even the whole of ancient Chinese cultural ideologies there was a Heaven that was concerned with the human world, and this was similar to the God of Christianity who has concern for the secular world. Second, Chinese people, especially ancient Confucians, emphasized the reward and punishment of Heaven, and there existed an idea of a world to come in China. Third, there was an idea of immortality in China and especially in Confucianism. These three features gave Confucianism a transcendental religious characteristic; thus, Confucianism could also be considered a religion.

For Matteo Ricci the religious feature of Confucianism was a potential resource for Christianity in starting a dialogue with Chinese Confucians. On the other hand, in order not to lose the essence of Christianity in the process of dialogue with Confucianism, even though Ricci had shown his understanding of Confucianism, he continually insisted on the special Christian understanding of theism and criticized Confucianism as a nonreligion,[13] since idol worship remains in Confucianism (worshiping ancestors, ancients, and sages), it lacks a professional religious clergy and official liturgy, and there is no doctrine of creation, etc.

It may seem that Ricci had a vague understanding of Confucianism, but in fact, his attitude was not confused at all. To recognize the religious features of Confucianism was to offer a spiritual platform for a dialogue between Christianity and Confucianism, since transcendental spirituality was the real topic that could be discussed between Christianity and Confucianism. And the claim that Confucianism was not a real religion justified Christian missionary work, since Confucian China lacked a real religion. Therefore, Christianity was needed for the Chinese people. In this way Ricci, on the one hand, maintained the superiority of Christianity and justified the mission of Christianity to China and, on the other hand, opened the possibility for dialogue between Christianity and Confucianism. Ricci also considered that there was no conflict between religious Christianity and secular Confucianism, since they could complement each other. Christian understanding and tolerance toward Confucianism enabled the former to easily enter China and Confucian understanding and faith; if the Christian mission succeeded in converting Confucians, it enabled Confucianism to gain more spiritual resources.[14]

13. Cf. *Li Madou quanji, Diyice,* pp. 83, 85-86.
14. *Li Madou quanji, Diyice,* p. 86. Ricci says: "Confucianism is not a real religion, and it

In the twenty-seventh year of Wanli in the Ming dynasty, Matteo Ricci observed a discussion on human nature between the School of Mind of Wang Yangming and their opponents in Nanjing. One group insisted on the idea of Wang — that the nature of heart (mind) is neither good nor evil. Their opponents considered human nature as originally good. This was an old topic that had been discussed between the Mencian school and the followers of Xunzi among Confucians since the pre-Qin dynasty (before 221 BCE), and no authoritative conclusion had been achieved. Thus, this question was difficult for Confucians themselves, not only for different schools of Chinese philosophy. However, this discussion in Nanjing interested Matteo Ricci, who had started to compile his book *The True Meaning of the Master of Heaven* in response to this issue. Ricci's participation in this discussion became a chance for him to have a dialogue with Confucians.

Risking misunderstanding, Ricci chose to argue the position that human nature was originally good. His opinion seemed to be in conflict with biblical teaching, since human beings have original sin. If human nature was good originally, how could one interpret the Fall of Adam and Eve in the Garden of Eden? Ricci knew this issue very well, and he employed the doctrine of Thomas Aquinas to distinguish "natural" and "moral" goodness and evil. Through this distinction Ricci argued the meaning of human morality and the theological meaning of original goodness according to the doctrine that God is perfectly good. Since human beings were created by and in the image of God, like the human body, human nature would have been good originally. Human beings committed sin, though not because of God but because of human beings having lost their basic rationality. Thus, the human hope and wish to be saved by God becomes natural and necessary. The essence of human evil is to turn away from the highest *noumenon* (i.e., the Master of Heaven, or God), and the fact that human beings are able to commit sin shows that human beings are finite beings who may turn away from the Master of Heaven and fall into despair. Therefore human beings need the salvation of the infinite God.

Obviously Ricci's optimistic interpretation of human nature did not completely fit with Christian biblical teaching, but he had skillfully ex-

---

is only a school, which is established in order to rule family and country. Thus, they [Confucian intellectuals and the class of officials] can belong to this school while they become Christians. Since in principle there is no place of conflict with Catholics, Catholic faith is not harmful for the fulfillment of peace and social harmony in Confucian classics, in fact, it offers a great help for that."

plained the basic spirit of Christian doctrine, and he had clearly expressed the ultimate concern of Christianity as to the meaning of human life and the highest ideals in the context of Chinese traditional culture. Ricci's claim seems not to fit with the Chinese Confucian theory of human nature either, regardless of his emphasis on the original goodness of human nature. But if we look at this issue from the viewpoint of ethics we will find that Ricci's theory can reach the same result as Confucianism.

From Confucius's idea of "being benevolent from oneself" to the Song-Ming dynasties' neo-Confucian theory of ethical practice, there always existed a transcendental ideal spirit of moral perfectionism. The difference exists only in that Christianity considers human final perfection as a religious event that relies on a perfect God, and Chinese Confucianism considers it as an individual personal event that relies on the human search for morality and ethical practice. In this sense one may say that there is a similarity of religious transcendence in Christianity and Confucianism. Christian salvation by God, the future world, and the kingdom of heaven can be considered a kind of theistic ideal of human perfectionism. Christianity and Confucianism are the same in seeking human perfection; in religious terms they both are not only concerned with functional values in real lives but also with the ultimate meaning.[15]

In fact, there are many other similarities between Christian religious ethics and Confucian morality. For example, Confucian benevolence and Christian love, Confucian reverence for perfect persons (sages) and Christian worship of the perfect God, Confucian appreciation of political ceremonies and Christian obedience to the state, Confucian loyalty and forgiveness and Christian righteousness and mercifulness. Both Confucianism and Christianity emphasize the unity of knowledge and morality, appreciate the idea of immortality, etc. Although many differences exist between Christianity and Confucianism with respect to these subjects, it is also true that they both share many similarities that are worthy of our attention.

Modern Confucianism and Christianity

If Matteo Ricci's cultural approach and religious-ethical method of dialogue made it possible for Christianity to enter China with a status of "foreign culture," the similar fate of Confucianism and Christianity in the modern pe-

---

15. Cf. Sun Shangyang, *Zongjiao shehui xue* (Beijing: Beijing daxue chubanshe, 2001).

riod has rendered this possibility a reality. After studying the process of their modernization, we have a stronger faith that they should start a new dialogue rather than a cultural conflict (conflict of civilizations) as Professor Huntington predicts.

Among the world's main religions, no other religion has been able to adjust to Confucianism as Christianity has done, and their similar modern fate has become the basis for their contemporary dialogue. In contemporary China the main religions are Christianity, Buddhism, Islam, Taoism, and semi-religious Confucianism.[16] It should be noted that Taoism and Confucianism are Chinese local religions or semi-religions, and Chinese Buddhism is different from the original Buddhism of India although it originally came from there. Since its transmission into China long ago, it has adopted a Chinese style, especially the school of Ch'an (Zen). Islam in China is mainly an ethnic religion that does not have an influence over peoples of other ethnicities. Nor has it engaged in much dialogue with Confucianism.

Dialogue between Buddhism and Confucianism occurred during the dynasties of Sui, Tang, Wei, Jin, and the dynasties of South and North; this encounter was the primary cultural reason for the birth of Chinese Ch'an-Buddhism. However, in the modern period there have been few dialogues between Buddhism and Confucianism. Christianity has not only maintained its traditional dialogue with Confucianism but also has engaged in more frequent exchanges with Confucianism in the modern era. The phenomenon of Cultural Christians in today's China is one evidence of this. In this sense we may say that my claim according to which Christianity is more easily able to enter Chinese culture than other foreign religions is not only historically true but also constitutes a cross-cultural judgment on the present and future.

All who know Western and Chinese modern history understand that both Christianity and Confucianism have been challenged and attacked by modern society and that they both became the critical objects of the Enlightenment movement. This is not an accident but an evidence of the uni-

16. There has been a dispute concerning whether Confucianism can be considered a religion. Since the beginning of the 1980s some scholars, represented by the philosopher and historian Ren Jiyu, affirm the religious status of Confucianism. Other scholars oppose such a claim. Among overseas Confucian scholars, there are also different opinions on this issue. Du Weiming at Harvard University and the so-called Boston Confucians believe that Confucianism has the basic features of a religion; but other scholars hold an opposing view. Based on this situation, I employ the term "semi-religion" to describe the basic features of Confucianism, and I believe that this is close to Ricci's judgment.

versal spiritual tension between cultural traditions and modern society. After the Nicene Council of 325, Christianity was united with the Roman Empire and subsequently dominated the Western world spiritually for over one thousand years. Together with Greek philosophical culture, Christianity became one of the two cultural traditions underlying the Western spiritual civilization. However, since the middle of the Renaissance, Christianity has been criticized as an obstacle to the development of modern civilization. The Enlightenment movement that began in France in the eighteenth century has treated Christianity as an object of rational criticism.

Since the work of Max Weber, numerous scholars have shown that many Christian cultural values became the spiritual power for the development of modern Western capitalist and socialist societies. For example, the market economy theory of Adam Smith and the influence of Protestant ethics led to the appearance of capitalist commerce. The theories of freedom and human rights of John Locke and the influence of early Christian ethics of law led to the establishment of the modern democratic political system. And the influence of the natural rights ideas of medieval theologians such as Thomas Aquinas led to the ideal of freedom in modern political thought. However, in the history of modern Western European development, Christianity has been criticized and attacked at almost every turn.

Since the middle of the twentieth century, the Western world seems to have awakened from Nietzsche's declaration that "God has died." The disaster of two world wars has shown that one can do anything in a world without God. However, a world where one can do anything and where one follows his inclinations is not better than a world of order that is governed by God. On the contrary, human disaster and the technological control of human beings, which have been criticized by phenomenology and existentialism, have taught human beings that without an ultimate concern and final meaning human beings and the world will fall into disaster and disorder. The modern Western world is now calling once again on a Christian spirit, and this enables Christianity once again to find its cultural role in modern society. This is to say that, as the tradition underlying Western modernization, Christianity has found the power and resources for continuous growth in the modern world and has become one of the spiritual pillars of modern Western civilization.

Similarly, Chinese Confucianism has also been experiencing a process of movement from guilt to freedom and from crisis to new life. Since the May Fourth Movement of 1919, in the process of China's modernization as a technological and political civilization, with the ultimate vision of a moral or spiritual civilization, Confucianism has been criticized as a spiritual burden that should be rejected. Getting rid of Confucianism has been considered "the waking up of the last waking up" (words of Chen Duxiu). However, whether China can be modernized will not depend on rejecting Confucianism. The essential element is the change of the social system, especially the modern change of the socioeconomic and political system. This social change needs a cultural change as its precursor; however, the change of cultural values does not mean rejection of its own cultural tradition.

The successful experience of modernization of the Four Small Dragons of Asia indicates that, as Christianity has influenced European capitalist development, Confucianism and its ethical spirit can play a special role in Asian social modernization and development. It is not reasonable to consider a spiritual revolution as a total change of society, since it is impossible to change a whole society through ideological revolution alone. To modernize the whole society, it is impossible to rely on ideological and spiritual change alone; the Cultural Revolution (1966-76) made the Chinese people well aware of this. The rejection of Chinese traditional culture is the main reason that contemporary China is facing a shortage of cultural resources. Confucianism, however, has not been eliminated but has received a new life in the process of Chinese modernization. Since the mid-1980s, traditional culture, especially Confucianism, has interested many people both inside and outside China.

Christianity has maintained its independent position in the Western world, and it retains a critical attitude toward modern social/cultural values. In the same way, Confucianism has also retained its spirit; it has kept a critical attitude and adjusted its function within modern China. This becomes clear by observing the powerful resurgence of folk and ethnic customs. Both Christianity and Confucianism have a strong influence on cultural life. The strength of Christianity and Confucianism is found in their ultimate concern with values and inner spiritual resources. It is this inner spiritual energy that enables them to revitalize themselves and to play special roles in satisfying the spiritual needs of modern society. As a religion, Christianity has relinquished its original quest for power and wealth, but it has not given up its cultural responsibility and spiritual ideals. On the contrary, with a new form of faith (freedom of faith) and religious ethics, Christianity is fulfilling her cultural responsibility and spiritual ideals.

The basic promise of Christianity to Western social life is its ethical religious culture. Similarly, the Confucian promise to Chinese social life is through religious morality, i.e., in seeking the utmost individual morality and spiritual freedom. Confucian ethics is no longer the essential precondition of becoming a sage, nor is it the sole spiritual avenue for intellectuals to enter official positions so as to finally rule the country. Rather, today it is only a spiritual foundation for individuals in their modern social lives. As long as human beings are not satisfied with being controlled by modern technology and capitalism, it will be meaningful to seek such a spiritual foundation of life in the world. As a Chinese cultural tradition with a history of more than three thousand years, Confucianism clearly finds its contemporary meaning in providing this foundation.

If my interpretation can stand, we will be surprised to find that modern Christian ethics and modern Confucian ethics can establish the basis for a new cultural dialogue and spiritual encounter. Since there is an incentive within them to approach each other and to understand each other, their ultimate concern and spiritual search have a broad area in which to grow in the modern world. Thus, they have more possibilities for dialogue and for mutual encounter. More important is the fact that the religious ethics of love and the moral ethics of benevolence are universally meaningful for an ethics of human beings in the process of globalization. Of course, many elements of each system should be analyzed and criticized in detail. Based on such an ethical judgment and academic faith, I would expect a positive exchange between Western Christianity and Chinese Confucianism, and I would like to disagree with Professor Huntington's judgment that these two cultures are in conflict with each other.

5 *Ren* as a Fundamental Motif: The Promise and Problem of a Contextual Theology of an *Agape-Ren* Synthesis — A Dialogue with Anders Nygren

Lo Ping-cheung

On this historic occasion of the first Sino-Nordic theological conference, I want to pay tribute to a great Swedish theologian, Anders Nygren (1890-1977). His book *Den kristna kärlekstanken* (The Christian Idea of Love) was published in 1930, when he was just 40 years old. The revised, complete English translation, known as *Agape and Eros*, was published in 1953. The Chinese translation, in two volumes, was published in 1950 and 1952 in Hong Kong. It is long out of print, and fortunately will be reprinted in China soon. This book is a masterpiece and a modern classic, which should continue to be read by theologians of both West and East. I read it for the first time more than twenty years ago, and reread it again and again.

Most English discussions on this book (under the influence of Reinhold Niebuhr, Paul Ramsey, Gene Outka, Edward Collins Vacek, etc.) are on the ethics of *agape* or on the typology of love, which constricts the scope of Nygren's concern, viz., motif research. This essay will focus on the following topics: (1) motif research in religious studies, (2) *agape* as a distinctive fundamental motif of Christianity, (3) *ren* as a fundamental motif in Confucianism, and (4) the possibility and difficulty of a contextual theology involving an *agape-ren* synthesis.

Anders Nygren's Idea of Motif Research in Religious Studies

Nygren makes himself very clear about the nature of a "fundamental motif" in *Agape and Eros*. He first briefly describes it as "a general attitude of mind"[1] and "an attitude to life."[2] He then speaks more precisely: "For this purpose the following definition may be given: *A fundamental motif is that which forms the answer given by some particular outlook to a question of such a fundamental nature that it can be described in a categorical sense as a fundamental question.*"[3] Regarding fundamental questions Nygren explains, "Quite early in the history of thought we find the great fundamental questions asked concerning the True, the Beautiful, the Good, and — to crown them all — the Eternal. . . . the problems of Knowledge, of Aesthetics, of Ethics, and of Religion. . . . The fundamental motif is the answer given by some particular type of outlook to one or more of these questions."[4]

Motif research as a methodology in religious studies is built upon such an understanding of fundamental motif. Nygren explains:

> The most important task of those engaged in the modern scientific study of religion and theological research is to reach an inner understanding of the different forms of religion in the light of their different fundamental motifs. For a long time they have been chiefly occupied in collecting a vast mass of material drawn from different religious sources for the purposes of comparison. . . . In other words, we must try to see what is the basic idea or the driving power of the religion concerned, or what it is that gives it its character as a whole and communicates to all its parts their special content and color. It is the attempt to carry out such a structural analysis, whether in the sphere of religion or elsewhere, that we describe as motif-research.[5]

In other words, motif research in religious studies attempts to find "the center" of a religious system lest we miss the forest for the trees.[6] Nygren

---

1. Anders Nygren, *Agape and Eros,* trans. Philip S. Watson (Philadelphia: Westminster Press, 1953), p. 33.

2. Nygren, *Agape and Eros,* p. 34.

3. Nygren, *Agape and Eros,* p. 42.

4. Nygren, *Agape and Eros,* pp. 42-43.

5. Nygren, *Agape and Eros,* p. 35.

6. "The purpose of the scientific study of religion is not merely to record the actual conceptions, attitudes, and so forth, that are found in a particular religious milieu, but more especially to find out what is characteristic and typical of them all. That is what motif-research deliberately and consistently seeks to do, and is indeed fully capable of doing. . . . A religion deprived of its fundamental motif would lose all coherence and meaning; and therefore we cannot rightly regard anything as a fundamental motif unless its removal would have such an effect." *Agape and Eros,* p. 37.

then proceeds to propose that *agape* is the fundamental motif of Christianity. In his own words,

> In the case of two of these great fundamental questions, the ethical and the religious, Christianity has brought a revolutionary change not only with regard to the answers but with regard to the questions themselves. . . . This change, in respect both of questions and answers alike, is essentially bound up with the idea of Agape. . . . We have therefore every right to say that Agape is the centre of Christianity, the Christian fundamental motif *par excellence*, the answer to both the religious and the ethical question.[7]

Furthermore, and even more controversially, Nygren argues in the book that, as fundamental motifs,[8] the motif of *agape* is antithetical to the motif of *eros*, which stems from Hellenism. His thesis is that "Platonic *eros* and Pauline *agape* have, so to speak, no common denominator; they are not answers to the same question."[9] The following summary table on page 210 of his book is well known:[10]

Eros is acquisitive desire and longing.	*Agape* is sacrificial giving.
Eros is an upward movement.	*Agape* comes down.
Eros is man's way to God.	*Agape* is God's way to man.

7. Nygren, *Agape and Eros*, pp. 44, 48. There were theological criticisms, from within the University of Lund, against both Nygren's program of motif research and Nygren's thesis that *agape* is the fundamental motif of Christianity. See William A. Johnson, "Development in Swedish Theology, 1939-1966," in Nels F. S. Ferré, *Swedish Contributions to Modern Theology: With Special Reference to Lundensian Thought*, updated edition (New York: Harper & Brothers, 1968), pp. 242-95, especially pp. 265-70 on Gustaf Wingren's criticism of Nygren; Valter Lindstrōm, "The Method of Motif Research," in *The Philosophy and Theology of Anders Nygren*, ed. Charles W. Kegley (Carbondale: Southern Illinois University Press, 1970), pp. 95-100. The purpose of this present essay does not allow me to digress into these discussions. As a whole I still find Nygren's project very helpful for a Sino-Nordic theological dialogue.

8. In other words, the incompatibility between *agape* and *eros* is on the level of fundamental motif, not on the level of aspects of love. Nygren does not deny that *eros* has a rightful place in a Christian's life. See the last section of this essay.

9. Nygren, *Agape and Eros*, p. 33.

10. "Agape and Eros are contrasted with one another here, not as right and wrong, not as higher and lower, but as Christian and non-Christian fundamental motifs." *Agape and Eros*, p. 39.

Eros is man's effort: it assumes that man's salvation is his own work.	*Agape* is God's grace: salvation is the work of Divine love.
Eros is egocentric love, a form of self-assertion of the highest and noblest kind.	*Agape* is unselfish love, it "seeketh not its own," it gives itself away.
Eros seeks to gain its life, a life divine, immortalized.	*Agape* lives the life of God, therefore dares to "lose it."
Eros is the will to get and possess which depends on want and need.	*Agape* is freedom in giving, which depends on wealth and plenty.
Eros is primarily *man's* love; God is the *object* of eros. Even when it is attributed to God, *eros* is patterned on human love.	*Agape* is primarily God's love; God is *agape*. Even when it is attributed to man, *agape* is patterned on Divine love.
Eros is determined by the quality, the beauty and worth, of its object; it is not spontaneous, but "evoked," "motivated."	*Agape* is sovereign in relation to its object, and is directed to both "the evil and the good"; it is spontaneous, "overflowing," "unmotivated."
Eros recognizes value in its object . . . and loves it.	*Agape* loves — and *creates value in* its object.

In short, this book is about *agape* (the Christian motif), *eros* (the non-Christian and Platonic motif), and their incompatibility with one another as fundamental motifs. The title of the Chinese translation *(Views on Love in the History of Christian Thought)* does not grasp it well.

Application of Motif Research to Chinese Religious Thought

Since motif research is a method in the scientific study of religion, it can be applied to other religions as well,[11] Chinese religions included. Gunnar Sjöholm (a Swedish missionary in China in the 1930s), in the preface to the Chinese translation of *Agape and Eros,* applied this method to analyze the

11. Bernhard Erling, "Motif Research as a General Historical Method," in *The Philosophy and Theology of Anders Nygren,* ed. Charles W. Kegley (Carbondale: Southern Illinois University Press, 1970), pp. 117-18.

thought of Mozi of ancient China, c. 476–c. 390 BCE (which was based on his earlier publication, *Den motistiska filosofiens kärlekstanke*, pp. 9-29 of the Chinese translation). This method can be applied to Confucianism as well, which is more significant, because Mozi's school of thought was no longer influential in China after the pre-Qin period, whereas Confucianism still exerts its influence in the mind of many Chinese intellectuals.

One might wonder about the legitimacy of including Confucianism in religious studies. However, to raise the question "Is Confucianism a religion or a philosophy?" can be anachronistic, because the presently used Chinese terms for "religion" *(zhongjiao)* and "philosophy" *(zhexue)* did not exist before the twentieth century, and hence there was no distinction between religion and philosophy in premodern China. Similarly, the distinction between faith and reason was nonexistent. However, after the terminology was coined in the early twentieth century, there has been an almost unceasing debate on whether Confucianism should be considered a religion or a philosophy. There have been many materials on this debate in Chinese, and the options are:

1. Confucianism per se is a religion;
2. Confucianism per se or as a whole is not a religion in the full sense, but it has a religious dimension, character, import, or sentiment;
3. Confucianism is a religious philosophy;
4. Confucianism is a philosophy, but to a certain extent provides the functional equivalence of a religion;
5. Confucianism is a philosophy, and a philosophy only.

Recently English materials on this topic have also begun to emerge, with a different account of Confucian religiosity or religiousness.[12]

---

12. Cf. John Berthrong, "Confucian Piety and the Religious Dimension of Japanese Confucianism," *Philosophy East and West* 48, no. 1 (Jan. 1998): 46-79; Julia Ching, *Chinese Religions* (Maryknoll: Orbis Books 1993), pp. 51-67; Hans Küng and Julia Ching, *Christianity and Chinese Religions* (New York: Doubleday, 1989), pp. 61-127; Shu-hsien Liu, "The Religious Import of Confucian Philosophy: Its Traditional Outlook and Contemporary Significance," *Philosophy East and West* 21, no. 2 (April 1971): 157-75; Lauren Pfister, "The Different Faces of Contemporary Religious Confucianism: An Account of the Diverse Approaches of Some Major Twentieth Century Chinese Confucian Scholars," *Journal of Chinese Philosophy* 22 (1995): 5-79; Rodney L. Taylor, *The Religious Dimensions of Confucianism* (Albany: State University of New York Press, 1990), "The Study of Confucianism as a Religious Tradition," *Journal of Chinese Religions* 18 (1990): 143-59, "The Religious Character of the Confucian

Many overseas neo-Confucian thinkers in the second half of the twentieth century argued that though Confucianism *per se* is not an organized religion, Confucian thought has a definite religious dimension or religiosity (option 2 above). This is because an important theme in Confucian thought revolves around the Heaven-human relationship, and Heaven in Confucianism is equivalent to God in theistic religions. In the People's Republic of China, for a long time Confucianism was regarded as a philosophy (options 4 and 5 above). Some important scholars (Ren Jiyu, Li Sun, He Guanghu) in the past decade, however, have articulated a vocal minority voice that argues for either option 2 or option 3 above. My own position is option 2 above, for the reason that for most Confucians *Tian* (Heaven) does play a role similar to that of God in theistic religions.

There are many branches of Confucianism. In the neo-Confucianism of the Song and Ming period, the two major schools are the School of Cheng-Zhu and the School of Lu-Wang. I submit that *ren* is the fundamental motif in the former, especially in the thought of Zhu Xi (1130-1200 CE). Though all Confucians regard *ren* as the supreme virtue and the basis of all moral goodness, many Confucians confine *ren* to ethics. It is Zhu Xi, in particular, who has expanded *ren* to the religious dimension as well. Hence *ren* in Zhu Xi is qualified to be regarded as a fundamental motif, whose role in his thought resembles the role of *agape* in Christian thought as Nygren articulates it.

Basic Features of the *Ren* Motif in Confucianism[13]

The rise of neo-Confucianism since the Northern Song dynasty produced some innovative views on *ren* (generally translated as benevolence or cohumanity in English),[14] and they are all elaborated and synthesized by Zhu

---

Tradition," *Philosophy East and West* 48, no. 1 (Jan. 1998): 80-107; Rodney L. Taylor and Gary Arbuckle, "Confucianism," in "Chinese Religions: The State of the Field," *Journal of Asian Studies* 54, no. 2 (May 1995): 347-54; Laurence G. Thompson, *Chinese Religion: An Introduction*, 4th ed. (Belmont: Wadsworth, 1989), pp. 75-88; Mary Evelyn Tucker, "Religious Dimensions of Confucianism: Cosmology and Cultivation," *Philosophy East and West* 48, no. 1 (Jan. 1998): 5-45.

13. A slightly different version of this section is published in Lo Ping-cheung, "Agape, *Ren*, and Altruistic Suicide," *Ching Feng*, New Series, vol. 2, nos. 1-2 (Fall 2001): 89-112.

14. In the older system of transliteration the word is rendered as "*jen*." Some quotations in the rest of this paper use this transliteration; it should be understood as the same as "*ren*."

Xi. Hence Wing-tsit Chan says, "Historically speaking, Chu Hsi [Zhu Xi] represents the summit of development in the theory of *jen* [*ren*]."[15]

Like most Confucians before him, Zhu Xi understands *ren* in the following ways: (1) *Ren* is both one cardinal virtue among others (*ren* in the narrow sense) and the leading virtue (*ren* in the wide sense) that includes the other cardinal virtues; in the wide sense, *ren* is the supreme moral principle and the *summum bonum*. (2) *Ren* in the narrow sense leads to love (*ai*).[16] (3) Love should both be inclusive and be practiced with a preferential order, beginning with one's parents and relatives, then extending to other people, and finally to other living things as well.[17]

Zhu Xi's neo-Confucian theory of *ren* has significant innovative elements, and for our purpose, the following features are noteworthy. First, *ren* is both the "mind" of Heaven and Earth and the "mind" of human beings. In other words, there is a cosmic as well as a human, a metaphysical as well as an ethical dimension to *ren*. Besides, there is a correspondence between these two dimensions.

> The Mind of Heaven and Earth is to produce things. In the production of man and things, *they receive the mind of Heaven and Earth as their mind.* Therefore, with reference to the character of the mind, although it embraces and penetrates all and leaves nothing to be desired, nevertheless, one word will cover all of it, namely, *jen* (humanity).[18]

Second, in Zhu Xi's time as well as today, the word "*ren*" is also used to mean the kernel of a fruit, as in "fruit kernel," "peach kernel," "apricot kernel" (almond). Zhu Xi thinks that this linguistic usage of *ren* is no coincidence, and argues that both the Heavenly *ren* and the human *ren* should be understood accordingly. In other words, *ren*, as kernel, is the seed, the source, the spring, or the full potentiality of life waiting to be unfolded or developed.[19]

15. Wing-tsit Chan, "The Evolution of the Confucian Concept of *Jen*," *Philosophy East and West* 4, no. 1 (Jan. 1955): 295-319. Reprinted in Wing-tsit Chan, *Neo-Confucianism Etc.: Essays by Wing-tsit Chan* (Hanover: Oriental Society, 1969), p. 31.

16. "*Ren-ai*" is a common Chinese phrase both in ancient times and today.

17. *Zhuzi Xin Xue An* (A New Anthology of Master Zhu's Writings), vol. 2, ed. Qian Mu (Taipei: San Min, 1971), p. 52. All subsequent quotations from this anthology are my English translations.

18. Zhu Xi (Chu Hsi), "A Treatise on *Ren* (*Jen*)," in *A Source Book in Chinese Philosophy*, trans. and ed. Wing-tsit Chan (Princeton: Princeton University Press, 1963), pp. 593-96; emphasis added.

19. Zhu, quoted in Chan, *A Sourcebook in Chinese Philosophy*, p. 633.

As the mind of Heaven and Earth, *ren* gives rise to all kinds of biological life and biological flourishing. As the mind of human beings, *ren* gives rise to moral life and moral flourishing.[20] In his own words:

> What mind is this? In Heaven and Earth it is the mind to produce things infinitely. In man it is the mind to love people gently and to benefit things. It includes the four [cardinal] virtues (of humanity, righteousness, propriety, and wisdom) and penetrates the Four Beginnings [of cardinal virtues] (of the sense of commiseration, the sense of shame, the sense of deference and compliance, and the sense of right and wrong).[21]

In other words, *ren* in human nature is "the spring of all virtues and the root of all good deeds."[22]

Third, though he agrees that *ren* gives rise to love *(ai)*, he denies that *ren* is to be defined as love.[23] He articulates the relation between *ren* and love in the following famous dictum: *ren* is "the character of the mind and the principle/ground of love." *Ren* and love are closely related without being identical. *Ren* is the ultimate reality in human nature; hence it is called the "character of the mind" or "essence of the mind." *Ren* manifests itself in love (hence it is called the "principle/ground of love"). In other words, love is the empirical manifestation *(yong)* of *ren,* and *ren* is the transcendental nature *(ti)* of love. *Ren* is love-not-yet-manifested, and love is *ren*-already-manifested. Analogously, *ren* to love is like root to shoot, or like sugar to sweetness.[24] *Ren* is nature *(xing)*, whereas love is sentiment *(qing)*.

Fourth, Zhu Xi repeatedly asserts that an essential manifestation of *ren* is impartiality *(gong)*. A preference for partiality, or selfishness *(shi)*, is contrary to *ren*. In his own sayings:

> Jen is the principle of love, and impartiality is the principle of *jen*. Therefore, if there is impartiality, there is *jen*, and if there is *jen*, there is love.[25]

> Whenever selfish desires can be entirely eliminated and the Principle [of Heaven] freely operates, there is *jen*.[26]

---

20. Zhu Xi also compares *ren* to a seed of grain and explains *ren* as *"shengsheng,"* i.e., the generative force of all things that leads to unceasing growth.

21. Zhu Xi, "A Treatise on *Ren (Jen),*" p. 595.

22. Zhu Xi, "A Treatise on *Ren (Jen),*" p. 594.

23. It is well known that Han Yu of the Tang dynasty defines *ren* as "universal love," *bo ai.*

24. Zhu Xi, *Zhuzi Xin Xue An,* vol. 2, pp. 50-51, 60-61.

25. Zhu Xi, "A Treatise on *Ren (Jen),*" p. 633.

26. Zhu Xi, "A Treatise on *Ren (Jen),*" p. 633.

Lo Ping-cheung

Impartiality is not equivalent to *ren*. Impartiality is the elimination of partiality. When partiality is eliminated, there is the outflow of *ren*.[27]

Just as clouds covering the sun or the moon block the sunlight or moonlight, to say that the removal of clouds is equivalent to the sun or moon is wrong.[28]

The eradication of selfish desires is like removing the obstacles that block the flow of water in an irrigation ditch.[29]

Fifth, if a feature of *ren* is impartiality, it is only natural that Zhu Xi reiterates what Confucius has already affirmed, viz., *ren* is considerateness *(shu)*. As he explains,

> *Jen* is the principle originally inherent in man's mind. With impartiality, there is *jen*. With partiality, there is no *jen*. But impartiality as such should not be equated with *jen*. It must be made man's substance before it becomes *jen*. Impartiality, altruism [*shu*], and love are all descriptions of *jen*. Impartiality is antecedent to *jen*; altruism [*shu*] and love are subsequent. This is so because impartiality makes *jen* possible, and *jen* makes love and altruism [*shu*] possible.[30]

Last, but not least, Zhu Xi makes it very clear that human *ren* is to be patterned after Heavenly *ren*. In his own words again,

> Our mind is also the mind of Heaven and Earth. However, the Heavenly mandate is upright, whereas the human mind is evil. The Heavenly mandate is impartial, whereas the human mind is partial. The Heavenly mandate is great, whereas the human mind is small. Hence our mind does not resemble that of Heaven and Earth. The purpose of learning is to eliminate that which does not resemble Heaven and Earth, so that we can resemble Heaven and Earth.[31]

When the mind is without partiality or selfishness it corresponds to Heaven and Earth; this is *ren*.[32]

27. Zhu Xi, *Zhuzi Xin Xue An*, vol. 2, p. 69.
28. Zhu Xi, *Zhuzi Xin Xue An*, vol. 2, p. 66.
29. Zhu Xi, *Zhuzi Xin Xue An*, vol. 2, p. 66.
30. Zhu Xi, quoted in Chan, *A Sourcebook in Chinese Philosophy*, p. 633.
31. Zhu Xi, *Zhuzi Xin Xue An*, vol. 1, pp. 357-58.
32. Zhu Xi, *Zhuzi Xin Xue An*, vol. 1, p. 362; paraphrase.

Ren is like the way Heaven and Earth produce a myriad of things. When human beings are without selfishness they will then resemble Heaven and Earth.[33]

In short, *ren* in Zhu Xi is more than a moral norm or an ethical ideal. *Ren* has both a Heavenly and a human dimension. *Ren* is the key to understanding both the nature of Heaven and the nature of human beings. It is a fundamental motif in the sense of Nygren's. Since Zhu Xi's school of Confucianism is one of two dominant schools of Confucianism in the last eight hundred years, *ren* can arguably be said to be a, if not *the,* fundamental motif of Confucianism.[34]

Is an *Agape-Ren* Synthesis Promising or Problematic?

My preliminary understanding of contextual theology is as follows. It is a methodological insistence on the priority of a particular, local, and contemporary context for doing theology. The context can be religious, philosophical, literary, political, economic, social, or ideological. Though many contemporary contextual theologies emphasize the contexts of political and economic oppression, racism, sexism, Eurocentrism, colonialism and postcolonialism, and post-Communism, my concern in this paper is the religious and philosophical contexts of the Chinese people. In particular, it is the context of the Confucian legacy that is my major focus.[35]

Since both *agape* and *ren* are expressions of love, and both are fundamental motifs, it seems obvious to many that a Chinese contextual theology and ethics has to incorporate some kind of an *agape-ren* synthesis. We often hear views like: "Jesus and Confucius have similar ideas about the Ultimate Reality"; "*agape* and *ren* are only two different aspects of the same love, not two different loves." Hence an *agape-ren* synthesis seems to look promising.[36]

However, a major argument in Nygren's masterpiece is that the synthe-

---

33. Zhu Xi, *Zhuzi Xin Xue An,* vol. 1, p. 362.

34. Put differently, no Confucian scholar would deny that *ren* is "the center" of Confucianism. It is Zhu Xi, however, who has elaborated *ren* into part of a comprehensive moral-religious worldview.

35. Accordingly, Chinese contextual theologies are bound to be pluralistic.

36. In this connection, one should note that Nygren's name in Chinese transliteration contains the Confucian term "*ren.*" I do not think this is only a coincidence.

sis of *agape* with *eros* destroys the integrity of the *agape* motif. That is why Nygren is so critical of Augustine's *caritas*, which is a synthesis of *agape* and *eros*; that also explains why he stops his treatment at the Reformation, in which the *caritas* synthesis is broken down and the *agape* motif is renewed. The finding of Nygren raises important theological-methodological issues: Is it ever theologically advisable to seek an *agape*-X synthesis, where X is a fundamental motif of another culture? Can there be such a synthesis without losing one's identity, say, both as a Christian and as a Chinese? What follows here is a brief investigation.

Nygren and subsequent theologians have written and spoken extensively about the nature of *agape;* none of it needs to be repeated here. I have two major theses-in-tension about *agape* to advance, to which I think not much attention has been given. First, there is a correlation between neighbor-love and the imitation of God or of Christ. Christian love for others should imitate God's or Jesus Christ's love for us. This is Thesis One. However, that our love for others should be continuous with God's love for us (through imitation) should not overshadow the fact that there should also be discontinuity between divine love and human love. In some crucial ways, human beings cannot and should not love as God or Jesus Christ loves. There should be contrast or divergence as well as resemblance or correspondence between these two kinds of love. This is Thesis Two.[37]

According to Thesis One, first of all, God's or Jesus Christ's loving action is the measure, yardstick, standard, or norm of our loving action. Such a divine love provides both the content and the justification of Christian love.

Among recent theologians and ethicists Nygren and Allen self-consciously use a divine exemplar model to understand Christian love. For Nygren, the four major features of God's love for us are also the four features of Christian love.[38] For Allen, the six major characteristics of Christian love correspond closely to the six major characteristics of God's covenant love.[39] Ramsey's programmatic statements on Christian love also exhibit a divine

37. I do not have the room to substantiate these two theses in this paper. See Lo Ping-cheung, *Love and Imitation in New Testament and Recent Christian Ethics* (Ann Arbor: University of Michigan Dissertation Services, 1990); Lo Ping-cheung, "Love and Imitation: A Dialogical and Hermeneutical Theological Ethics," *CGST Journal* 35 (July 2003): 67-96 (in Chinese).

38. Nygren, *Agape and Eros*, pp. 91, 96, 97.

39. Joseph Allen, *Love and Conflict: A Covenantal Model of Christian Ethics* (Nashville: Abingdon, 1984), pp. 56-59, 60-81.

exemplar model.[40] For Niebuhr, it seems that he is willing to use Jesus' love for us as the model of our love for others in personal morality ("Christ as the norm of human nature defines the final perfection of man in history").[41] But since he thinks that Jesus' ethic is only a personal one, not a social one, he does not think that Jesus' love for us can be the model of social morality.[42] Only indirectly, through justice, is Jesus' love relevant to our social life.[43] In short, my Thesis One is a consensus among major Christian theologians and ethicists, though in different degrees.

The same, however, cannot be said about Thesis Two. Gene Outka is the only Protestant ethicist of love known to me who is acutely aware of this important issue, and I am indebted to him for this important reminder. By incorporating Hans Frei's insight, he stresses that there should be both differences and points of correspondence between Jesus and the believer. Christians should only follow their Lord at a distance.[44] A theocentric love should honor both the differences and the likenesses between God and ourselves.[45] This formal principle can be filled with content by studying carefully the New Testament writings on love, which I have done elsewhere.[46]

40. Paul Ramsey, *Basic Christian Ethics* (New York: Charles Scribner's Sons, 1950), pp. xii-xiv, xvii, 5, 16-21, 24, 43-44, 102. But in his actual exposition of Christian love it seems that Ramsey does not follow this model faithfully (e.g., for him the hallmark of Christian love is a disinterested concern for others, but he does not elaborate how Jesus' love for us is also of, and largely, this nature).

41. Reinhold Niebuhr, *The Nature and Destiny of Man: A Christian Interpretation*, vol. 2, *Human Destiny* (New York: Charles Scribner's Sons, 1963), p. 68.

42. Reinhold Niebuhr, "The Ethic of Jesus and the Social Problem," in *Love and Justice: Selections from the Shorter Writings of Reinhold Niebuhr*, ed. D. B. Robertson (Philadelphia: Westminster Press, 1957), p. 30.

43. Reinhold Niebuhr, *An Introduction to Christian Ethics* (New York: Seabury, 1979), pp. 64-68. As for those Christian ethicists who want to render the Christian ethic of love into the moral philosophy of beneficence or respect for persons, given the very nature of their enterprise, they have to exclude Jesus Christ's love (through an appeal to scriptural authority) from being the exemplar of human love (beneficence, respect) for others.

44. Gene Outka, "Following at a Distance: Ethics and the Identity of Jesus," in *Scriptural Authority and Narrative Interpretation* (Philadelphia: Fortress Press, 1987), pp. 144-60.

45. Gene Outka, "Theocentric Love and the Augustinian Legacy: Honoring Differences and Likenesses between God and Ourselves," *Journal of the Society of Christian Ethics* 22 (Fall 2002): 97-114.

46. Lo Ping-cheung, *Love and Imitation in New Testament and Recent Christian Ethics*, pp. 411-16.

To employ the four-component analysis of *agape* advanced by Outka,[47] the discontinuities between divine and Christian love can be formulated as follows. (1) God bestows worth upon human beings regardless of their merits or demerits, whereas Christians can only affirm and appreciate others' worth regardless of their merits or demerits (both divine and Christian valuation of others are universal, though). (2) Divine commitment to the well-being of human beings is universal and redemptive, whereas Christian commitment to others' well-being is inclusive but neither universal nor redemptive. (3) God and Christ can seek communion with human beings universally, whereas Christians' scope of seeking communion with others is even narrower than that of agent commitment (in virtue of the high demand in communion and of human finitude). (4) An important characteristic of divine sacrificial love is the substitutionary death of the Son, whereas Christian sacrificial love does not require death, still less a substitutionary one, as a necessity.[48]

I have said in the discussion of Thesis One above that Nygren and Allen are the ones who most consciously use a divine exemplar model. In his book *Love and Conflict*, though Allen never explicitly affirms the discontinuity between divine and human love, he is not entirely insensitive to this issue either. Thus the first characteristic of God's covenant love is "God binds us together as members of a covenant community,"[49] whereas the first characteristic of Christian covenant love is "to see self and others as essentially belonging together in community";[50] the second characteristic of divine covenant love is "God creates and affirms the worth of each covenant member,"[51] whereas the second characteristic of Christian covenant love is only "to affirm the worth of each covenant member."[52] But for the sake of a more accurate understanding of Christian covenant love, the discontinuities between divine and Christian love need to be articulated explicitly.

---

47. Gene Outka, *Agape: An Ethical Analysis* (New Haven: Yale University Press, 1972), pp. 9-44.

48. We should note that the function of this thesis is only to point out that there are things that God and Christ can do for us that we cannot and should not do for one another, but not to lower the standard of love. Compared with some secular understanding of moral norms, Christian love that is patterned after divine love is still very demanding. There is much less room for supererogation, for example.

49. Allen, *Love and Conflict*, p. 61.

50. Allen, *Love and Conflict*, p. 77.

51. Allen, *Love and Conflict*, p. 62.

52. Allen, *Love and Conflict*, p. 78.

Nygren's case is more complicated, however. He certainly is acutely aware of the discontinuity between God's *agape* and our *agape*. His awareness is so keen that he probably has overblown it. He sees such an unbridgeable *de facto* gulf between divine and human love that he attempts to deny human agency in Christian love. The following statements in the last chapter of his masterpiece are well known, for good or for bad: "The subject of Christian love is not man, but God himself. . . . Divine love employs man as its instrument and organ. . . . He [i.e., the Christian] is merely the tube, the channel, through which God's love flows."[53]

A more sympathetic reading of Nygren needs to go back to his earlier chapter on Paul, in which he explains why he considers a Christian to be an instrument of *agape:* "When Paul speaks of Agape he always means the Divine love, never a merely human love. The Christian's love for his neighbor is a manifestation of God's Agape, which in this case uses the Christian, the 'spiritual' man, as its instrument. . . . It is not the case that I possess in my religious life the effective basis of my ethical life; were it so, it might look as if I were resting in myself and simply drawing on my own inner resources. Paul's entire religion and ethics are theocentric, and he cannot rest until he has referred everything to God."[54] We can share Nygren's vigilance against Pelagianism in Christian life, but the solution to this problem does not have to be purchased with the high price of human agency. Though divine love is wholly other than *human* love, divine love is not necessarily also wholly other than *Christian* love. As mentioned before, a Christian is able to follow the shape of Jesus Christ's love because this very love has shaped his or her love. Jesus Christ in his love is not only the exemplar of Christian love, but also the Savior and the enabler of Christian loving conduct. Hence a theocentric account of Christian life is not incompatible with a double-agency approach of explaining Christian life.

Can we find these two theses-in-tension about love in Zhu Xi? Yes and no. On the one hand, as explained in the earlier section, Zhu Xi deems that human *ren*-love should be patterned after the *ren* of Heaven and Earth. This corresponds to the thesis of continuity — a correlation between love and imitation — in the Christian ethics of *agape* articulated above. However, there is no discussion in Zhu Xi on the possible discontinuity between the human *ren* and the Heavenly *ren*. In fact, the overall shape of Zhu Xi's philosophy makes this discontinuity rather unlikely, because, like

---

53. Nygren, *Agape and Eros*, pp. 733, 734, 735.
54. Nygren, *Agape and Eros*, p. 130.

other neo-Confucians, Zhu Xi subscribes to the position of the immanentism of Heaven.

"Immanentism" can be understood as "a view of God which stresses his immanence or indwelling in the world at the expense of his transcendence. . . . The symbol of depth rather than height has been applied to God, suggesting that he is the inner principle that expresses itself in the world-process rather than an external power separate and independent from the world."[55] If we replace the word "God" with the word "Heaven" in the quotation above, I think it will be a fair summary of Zhu Xi's view of Heaven. In fact, in some typical sayings Zhu Xi remarks, "Heaven is human beings, and human beings are Heaven. . . . Heaven is human beings writ large, and human beings are Heaven writ small. . . . Ultimately Heaven and human beings are but one principle."[56]

In short, the idea that the *ren* of Heaven is in some way wholly other than the *ren* of human beings is rather unintelligible to Zhu Xi. Here lies the crucial difference between the fundamental motif of *agape* and the fundamental motif of *ren*, viz., Thesis Two is applicable to the former but not to the latter. The anthropological implications of this difference are enormous. For Zhu Xi, in virtue of "the oneness or identity of Heaven and human beings," the Heavenly *ren* and the human *ren* are in fact one and the same. *Ren* is a natural endowment in human nature from Heaven. *Ren* is the ultimate reality in human nature; hence it is called the "character of the mind" or "essence of the mind." Such a *ren* nature in us is always pure and uncorrupted; its potential is eternally infinite and its strength inexhaustible. Hence the metaphor of the beaming moon and the cloud: evil is only like a cloud, which is extrinsic to the moon. No matter how wicked and perverse one is, one's boundless moral goodness remains intact. This firm belief in one's innate and infinite goodness is certainly antithetical to Nygren's theocentrism as quoted above, viz., "It is not the case that I possess in my religious life the effective basis of my ethical life; were it so, it

55. John Macquarrie, "Immanentism," in *The Westminster Dictionary of Christian Theology*, ed. Alan Richardson and John Bowden (Philadelphia: Westminster Press, 1983), p. 287.
56. Zhu Xi, "A Treatise on *Ren* (*Jen*)," pp. 366, 375. It should be noted that "immanentism" is not only a characteristic in Confucianism, but also a hallmark in other Asian religions, as a famous scholar on the Asian religions observes: "[In Asian religions] Immanence of the sacred rather than its transcendence is emphasized. Thus Hinduism, Buddhism, and Taoism characteristically find the truly transcendent within the human self itself." Winston L. King, "Religion," in *The Encyclopedia of Religion*, vol. 12, ed. Mircea Eliade (New York: Macmillan, 1987), p. 284.

might look as if I were resting in myself and simply drawing on my own inner resources."

No one has done a full-scale comparison of the motif of *agape* in Christianity and the motif of *ren* in Confucianism in the way Nygren has done for *agape* and *eros*. My treatment above is still sketchy, and other treatments are usually confined to the ethical realm.[57] My preliminary finding is that though *agape* and *ren* might not be as antithetical to one another in as many aspects as *agape* and *eros* are (see Nygren's summary quoted above), *ren* as a fundamental motif still conflicts with the fundamental motif of *agape*.

Religious Syncretism and Contextual Theology

From the perspective of Nygren in *Agape and Eros,* accordingly, the *agape-ren* synthesis is undesirable. He would disapprove of the view that the *ren* fundamental motif and the *agape* fundamental motif are more or less the same. This is confirmed by his interpreters, such as Bernhard Erling, and by his own statement forty years later. Commenting on Nygren's program of motif research, Erling writes, "Nygren is not suggesting that these motifs either do or should exist in a pure form. He does argue, however, that the *agape* motif, at least, resists synthesis with the other motifs, and must assert its predominance in a given religious orientation in so far as it encounters elements characteristic of these other motifs."[58] Furthermore, "At the same time this method suggests that the answer to the problem posed by this [religious] pluralism is not an attempted syncretism. Each of these faiths has its own characteristic uniqueness. The significance of the faith decision is that one must choose between them. It is not possible to serve two masters."[59]

In his replies to critics and interpreters forty years after the publication of his masterpiece, Nygren the bishop displays some openness to the idea of synthesis, though still with caution. He writes,

If one wishes a synthesis of Agape and Eros, one may seek to build one. There is nothing that hinders; this has happened many times before. But to maintain for this reason that Paul, in speaking of God's Agape or of Christ's Agape, should mean about the same as Plato means with Eros,

---

57. E.g., Yao Xinzhong, *Confucianism and Christianity: A Comparative Study of Jen and Agape* (Brighton: Sussex Academic Press, 1996).

58. Erling, "Motif Research as a General Historical Method," pp. 107-8.

59. Erling, "Motif Research as a General Historical Method," p. 118.

only that he develops another *aspect* or lets the accent fall at a different point — this it would seem is to force the meaning of the texts far beyond what any useful purpose requires. Why is one eager that great men should think in about the same way? Actually they think quite differently — and it is just in this that the richness of the history of humanity consists. . . . [Ulrich von] Wilamowitz[-Möllendorf] is correct. He who says that it is love of the same kind, only under a different aspect, is in error.[60]

In other words, Nygren would certainly agree that the moral norm and virtue of *ren,* theologically specified, has a legitimate place in a Chinese Christian ethics. In that sense *agape* and *ren* are in synthesis. One should not jump to the next step, Nygren would say, and assert that *ren* is more or less the Chinese name for *agape,* and the *agape* motif can best be explained as *ren* in a Chinese context.

To put it differently, Nygren explains his openness and caution in this way:

> There is a difficulty which easily arises when there is discussion of "basic motifs" that one tends to think that the basic motif is the whole and excludes all other elements. No, the basic motif is in this respect not exclusive, but inclusive. It is, to be sure, exclusive over against competing basic motifs, but inclusive with respect to the different elements in the religious life. . . . When "the problem of culture" is brought over to the theological domain, it receives a wholly concrete content. During its almost two-thousand-year history the Christian faith has entered into relationship and interaction with widely differing cultures. This is inescapable and of the greatest significance for both parties. The risk is only that in this way a religious syncretism can creep in, which robs the Christian faith of its meaning and power. . . . It is to set up a defense against this that I have said yes to "cultural synthesis" and *no* to "religious synthesis," however difficult it may be to maintain this distinction concretely.[61]

Nygren's advice, at age 80, is quite intriguing. From the perspective of Chinese contextual theology one needs to ask, "Can we do a Chinese contextual theology of *agape* that involves only a cultural synthesis but not a reli-

---

60. Anders Nygren, "Reply to Interpreters and Critics," in *The Philosophy and Theology of Anders Nygren,* ed. Charles W. Kegley (Carbondale: Southern Illinois University Press, 1970), pp. 361-62.

61. Nygren, "Reply to Interpreters and Critics," pp. 365, 373.

gious synthesis? What specific place for *ren* is there in this contextual theology and ethics of *agape* then?" This is a Nygren legacy that we need to probe further in the future.

On the other hand, some theologians, Chinese and Western, might be shocked by Nygren's insistence against religious synthesis and his exclusiveness against other competing fundamental motifs. Nygren's old-fashioned view is no longer tenable in this age of religious pluralism, they deem. If that is the case, we even need to call into question the value of motif research, which emphasizes the uniqueness of each religion and the structural differences among them.

Whether Nygren's motif research is helpful or not for the construction of Chinese contextual theology of *agape* is open to dispute. What is indisputable is the value of his program for the prolegomenon of any future Chinese contextual theological work. Hence Sino-Nordic theological dialogue through the Nygrenian bridge should continue.

A Response to Professor Lo Ping-cheung

You Bin

First of all, I would like to introduce some of the latest research in the Chinese academy concerning Anders Nygren's master work, his *Agape and Eros*. Within the short history of theological study in China, we need to recognize that Nygren and his works have attracted much attention from Chinese scholars.

A paper titled "Agape and Eros" by Mr. Yu Zi was published in *Christian Cultural Review* 7 (1998), and a doctoral thesis titled *Agape and Eros: An Approach to the History of Christian Thought* by Dr. You Guanhui was published in 2002. Besides these specific pieces of research, the motif research methodology, the *agape* motif of Christianity, and the distinction of Christian *agape* from all other *eros* cultures, all considerations of Nygren are quite well known among Chinese scholars.

I think Professor Lo's paper is resourceful, insightful, and open-ended. It applies the methodology of motif research in the analysis of Chinese culture. Lo draws the conclusion that *ren* can be seen as the motif of Confucianism. His comparison between *ren* and *agape*, especially the interpretation of the metaphysical dimension of *ren*, is very impressive. Though Professor Lo's paper seems to aim at some kind of *agape-ren* synthesis in Chinese contextual theology, it also pays attention to the differences between the two motifs and cautions against any hasty religious synthesis. These statements and the questions he raises are all worthy of our further discussion.

In the following, I shall raise some questions with respect to Professor Lo's paper, about both its methodology and concrete conclusions. First, I would like to call into question the methodology of motif research as such, in the study both of Christianity and of Chinese culture, by both Anders Nygren and Professor Lo. It is well known that Nygren followed the methodology of Max Scheler and Max Weber, i.e., cultural/structural comparison or cultural typology, but it seems that Nygren reduced it further into motif research. The risk here is in isolating the motif from its network of meaning, and reducing it to an abstract concept. But the fact is, if we take any culture or religion as an integrated whole, then every concept in that system must adhere to some other concepts or ideas. There is never an "A" as itself, but an "A" in realation with "B," "C," and "D." "A" is alive only in an integrated system, and its meaning varies with its position and role in the order and structure of different systems.

The so-called motif is like this "A." Furthermore, motif research can hardly cover all-important historical expressions of one particular culture. It must be limited to some features of that culture. In the history of Christian thought, *agape* is surely the fundamental motif for most Christian theologians, but in terms of its relationship with other motif(s), the differences will be more obvious. Take the example of relationship between the motif of *eros* and the motif of *agape* in Augustine and in Thomas Aquinas. Thomas is more likely to synthesize them. Paul Tillich goes as far as seeing the Christian *agape* as equal in essence to Platonic *eros,* both being clearly different from Nygren's antithetical position between *agape* and *eros.* In this sense, it is too simple to say that "*agape* is the center of Christianity."

Most important, as Professor Lo also stated in the last part of his essay, the methodology of motif research implies a theological presupposition, i.e., the uniqueness of each religion and the structural differences among religions. This is probably the reason why Nygren believed that *agape* is the distinctive characteristic of Christian faith, whereas other religions and philosophies are more or less driven by the motif of *eros.* In this way Nygren defends the particularity and integrity of the Christian faith. Therefore, we can rightly say that Nygren's resistance to religious synthesis is actually predetermined by this theological or even religious basic motivation of his motif research methodology.

Second, I would like to turn to Professor Lo's treatment of *ren* as a leading motif of Confucianism. To discover a single motif for such a long-lived and abundant philosophical-ethical tradition is a hard job. But we have to admit that taking the Northern Song philosopher Zhu Xi as a gateway is legitimate. And his view, according to which "*Ren* in Zhu Xi is qualified to be regarded as a fundamental motif, whose role in his thought resembles the role of *agape* in Christian thought as Nygren articulates it," can be appreciated.

But Professor Lo's saying that "*Ren* is both cosmic as well as human, with a metaphysical as well as an ethical dimension" needs some refinement. We can hardly say that *ren* in Confucianism is as metaphysical a concept as *agape* in Christianity. *Agape* in Christianity is a metaphysical concept in the sense that it expresses the power of God to create the world *ex nihilo*, God's election of Israel as his chosen people in history, and sending his only Son to be crucified for the redemption of the world. In this sense, *agape* is the cornerstone of the whole Christian theology, while *ren* in Zhu Xi is essentially an ethical concept.

Third, I would like to comment on Professor Lo's understanding of contextual theology. According to him, "it is a methodological insistence on the priority of a particular, local, and contemporary context for doing theology. The context can be religious, philosophical, literary, political, economic, social, or ideological. . . . My concern in this essay is the religious and philosophical contexts of the Chinese people. In particular, it is the context of the Confucian legacy that is my major focus." A few more points need to be taken into consideration here. To begin, the role of Confucianism in contemporary China needs to be newly evaluated. A leading contextual theologian in East Asia, Choan-seng Song, stated that Confucianism is out of date and plays only a small role in contemporary society. For him, to incorporate Confucianism into contextual theology is like finding a wrong dialogue partner. Though Dr. Song's judgment may not be accepted, it is important to bear in mind his criticism. Thus, the incorporation of Confucian legacy into Christian contextual theology should be oriented to the contemporary sociocultural reality.

Furthermore, emphasizing the "religious and philosophical contexts of the Chinese people" should not mean isolating these contexts from the sociopolitical reality of Chinese culture, both ancient and modern. Taking the motif of *ren* as an example, Professor Lo also points out that *ren* in Zhu Xi should both be inclusive and be practiced with an order. This order is actually the model of the hierarchic society (*zongfa shehui*) of classical China. Therefore, doing theology within the religious and philosophical contexts of the Chinese people might include two steps: (1) detaching the ethical and spiritual content of *ren* from the hierarchic order; and (2) implanting it into the situation of modern society. At any event, true contextualization is never just a pure theoretical interpretation, but an engagement with the sociopolitical reality.

Fourth and finally, I would like to conclude my response by discussing some fundamental questions of contextual theology stimulated by Professor

Lo's essay. My first remark is on his idea of "the priority of a particular, local, and contemporary context for doing theology." This is surely a very important principle, but on the other hand, theology is also the "logos of God." It concentrates on the interpretation of God's word but it is also a reflection *about* God. In this sense, theology should transcend any locality and temporality, and be a universal enterprise. Therefore, the dual aspect of contextuality and universality are equally important for constructing Chinese theology. They are like the two wings of a bird or the two wheels of a cart.

My second remark is on the synthesis (or conflict) between God's revelation and human culture, or "Jerusalem and Athens." As Nygren argued, the synthesis of Christian *agape* and Platonic *eros* will destroy the integrity of the *agape* motif. Thus, he is against any attempted syncretism between Christian revelation and other religions. But the history of Christian thought has revealed to us that most of the fruitful works of Western theology are actually results of some kind of synthesis, even those that we regard as "classical" ones, such as the theology of Augustine or of Thomas Aquinas. Therefore, as generally proposed, the dialectic between Jerusalem's revelation and Athens's reason is the driving power for Western civilization. It also might be the dialectic between *agape* and *ren* that would bring the power of life for Chinese contextual theology!

6 Dialogue between Christianity and Taoism: The Case of Lin Yutang

He Jianming

Lin Yutang was a famous scholar and writer in the history of modern China and also a famous religious explorer. In his teenage years, he was a Christian. He became a humanist Taoist in his middle age, but he returned to Christianity in his old age. His experience has shown the uniqueness of the dialogue between Christianity and Taoism in twentieth-century China.

In his youth, Lin accepted Christianity naturally, for he had been influenced by his family, his place of residence, and his educational environment. After becoming a university student, he experienced the impact of scientific thinking through the New Culture movement in China. A search for rationality led him to reject Christianity and to accept traditional Chinese Taoist humanism. After forty years of life amid social change, Lin returned to Christianity. His was not a simple return; it had two distinct characteristics: on the one hand, he was a Taoist Christian; on the other hand, Christianity proved most compelling in the encounter among religions in the poly-religious environment of twentieth-century China.

The encounter between Christianity and Chinese culture is an important field that interests contemporary scholars. In the past, scholars focused on the encounter between Christianity and Confucianism or Buddhism;[1] few have studied the encounter between Christianity and Taoism. This situa-

1. There are many works on the relationship between Christianity and Confucianism, for example, Whalen Lai and Michael von Bruck, *Christianity and Buddhism: A Multi-Cultural History of Their Dialogue* (New Haven: Overseas Ministries Study Center, 2001); Lai Pinchao and He Jianming, *Jindai Zhongguo fojiao yu jidujiao de xiangyu* (Hong Kong: Hanyu jidujiao wenhua yanjiusuo, 2003).

tion has been changing recently,[2] but there are not yet deep case studies or motif studies. This essay takes Lin Yutang as a case study.

In the history of modern Chinese culture, Lin Yutang is a distinctive cultural figure, since he lived in both Eastern and Western cultures and he sought to write in a universal way. After his death, an editorial in Taiwan's *Lianhebao* newspaper said:

> The biggest contribution of his life should be, and is also generally accepted by people, the facilitation between Chinese and Western cultures. As far as the importing of Western culture into China, there have been many people since the generation of Yan Fu and Lin Su. However, as far as the introducers of Chinese culture to the West, except Matteo Ricci and Tang Ruowang, Lin Yutang was one of the few successful people.[3]

In addition, among modern Chinese writers, no one has done better than he in the dialogue between Christianity, Taoism, and Buddhism. Lin Yutang was especially fond of Taoism both as a philosophy and as a religion. His most representative novel, *Shunxi jinghua*, begins with a subtitle: "The two daughters of the Taoist." However, his understanding and experience of Taoism was not purely traditional, since Christianity had influenced him. It can be said that the most noticeable phenomenon of Lin Yutang's cultural thought is the encounter between traditional Chinese local Taoism and Western Christianity. The present paper explores this encounter.

Some other scholars have also studied the relationship between Lin Yutang and Taoism. The most representative works include Fei Leren's "Xiandai Zhongguo wenhua zhong jidujiao yu daojiao de xiangyu, bianun, huxiang tansuo" (Encounter, Argument, and Mutual Exploration between Christianity and Taoism in Modern Chinese Culture), Yang Yi's "Lin Yutang: Daojia wenhua de haiwai huiguizhe" (Lin Yutang: The Overseas Returner of

---

2. Cf. Knut Walf, "Christian Theologoumena in Western Translations of the Taoists," in *Bible in Modern China: The Literary and Intellectual Impact*, ed. Irene Eber, Sze-Kar Wan, Knut Walf, and Roman Malek (Nettetal: Steyler Verlag, 1999), pp. 123-33; Fei Leren, "Xiandai Zhongguo wenhua zhong jidujiao yu daojiao de xiangyu, lunbian, xianghu tansuo," in Luo Bingxiang and Zhao Dunhua, *Jidujiao yu jindai zhongxi wenhua* (Beijing: Beijing daxue chubanshe, 2000); He Jianming, "Lue lun jindai jidujiao laihua dui daojiao de tiaozhan," in *Daojiao jiaoyi yu xiandai shehui guoji xueshu yantaohui lunwenji* (Shanghai: Shanghai guji chubanshe, 2003).

3. Quoted from Lin Taiyi, *Lin Yutang zhuan* (Xian: Shaanxi shifan daxue chubanshe, 2002), p. 291.

Taoist Culture),[4] and Liu Yong's "Shunhu benxing, jiushi shen zai tiantang — Lin Yutang jiqi chuangzuo dui zongjiao wenhua de lijie yu kunhuo" (Following the Original Nature Is in Heaven — Lin Yutang: Understanding and Puzzling His Writing on Religious Culture).[5]

Yang's article mainly analyzes how the thinking of Laozi and Zhuangzi influenced Lin's writing. In another article, "Daojia wenhua yu xiandai wenxue" (Taoist Culture and Modern Literature),[6] Yang has also shown how Chen Duxiu, Hu Shi, Lu Xun, Guo Moruo, Liang Shiqiu, Lin Yutang, Zhou Zuoren, and Cao Yu treat Taoist culture and how Taoist culture has influenced them. Liu Yong points out that the Taoist daughter Yao Mulan in Lin Yutang's *Shunxi jinghua* is "not only a Taoist daughter, but a combiner of Christianity, Taoism, Buddhism, and Confucianism."

However, Yang Yi and Liu Yong have not analyzed Lin Yutang from the viewpoint of religious encounter. Compared with Yang and Liu, Fei has really explored Lin Yutang's relationship between Christianity and Taoism in light of the encounter between Christianity and Taoism in modern China. Fei points out that Lin Yutang criticizes Taoism as a religion but appreciates the Taoism of Laozi and Zhuangzi. Fei has also studied the important connection between Taoist classics and the Bible by the method of comparison. Fei says, "By the Christ-like figure in this important Taoist classic Lin has once again established his identity as a Christian." Fei here has clearly emphasized the later thought of Lin in his old age, and he has not studied this issue in detail.

The present paper intends to explore mainly the following two issues on the basis of Fei's study: the importance of Taoism in the change of Lin Yutang from a young Christian to a gentile and then again to a Christian in his old age, and the characteristics of Lin Yutang's dialogue between Christianity and Taoism.

---

4. Yang Yi, "Lin Yutang: Daojia wenhua de haiwai huigui zhe," *Huawen wenxue* 2 (1991).

5. Liu Yong, "Shunhu benxing, jiu shi shen zai tiantang — Lin Yutang jiqi chuangzuo dui zongjiao wenhua de lijie yu kunhuo," in Liu Yong, *Zhongguo xiandai zuojiade zongjiao wenhua qingjie* (Beijing: Beijing shifan daxue chubanshe, 1998).

6. Yang Yi, "Daojia wenhua yu xiandai wenxue," *Zhongguo shehui kexue* 1 (1997). See also Yang Yi, *Wencun. Zhongguo xiandai wenxue liupai*, vol. 4 (Beijing: Renmin chubanshe, 1998).

Early Christian Impact and Taoist Elements in Lin Yutang's Heart

Although Lin Yutang was born into a Christian family, as he says, "there were Taoist elements in [his] blood."[7] Lin Yutang was born in 1895 in a coastal village called Banzi in Zhangzhou's Longxi county of Fujian Province. In that year China was defeated by Japan in the Ocean War of Jiawu and was forced to sign an unequal agreement giving Taiwan to Japan. Although Lin Yutang could not feel anything from such an important event when he was born, this national shame had an unforgettable impact on his later life. He once said that there were three important influences on his early life. First was the mountain view where he was born, second was his father, and third was his "strict Christian family."[8] This is also to say that, from his childhood, traditional Chinese Confucianism, Taoism, and foreign Christianity influenced him.

Lin's grandparents and parents were Christians, and they usually prayed every evening before going to bed. This experience deeply influenced Lin Yutang. Some of his "earliest memories of childhood were to slip down from the roof of the church building" and "to [be] amazed at the omnipresence of God."[9] His father was a well known village pastor in the local area; "the best nature of his was to love his congregation members very much. It was not because he would like to be responsible by loving his congregation members, but because he really loved them, because he was also born in a poor family." Lin thinks that the influence of his father's benevolent nature on him "was very important."[10] This suggests that Lin Yutang appreciated his father's simple spirit of universal love. Since his father had this spirit of love, he "was not only a preacher in the church, but was also a problem-solver among the conflicts of the local people, the lawyer in the court, and a person who helped people both in the great and small things of local inhabitants' family affairs."

More important was the fact that his father "was a pioneer of that time. He was a dreamer who was sharp, full of imagination and humor, and he never stopped. He transferred to us kids a strong interest in all the new and modern things, which were called 'New School' knowledge."[11] He also men-

---

7. *Lin Yutang zizhuang*, ed. Liu Huiying (1995), p. 18.
8. *Lin Yutang zizhuang*, p. 50.
9. Lin Yutang, *Xinyang zhilü — Lun dongxifang de zhexue yu zongjiao*, trans. Hu Zhanyun (Taipei: Daosheng chubanshe, 1994), p. 20.
10. *Lin Yutang zizhuang*, p. 10.
11. Lin Yutang, *Xinyang zhilü*, p. 22.

tioned that his father "was humorous by nature, and he often told jokes when he preached."[12] From the figure of Yao Si'an, the father of Yao Silan in the novel *Shunxi jinghua*, we can find some shadow of Lin Yutang's own father. Yao Si'an was a Taoist who was fond of New School and New Knowledge. Lin later wrote that the humorous feature of his father derived from the Chinese Taoist tradition.[13] For Lin Yutang, his father was not only a Christian and a Confucian[14] but, in fact, was also a Taoist.

In his writings Lin Yutang often mentioned that the mountain and water of his home village had influenced him deeply. On the one hand, the scene of his home village made him realize the omnipresence of God, as he himself said:

> something is related to the fact that [I] lived in the mountain area, since to be close to those high mountains is to be close to the greatness of God. I often stood there looking far away at the change of the mountain blues, the strange and free movement of white clouds on the tops of mountains, and I was amazed and felt puzzled. This made people look down on all those low mountains and all those unreal and small things which were made by human hands. These high mountains had become a part of me and of my religion since they made me rich and contented, and they gave me a feeling of inner power and independence which cannot be taken away by anyone. These mountains also brought me the true feeling of the Biblical words. "How beautiful it is when the feet of people are on the mountain." I started to believe that if one had not experienced the enjoyment of putting his feet in the wet grass he could not really know God.[15]

Every time Lin Yutang mentioned his life history, he always emphasized the beauty of the mountain and water in his home village. The elements that had influenced his childhood most deeply were "the mountain and water of Xixi." His home village Banzi was also called "Donghu" (East Lake). It was surrounded by high mountains. To the south was the ten tops mountain; to the north was a cliff that rises steeply. "The sun rises from the east and goes down to the west, both the early sunrise and the evening sunset receive the straight air of Heaven and Earth. It is not strange if you say it is not. It is a

12. *Lin Yutang zizhuang*, p. 273.
13. Lin Yutang, "Lun youmo," in *Youmo rensheng* (Xian: Shaanxi shifan daxue chubanshe, 2002).
14. Lin Yutang, *Xinyang zhilü*, p. 23.
15. Lin Yutang, *Xinyang zhilü*, p. 21.

trick of nature if you say it is strange. Looking far to the south, you will find the appearance and disappearance of clouds." "My view of human life is based on such a picture of mountain and water. Because the world is full of huge ocean and high sky, I have not seen the limit of human nature and the disorder of human affairs, nor I have forgotten them. If one wants to observe the smallness of humankind, he has to first look at the greatness of the universe."[16] Living in such a place of mountain and water, Lin Yutang experienced the presence of God and the influence of Taoist culture.

The mountain and water of Banzi revealed the simple spirit of Taoism. As Lin Yutang said, in his childhood he lived close to nature, where there are mountains, water, and farm life.

Such a close contact with nature makes my thinking very simple. I greatly emphasize this point, since it has given me a super idea of being human and of dealing with the world. Because of this, I would not become a politician, academic, or other kind of cheater. . . . If I have some healthy ideas and simple thoughts, it is because of the beautiful mountains of Banzi in the south of Fujian Province, since I believe that I still observe human life with the eyes of a simple farmer's son.[17]

There were also numerous Taoist celestial legends associated with the mountain and water of Banzi, and they interested Lin Yutang. When he was a child, he "often wondered how one could get out of such a valley, which is surrounded by steep cliffs. It is said that the high mountain in the north was opened once from the middle, and a celestial being had walked here, but his toe was mistakenly trapped in the hole in the rock. Thus, the mountain in the north appeared often in my mind."[18]

Of course, the practice of folk Taoist religion was the local custom, which was most easily felt in the area of Banzi, and the larger area of Zhangzhou, where Banzi was located, was full of beliefs in Mazu and Guangong. While Lin Yutang received Christianity, it was also natural to be influenced by local Taoist culture at the same time. He remembered that after he became ten years old, he often went to a primary school on Gulang Island in Xiamen with his older brother. They had to travel many days by boat to reach the school, and this enabled him to "enjoy the spiritual air of these mountains and the scene of the moon. The boat usually stopped in the river

---

16. *Lin Yutang zizhuang,* p. 272.
17. *Lin Yutang zizhuang,* p. 5.
18. *Lin Yutang zizhuang,* p. 9.

in the evenings, and there was an altar with several joss sticks in the back of the boat, since Mazu Grandma or Duke Guangong were worshipped. Since the Chinese masses always respect loyal and brave people, Guan Yu had also become an idol of worship in the hearts of the people."[19]

Among those Taoist elements, which were deeply rooted in Lin Yutang's heart, there was also the great love of his mother. In his biography Lin Yutang told an interesting detail concerning his marriage to Miss Liao Cuifeng. The night before the wedding, Lin Yutang hoped to sleep with his mother, and he said: "I am very close to my mother. It was the last night when I could sleep with my mother. I had a habit to play my mother's breasts till I was ten years old. Because of that kind of wish, which cannot be expressed clearly, I hoped to sleep beside her. Then I was still a virgin boy."[20]

Such a deep love for his mother was expressed when he wrote:

> I had a mother, who is kind and humble, and one cannot find another similar one under the sky. She gave me the limitless love of a mother, she never scolded me but loved me only. Such a love was endless without day and night; one cannot find its sign, but it has covered everything. I cannot express how she had influenced me; if one says that she had not influenced me, she exists always in front of and in back of me. This is similar to the change of spring wind into rain. I grew up in the protection of such a mother love, which is similar to the spring wind changing into rain. I grew up and became an adult, but she had become old till she left me alone in the world. . . . There is no endless love in the world, only mother's love is endless. Such an endless love, how can one forget? Since every person has only one such love.[21]

Such a profound love of mother reveals the Taoist spirit.

Therefore, although Lin Yutang had been influenced by a Christian family background, his family was also influenced by the Taoist spirit. From the mountains and water in Banzi he had realized the presence of God, and in the meantime he had also experienced the simple spirit and folk-religious beliefs of Taoism. He later criticized Christianity and tried to sever the relationship between Chinese Christianity and Chinese traditional culture, yet he had to admit that Chinese Christians who live in the context of Chinese culture will always experience the influence of traditional Chinese culture.

19. *Lin Yutang zizhuang,* p. 273.
20. *Lin Yutang zizhuang,* p. 76.
21. *Lin Yutang zizhuang,* p. 272.

This suggests that the conflict between Christianity and the Chinese cultural tradition is not precisely expressed as a conflict of cultures and is more adequately expressed as the human conflict between church and society. From his early years, Lin Yutang's ideas of Christianity and Taoism were not in conflict but rather in harmony.

Lin Yutang's View of Christianity and Taoism When He Became a Gentile

In outward appearance, Lin Yutang became a "gentile," i.e., he left Christianity for Chinese culture because of the conflict between his Christian faith and Chinese culture. In fact, his apostasy was more closely related to the social and cultural context of the time and the methods employed by Western missionaries in China. The scientific movement of New Culture at that time led Lin Yutang to replace his faith in the Christian God with faith in the Taoist *Dao*. Consequently, he became a humanist scholar in modern China.

Lin Yutang became a pious Christian in his childhood because of the influence of his family. "When he was a teenager, he often thought about things, which other people usually do not think about," and he felt that "God is omnipresent."[22] As a Christian, he was able to complete his middle school education in a church school in Xiamen free of charge; and, under the influence of his father, he made a further decision to attend St. John's University in Shanghai to study theology in preparation for becoming a pastor. Instruction at St. John's was in English.

However, after he entered St. John's University, he gradually realized that theology was in conflict with then-popular new ideologies. He said, "Not long after I arrived in Shanghai, I chose to study theology in order to make a preparation for working in the church. However, many trickeries of theology made me sick of it. Although I believed in God, I opposed doctrines; thus I left theology and church."[23] As he reflected on church education in China, he believed that many mistakes were being made. For example, English education was especially emphasized at St. John's University, but Chinese education was neglected. This led him later to oppose Christianity strenuously.[24] This intellectual struggle led him to commence "a great journey of spirit."

---

22. *Lin Yutang zizhuang,* p. 59.
23. *Lin Yutang zizhuang,* p. 197.
24. *Lin Yutang zizhuang,* p. 136.

Since traditional Chinese Confucian and Taoist culture had influenced him from a very young age, Lin Yutang felt that "for a Chinese intellectual, it was a natural wish to join in the mainstream of the Chinese tradition and not to be a Chinese who had been robbed of his citizenship."[25] However, after he entered St. John's University, Lin Yutang observed that a person "could be educated as a Christian, which meant to become a progressive person who appreciated Western culture, the New School, and the New Knowledge. Anyway, it meant that such a person accepted Western culture and especially appreciated its microscope and medical surgery." However, this also meant that in the meantime he felt that he "was separated from that contented and glorified gentile society [Chinese society] in rationality and aesthetics." More profoundly, he felt that "we are not only separated from Chinese philosophy but also separated from Chinese folk legends. It is tolerable for a Chinese if he does not understand Chinese philosophy, but it is ridiculous if one neither understands the stories of evil and ghosts nor Chinese folk legends."[26] Taoist content and form fill Chinese legendaries of evil and ghosts, and this indicates that Lin Yutang was unwilling to give up Chinese legends and Taoist culture, although one cannot say that his criticism of Christianity derived from faith in Taoism.

On the other hand, Lin Yutang was also dissatisfied with the college education at St. John's University. Essentially Lin did not like theology or philosophy, since both theology and philosophy were characterized by church or scholastic exclusiveness. He mentioned that

> a professor tried to persuade me to believe in the need of the Holy Spirit in theology through an example that if A and B exist, there must be a line C to connect them. Such scholastic pride and spiritual exclusiveness hurt my consciousness. These doctrines came from corrupt hearts, since they dealt with spiritual issues in the same way as they dealt with material issues, and they even appealed to God's justice together with their arguments. Those theologians were so sure about themselves; they thought that their conclusions must be the final ones, which will be kept forever in the form of books in boxes. I, of course, opposed them. There were many things in these doctrines that were not interrelated, and they had obscured the truth.

25. *Lin Yutang zizhuang,* p. 144.

26. *Lin Yutang zizhuang,* p. 138. Concerning the relationship between the education of St. John's University and Chinese culture, see He Jianming, "Shanghai Sheng Yuehan daxue de Zhongguo wenhua jiaoyu," in *Shehui zhuanxing yu jiaohui daxue,* ed. Zhang Kaiyuan (Wuhan: Hubei jiaoyu chubanshe, 1998), pp. 46-47.

Thus, Lin "had lost his sure faith, but he still grasped indomitably a belief in the Father God."[27]

After he graduated from St. John's University, he worked as a teacher in Tsinghua University in Beijing, and he still taught at Sunday schools then. However, Beijing was the center of the New Culture movement, which was promoted by Chen Duxiu and Hu Shi. Under the attack of New Culture and the Scientific movement, Lin's belief in the Father God was shaken. Later, under the impact of Gu Hongmin, who understood both Western and Chinese culture but criticized Christianity, Lin Yutang "returned to the mainstream of Chinese thought."[28] This means that he left Christianity voluntarily.

It is obvious that Lin Yutang started to abandon the Christian faith while he was a teacher in Tsinghua University. Although the mistakes of church education in separating Christianity from Chinese culture and the exclusiveness of scholastic theology had influenced Lin Yutang's attitude to Christianity, the more important reasons were the generational influence of society, politics, and culture. He wrote, "For a Chinese intellectual . . . [the] natural wish to join in the mainstream of the Chinese tradition and not to be a Chinese, who had been robbed of his citizenship." What did it mean when he said "to return to the mainstream of Chinese thought"? This question may be answered by observing his behavior after he left Christianity.

Lin Yutang said that, after he left Christianity in Tsinghua, he "studied only Chinese literature and philosophy, and was sick of all the education and other instruction which I received from church." Thus, he became a humanist.[29] In his *Sishi zixu* (Self Story at Forty) he mentioned that "there are endless contradictions in his entire life," and that he "came and went out and came into Christianity and Confucianism but that his luck of the Dao was shallow." He said that he "was both a Christian and a Confucian." It was true that, under the influence of his father who was both a Confucian and a Christian pastor, he had read the Confucian Four Books and Five Classics from the time he was very young.[30] Later, under the influence of Gu Hongming, he officially gave up the Christian faith. And on the same day he gave up Christian faith, a colleague of his in Tsinghua led Lin to believe in humanism and to affirm that, "according to Confucian humanity," "human rationality is able to change human beings themselves and the

27. *Lin Yutang zizhuang*, p. 147.
28. *Lin Yutang zizhuang*, pp. 148-61.
29. *Lin Yutang zizhuang*, pp. 196-97.
30. *Lin Yutang zizhuang*, p. 130.

world."[31] All these statements seem to indicate that, after he gave up Christianity, Lin Yutang was only a Confucian humanist. In fact, it is more accurate to say that Lin was a Taoist than to call him a Confucian at this time.

The first evidence of this is the fact that, during the thirty years after he gave up the Christian faith, all of Lin Yutang's representative works took Taoist philosophy or Taoist religion as their main lines. *Shunxi jinghua, Fengsheng heli,* and *Hong mudan* were his most representative writings of this period. All these works clearly reveal Taoist characteristics. As he himself said, "There is appearance and disappearance for all things in the human world. What interests people are usually the figures in books." Taoism's entire meaning has been expressed in Old Mr. Yao, the father of Yao Mulan in *Jinghua yanyun* (i.e., *Sunxi jinghua*), in Old Peng in *Fengsheng heli,* and in Liang Hanlin in *Hong mudan.*[32] His most important work, *Shunxi jinghua,* especially "is penetrated with the Taoist spirit and Zhuangzi's philosophy."

He quotes from Zhuangzi's *Qiwulun* by saying: "In a dream he met a person who drank and cried in the morning; he met another person who cried and hunted in the morning. Such words are called paradoxical. Ten thousand years later, I met a great sage who can understand this, and such a meeting is like a happening between morning and evening."[33] During these thirty years Lin Yutang proposed to express a natural spirit and to promote humor in literature, and his style of literature was also formed during this period. He considered the Chinese cultural tradition of natural spirit and humor as characteristic of Taoists such as Laozi, Zhuangzi, and Tao Qian.[34] He even expressed his gratitude to history, since many historical figures such as Zhuangzi, Tao Qian, Bai Juyi, Su Dongpo, and Yuan Zhonglang were his spiritual friends and influenced him very much. He said that "this kind of impact is like parents' influence on their children in the family."[35]

Second, during this period, Lin Yutang frequently mentioned his Taoist nature and often expressed his identification with Taoism. In his autobiography he wrote that there are two kinds of animals in the world: one cares only for himself, another cares for others' affairs. The former are the people who eat plants and think much, and the latter are the people who eat meat and act. He said that he himself "would never be able to become a person of action," since

31. *Lin Yutang zizhuang,* p. 198.
32. See Lin Yutang's "Jingcha qingdian," in *Lin Yutang zizhuang,* p. 122.
33. Lin Yutang's "Guanyu Shunxi jinghua — Gei Yu Dafu de xin," in Lin Yutang, *Shunxi jinghua,* trans. Yu Fei (Changsha: Hunan wenyi chubanshe, 1991), p. 785.
34. Lin Yutang, *Youmo rensheng* (Xian: Shaanxi shifan daxue chubanshe, 2002), pp. 3-7.
35. Lin Yutang's "Guanyu shenghuo de yishu," in *Lin Yutang zizhuang,* pp. 250-52.

he "usually liked to follow his own original nature and to act according to his own wish"; he especially liked to decide by himself "what goodness is, what beauty is, and what non-being is. . . . And individual life is most important for me. Perhaps in essence, if not in sure confidence, I am an anarchist or Taoist."[36]

Although he did not believe exclusively in Taoism, he appreciated Taoism very much. *Su Dongpo zhuan* (Biography of Su Dongpo) was perhaps his only work written because of his personal interest, with no other purpose in his whole life. He considered "Su Dongpo as a person, who was perhaps not the only one in the world, but it was almost impossible to find another similar one," since Su Dongpo "took Confucianism as his standard of ethics, but he was a pure Taoist inside his bones."[37] In fact, Lin Yutang was expressing his own opinion and told about himself with the help of Su Dongpo.

Of course, the most important thing was that Lin Yutang's faith object at that time was no longer the Christian God but the *Dao* of Taoism. When he mentioned his journey of leaving the Christian faith, Lin Yutang said, he "always liked science." "Since Galileo, science has had a profound influence; no one has escaped its impact. Thus all those ideas according to which souls do not die and that God rewards and punishes human beings should be reconsidered." He especially considered the Christian doctrine of original sin ridiculous, and he "really could not understand" the best theories of Christianity. He thought that "both Moses and Confucius gave rules for human behavior which constitute the meaning of religion, and they followed the method of wisdom. However, in modern society we can neither produce a Moses nor a Confucius. The only way which we can follow, is mysticism such as Laozi proposed. In the broad sense, mysticism refers to respecting the natural order between Heaven and Earth, following nature and blending the individual into the order of nature."[38]

It is obvious that Lin Yutang did not totally deny Christianity when he became a gentile. He thought that in modern scientific society, the *Dao* of Taoism better served the need of his spirituality. Therefore, he did not claim that Christianity is contrary to Taoism or Buddhism. Lin Yutang was not in fact a pure Taoist at that time. For example, he considered Su Dongpo as "taking Confucianism as the standard for the sake of brothers and fathers, but he was a pure Taoist inside his bones." In fact, Lin Yutang himself was also a Taoist inside his bones; of course, this did not mean that he was no

---

36. *Lin Yutang zizhuang*, p. 38.
37. Lin Yutang's "Guanyu Su Dongpo zhuan," in *Lin Yutang zizhuang*, pp. 256-59.
38. Lin Yutang's "Wo de xinyang," in *Lin Yutang zizhuang*, pp. 187-94.

longer a Confucian. For him, to be a Chinese intellectual, one should be both a Taoist and a Confucian, and these double identities do not conflict with each other, since this feature fits the cultural spirit of the Chinese.[39] Because of this, Lin Yutang said that, during the period of more than thirty years when he left Christianity, "the only religion of his was humanism."[40] His good friend Jiang Fuzong thus called him "both Buddhist and Taoist."[41]

Lin Yutang's View of Christianity and Taoism When He Returned to Christian Faith

Lin Yutang gave up the Christian faith at the end of 1910 when he taught at Tsinghua University in Beijing. After nearly forty years of exploration, he returned from humanism to the Christian faith in 1958.[42] There have not been many people in Chinese history like Lin Yutang, who first gave up Christianity and then returned to the Christian faith. More significantly, Lin Yutang's return was not a simple return to the Christianity of his earlier faith when he was a child, teen, and youth. Rather, he returned because he had a newer and better understanding of Christianity. This is apparent in his dealing with the relationship between Christianity and gentile religions (e.g., traditional Chinese Confucianism, Buddhism, and Taoism), especially in his dealing with the relationship between Christianity and Taoism, which he had believed in for many years.

When he mentioned why he had returned to Christianity in his old age, Lin Yutang said:

> During the past thirty years, the only religion of mine was humanism, i.e., I believed that it was enough if a person had rationality and that the de-

39. Concerning Lin Yutang's opinions on the role of Confucianism and Taoism in Chinese and other cultures, see "Wuguo wumin," in *Lin Yutang wenji*, vol. 8 (Beijing: Zuojia chubanshe, 1996). See also Lin Yutang, *Shengzhe de zhihui* (including two books: *Kongzi de zhihui* and *Laozi de zhihui*) (Xian: Shaanxi shifan daxue chubanshe, 2002).

40. Lin Yutang's "Cong renwen zhuyi huidao jidujiao xinyang," in *Lin Yutang zizhuang*, p. 196.

41. Lin Taiyi, *Lin Yutang zhuan*, p. 285.

42. Concerning the date when Lin Yutang returned to Christian faith, the present essay is based on the opinion of Jiang Fushen, who was the dean of the Taiwan Academy of the Forbidden City and an old friend of Lin Yutang. In 1958 Jiang told this in his speech to celebrate Lin Yutang's 80th birthday, where Lin Yutang was present. The second daughter of Lin Yutang, Lin Taiyi, recorded this date in her *Lin Yutang zhuan*, pp. 284-86.

velopment of knowledge would certainly change the world. However, after observing the material development of the 20th century and the behavior of those nations which do not believe in God, now I believe that humanism is not enough. For the sake of its self-existence, human beings need an extra and greater power to connect them. This is the reason that I returned to Christianity. I would like to return to the love of God, which was expressed by Jesus, and to the knowledge of it.[43]

During that time, Lin Yutang sought for a religion that could "fit those people who had received a modern education." He did not return to Christianity immediately after he doubted humanism; in fact, he had thought long and hard. For him, besides Confucianism, there were still Buddhism and Taoism in Oriental society. However, they could not satisfy him. Buddhism is based on the idea of mercy, and considering the world as unreal. Thus, everything in human life is very pitiful, the only hope is in the future world, and humankind cannot positively face the real world.

He especially reconsidered Taoism, which he had appreciated for many years. He said, "Taoism appreciated worship of the Dao, which is unreal, nameless, untouchable and exists everywhere, and this Dao is the ruler of Heaven and Earth, its rule controls the universe in a mystical and certain way; thus, the humility of Taoism and Jesus' Sermon on the Mountain recorded in the New Testament are quite similar. The Taoist prophet Laozi was indeed an outstanding teacher, but his essence of returning to nature and refusing to go forward cannot make any contribution to solving the problems which are faced by modern humankind." Since Daoism could not satisfy his spiritual need at that time, after he went to church many times accompanying his wife, he was moved by sermons and the Christian faith of his childhood gradually reasserted itself. In Lin's own words, he "was inclined to the Christian faith of his childhood without noticing."[44]

It is obvious that Lin Yutang appreciated the Taoist emphasis on returning to nature when he gave up Christianity. However, after experiencing many things in his life, finally Lin Yutang criticized Taoism as too negative in emphasizing a return to nature. The attitudes of Lin Yutang to Taoism and Buddhism are different. He affirmed the Taoist content, which is similar to Jesus' Sermon on the Mount. Since Jesus' teaching plays an important role in Christianity, Lin's employment of it indicates that he did not consider Tao-

---

43. Lin Yutang's "Cong renwen zhuyi huidao jidujiao xinyang," in *Lin Yutang zizhuang*, p. 196.

44. *Lin Yutang zizhuang*, p. 198.

ism as contrary to Christianity in every aspect. Lin Yutang treated Taoism quite specially. In fact, the return of Lin Yutang to Christianity meant that he gave up humanism, which he had believed in for forty years, but it is questionable to say that he also totally gave up Taoism, which he appreciated very much.

Here two things need to be emphasized. First, his return to the Christian faith of his childhood was closely related to his respect for Taoism. This not only indicated that Lin appreciated the Taoist content, which is close to Jesus' Sermon on the Mount, it also indicated his Taoist understanding of Christianity. As he said, "Now I re-experience Jesus' teaching, which is brief, simple, respectful and makes people reconsider themselves deeply."[45] Although Jesus' teaching of forgiveness is different from Taoist teaching, they share a similar form in brevity and simplicity.

More representative was the fact that Lin Yutang considered himself full of contradictions. In his *Bashi zixu* (Self Story at Eighty) he said: "I am nothing but a bundle of contradictions, but I am happy with my self-contradictions." Why? On the one hand, he described himself as "a gentile who in his heart was a Christian." On the other hand, he considered himself as "a Taoist disciple of Laozi and Zhuangzi." He was different from those Christians who were keen in doing missionary work; he was rich in the Taoist features of following nature and forgiving others,[46] and he "never persuaded gentiles to turn towards the Lord Jesus."[47] When he summarized his writings of his whole life, Lin Yutang mentioned especially *Shunxi jinghua, Fengsheng heli,* and *Hong mudan,* since they showed a Taoist spirit, and he affirmed that "Taoists were great people."[48]

Second, Lin Yutang considered Taoism as the top of the Taoist mountain but spoke of "the dense fog of Buddhism." This view was expressed in a book written after he returned to Christianity in his old age: *Cong yijiaotu dao jidutu* (From a Gentile to a Christian), i.e., *Xinyang zhi lu: Lun dongxifang de zhexue yu zongjiao* (The Journey of Faith: On the Eastern and Western Philosophies and Religions). In this book, although he criticized certain superstitions of Taoism, he highly praised the thought and wisdom of the fundamental Taoist representatives such as Laozi and Zhuangzi. He

---

45. *Lin Yutang zizhuang,* p. 199.
46. In his *Xinyang zhilü* (The Journey of Faith) Lin Yutang appreciated the tolerant spirit of Chinese Taoism. He said: "Chinese religions do not hold an exclusive attitude, and this is different from Christianity." See *Xinyang zhilü,* p. 154.
47. Lin Yutang's "Bashi zixu," in *Lin Yutang wenji,* vol. 8, pp. 43-49.
48. Lin Yutang's "Bashi zixu," in *Lin Yutang wenji,* vol. 8, p. 122.

insisted that the nineteenth-century American writer Ralph Waldo Emerson (1803-82) appreciated the value of Laozi's thought and that the seventeenth-century French Christian philosopher Blaise Pascal (1623-62) held views in accordance with those of Zhuangzi.

In interpreting the Chinese cultural spirit, on the one hand, Lin Yutang considered the Confucianism of Confucius and Mencius and the Taoism of Laozi and Zhuangzi as two sides of Chinese culture, neither of which could be omitted. He said, "When a Chinese person is successful, he is a good Confucian. When he is surrounded by difficulties and failings, he is a Taoist." Meanwhile, he emphasized also that the "failings of a person are more than the successes of a person; even those people who seem to be successful on the surface have their own secret worries when they consider themselves alone in the night. Therefore, the Taoist impact is greater than that of Confucianism."[49] In fact, this indicates also that Lin Yutang placed greater emphasis on the Taoist elements in Chinese culture.

After he returned to the Christian faith, Lin Yutang constantly emphasized the identification between Christianity and Taoism. He said, "Confucius mentioned that 'if one does not know life, how can one know death?' It is real knowledge when one knows what he knows, and when one knows what he does not know." In fact, these words of Confucius "make one keep distance from God himself." However, Laozi persuaded Confucius "to wash yourself and to get rid of all of your morality of benevolence and righteousness so that you can be saved." This is, in fact, in accordance with Jesus' words, "If your righteousness is not better than that of the teachers of the law and Pharisees, you will certainly not be able to enter the kingdom of heaven."[50]

Lin praised Laozi as "the first philosopher, who hid himself, refraining from expressing himself," and he said that many teachings in the *Daodejing* are totally the same as biblical teachings. The doctrines of weakness and humbleness by Laozi are "like the rationalization of Jesus' Sermon on the Mountain." He said, "Laozi's teaching concerning the power of love and humbleness is not only similar to Jesus' special, outstanding teachings in spirituality, their literal expressions are sometimes also astonishingly similar."[51]

Lin Yutang also greatly appreciated another Taoist representative, Zhuangzi. Lin called him "the greatest and deepest philosopher ever born in

49. *Xinyang zhilü*, p. 114.
50. *Xinyang zhilü*, pp. 111-12.
51. *Xinyang zhilü*, pp. 128-30.

China" and considered Zhuangzi "a keen religious mystic like Blaise Pascal, and the sayings of Blaise Pascal are easily interpreted in the light of Zhuangzi's viewpoint." For Lin, "Zhuangzi reached the pinnacle of 'accepting God's will' in Christianity," "in fact, Zhuangzi believes in the omnipresence of God."[52] Therefore, Zhuangzi was the Chinese Blaise Pascal, and Blaise Pascal the French Zhuangzi. Lin Yutang even criticized the stupidity of Christian theologians with the wisdom of Zhuangzi by saying: "The beauty of Zhuangzi's wisdom is that he knows where and when 'to stop and to rest' when he reached the border of Dao. The stupidity of Christian theologians is that they did not know where and when to stop but continued to define God with limited logic as a triangle-like shape, and further decided to satisfy their own will of seeking knowledge."[53] This indicates that his criticism of theology led Lin Yutang to give up Christianity and that forty years later after returning to Christianity he had no better feeling about theology.

In summary, after he returned to Christianity, Lin Yutang tried to distinguish Christianity from Taoism, but he did not reject the Taoist *Dao* as did other Christians. Lin distinguished Taoist philosophy from Taoist religion, and he interpreted Christianity in the light of Taoism and interpreted Taoism in the light of Christianity. This may indicate that he was a Taoist Christian or a Christian Taoist.

Conclusion

In his childhood Lin Yutang accepted the Christian faith, in his middle age he believed in humanism, and in his old age he again returned to Christianity. Concerning Christian faith and knowledge, Lin Yutang experienced a process from perceptual acceptance to rational rejection and finally to spiritual return. For Lin Yutang, the process was complex and long since it was based on historical reasons, i.e., the Taoist impact.

In his childhood, Lin Yutang longed for wisdom and knowledge. The influence of his family, hometown, and educational environment played an essential role in his acceptance of Christianity, which at that time was mainly perceptual rather than rational. In the meantime, although he accepted Christianity, he did not reject traditional Chinese Buddhism or Taoism, and in fact he retained "Taoist elements" in his heart. However, the "Taoist ele-

---

52. *Xinyang zhilü*, pp. 133-51.
53. *Xinyang zhilü*, p. 152.

ments" in the heart of Lin Yutang were not mainly the thought of Laozi and Zhuangzi but the folk-religious legends of faith in Mazu, Guangong, and celestial beings.

After he went to college, Lin Yutang came to know the New Culture movement that promoted science and opposed religious superstition, and he lived in Shanghai and Beijing, the centers of the New Culture movement. Thus, rationalism played an important role. First, he started to reject those ideas of Christianity that did not seem to be in accordance with science, e.g., that Jesus was born of a virgin and that he rose from the dead and ascended into heaven. He then looked for ideas that could satisfy human need and did not oppose science. Lin Yutang noticed that the Taoist *Dao* had both rationalist and humanist values. As he said, "The Taoist Dao had such a feature." Its meaning is so broad that it can include the most advanced recent and future worldviews. It is not only mystical but also fits reality.

Taoism holds a tolerant attitude to materialism. For Taoists materialism is rather stupid but is not evil. Taoists laugh at hatred and jealousy. For people living in luxury they propose simplicity. For people living in a capital city, they emphasize the beauty of the nature. For competition and struggle, they propose the theory of emptiness and the principle of softness. For people who hoped to live forever, they teach the theory that the universe is material and will never die out. For radicals, they teach theories of nonaction and quietness. For people who hoped to achieve great things, they teach paying attention to the arts of life. For hard people, they teach them with softness.

As to those people in recent history who worshiped war, e.g., the followers of Fascism, Taoism asked them to realize that they are not the only wise people in the world and that, if they continue in the same way, they will receive nothing. Some change for the better will certainly take place if a stupid person thinks one thousand times; if anyone is against such a principle, he faces a terrible result. The Taoist attempt to reach peace starts from harmony. Lin even felt that in an era that is full of killing, "Only Taoism, which criticizes the world and secularism, is not cold and terrible."[54] Since the Taoist *Dao* has both rationalist and humanist values, it became for Lin Yutang an alternative to Christianity and replaced the Christian God as an object of faith.

At the end of the 1950s Lin Yutang returned to Christianity, after many years of change and experience. He felt that the twentieth century was a period of rationalist materialism, that material had prevailed over spirituality,

54. Lin Yutang's "Wo de xinyang," in *Lin Yutang zizhuang,* pp. 194-96.

and in following materialism human hope had collapsed. "In addition to the basic doctrine of Jesus, nothing can change it," since the root of freedom and democracy is in the words of Jesus. Even so, Lin Yutang did not totally reject the values of Taoism. The difference was that he intentionally distinguished Taoist philosophy from Taoist religion. He criticized Taoist religious superstition, but he appreciated the Taoist philosophy of Laozi and Zhuangzi; for Lin Yutang the latter was not in conflict with Christianity. He said:

> The Taoism of Zhuangzi was most directly helpful to the liberation of spirituality. He had a realization, which was rare among rationalist philosophers. The standing position of Zhuangzi was similar to that of Blaise Pascal, and they were really religious. . . . Sometimes Laozi lifted this element to a very high position; for example, he had faith in the power of love and humbleness, and in order to bring peace to humankind, he looked down upon all human measures such as governments, punishments, and wars. Laozi and Jesus were brothers in their spiritualities.[55]

In the journey of Lin Yutang's exploration of faith, he accepted Christianity in his childhood, and he also accepted the Chinese folk-religious Taoist faith in his subconscious, but such an inherited Taoism was not in conflict with Christianity. After giving up Christianity and accepting the Taoist *Dao,* he did not distinguish Taoist philosophy strictly from Taoist religion, but regarded Taoism as contrary to Christianity. After returning to Christianity in his old age, he gave up Taoist religious superstition but affirmed the positive value of Taoist philosophy and affirmed that the thought of Laozi and Zhuangzi was not in conflict with Christianity but identical with it. Thus, Lin Yutang accepted Christianity but did not reject traditional Chinese culture, especially the Taoist tradition. As he commented regarding his own father, "My father was a pastor, but this did not mean that he was not a Confucian."[56] We may also say that, although Lin Yutang again became a Christian in his old age, this did not mean that he was not a Taoist.

Interreligious dialogue is different from intrareligious dialogue, since the former faces a possibility of changing religion. Interreligious dialogue is, in fact, a dialogue within one's own heart, which is influenced by the living environment and experience rather than by any pressure or temptation from other religions. Therefore, the change of Lin's religion was a change of mental environment rather than a result of some urgent influence of a gen-

55. *Xinyang zhilü,* pp. 240-45.
56. *Lin Yutang zizhuang,* p. 130.

tile religion. With changes in society, politics, and life situations, an interreligious dialogue can lead to conflicts or new syntheses at any time; it is impossible to have any kind of pure religion. Dialogue between Christianity and Taoism in Lin Yutang's case exhibited such a feature of religious contextualization. Thus, contextualization is the natural way of religion's existence and development.

Raimondo Panikkar observed that interreligious dialogue must rid itself of special and common apologetic positions.[57] In fact, this means that one should get rid of the limits of churches and denominations. After he returned to Christianity in his old age, Lin Yutang did not return to church and did not accept a denominational theology. However, this did not mean that he lacked a pious faith in God. As he said:

> What makes me feel abnormal and upset is that, in Christian countries, educated people found it easier to have sympathy with rationalism and humanism than with their fellow-Christians. On the other hand, a gentile, who publicly proclaimed his return to Christianity, certainly did not give up his faith in the power of reason or denigrate wisdom. I have observed for many years, I believed in God, but I cannot join any church. I will never be satisfied with such a situation, but in the confusion of faith, creed and doctrine, it is very difficult to express one's faith in God.[58]

This was a worry but also a reality, which no one could doubt.

It is not abnormal that interreligious dialogue leads to a change of religion. Such a change is not a wrong way but a natural result. If one accepts the necessity of dialogue in the polyreligious context, one has also to accept the possibility that one may change one's religious identity. Such a change of faith may lead one to become a gentile and may also lead to a return to the original faith that one had earlier. However, the return to faith cannot be a simple repetition; it is more likely a reunification and a higher level of spirituality and rationality. The content of faith may not change, but the form of faith may change significantly. It was a typical example of such a movement that Lin Yutang returned to the Christian faith in his old age since, as a Christian, Lin Yutang was also a gentile Taoist at the same time.[59] Thus, he

---

57. Raimondo Panikkar, *Zongjiao nei duihua,* trans. Wang Zhicheng (Beijing: Zongjiao wenhua chubanshe, 2001), p. 81.

58. *Xinyang zhilü,* p. 195.

59. Concerning the concept "gentile," Lin Yutang interpreted it by saying: "Since religious faiths are confused and there are many denominations among them, I tried to go

could retain the same critical attitude to church and theology that he had when he gave up Christianity earlier. However, this critical attitude did not signify that he had rejected Christianity again or that he did not believe in God.

---

through the cursed fire of Hell, the beach of Greece, and the female ghost of the Pharisees, and I called myself a gentile. Since I stood in the positions of rationalism and humanism, I remembered all the adjectives every religion gave to others; thus, I believed that the term 'gentile' might avoid the criticism of believers. It is amazing that the English term 'gentile' can usually not be used in the major religions such as Christianity, Judaism, and Islam." See *Xinyang zhilü*, p. 193.

7 Reflections on the History of Buddhist-Christian Encounter in Modern China

Lai Pan-chiu

Studies on Christian-Buddhist dialogue have become one of the important areas of religious studies, and large numbers of works in English are published as the result of such studies. In Japan, Europe, and North America, several societies and organizations have been established to study and promote the dialogue between Christianity and Buddhism. In view of the current publications, Buddhist-Christian studies at the international level seem to be dominated by the discussion among the American and Japanese scholars. The most active figures, including D. T. Suzuki (1870-1966), Hisamatsu Shinichi (1889-1980), Masao Abe, and Seiichi Yagi, etc.,[1] are from Japan, and the discussion so far has been focused on Japanese Buddhism, especially Zen Buddhism. In comparison, the contributions of Chinese scholars, as yet, have been far from substantial.[2] Apart from the language barrier, this situation may also reflect, to a certain extent, the underdevelopment of Christian-Buddhist dialogue in Chinese society.[3]

1. Among them, Seiichi Yagi is perhaps the least known for work in English. For an introduction to his thought, see Masaya Odagaki, "An Introduction to the Religious Thought of Seiichi Yagi," *Buddhist-Christian Studies* 9 (1989): 271-81.

2. For instance, in the twenty-two volumes of *Buddhist-Christian Studies* published as of 2002, fewer than ten articles are written by Chinese. There are three articles by Julia Ching (including a respondent article), three by Whalen Lai, one by Darui Long, and one by Lai Pan-chiu. In addition, there is an article on the early encounter between Buddhism and Taoism in China by Liu Chia-ho (presumably Chinese) and translated by D. Shao.

3. For the encounter of Christianity and Buddhism in different cultures, see Whalen Lai and Michael von Brück, *Christianity and Buddhism: A Multi-Cultural History of Their Dialogue*, trans. Phyllis Jestice (Maryknoll: Orbis Books, 2001).

It is evident that the encounter between Christianity and Buddhism started rather early, in the Tang dynasty (618-907).[4] Nevertheless, in the years that followed, such encounters did not fully blossom, nor did they give rise to fructification, largely due to historical reasons.[5] In Japan, the encounter between the two religions transformed from mutual antagonism to dialogue in the second half of the nineteenth century.[6] During the twentieth century, Japanese scholars from both the Buddhist and Christian sides actively engaged in the dialogue. In addition to the scholars from the Kyoto school, many Catholic scholars, particularly those from the Jesuit-founded Sophia University, contributed tremendously to the dialogue. Some of them were equipped with a profound understanding of Zen, for instance, Heinrich Dumoulin,[7] William Johnston,[8] and J. K. Kadowaki.[9] In addition, Protestantism in Japan, especially the Nanzan Institute for Religion and Culture, has also actively contributed to this dialogue. In contrast, it should be admitted that the Buddhist-Christian dialogue in China as well as research related to it have lagged far behind.

Whalen Lai, who has made valuable contributions to the studies on the encounter between Buddhism and Christianity in China, raises the question as to why there is no Buddhist-Christian dialogue in China.[10] Of course, this does not mean that there has been no contact or dialogue whatsoever between Christianity and Buddhism in China. Instead, it implies that the en-

---

4. See Sverre Holth, "The Encounter between Christianity and Chinese Buddhism during the Nestorian Period," *Ching Feng* 11, no. 3 (1968): 20-29.

5. For the history of the encounter between Buddhism and Christianity in China, see Whalen Lai, "The Buddhist-Christian Dialogue in China," in *Religious Issues and Interreligious Dialogue,* ed. Charles Wei-hsun Fu and Gerhard E. Spiegler (New York: Greenwood, 1989), pp. 613-31.

6. Notto R. Thelle, *Buddhism and Christianity in Japan: From Conflict to Dialogue, 1854-1899* (Honolulu: University of Hawaii Press, 1987).

7. Heinrich Dumoulin was an expert in Zen studies. In addition to the works that discuss Zen, he also wrote on the encounter between Christianity and Buddhism. For example, Heinrich Dumoulin, *Christianity Meets Buddhism* (LaSalle, IL: Open Court, 1974).

8. William Johnston wrote several other books on Buddhist meditation and Christian spiritual practice, for example, *The Mirror Mind: Zen-Christian Dialogue* (New York: Fordham University Press, 1990). See also So Yuen-tai, "William Johnston's Contemplative Approach to Buddhist-Christian Dialogue," *Ching Feng* 42, nos. 1-2 (March-June 2000): 83-110.

9. J. K. Kadowaki, *Zen and the Bible: A Priest's Experience,* trans. Joan Rieck (London: Routledge, 1980).

10. Whalen Lai, "Why Is There Not a Buddho-Christian Dialogue in China?" *Buddhist-Christian Studies* 6 (1986): 81-96.

counter between Chinese Buddhism and Christianity is rather full of mutual confrontation and conflict, and little has been achieved in the dialogue. No mutual understanding and intercommunication, as occurred in Japan, have taken place in China. Whalen Lai's observation is certainly true that the Buddhist-Christian dialogue never thrived in China as it did in Japan and North America. However, should it be then concluded that nothing in the Christian-Buddhist dialogue in China deserved to be studied? If so, does this indicate that there is nothing but a dead end for the dialogue between the two religions in China? Or, if a certain historical foundation was already laid down for the encounter between Chinese Christianity and Buddhism in the past, can it successfully pave the way for dialogue in the future? All these questions are worthy of further discussion.

As a person who has been interested in Christian-Buddhist studies for many years, I would like to take this opportunity to reexamine my own studies and to share some of my personal reflections on the topic. It is my hope that this may arouse the interest of scholars in the subject.

The (Re-)Discovery of Historical Materials

A few years ago, Professor He Jianming (formerly at Central China Normal University and now People's University) and I conducted a research project on the Buddhist and Christian publications in China during the first half of the twentieth century. We discovered that although the encounter between Buddhism and Christianity at that time was also marred by intermittent heated disputes, a number of constructive and open-minded dialogues had indeed taken place from the late Qing dynasty and continued during the Republican Era. The contact between Timothy Richard (1845-1919) and Yang Wenhui (1837-1911) enabled them, a Christian missionary and a lay Buddhist, to cooperate on a project to translate the *Treatise on the Awakening of Faith* (*Mahāyāna Śraddhotpāda Śastra*) and the *Lotus Sutra* (*Sadharmapundarīka Sūtra*) into English in hope that Mahayana Buddhism might be introduced to the West.[11]

Timothy Richard also attempted to initiate dialogue with Buddhists.[12]

---

11. Timothy Richard, *The New Testament of Higher Buddhism* (Edinburgh: T. & T. Clark, 1910).

12. Timothy Richard, *Liti Motai zhi shijia shu* (Timothy Richard's Letters to Buddhists) (Shanghai: Guangxuehui, 1916).

Later on, he introduced Dhammapala (1865-1933),[13] a pioneer for the Buddhist revival movement in India, to Yang Wenhui. To a certain extent, the Buddhist reform advocated by Yang was inspired by his personal contact with Christianity.[14] Unfortunately, most of the existing studies on Timothy Richard have concentrated on how he, as a Christian missionary, contributed to the sociopolitical reform and modernization of China, while his efforts as well as contributions to Christian-Buddhist dialogue largely have been neglected.[15] Meanwhile, some eminent Buddhist monks in the Republican Era also adopted open and positive attitudes toward Christianity. They believed that Buddhism could learn from Christianity in many ways, especially its missionary method and its involvement in education and charity.[16] Within the Buddhist circle, some Buddhist journals also published Buddhist responses to the challenges coming from Christianity. Many of the respondents were not well-known monks, but ordinary Buddhist intellectuals. Their responses, which revealed the attitudes among ordinary Buddhists, showed that the concern about Christianity was not limited to the Buddhist hierarchy, but extended to the broader Buddhist community.[17]

Within the Christian circle, in addition to the small numbers of missionaries who extended their goodwill toward Chinese Buddhists, many Chinese Christian intellectuals also endeavored to study the indigenization of Buddhism in China in order to learn the way of indigenizing Christianity with a view to making Christianity more suitable and acceptable to the Chinese.[18] Furthermore, many intellectuals such as Xu Songshi (1900-1999) and Zhang

13. Yu Linpo, *Yang Renshan jushi pingzhuan* (A Critical Biography of Yang Renshan) (Taipei: Xinwenfeng, 1995), pp. 223-28.

14. He Jianming and Lai Pan-chiu, "Christianity and the Reformation of Modern Chinese Buddhism," in *Jinxiangdai Zhongguo fojiao yu jiduj zongjiao de xiangyu* (The Encounter between Buddhism and Christianity in Modern China), ed. Lai Pan-chiu (Hong Kong: Institute for Sino-Christian Studies, 2003), pp. 74-80.

15. For an exceptional example, see Andrew F. Walls, "The Multiple Conversions of Timothy Richard," in *The Cross-cultural Process in Christian History* (Maryknoll, NY: Orbis Books, 2002), pp. 236-58; see also Lee Chi-ho, "Timothy Richard's Response to the Challenges to Christianity in China," in *The Second International Seminar on the Studies of History of Christianity in North East Asia for Graduate Students and Junior Scholars*, Kanagawa, Japan, September 21-23, 2002, pp. 87-104.

16. He Jianming and Lai Pan-chiu, "Christianity and the Reformation of Modern Chinese Buddhism," pp. 80-124.

17. He Jianming, "Buddhist-Christian Encounter in Modern China: A Case Study of *Ren Jian Jue Banyuekan*," *Ching Feng* (New Series) 1, no. 2 (Fall 2000): 121-42.

18. Lai Pan-chiu, "Influence of Chinese Buddhism on the Indigenization of Christianity in Modern China," *Ching Feng* (New Series) 1, no. 2 (2000): 143-60.

Chunyi (1871-1955), who were knowledgeable in both Buddhism and Christianity, attempted to synthesize Buddhism and Christianity by proposing a "Mahayana Christianity."[19] Although Xu Songshi was a Christian, he often had his articles published under a Buddhist name "Zhao-liu ju-shi" (the term "ju-shi" usually refers to the lay Buddhist) in an attempt to reconcile the conflict between the teachings of Christianity and Buddhism. He even elaborated on "the Buddha's flavor in Christianity" and "the Christ's flavor in Buddhism."[20] Zhang Chunyi, who had been a Christian but embraced Buddhism later on, composed eight books to discuss how Christianity could be transformed through Chinese culture, including Chinese Buddhism.[21]

In addition to these attempts to harmonize Buddhist and Christian doctrines, many Chinese intellectuals managed to deal with the practical issues of coexistence between Buddhism and Christianity in their daily lives, and some of them provided unique solutions. For instance, Xu Dishan (1893-1941), a well-known writer, not only cherished the idea of harmony between Buddhism and Christianity in his daily life, but also displayed it in his literary works.[22] Nevertheless, since previous studies of the Buddhist-Christian encounter have been focused on how Western missionaries such as Karl Ludvig Reichelt (1877-1952) exerted influence on Buddhism,[23] and on how

19. Lai Pan-chiu and So Yuen-tai, "Zhang Chunyi de fohua shenglinglun" (Zhang Chunyi's Buddhist-Christian Pneumatology), in *Shengling: Huaren zongjiao ji wenhua chujing xia de fansi* (Holy Spirit: Reflections in the Chinese Religious and Cultural Context), ed. Deng Shaoguan (Andres Tang S.K.) (Hong Kong: Lutheran Theological Seminary, 2002), pp. 181-203; So Yuen-tai and Ho Hing-cheong, "Baoshou yu kaifang: shilun Xu Songshi zaoqi de zongjiao duihua" (Conservative and Open: On Religious Dialogue in Xu Songshi's Early Career), *Jian Dao: A Journal of Bible and Theology (Jiangdao xuekan)* 18 (2002): 47-66.

20. Xu Songshi, *Jidujiao de fowei* (Buddha's Flavor in Christianity) (Shanghai: Qingnian jiehui shuju, 1935).

21. Zhang Chunyi, *Laozi tongshi* (Concise Commentary on Laozi) (Shangwu yingshuguan, 1946), p. 3.

22. I have recently supervised three graduate students, who undertook studies on Xu Dishan, Xu Songshi, and Zhang Chunyi, respectively. Their research results are incorporated as three chapters in *Jindai Zhongguo fojiao yu jidujiao de xiangyu* (The Encounter between Buddhism and Christianity in Modern China), ed. Lai Pan-chiu. The students are So Yuen-tai, "Buddhicizing Christianity: Zhang Chunyi's Mahayana Theology," pp. 147-211; Ho Hing-cheong, "Reinterpreting Christianity with Buddhism: Xu Songshi's Indigenous Theology," pp. 213-73; and Chan Wai-keung, "Transcending the Difference between Christianity and Buddhism with Love: Xu Dishan's Life and Literary Work," pp. 275-311.

23. Winfried Glüer, "The Encounter between Christianity and Chinese Buddhism during the Nineteenth Century and the First Half of the Twentieth Century," *Ching Feng* 11, no. 3 (1968): 39-57; Timothy Man-kong Wong, "Protestant Missionaries' Images of Chinese Bud-

eminent Buddhist monks such as Taixu (1890-1947)[24] looked upon Christianity, no attempt has so far been made to study the creative attempts made by Chinese intellectuals like Xu Songshi and Zhang Chunyi to harmonize Christianity and Buddhism. Because of the difficulty of locating related documents, which are scattered here and there, records of their experiments in uniting Christianity and Buddhism have not been properly organized, despite the fact that they thoroughly deserve to be studied carefully.[25]

Our discussion so far has concentrated on the materials related to the Buddhist-Christian encounter in the China of the past. With regard to the research methodology, it is found that more attention must be paid to the differentiation between *inter*religious dialogue and *intra*religious dialogue when we embark on studies of the encounter between Christianity and Buddhism.[26] While "interreligious dialogue" refers to the audible and visible conversations conducted outwardly between two or more persons representing

---

dhism: A Preliminary Study of the Buddhist Writings by Joseph Edkins, Ernest John Eitel, and James Legge," *The HKBU Journal of Historical Studies* 1 (1999): 83-204; and Eric J. Sharpe, *Karl Ludvig Reichelt: Missionary, Scholar and Pilgrim* (Hong Kong: Tao Fong Shan Ecumenical Centre, 1984).

24. Don A. Pittman, "The Modern Buddhist Reformer T'ai-hsü on Christianity," *Buddhist-Christian Studies* 13 (1993): 82-109; Darui Long, "An Interfaith Dialogue between the Chinese Buddhist Leader Taixu and Christians," *Buddhist-Christian Studies* 20 (2000): 167-89.

25. For instance, Zhang Chunyi's idea about the Holy Spirit under the influence of Buddhism is a great contribution to Chinese theology. See Lai Pan-chiu and So Yuen-tai, "Zhang Chunyi de fohua shenlinglun" (Zhang Chunyi's Buddhist-Christian Pneumatology), pp. 181-203. Xu Songshi emphasized the concept of skillful means, which can provide a new approach to the question of biblical theology. See Lai Pan-chiu, "Zhongguo fojiao de panjiao dui 'Shenjing' shenxue de qifa" (The Inspiration of Chinese Buddhist Doctrinal Categorization to Biblical Theology), in *Wujing de zhuiqiu* (Endless Search), ed. Chen Zuoren (Stephen Chen Tso-Jen) (Hong Kong: The Religion Society, Chinese University of Hong Kong, 1988), pp. 36-62. Although this article has no direct connection with Xi Songshi, it points out that the theory of doctrinal categorization in Chinese Buddhism is a way to deal with the diversity among different scriptures and teachings. Similar problems also occur with the Bible, which consists of both the Old Testament and the New Testament. There are theological diversities between the two Testaments as well as within each Testament. For instance, there are tensions between the Pauline letters and James with regard to their understandings of the relations between faith, work, and salvation. It may be beneficial to consult the Buddhist method of doctrinal categorization, which is based on the concept of skillful means. Meanwhile, in the Christian tradition, there are some concepts similar to that of skillful means, and even the embryo of theological categorization can be found.

26. Raimondo Panikkar, *The Intrareligious Dialogue*, rev. ed. (New York: Paulist Press, 1999), pp. 111-17.

different religious traditions, "intrareligious dialogue" refers to the dialogue between two or more religious traditions occurring inwardly within an individual. The distinction between the two sorts of dialogue is merely a conceptual classification for the facilitation of discussion. Actually, when an interreligious dialogue takes place, an intrareligious dialogue occurs concurrently, so that more than two religious traditions can be compared, evaluated, mutually interpreted, or harmonized. The religious attitude of those who are engaged in the interreligious dialogue, which inevitably involves some sort of intrareligious dialogue, may thus be changed and readjusted. The differentiation of the two sorts of dialogue is vital for the understanding of the Christian-Buddhist dialogue in China.

In Western society religious identity is basically exclusive, and each person tends to have only one particular religious identity. In general, it is very rare to find overlapping religious identities in an individual, even though Judaism, Christianity, as well as Islam were derived from cognate Abrahamic faith and were closely interrelated in history, and even though there are relatively few Jewish or Arab Christians. In contrast, in the Chinese religious tradition, a large number of people can simultaneously accept three religions, and their religious identities can be multiple. Due to their social and cultural background, some Chinese Christians may possess a certain understanding about Buddhism, or they might have been themselves Buddhists before converting to Christianity. It is quite easy or natural for them to undertake some sort of dialogue in their own minds between the religion of their past and the religion they now embrace. Some of them may consider whether Buddhism should be completely rejected or whether it is endowed with some truth and worth preserving. The occurrence of such issues in the individual mind will inevitably give rise to intrareligious dialogue. Since this dialogue is within an individual, it reflects one's own genuine belief and can be free from the pressure of the official position of the religious tradition. It can thus be more penetrating and creative. Therefore, so far as the studies of Buddhist-Christian dialogue are concerned, it should not be limited to the visible and outward interreligious dialogue, but more attention should be paid to the intrareligious dialogue of individuals.

In the history of the encounter between Christianity and Buddhism in China, apart from the several incidents of contention and conflict, there were also some notable endeavors toward synthesizing and harmonizing the teachings of the two religions. Furthermore, there were also attempts to harmonize the two religions in daily life and literature. All these have left us with a great volume of material that is worthy of further study.

Reflection on the Attitudes toward the Dialogue

In examining the encounter and dialogue between Christianity and Buddhism in China during the first half of the twentieth century, two contributing factors are found to be influential in the positive development of Buddhist-Christian dialogue. One is the external sociopolitical environment and the other is the internal quest within each of the two religions. With regard to the latter, while Christianity looked for its indigenization in China, Buddhism searched for its modernization. From the Christian side, a large number of Christian intellectuals believed that Christianity needed to double its effort for indigenization in order to be free from occidental ideology. Only then would Christian faith integrate better into Chinese culture and Christianity take root in Chinese soil and grow accordingly. The successful experiences of the indigenization of Buddhism in China seemed to provide good examples for Christianity to follow. From the Buddhist side, Buddhism witnessed the advanced methods of Christianity in missionary work, organization, education, and social service. All of these were recognized by Chinese Buddhists as good examples, deserving to be adopted for Buddhist reform so that Buddhism would not lag behind contemporary society.

Quite amazingly, most Buddhists were only interested in learning what was called "external forms," such as the skill and strategy of religious missions, design of theological curricula, and expansion of charitable activities. They neglected or even denounced the Christian "inner learning" [nei xue] (doctrine and spiritual discipline), disregarding all of them as too little and too superficial to be studied.[27] They were quite similar to some of the contemporary Confucians who considered that Confucianism had been perfect with regard to the aspect of "inner sagehood" so that nothing could be learned from Christianity except that which pertained to the aspect of "outward kingship." This kind of attempt to learn from the other, highlighting the value of superficial copying and emulation without entering into the depth of the other religion, is no different from the approach called "Chinese substance with Western function," a famous slogan articulating the half-baked attitude of many Chinese intellectuals toward Western learning, especially Western science and technology.

27. He Jianming and Lai Pan-chiu, "Christianity and the Reformation of Modern Chinese Buddhism," pp. 122-24; see also Lai Pan-chiu, *Jinxiangdai Zhongguo fojiao yu jidujiao zongjiao de xiangyu* (The Encounter between Buddhism and Christianity in Modern China), pp. 313-14.

As for the Christian side, although a number of Christians appreciated the merits of Buddhist philosophy, they never thought that Buddhism in contemporary China could provide any special inspiration to the Christian mission. This is because what they were interested in was merely the successful examples of Buddhist indigenization in the past, not the present practices of contemporary Chinese Buddhism. They came to the conclusion that as the accomplishment of Buddhism in the past could be attributed to its indigenization in local Chinese culture, contemporary Christianity should also endeavor to be integrated into Chinese culture, especially Confucianism. An implication of this is that communication with contemporary Buddhism or Buddhists is relatively nonessential, if not entirely irrelevant. Ironically, since the aim of indigenizing Christianity was to proselytize more Chinese people, this rationale for the learning from Buddhism could be understood as a strategy for "overcoming the barbarians through learning the strength of the barbarians," another famous slogan, articulating an agonizing and antagonistic attitude of some Chinese toward the invasion of Western culture. According to this understanding, Buddhism in contemporary China is not taken seriously as a living partner in actual dialogue.[28]

It can thus be said that this mutual learning between Buddhism and Christianity was the result of a practical, if not pragmatic consideration. One's being interested in the other religion was not motivated by one's interest in another religion as such. Furthermore, the possible areas of dialogue had been delimited even before any dialogue was undertaken. The dialogue between the two was thus by no means open, and the foundation for dialogue was far from solid. Inevitably, with the change of external factors or environments, such interest would easily be lost. Since 1949, religious organizations in mainland China had to focus their efforts on how to adapt to the new sociopolitical system, and interreligious dialogue became superfluous. The situation is quite different in Hong Kong and Taiwan. On the one hand, Chinese Buddhism, especially in Taiwan, underwent undisturbed development and modernization, and its social and cultural influence was second to no other religions. On the other hand, as the influence of traditional Chinese culture on the Chinese people has gradually lost ground, the demand for indigenization on the Christian side has also weakened. There has been less and less interest in Buddhist-Christian dialogue. Besides the apologetic contention, only a few occasions occurred for fair and serene contact

28. Lai Pan-chiu, *Jinxiangdai Zhongguo fojiao yu jiduj zongjiao de xiangyu* (The Encounter between Buddhism and Christianity in Modern China), pp. 313-15.

between the two religions.[29] The situation was improved only recently at the turn of the century.[30]

In order to pave the way for Christian-Buddhist dialogue in the twenty-first century, we have to rethink or remove some of the presuppositions that might impede Buddhist-Christian dialogue in China. Buddhism needs to re-examine the prejudice that the doctrine of Christianity is naïve and defective, and that its spiritual discipline has nothing to be recommended. This kind of pre-understanding was largely derived from the impressions given by Western missionaries as well as Chinese Christians in the past. If such an impression is generalized to pass judgment on Christianity as a whole, it will not only underestimate the diversity of the Christian tradition, but will also betray ignorance concerning the accomplishment of Christian theology, philosophy, and spirituality in the past two millennia. It may even undermine the organic relation between external practices and internal faith as well as spiritual discipline. Buddhism and Christianity use Nirvana and the kingdom of God respectively as symbols for the ultimate state, yet they may also have different emphases in social ethics.[31] If Buddhists can take seriously the longstanding and well-established spiritual and mystical tradition of Christianity, they may not hastily comment that Christianity is lacking of "inner learning" and fine doctrine.[32] In fact, the study of spirituality and mysticism has become one of the most important topics for Christian-Buddhist comparison and dialogue in the international academic circle in the past decades.[33] Based on the profound resource of Chinese Ch'an Bud-

29. K. H. Lee and Shih-Heng-ching, "A Christian-Buddhist Dialogue on Causality and Good and Evil," *Ching Feng* 30, nos. 1-2 (May 1987): 39-57; and "Karma and Christ," *Ching Feng* 31, no. 1 (March 1988): 24-47.

30. Lai Pan-chiu, "Prospect of Buddhist-Christian Dialogue in China: With Special Reference to the Case of Hong Kong," unpublished paper presented at the Workshop on Chinese Religion and Traditional Culture, Hong Kong, March 17-19, 2003. The conference was co-organized by the Department of Religion, Chinese University of Hong Kong; Hong Kong Institute for Culture, Commerce and Religion; and Centre for Anthropological Research, University of Hong Kong.

31. Lai Pan-chiu, *Bianyuanshang de shenxue fansi* (Theological Reflections on the Boundaries) (Hong Kong: Christian Literature Council, 2001), pp. 160-61.

32. For a survey of the origin and development of Christian spirituality, see *Christian Spirituality I: Origins to the Twelfth Century,* ed. Bernard McGinn, John Meyendorff, and Jean Leclercq (New York: Crossroad, 1985); *Christian Spirituality II: High Middle Ages and Reformation,* ed. Jill Raitt, Bernard McGinn, and John Meyendorff (New York: Crossroad, 1988); and *Christian Spirituality III: Post-Reformation and Modern,* ed. Louis Dupre, Don E. Saliers, and John Meyendorff (New York: Crossroad, 1989).

33. For instance, Donald W. Mitchell, *Spirituality and Emptiness: The Dynamics of Spiri-*

dhism, the right attitude of acknowledging the value of the Christian spiritual and mystical tradition may open a way for further exchange between the two religions in the future.[34]

For Christianity, reflection perhaps should be undertaken immediately to review the mentality of taking interreligious dialogue as a direct (for proselytizing under the name of dialogue) or indirect (for learning the way of indigenization) instrument for evangelization. As pointed out by John B. Cobb, Jr., who has made a great contribution to Christian-Buddhist dialogue, this kind of mentality only forces the participants of the dialogue to bind themselves to the official standpoint, preventing any open and penetrating dialogue on equal footing, not to mention mutual creative transformation through dialogue.[35] In recent years, many Chinese Christian theologians have queried the proposal of theological indigenization. The scheme of indigenization used in the dialogue between Confucianism and Christianity has also gradually been cast aside. This gives way to an examination of how dialogue between Christianity and Confucianism, as two spiritual traditions, can be carried out and how they can contribute to solving the issues confronting humankind here and now.[36] Recently, the Buddhist-Christian dialogue at the international level has shown a trend toward focusing more on the global issues related to ecology and economy.[37] In contrast, in the Chinese academic circle, there is only some primary research on Christian and Buddhist ethics conducted and there is more work to be done.[38]

---

tual Life in Buddhism and Christianity (New York: Paulist, 1991); *The Gethsemani Encounter: A Dialogue on the Spiritual Life by Buddhist and Christian Monastics*, ed. Donald W. Mitchell and James Wiseman (New York: Continuum, 1999); and Paul Mommaers and Jan van Bragt, *Mysticism Buddhist and Christian: Encounters with Jan van Ruubroec* (New York: Crossroad, 1995).

34. Some works have already been done in this area. For instance, Tan Peiquan (Ekman Tam), "Chanzong de jingmoguan he jidutu yu shen de jingli" (The Silent Illumination of Chan and the Experience of Christians with God), in *Chuancheng yu shiming: Aixiangde boshi shishi sishiwu zhounian jinian xueshu wenji* (Heritage and Mission: Memorial Volume to Rev. Karl Ludvig Reichelt), ed. Chen Guangpei (Frank K. P. Chan) (Hong Kong: Tao Fong Shan Ecumenical Centre, 1998), pp. 131-46.

35. John B. Cobb, Jr.'s ideas on religious dialogue can be referred to in Lai Pan-chiu, "Cobb's Theory of Inter-religious Dialogue and the Buddhist-Christian Encounter in China," *Ching Feng* 40, nos. 3-4 (Sept.-Dec. 1997): 261-90.

36. For example: "Special Issue: Christian Dialogue on Life and Ethics," ed. Lai Pan-chiu, *Ching Feng* (New Series) 2, nos. 1-2 (Fall 2001): 1-212.

37. The first four articles in *Buddhist-Christian-Studies* 22 (2002) discuss these issues.

38. You Huizheng and Cui Benrui, "Jidujia aiguan yu fojiao cibeiguan de bijiao — zongjiao shehui guanhuai de lunli jichu" (The Comparison between Christian "Love" and

So far as Buddhism and Christianity in the contemporary world are concerned, the most urgent issues, which need to be dealt with properly, are related to globalization, such as environmental protection, human rights, and world peace, as well as the unsettling of the human soul and the collapse of ethical values. These current challenges may stimulate Christians and Buddhists to think again about the shortcomings of their own religions and to ponder how they should face these common issues through dialogue and cooperation. This may also be a possible way for Christian-Buddhist dialogue in China to go forward.[39]

Reflection on the Philosophical Issues

In the Christian-Buddhist comparison and dialogue, one often comes across the stereotype that while Christian theology is based on the notion of "being," Buddhism expounds a doctrine of "emptiness." This kind of labeling often gives rise to a view that Christianity and Buddhism cannot communicate, but contradict each other. Matteo Ricci (1552-1610), a Jesuit missionary, dressed like a Buddhist monk for the first nine years after arriving in China at the beginning of the seventeenth century. After discovering that Confucian ideology was in fact cherished by most Chinese gentry, he began to wear Confucian robes.[40] This incident shows that Matteo Ricci had initially attempted to indigenize or "Sinicize" Christianity through some kind of superficial "Buddhistization," so that Chinese people could embrace easily the Christian religion. It is clear that the motivation behind this kind of dialogue with Buddhism was to propagate Christianity rather than to understand or study Buddhism.

What is more unfortunate is that Matteo Ricci and many of his followers severely criticized Buddhism as superstition and idolatry, and attempted to adopt and implement the strategy of "replacing Buddhism and supple-

---

Buddhist "Compassion": The Foundation of Religious Social Concerns and Ethics), in *1996 nian foxue yanjiu lunwenji — dandai zongjiao de fazhan qushi* (The Collection of Buddhist Studies 1996: Trend of Contemporary Religious Development) (Taipei: Foguan chubanshe, 1996), pp. 299-320.

39. Lai Pan-chiu, "Cobb's Theory of Inter-religious Dialogue and the Buddhist-Christian Encounter in China," *Ching Feng* 40, nos. 3-4 (Sept.-Dec. 1997): 280-84.

40. See Gianni Criveller, *Preaching Christ in Ming China* (Taipei: Ricci Institute for Chinese Studies, 1997). Cited from the Chinese translation by Wang Zhicheng, Sizhu, and Wan Jiangda, *Wan Ming Jidu Lun* (Chengdu: Siquan renmin chubanshe, 1999), pp. 68-71.

menting Confucianism." The confrontation or contention between Christianity and Buddhism was thus quite unavoidable, because both sides endeavored to promote their own religion and to denigrate that of the other. Each side failed to understand the thought system of the other with an open mind.[41] Based on the available documents, especially those from the Catholic side, one may find that due to their intellectual background, the Catholic theologians took seriously the concept of "being" and failed to understand the Buddhist doctrine of "emptiness" *(kong)* or the Taoist concept of "nothingness" *(wu)*. Assuming that these concepts are directly opposed to Christian theology, they rigorously denounced the Buddhist idea of "emptiness" and the Taoist doctrine of "nothingness," arguing that these concepts would only lead to nihilism, arbitrarily denying phenomenon/reality, and scientific discovery.[42]

In reverse, the Chinese Buddhist circle, being based on the viewpoint of emptiness, also criticized the philosophical realism advocated by the Catholic missionaries.[43] This seems to be an irreconcilable dichotomy or contradiction. As He Guanghu once pointed out, the most fundamental barrier to communication between Christian theology and Chinese religious philosophy seems to be that they hold two incompatible views on the ultimate reality or origin. While the former stresses the notion of "Shi-You-She" (Reality-Being-Affirmation), the latter upholds a philosophy of *Kong-Wu-Fei* (Emptiness-Nothingness-Negation). However, He Guanghu argues that the contradiction is not absolute and it is not as serious as imagined, if the two traditions are carefully examined. Just as the notion of "Shi-You-She" also appears in Chinese religious philosophy, the idea of *Kong-Wu-Fei* also can be found in Christian theology.[44]

Using the theory of complementarity in quantum physics, especially the complementarity between the models of "wave" and "particle" advocated by

---

41. Matteo Ricci, *China in the Sixteenth Century: The Journals of Matteo Ricci (1583-1610)*, trans. Louis Gallagher (New York: Random House, 1953). For the Buddhist response to Catholics, see Jacques Gernet, *China and the Christian Impact: A Conflict of Culture*, trans. Janet Lloyd (Cambridge: Cambridge University Press, 1985), pp. 72-82.

42. Gianni Criveller, *Preaching Christ in Late Ming China*, Chinese translation, pp. 72-73.

43. Gernet, *China and the Christian Impact*, pp. 214-21.

44. He Guanru, "'Shiyoushi' yu 'kongwufei' — Zhongguo zongjiao zhexue yu jidujiao zhexue xiangtong de yida zhangai" (Being vs. Nothingness: A Challenge to the Compatibility of Chinese Religious Philosophy with Christian Philosophy), *Daofeng: Jidujiao wenhua pinglun* (Logos and Pneuma: Chinese Journal of Theology) 12 (Spring 2000): 165-85.

Niels Bohr (1885-1962), I have attempted to point out that comparable examples of complementarity can be found in Christianity and Buddhism. Notable examples include the *Mādhyamika* school in Buddhism and "the Middle Way of Fourfold Negatives" in the Chalcedonian Creed (451). Furthermore, Augustine (354-430), who made a great impact on the theology of both Catholicism and Protestantism, also expounded that all phenomena can be characterized as "both 'being' and 'nonbeing'" or "neither 'being' nor 'nonbeing.'" Besides, according to the study of Western theology made by John Macquarrie, there is a longstanding and well-established tradition of dialectical theism, which believes that God can be said to be both being and nonbeing, one and many, knowable and incomprehensible, transcendent and immanent, passible and impassible, eternal and temporal, etc. Accordingly, both Christianity and Buddhism employ the method of complementarity as well as the expressions of "Shi-You-She" and *Kong-Wu-Fei* (borrowing He Guanghu's terms) concurrently. It is clear that the two traditions not only do not contradict each other, but also possess some similarities. Moreover, we may be able to talk about the complementarity between Christianity and Buddhism in a loose sense.[45]

Through a study of the theory of complementarity, I also found that the Chalcedonian Creed could be read from the Mahayana perspective, so that Christianity might be able to formulate a Christology more in line with traditional Chinese culture. This also made me aware of John Keenan's proposal for a Mahayana Christology. After examining his award-winning *The Meaning of Christ: A Mahayana Theology*,[46] I find that the proposal of Mahayana theology advocated by Keenan is based mainly on the *Yogācāra* school, supplemented by some ideas from the *Mādhyamika* school, but it neglects or underestimates the potential of the *Tathāgatagarbha* tradition for Mahayana Christology.[47] Furthermore, Keenan's discussion of Mahayana theology is primarily derived from the *Problematik* in Western Christianity, which tends to separate religious doctrine from religious (mystical) experience or subordinate mystical experience to doctrinal formulation. He tries to make use of Buddhist philosophy, especially the *Mādhyamika* and *Yogācāra*, as a handmaid of theology *(ancilla theologiae)*, facilitating the res-

---

45. Lai Pan-chiu, "Buddhist-Christian Complementarity in the Perspective of Quantum Physics," *Studies in Inter-religious Dialogue* 12, no. 2 (2002): 148-64.

46. John Keenan, *The Meaning of Christ: A Mahayana Theology* (Maryknoll: Orbis Books, 1989).

47. Lai Pan-chiu, "Cong dasheng foxue kan Jia-ke-dun jidu lun" (Chalcedonian Christology from a Mahayana Perspective), *Fujen Religious Studies* 2 (Dec. 2000): 231-62.

toration of mystical experience to the center of Christianity and establishing the connection between mystical experience and Christian doctrine.

I find that Keenan's approach is merely one of the possible ways of doing Mahayana theology. It is also possible to establish a Mahayana theology based on the theory of *Tathāgatagarbha* to affirm the nonduality of human nature and divine nature. According to this view, human beings may participate in the divine life, or every human being can become Christ. In comparison with the *Yogācāra* doctrine, the *Tathāgatagarbha* doctrine may reflect even more clearly the character of traditional Chinese culture. This may be helpful for the development of Christian theology in the Chinese world. Nevertheless, this is only a tentative attempt with a view to demonstrating that between Christianity and Buddhism there can be a mutual interpretation, or a "fusion of horizons."[48] This fusion involves not only the horizons of Christianity and Buddhism, but also some other background of the interpreter, including the traditional Chinese culture. With the participation of Chinese culture, this fusion of horizons may carry the characteristics of Chinese culture and make a unique contribution to international Christian-Buddhist studies.

Conclusion

It should be admitted that Buddhist-Christian study in contemporary China is still in its formative stage. However, it is evident that the dialogue, communication, and even mutual transformation between Chinese Christianity and Buddhism has taken take place in the past, and the prospect for further development is vast. The dialogue and exchange between these two religions may prosper in the twenty-first century, if the two sides make efforts to eradicate misunderstanding and prejudice against each other. Since Buddhism has undergone drastic developments in China and become an integral part of Chinese culture, Christian-Buddhist dialogue in China may be rather different from those in America or Japan, and will thus make some special contributions to Christian-Buddhist dialogue worldwide.

48. Hans-Georg Gadamer, *Truth and Method*, trans. Joel Weinsheimer and Donald G. Marshall (New York: Continuum, 1998), pp. 306-7, 374-75.

A Response to Professor Lai Pan-chiu

Jorgen Skov Sorensen

In my response I will attempt to point toward what I perceive to be two significant issues or concerns that arose for me while reading through Professor Lai's paper. Eventually, I will also venture into a brief personal response to the three questions raised by Professor Lai in his essay: "Does nothing in the Christian-Buddhist dialogue in China deserve to be studied?" "Is there nothing but a dead end for the dialogue between the two religions in China?" And, "Can a certain historical foundation already laid down for the encounter between Chinese Christianity and Buddhism successfully pave the way for dialogue in the future?"

However, first let us turn to my two issues or concerns, which are:

1. Dialogue, yes, please! But whose dialogue are we talking about?
2. Aims and objectives: what are the role and goal of dialogue?

Dialogue, Yes, Please! But Whose Dialogue Are We Talking About?

When the discussion falls on interreligious dialogue, I must confess that I am rather much for it. I think it is a splendid idea that we talk together, and broadly speaking I try to live a life in dialogue with my fellow Muslim, Buddhist, Hindu — or whatever tradition they adhere to — fellow citizens. To be honest I must say that to do so is not particularly difficult for me, i.e., if I can find the time in a usually packed and busy schedule.

However, my schedule is a practical thing. But even as an existential, or

160

theological, exercise, to live a dialogical life in conversation with other religious people is not so difficult either. I love to challenge others and to be challenged in my own faith, too. I fancy participating in what Professor Lai (with the terminology of the Indian theologian Raimondo Panikkar) points out in his essay as an "intrareligious dialogue." Thus, I find no theological difficulties or spiritual dangers in engaging with interreligious dialogue. I find no problems in overruling what Professor Lai terms the "official standpoint" of my church and immerse myself in an open-minded and open-ended dialogue.

In fact the most difficult issue for me is to find likeminded representatives from the Muslim, Buddhist, and Hindu communities in my hometown. They are there, for sure, but they are few and scattered and mostly intellectuals. This has brought me to wonder: May it be that I have no problems with dialogue because I am the powerful partner in the vast majority of dialogues that I enter into? I represent by far the largest state-recognized church in my country, Denmark, and no doubt the most favored religion in the majority of Western countries. On top of that, I embody through my work a strong and well-established institution, a university with a long history of impeccable scientific research.

I try to dialogue with Muslims, who are perceived by many people in the Western world as the root of the world's evil, terror, and random killings and therefore looked down upon both politically and religiously by the majority culture. Many Muslims react by attempting to preserve what they have in their traditions by becoming inward looking and isolated in their communities, seeking refuge from strong external pressures. It all adds up to making the wish for dialogue on my side rather easy and joyful and on the Muslim side rather difficult and potentially risky.

If we look to other parts of the world, things do, however, look pretty different. In, say, Pakistan or India, from which I have gained some experience, Christians are a minority. Here they are the ones to hesitate to enter into a mind-blowing interreligious dialogue with Hindu or Muslim majority cultures, in which they are forced to reconsider their usually rather traditional theological viewpoints. The American researcher in religion Susan Billington Harper documents this tendency in an article in the *International Bulletin of Missionary Research,* where she recollects her sociological research among typical Indian Christian Dalits.[1]

---

1. Susan Billington Harper, "Ironies of Indigenisation: Some Cultural Repercussions of Mission in South India," *International Bulletin of Missionary Research* 19 (Jan. 1995).

According to Harper, for these Christians their unwavering Christian identity is what keeps them together and alive as a community in a dominant, occasionally hostile, Hindu culture, a culture that is increasingly prevailing in all aspects of Indian life. Some of them opted for conversion to Christianity exactly to avoid this Hindu culture and to get an alternative identity through the Christian faith. For them, to open up for a self-challenging "intrareligious" dialogue is simply a luxury they cannot afford as a minority community, and they have no intentions whatsoever to "be free from the pressure of the official position of the[ir Christian] tradition." Neither do they find it "natural . . . to undertake some sort of dialogue in their own minds between the religion of their past and the religion they now embrace."

Given this background, and although I support dialogue in every sense of the word, I cannot but question the conception of "intrareligious dialogue" as a precondition or an integral part of all interreligious dialogue. Rather I must see that as a luxury for intellectuals like myself, and those of us who are present here at this conference. This does not mean that we as academics must or indeed should quit our inter- and intrareligious dialogues — by no means so — but when we analyze the phenomenon of dialogue, we have to keep in mind that there are people of different faiths around us with substantially different prerequisites than the ones we work under as resourceful intellectuals.

Emerging postcolonial theory urges us not to assess the "other" with our own standards. In my experience, the dialogue (or lack of dialogue) that I have just described is of a substantially different character than any resourceful intellectual dialogue between the religions, and nobody should be surprised that the outcome is also different from what we as intellectuals would expect — maybe an outcome is even nonexistent. As to the apparent lack of Buddhist-Christian dialogue in contemporary China, one of the main reasons could be that the vast majority of Chinese Christians carry so much identity with them as distinctively Christians that they have no interest in engaging with that which they themselves or their parents or grandparents turned their backs on in order to opt for the religion named Christianity.

Aims and Objectives: The Role and Goal of Dialogue?

This brings me conveniently to my second item: What is the role and goal of dialogue? This is a question that cannot possibly be answered in my brief response with such limited time and space available. Even the shortest of introductions to the topic would be sizeable. Furthermore, the question reflects a perennial problem that requires our constant concern and theological consideration. What is the role and goal of dialogue? Fortunately, I need not deal with all aspects of the question here, but feel that I must address at least a single issue related to the topic, inspired by Professor Lai's paper.

Professor Lai several times uses a certain terminology in his paper when he directly or indirectly touches upon the role and goal of dialogue between the religions, in this case between Buddhism and Christianity. Professor Lai's paper does not reveal whether he applies this particular use of language to his thoughts on dialogue deliberately or not. It does not stand out clearly in the text. However, when I read terms like "synthesize," "harmonize," "uniting Buddhism and Christianity," or terminology derived from these words, I sense that Professor Lai through the application of such terms and words implies that this particular understanding of dialogue is taken for granted as an indisputable prerequisite for a common understanding of what — in our case — dialogue between religions will and must(?) bring with it.

Unfortunately I have not had access to Professor Lai's Chinese text and thus I have been unable to check the terminology used in it to investigate what kinds of connotations the Chinese text may bring to the table. However, as it stands in its English-language form, it brings (at least to me) the feeling that Professor Lai sees harmonization, ultimate unity, and synthesis evolving between the two religions as an actual goal of dialogue.

In my mind this is far from being the goal of interreligious dialogue. We may get to know one another better, and in some good cases prejudice about the other may be avoided as a result of dialogue. Inevitably, in some individual cases dialogue partners may in fact end up with a harmonized or unified understanding of what, say, Buddhism and Christianity are, and they may eventually become "Christian Buddhists" or "Buddhist Christians," but these are rare cases and to my mind this is not the primary goal of a dialogue, i.e., primary in the sense that if such does not happen, the dialogue has not succeeded. Deep down I think I share this conviction with Professor Lai, but from his text I also see something else peep through.

I have much respect for people who are searching for contact points between the different religious and philosophical traditions, e.g., between Buddhism and Christianity. We have for too long focused on the differences — and that does, admittedly, get a little tedious after a few centuries — but on the other hand we must also acknowledge that our different traditions really are different traditions, evolved over several millennia, in substantially different contexts, asking substantially different questions, and offering, subsequently, substantially different answers. They may change and evolve further over time and indeed they do already. Religions are human constructions and not static entities, but basically and realistically speaking there are no signs that they are about to become one in unity.

With the South African philosopher and professor of physics Paul Cilliers, I would — in something that may admittedly look like a departure from the subject — venture to suggest that ideals of harmonization in fact belong to Enlightenment thought and derived patterns of modernity, and that it basically reflects or reveals a suspicion toward difference, which is then as a result problematized. Cilliers goes on to suggest that the recognition of complexity in postmodern reflections will eventually remove the problematization of difference and otherness and potentially liberate us from the harmonizing tendencies of a modern epistemology or mindset.[2] I realize, however, that the point of view I here share with Paul Cilliers probably is possible for me, only because I am a relatively resourceful intellectual to whom difference and otherness do not represent a real risk in my daily life.

Epilogue

Finally let me return, as a last gesture, to the three questions raised in the beginning of Professor Lai's paper:

- "Does nothing in the Christian-Buddhist dialogue in China deserve to be studied?"
- "Is there nothing but a dead end for the dialogue between the two religions in China?"
- "Can a certain historical foundation already laid down for the encounter between Chinese Christianity and Buddhism successfully pave the way for dialogue in the future?"

---

2. "The obsession to find one essential truth blinds us to the relationary nature of complexity, and especially to the continuous shifting of those relationships. Any acknowledgement of complexity will have to incorporate these shifts and changes, not as epiphenomena, but as constitutive of complex systems." Paul Cilliers, *Complexity and Postmodernism: Understanding Complex Systems* (London and New York: Routledge, 1998), p. 112.

I shall attempt to be brief in my answers to these questions and state that, first, I do firmly believe that there are plenty of issues relating to Buddhist-Christian dialogue in China that need to be studied, and that all of us who are capable and have a research interest in the topic must engage sincerely with the many questions raised — not only in Professor Lai's thought-provoking paper but through our individual studies and experiences with Buddhist-Christian dialogue. I thank Professor Lai wholeheartedly for raising this important issue in his paper.

Second, there is by no means only a "dead end" left for the dialogue between the two religions. On the contrary, it is very true when Professor Lai points to the fact that Buddhist-Christian dialogue in mainland China has suffered from little or no interest so far. Maybe we should not expect too much engagement in the short term from regular Christian congregations in China, but with the growing interest from China's intellectuals in religion and in the dialogue between the traditions, I cannot but believe that the future for Buddhist-Christian dialogue in China is a bright one.

Finally, I find it much easier and usually more fruitful and constructively sound to look forward instead of backward. If there is a historical foundation for the encounter between Buddhism and Christianity, and I believe there is, I hesitate to say that it will help us much in our future dialogue between the two traditions. We live in a fluctuating world. Tomorrow is unlike today, which is unlike yesterday. China is undergoing tremendous changes these years, and both Buddhism and Christianity are two traditions, or perhaps two "conglomerates" of various traditions, that are taking new shapes in different contexts every day. We need to look at "real-time" expressions of both Buddhism and Christianity in order to engage in a meaningful, constructive, and relevant dialogue.

Hence, to conclude, my answer to Professor Lai's third and final question must be "yes," there is a historical foundation available, but also I must honestly confess that I hesitate to recommend it as a foundation for tomorrow's dialogue.

A Response to Professor Lai Pan-chiu

Jyri Komulainen

Professor Lai offered a very scholarly essay introducing us to various aspects of Buddhist-Christian dialogue in the Chinese context. The essay covers the subject matter in a balanced way, and hence provides us with a significant amount of knowledge on this important topic. Here I wish to explore further some important aspects indicated in the essay. My response primarily touches on methodological issues and requirements relevant for any interreligious dialogue. In his essay, Professor Lai points out rightly that future dialogue demands revisions of attitudes on both sides. He warns that Buddhists should not "underestimate the diversity of the Christian tradition." Neither should Buddhist-Christian dialogue repeat stereotypes such as "Christian theology is based on the notion of 'being,' while Buddhism expounds a doctrine of 'emptiness.'"

With these critical observations, we approach one of the most crucial principles in any dialogue that wishes to take seriously recent findings of theology and philosophy: namely, that dialogue should be aware of a danger of essentialism. One should resist the temptation to see the "other" through age-old stereotypes. Both Buddhism and Christianity are highly complex amalgams with millennia of history behind them. Moreover, both of these religions expanded across geographical and cultural boundaries. Therefore, they should not be essentialized as having some permanent and unchanging essence that could be neatly categorized and compared.[1]

1. See Thomas A. Tweed, "Who Is a Buddhist? Night-Stand Buddhists and Other Creatures," in *Westward Dharma: Buddhism Beyond Asia*, ed. Charles S. Prebish and Martin

It is widely acknowledged that the concept "religion" is highly problematic. This is more obvious in the context of Buddhist-Christian dialogue than in other areas. If there is any religious tradition that challenges our understanding of "religion," it is Buddhism with its agnostic attitude toward God.[2] Taking a critical stance toward the essentialist understanding of "religion," we can remind ourselves that both traditions, Buddhism and Christianity, warn us about human-made intellectual constructions. Engaging in dialogue requires a critical attitude toward one's own prejudices, not only regarding the "other" who is encountered, but also in relation to one's own way of constructing reality. Thus, as a preliminary to interreligious dialogue between Buddhism and Christianity, I will discuss in brief whether there is "religion" as a category of its own.[3]

The concept "religion" *(religio)* is burdened with an unwarranted ballast of Christianity and the Enlightenment. This is observable, for instance, in emphasizing the textual traditions and in the way religion is connected with the question of truth. The West has constructed the category of "religion" on the basis of Christianity and then commenced a search for similar phenomena in other cultures.[4] In fact, many of the phenomena categorized as "religion" are only a part of a complex and fluid network of traditions that form a wider cultural context. The original meaning of the Latin word *religio* could be interpreted as referring to rituals and practices inherited from the ancestors.[5] Therefore, traditions that are labeled religious are, in a certain

---

Baumann (Berkeley: University of California Press, 2002), pp. 17-33. An ample introduction to the multifaceted encounter between Buddhism and Christianity is Michael von Brück and Whalen Lai, *Buddhismus und Christentum: Geschichte, Konfrontation, Dialog* (München: C. H. Beck, 1997).

2. A lucid overview of Buddhism in this respect is provided in Hans-Martin Barth, *Dogmatik: Evangelischer Glaube im Kontext der Weltreligionen* (Gütersloh: Chr. Kaiser, 2001), pp. 312-20.

3. Another related issue is whether a commitment to the cause of interreligious dialogue requires a pluralistic theology of religions. A criticism of such demands is provided, e.g., in Jyri Komulainen, "Are Religions Only Different Ways to the Same Goal? Pluralistic Theology of Religions Discussed," in *Swedish Missiological Themes* 88 (2000): 577-91.

4. For a persuasive criticism of the term "religion," see Richard King, *Orientalism and Religion: Postcolonial Theory, India and "The Mystic East"* (London and New York: Routledge, 1999), pp. 35-72. See also, e.g., Heinrich von Stietencron, "Hinduism: On the Proper Use of a Deceptive Term," in *Hinduism Reconsidered*, ed. Günther-Dietz Sontheimer and Hermann Kulke (New Delhi: Manohar, 1997), pp. 32-53. For a concise introduction to the recent change in the field of religious studies, see also Max Charlesworth, *Philosophy and Religion: From Plato to Postmodernism* (Oxford: Oneworld, 2002), pp. 1-4.

5. See King, *Orientalism and Religion*, pp. 35-37.

sense, cultural traditions whose cognitive content is difficult to systematize. Millions of people follow these kinds of age-old rituals simply because they belong to a proper, traditional way of living one's life. In an epistemological sense, is it thus meaningful to ask whose rituals are right, and whose wrong?

There is no easy answer to the question to what measure it is reasonable to differentiate doctrinal elements, say, in rituals that are conducted in order to pay homage to the ancestors. Without doubt, rituals entail doctrinal implications to some extent; nevertheless, the communal character of rituals is even more vital.[6] Most of the so-called "religious" practices are thus part of local networks of different cultural traditions. Of course, these practices can be related to different theological ideas. It should be borne in mind that, in general, people are just practicing age-old rituals without knowing all the theological complexities that are elaborated by the elite.[7]

With these critical remarks, I do not wish to deny that there are, indeed, a number of worldviews. It is reasonable to distinguish Christian, Hindu, Buddhist, or Taoist theologies, to name a few. One can see certain structural ideas that give shape to, and also lend support to, an inchoate mass of cultural traditions and practices. Moreover, these theological ideas provide practices with a certain transcendental meaning — at least from the point of view of the intellectual elite. However, the existence of these kinds of interpretative "meta-levels" does not mean that one could uncritically speak about some monolithic totalities called "world religions." Instead of an essentialist understanding of Buddhism and Christianity, we should emphasize the open-ended and dynamic nature of these extensive traditions. Only this provides us with a realistic basis for dialogue, which is an open process.

Next to highlighting the amplitude of both Buddhism and Christianity, there is another significant throwaway remark in Professor Lai's paper. Utilizing a differentiation of Raimondo Panikkar, he says that Buddhist-Christian dialogue "should not be limited to the visible and outward interreligious dialogue, but more attention should be paid to the intra-religious dialogue of individuals." I agree with Professor Lai at this point. One of the most challenging and probably also most fruitful tasks for theology is to

---

6. See Theo Sundermeier, "Religion, Religions," in *Dictionary of Mission: Theology, History, Perspective,* ed. Karl Müller et al. (Maryknoll, NY: Orbis Books, 1997), pp. 388-89.

7. Cf. here a pertinent analysis of religious dynamics in Sundermeier, "Religion, Religions," pp. 392-93. An interesting account of down-to-earth motives of ordinary village Indians doing religious rituals is in A. M. Abraham Ayrookuzhiel, *The Sacred in Popular Hinduism: An Empirical Study in Chirakkal, North Malabar* (Madras: The Christian Literature Society, 1983), pp. 101-3.

study in detail those prominent figures that stand at the crossroads of different religious traditions.

In the modern history of multireligious Asia, a number of interesting and creative Asian thinkers have been Christians, or at least very open toward Christianity. At the same time, they have been imbued with another culture and its religious features. In other words, they have had a multireligious identity. In the Indian context, especially during the time of national awakening, there were some significant figures worth studying even today, such as Keshub Chunder Sen (1838-84) and Brahmabandhab Upadhyay (1861-1907).[8]

Without doubt, there must have been equivalent figures in China — people who opened themselves toward Christianity without rejecting the religious traditions of their ancestors. In fact, I believe that there must have been such people in any Asian country where the local intelligentsia has come into contact with the Christian faith. These kinds of people provide us, so to say, empirical material that could help us understand the hermeneutical laws that prevail in an interreligious encounter. This will facilitate Christian theology in its imperative task in constructing theological models that allow us both to keep Christian principles intact — the fullness of the Divine Love revealed in Jesus Christ (Col. 2:9) — and at the same time to recognize that God has not left the world without knowledge of him (Acts 17:27-28; Rom. 1:19-20).[9]

8. On these seminal figures in the history of Hindu-Christian dialogue, see, respectively, Manilal C. Parekh, *Brahmarshi Keshub Chunder Sen* (Rajkot: Oriental Christ House, 1926), and Julius Lipner, *Brahmabandhab Upadhyay: The Life and Thought of a Revolutionary* (New Delhi: Oxford University Press, 2001).

9. See, e.g., David Bosch, *Transforming Mission: Paradigm Shifts in Theology of Mission* (Maryknoll: Orbis Books, 1991), pp. 488-89.

8 The Impact of Contemporary Chinese Folk Religions on Christianity

Gao Shining

Since the reform of the 1980s, every major religion has experienced development in China; the growth of Buddhism and Christianity has been a special focus of attention. However, one phenomenon that has usually been ignored is the recovery of Chinese folk religion. As the most common phenomenon in daily life, folk religion has long been a part of Chinese traditional culture. Thus, in the process of transmission into China and establishing roots there, Christianity has been influenced by folk religion in a variety of ways. The present paper will explore this topic.

Deep-Rooted Folk Religion

Many scholars assert that the Chinese people have a weak sense of religion. The main reasons for such an argument are two. On the one hand, Chinese people focus on the present world, treat the human-divine relationship in the light of relations among people, do not have an idea of transcendence, and differ from Europeans, who place religion in a central, controlling position. On the other hand, the Chinese people do not have a monotheistic tradition comparable to Western people's Christianity. I am not going to comment on these arguments; I shall point out, however, that from ancient times until today many Chinese people who have a clear religious identity think in terms of buddhas, celestial beings, ghosts, and gods. This phenomenon, which is deep-rooted in the heart of the Chinese people, is termed "folk religion."

Folk religion is rooted in the people (especially in the rural masses), and its content is very complicated. The objects of people's faith include various natural things and powers, ancestors, ghosts, and spirits. These objects of faith involve different aspects of the world and human life and, as a subcultural system, have a very powerful influence. Folk religion has absorbed the polytheistic characteristics of primary religion, and the following ideas are especially important: longing for the blessing of ancestors, preferring death to life, believing in fatalism and preordained fate *(karma)*, test and verification of irritability, and the double-world of *yin* and *yang*.

Although folk religion has never entered the mainstream of Chinese faith, its history is much older than that of Catholicism, Protestantism, Buddhism, Taoism, and Islam; and its impact is also much greater and stronger than that of the above-mentioned five religions. During a long history, on the one hand Chinese religions, especially Taoism, have often promoted their transmission in Chinese society with the help of folk religion. On the other hand, folk religion has continually absorbed various religious ideas and doctrines and has become more formidable. For example, Buddhist concepts of transmigration and *karma,* Taoist gods, celestial beings, ghosts and forces of evil, Confucian ethics and morality, and even Christian ideas of heaven and hell have been accepted, absorbed, and changed by folk religion. In this process they have become more generally known and more easily understood by people.

Since the beginning of the twentieth century, folk religion has been considered a feudal superstition. It was heavily attacked after 1950, and its surviving forms were considered objects to be destroyed together with all religions during the Cultural Revolution. Since the 1980s, with the gradual opening of society, folk religion has begun to recover. Especially in the rural areas, the speed and scale of its development are much faster and larger than is the case with Buddhism and Christianity.

The rapid development of folk religion is mainly expressed in the following six ways:

1. All kinds of temples, which were in danger of disappearance, began to appear again both in cities and in the countryside all over the country. For example, in Zhejiang Province, where Christianity is better established than elsewhere, temples of folk religion are usually twenty or even a hundred times as numerous as Christian church buildings. Recently, over 17,900 temples that had been built without legal permission have been destroyed.[1]

1. See *Zongjiao wenhua* (Jan. 1998): 17.

2. Erection of luxury tombs for dead people and even for some who are still alive. In Ningbo city, Zhejiang Province, there is a tomb that occupies 532 square meters and has a reception room with an international telephone and other equipment. In 1996 alone, over 200,000 luxury tombs were destroyed along railways, highways, and in tourist areas.[2]

3. In the name of developing tourism, many ghost palaces and hell-buildings have been built. With the help of modern sound, light, and electric technologies, the atmosphere of *karma* and the fearful feeling of hell have been produced. There are at least ten such tourist projects in China.

4. More and more activities centered on ancestor worship are seen, especially in rural areas. Clan and family power again begin to play an important role; it becomes more and more common to build a family temple, to edit genealogy, etc.

5. Witches and shaman sorcerers are appearing again; increasing numbers of people are interested in divining — fortune-telling based on examination of face or hands or by studying Chinese characters. During the 1997 Spring Festival, 222 titles of books on such topics were found in Beijing.[3] More and more restaurants in cities, especially middle-sized and smaller cities, have put statues of the money-god in their dining areas, and it has also become common for urban citizens to participate in fortune-telling activities.

6. In order to attain peace and wealth, in addition to worshiping gods and selecting good dates for important activities, people have become fond of those numbers that sound similar to the Chinese word for "becoming rich" (8 = *ba*, which is similar to *fa* of *facai* = becoming rich) or for "smooth" (6 = *liu*, which is similar to *liu* of *shunliu* = smooth, smoothly). Therefore, the numbers 8 and 6 are popular and sought by people to use in their phone numbers and car registration numbers all over the country. Frequently people spend considerable money in buying these numbers.

After being limited and controlled for decades, folk religion is now recovering and developing quickly. The main reason is that these beliefs are rooted in the subconscious of the masses. Especially in rural and minority areas, folk religion has already become an important part of people's life-

---

2. *Zongjiao wenhua*, p. 17.
3. See *Dangdai zongjiao yanjiu* (Jan. 1997): 21.

styles. In China, with its vast area and population, there are many different nationalities. One common feature of these different nationalities is folk religion, with its belief in gods, ghosts, and ancestor worship. Of course, the content and extent of faith differ from one nation to another. However, there is a common feature among these phenomena.[4] The content of folk religion is complex, regardless of whether it is the continuation and confusion of various primary beliefs or the custom of a nationality. All of these folk religions are believed by many people, and they exist everywhere and in every generation. More important, these beliefs are deep-rooted in the ideas of the masses.[5]

Therefore, although folk religion has never become a part of Chinese mainstream faith, it has been closely connected with traditional Chinese Confucianism, Buddhism, and Taoism so as to become an important part of Chinese culture. Thus, folk religion will not disappear simply because of administrative orders and actions, and it cannot be eliminated from human hearts by administrative means. On the other hand, as a part of culture, folk religion participates in some features of the culture, for example, permeability and inclusiveness. Therefore, in traditional Chinese Confucianism, Buddhism, and Taoism we can find some features of folk religion, and there are also many historical examples of Confucianism, Buddhism, and Taoism having taken advantage of folk religion to promote themselves.[6] In addition to features of universality, decentralization, and spontaneity, Chinese folk religion has the two strong features of utilitarianism and pragmatism; in other words, these features have also influenced how Chinese people react to other religions. Thus, utilitarianism and pragmatism have also become strong features of Chinese attitudes toward religions in general.

As a religion coming from abroad, Christianity faced a problem in its encounter with Chinese traditional culture from the very beginning, and

---

4. See Wei Shigang and Li Zhi, *Zhongguo yuanshi xinyang, minjian xinyang, fengsu xinyang* (Beijing: Sanqin chubanshe, 1999), p. 183.

5. The "masses" refers to the common people who are living in the low level of society. The "idea of mass" refers to "the common psychological custom, value intension, morality, aesthetic judgment, religious faith, and ideal hope, which have been formed, inherited, and transmitted in the long and difficult process of producing, living, and other activities." Cf. Hou Jie and Fan Lizhu, *Zhongguo minzhong yishi* (Xian: Shanxi jiaoyu chubanshe, 1999).

6. For example, Buddhism was transmitted from India into China. During the process of transmission it followed the humanist tradition of China, and its objects of faith have also the color of Chinese folk religion, e.g., the Buddhist deity Guanyin, in the eyes of the common masses, long ago became a Buddha who gives people children. Cf. Hou Jie and Fan Lizhu, *Zhongguo minzhong yishi*, p. 194.

even now the problem has not been resolved. In fact, we can find evidence that folk religion has impacted Christianity in many aspects.

The Many-Layered Impact of Folk Religion on Christianity

As mentioned above, although folk religion does not belong to the mainstream of Chinese faith, it is powerful and popular, and Christianity has had to face it and has been impacted by it. Since folk religion is especially deep-rooted in the rural areas, its impact on Christianity is also especially clear in those areas.

In the beginning when Christianity came to China, its main transmission areas were along the east coast, the Yangtze River area, and the cities of middle China. Christianity was not especially popular in rural areas. This route of Christianity's transmission resulted from many factors, such as unbalanced economic development, difficult transportation in the rural areas, and relatively fewer inhabitants in Western China. In addition, one should notice the impact of folk religion on the route of Christianity's transmission. As Dr. Liang Jialing clearly points out, the existence of folk religion is the reason why Christianity cannot take root in the hearts of the masses even though it has been in China for a long time, and the general religious sense and attitude of the masses, which were formed by folk religion, have influenced people's reaction to Christianity.[7]

> The content of folk religion is complicated, but ancestor worship is its center, since Chinese people are family-centered, and this feature has influenced their religious faith. For the common mass, "respecting Heaven" is not as important as "to worship ancestors," and Christianity is a religion which does not respect ancestors and ghosts.[8] Thus, Christianity can be accepted neither by elites nor by the common mass in China.[9] This is especially obvious in minority areas. In those areas where nature is worshipped, "Christianity is popular in the area or within the same nation, since there is

---

7. Cf. Liang Jialin, *Gaige kaifang yilai de Zhongguo nongcun jiaohui* (Hong Kong: Jiandao shenxue yuan, 1999), p. 222. In the present work, I employ the term "folk belief" as a synonym of Liang's "folk religion."

8. See Wang Minglun, "Fan yangjiao shuwentie xuan," *Qilu shushe* (1984): 3.

9. Chen Zhiping, *Jin 500 nian lai Fujian jiazu shehui wenhua* (Shanghai: Sanlian shudian, 1991); Chen Zhiping, *Jidujiao yu Fujian minjian shehui* (Xiamen: Xiamen daxue chubanshe, 1992).

no effective limit to the transmission of Christianity." But in the areas where ancestors are worshipped, there is more resistance to Christianity.[10]

This is one of the factors that prohibit the transmission of Christianity. There are also contrary examples. For example, Zhu Jingyi mentioned Dunhuazhen Church in the book *A Test Rural Church*. This church instituted a contextual approach to make Christianity fit the local faith. Dunhuazhen Church seeks not only to reform the language used in evangelical activities but also tries to absorb the style that is close to Chinese traditional custom and folk religion in its services. In order to accommodate local customs, this church has arranged tree-planting services, anti-drug services, and relative-remembering services (to promote respect of parents and remembrance of relatives).[11] These efforts have attracted more people to the church and have enabled Christianity to become deep-rooted in the area. Of course, these services are different from traditional Christian liturgical services, and they have changed the meaning of Christianity in a certain sense.

On the other hand, there were more than 300 folk-religious organizations in the 1950s, but during the past period of more than thirty years most of these folk-religious organizations were destroyed, and now in many areas people no longer have faith in them.

In this situation of a lack of faith in traditional folk religion, Christianity has been able to develop since the 1980s, especially in rural areas where Christianity is developing more quickly than in the cities. Eighty percent of Chinese Christians now are living in rural areas, and this is a special situation in Chinese religions. Many scholars have noticed this and are interested in interpreting it. In my opinion, during the period from 1949 to 1978, there was no folk religion with official forms (organizations), but in the hearts of the people there remained a deep-rooted faith in gods and spirits, and people's need for religion was not reduced. Therefore, Christianity has filled the void of faith and has replaced deep-rooted folk religion in many respects. Some people have interpreted this situation as follows:

After Liberation, the visible aspects of god-authority have been destroyed by democratic reformation, propaganda, and education in antisuper-

---

10. See Han Junxue, *Jidujiao yu Yunnan shaoshu minzu* (Kunming: Yunnan renmin chubanshe, 2000), pp. 158ff.

11. Zhu Jingyi, *Yige shiyan de xiangcun jiaohui* (Hong Kong: Shengshu gonghui ban, 1954). Cf. *Daofeng: Hanyu shenxue xuekan* (Hong Kong Xianggang jidujiao wenhua yanjiusuo, 1998), pp. 285ff.

stition. These aspects included city-temple kings, the Earth-god, Buddhist idols, all kinds of small temples and gods, and the custom of sacrificing to ancestors and to the gods. However, the invisible aspects of god-authority, i.e., the ideas of ghosts and gods, still remain. Since Christianity has a strong evangelical emphasis, in certain situations quite a lot of people have become Christians. In a strict sense, these people were not converted from an atheist background; rather, they have found a new home for their original folk-religious faith to return to. . . . The universally existing ideas of ghosts and spirits among the Chinese people are the soil of Christianity's development.[12]

Such an interpretation has also been accepted by certain Christians in China. They believe that the development of Christianity (especially in the rural areas) "constitutes, in fact, a transfer of the faith objects of Chinese people who universally have the ghost-spirit idea."[13] However, the question is, why have most people chosen Christianity as the new home for their faith? The answer to this question is related both to features of Christianity and to those of other religions, including folk religion.

According to traditional folk-religious requirements, people have to spend considerable wealth on sacrifice and spiritual issues. For example, in one county in the northern part of Jiangsu Province, this kind of activity has recently consumed 46 percent of farmers' annual income, but the investment in agriculture requires only 17 percent of their income. Thus, the economic burden is quite heavy. Chinese people usually emphasize the yin-world and spend considerable wealth for the dead. For example, in a rural area in Shaanxi Province, *yin*-weddings, engagement and wedding festivals for dead people, are quite popular. In this one small place there are seventeen to twenty such weddings every year, and they cost 60,000 to 90,000 Chinese yuan. This kind of custom contributes to the prosperity of the joss stick industry, which earns as much as 200 billion yuan annually in China.[14]

Other religions such as Buddhism and Taoism also require joss sticks, but Christianity does not. Therefore, the economic factor must have also played a role in the development of religions in China. The following folk rhyme can help us understand this issue: "It is really worthwhile to believe in

12. Xiao Zhitian, *Dangdai zongjiao wenti sikao* (Shanghai: Shanghai shi shehui kexue xuehui, 1994), pp. 73, 164.

13. Cf. Wang Weipan, "Tan jidujiao de xianzhuang wenti," *Zongjiao* (Jan. 1991).

14. Cf. Xiao Zhitian, *Dangdai zongjiao wenti sikao.*

Jesus, one neither drinks (alcohol) nor smokes, one does not have to burn joss sticks and paper-money, and one will not gamble either; in such a way one can save much money every year. When money is saved, one may have better food and clothes; it will not be difficult any more to have a better life, and after death one can even go into heaven. Please tell me, whether this is worthwhile or not?"[15]

Folk Religion–Styled Christianity

Since the 1980s folk religion has been strongly influencing Christianity in China, and Christianity has received many folk-religious features, which are mainly as follows.

First, we pay attention to utilitarianism and pragmatism. Since 1980, although economic development has been rapid and extensive in China, many common people who belong to the lower socioeconomic level in society still often lack for food, clothing, and medical treatment. What is even worse is that these people cannot find other solutions for their difficulties. Therefore, for many common believers, Christianity offers the only hope of improving their living conditions, seeking security, and responding to sickness and poverty. In the eyes of many Christian believers, God is the same as the celestial beings and Buddhist idols in whom they believed earlier. Thus, many of them believe that God will grant everything asked for by the people, and those people who are suffering from sickness especially hope to be healed by God. In many places, once one sick person is healed because of belief in Jesus Christ, a whole family, a whole clan, and even a whole village may be converted to belief in Jesus Christ.

There are many such examples,[16] and some believers even say publicly: "I am a believer because I am sick and cannot be healed; otherwise I would not believe in Jesus Christ." Some people have asked shamans and witches to drive evil spirits out of their bodies, but this is usually expensive, and sometimes they cannot be healed. Once they hear that Jesus Christ is a "bigger" god who can heal them without their paying anything, they are usually very quickly converted to Christianity. In a word, if a miracle happens, even Buddhists and Taoists can go to a Christian church to ask for help. Some statis-

---

15. Quoted in *Han Junxue* (2000): 178.
16. Deng Zhaoming, *Chengshou yu chishou: Zhongguo dadi de fuyin huoju* (Hong Kong: Jidujiao Zhongguo wenhua yanjiushe, 1998).

tics suggest that in the rural area over 60 percent of Christians are converted to Christianity because of sickness.[17]

The pragmatic approach to religion shows also in other aspects. For example, for some believers the Bible has become a protective talisman or a magic weapon that can overcome evil. Many people bind the Bible with red cloth, place it beside their pillow at home, and take it with them when they go out. Jesus is considered a "bigger" god or similar to Chinese folk-religious idols such as the Earth-god, kitchen-god, harvest-god, or healing-god; and people worship Jesus with such an attitude. "Hallelujah" has become a magic word that can get rid of evil. In addition, when natural disasters happen, Christianity has also played the role of traditional folk religion in rural areas. For example, when flood or drought occurs, many Christians get together to pray to God and to fast in order to assure enough rain or good weather. Such strong utilitarian and pragmatic emphasis reflects the impact of folk religion in China. With such influence, many rural Christians neither understand nor care about Christian doctrine; what they pay attention to is the utilitarian effect. What they are interested in is whether miracles can happen.

Second, all kinds of superstition influence Christianity. It should be accepted that most rural believers are sincere and honest, but many misunderstandings occur because there are few qualified pastors; thus all kinds of superstitions have been confused with Christianity. For example, some pastors tell their congregations that there is visible evidence when a person is saved by God, and this signifies that the name of that person has been recorded in the Book of Life which is the register book in heaven. Consequently, Christians should seek such heavenly citizenship. In some places there are odd customs such as breathing spiritual air (i.e., breathing air into other Christians' bodies), spitting spiritual water (i.e., spitting food), touching the spirit (i.e., touching other Christians' bodies), and crying for the spirit (i.e., crying in the night during the time of prayer). Some sincere Christians with strong hope are victims of such misinformed teaching.[18]

In addition, since many rural Christians interpret Christianity in the light of their original folk-religious viewpoint, they have established many limitation rules for themselves. For example, certain days are understood as days of fasting during which people should not kill chickens to make food and women should not comb their hair. In some places during their menses

---

17. *Liang Jialing* (1999): 226.
18. One female youth in Jiangsu Province died because she fasted seven days for the kingdom of heaven. Xiao Zhitian, *Dangdai zongjiao wenti sikao*, p. 162.

women are not allowed to read the Bible, are not allowed to go church, and are not allowed to receive Holy Communion. The color yellow is not allowed in some places as it is believed to be a bad omen. Christians are not allowed to eat in the homes of non-Christians, since they are considered unclean, etc.[19] Such confused ideas of faith are quite popular among the masses, since many people do not know what Christianity is, and they do not understand the difference between Christianity and their original folk-religious faith.

Third, we pay attention to the different forms of religion. The pragmatism of Chinese rural Christianity leads believers to pay considerable attention to its form. As a result, different forms of Christian activities have been born. The spiritual hymn is one such form. Many Christians like to sing spiritual hymns since they are believed to have come from the Holy Spirit, and they have had a considerable impact on congregations. In fact, however, many spiritual hymns are composed by Christians themselves. For example, the melody of a popular Chinese People's Liberation Army song, *Three Principles and Eight Attentions,* has been employed as a spiritual hymn. The following words appear in this hymn: "I will sing Christ's spiritual hymns every day. I will have a new form of life for the sake of the Lord. Neither eating nor drinking, such a taste is strong. Relying only on the Lord, and the Lord will give me strength."[20]

Sometimes Christian activities are connected with local social activities such as weddings and funerals, and Christians sometimes sing spiritual hymns and dance spiritual dances on these occasions. In some places people arrange activities to assist them in seeking to be fully filled with the Holy Spirit, and some people even injure themselves in order to achieve the feeling of being filled with the Holy Spirit.[21]

Fourth, we must assess that rural Christians easily believe in rumors. Since many common rural Christians do not understand Christian doctrine well and do not have the ability to recognize truth from falsehood, it is quite common for them to believe in rumors. For example, some Christians hear that Jesus Christ will return on a certain date, and they may stop working in the field. Some Christians may even give up their secular life altogether and wait for Jesus to lift them into heaven. In some places accidents have oc-

---

19. *Liang Jialing* (1999): 418.

20. Deng Zhaoming, *Chengshou yu chishou,* p. 90.

21. Li Rui, "Shaoshu minzu jiaohui chengzhang," a presentation in the international conference on "Protestant Church Development in China" held by the Lutheran World Federation China Study Program and the Lutheran Theological Seminary, Hong Kong, December 2000.

curred as Christians competed to board a Holy Boat in order to go to heaven.[22]

Many factors contribute to the creation of such a situation in rural Christian life. First, folk-religious faith is deep-rooted and powerful. Second, living conditions in the rural areas are hard and difficult. As far as the demography of rural Christianity is concerned, the structure of the Christian community is characterized by the "Three mosts" (i.e., most Christians are aged, women, and illiterates). Since the opening up of China at the end of the 1970s, Christians have grown in number and become more active, sincere, and philanthropic, but they lack pastoral leadership.

For example, a congregation on Leizhou Peninsula, Guangdong Province, does not have its own pastor even though nineteen church buildings were erected in the late 1990s and the congregation numbers about 7,000 believers. Except for several Christians who were baptized before 1949, most have not been baptized, since there is no pastor in the congregation to handle baptism.[23] Thus, in many places there have been so-called "free-evangelists," and some of them try to attract people through all kinds of folk-religious elements such as miracles, dreams, and odd visions. Another problem is that pastors also lack opportunities for continuing education, and many rural congregations are disordered in organization. These weaknesses have enabled folk religion to have considerable influence upon Christianity.

Conclusion

One foreign scholar has summarized the features of Chinese people as follows: "In history we cannot find another nation who is more superstitious, more skeptical, more sincere, more rational, more secular, than Chinese people are, nor can we find another country more independent from the church than China is."[24] Although this statement seems paradoxical within itself, it does indeed indicate some features of Chinese people's religious life. I am

22. This kind of concrete statistics can be found in Sun Shanling, "Zhongguo minjian jidujiao," in *Jidujiao wenhua yu xiandaihua* (Beijing: Zhongguo shehui kexue chubanshe, 1996). See also Sha Guangyi, "Tan woguo zongjiao de qunzhong xing," *Zongjiao* (Feb. 1991).

23. Deng Zhaoming, *Chengshou yu chishou*.

24. Weier Dulan, *Shijiewenming zhisi: Zhongguo yu yuandong: Gangtai ji haiwai xuezhe lun Zhongguo wenhua, shangce* (Shanghai: Shanghai renmin chubanshe, 1988), p. 44. Quoted from Hou Jie and Fan Lizhu, *Zhongguo minzhong yishi*, p. 193.

not going to discuss the relationship between state and church, but the fact is that, since Christianity came to China, it has been influenced and limited by Chinese culture. Of course, we also must acknowledge that the great impact of folk religion on Christianity is most evident in rural areas and within the lowest socioeconomic strata of society. In cities such impact is less common.

The folk-religion style of Christianity in Chinese rural areas, in fact, has had some negative influences upon the development of Christianity in China. It has made Christianity cruder, less sophisticated, and less developed. It has also produced confusion in theology. Thus, many common Chinese rural believers cannot recognize normative Christian teaching. This situation has offered a possibility for heresies to appear. Examples include such groups as Eastern Lightning, Three Servants, and Word Becoming Flesh, which claim to be Christian but teach a very idiosyncratic doctrine. Such folk religion–styled Christianity is unable to make a positive contribution to the development of society in contemporary China.

However, it is not easy to change this situation. The China Christian Council has recently strengthened the training of rural pastors and preachers, and training has been arranged on numerous occasions.[25] Although many attempts have been made, the needs of congregations still cannot be met and the basic problem still remains. There is a paradoxical difficulty in Chinese rural churches: On the one hand, the church is continually influenced by folk religion. On the other hand, the Christian church has to compete with the revived folk religions in attracting believers.

This fact indicates that the folk-religion style of Chinese rural Christianity is determined by the actual conditions of Chinese rural life and the needs of the people at this level of society. This is reasonable since the present historical situation in China has shaped the developmental process and direction of Christianity in Chinese rural areas. Today, the development of Christianity in Chinese rural areas is rapid, and Christianity is more influential than it has been at any other time. Perhaps when living conditions are changed for the better in rural China, Christians will become more orthodox in their beliefs.

25. Zhao Zhien, "Zhongguo nongcun jiaohui de xianzhuang he qianjing," a presentation in the above-mentioned conference in Hong Kong: "Protestant Church Development in China" (2000).

PART II

CHRISTIANITY IN THE CONTEXT OF MODERN CHINA

9 Comprehensive Theology: An Attempt to Combine Christianity with Chinese Culture

Zhuo Xinping

Both Christianity and Chinese cultures are strong, influential cultures that have clashed in their relationship with each other. Both have strong subjective self-identities and wait for the other to make a compromise; thus either party refuses to budge from its own position. In addition to political and historical reasons, cultural and ideological factors have been essential in creating such a situation. Since the beginning of reform in the 1980s, a new generation of theologians and thinkers has appeared within the Chinese Christian church. They hold double identities as Chinese intellectuals and Christians, and they realize the importance of seeking similarities between Christianity and Chinese culture. Since seeking similarity is the precondition and basis of constructing a comprehensive theology, only through this approach can real Chinese Christianity and theology be developed. It can be said that such a direction is becoming the mainstream of developing Chinese contemporary Christianity.

In order to eliminate the tension and conflict between Christianity and Chinese culture so as to create a smooth way for both sides to exchange ideas and to develop, the attempt to combine them must involve comparison and comprehension. If the figurative approach of Jesuits' attempt in Chinese history reached only a low level of acculturation or acknowledgment of similarity in the forms of Christianity and Chinese culture, a further exploration in this field is now appropriate in order to reach a deeper level of inculturation or acknowledgment of similarity in their essences. Through comparison and judgment, the universal truth of Christianity should be able to find access into Chinese culture.

The Chinese church, which was born on such a basis, should become a church of cultural comprehension, and Chinese theology should also be a comprehensive theology that can combine components from both East and West. To compare Christianity with Confucianism so as to construct a comprehensive theology is very important. Comprehensive theology, as an attempt to combine Christianity with Chinese culture, was first put forward by He Shiming (Ho Sai Ming, 1911-96). He was from Shunde County of Guangdong Province, and he received the B.A. degree in literature from Zhongshan University. He Shiming had been a pastor in the Hong Kong Church of Luke, director of a middle school, director of a Christian publishing house, lecturer in a Baptist seminary, and president of the Christian Cultural Association.

Concerning the relationship between Christianity and Chinese culture, he published the following books: *A Dialogue between Christianity and Confucianism (Jidujiao yu ruxue duitan)*, *Four Lectures on Christianity and Confucianism (Jidujjiao ruxue sijiang)*, *A Perspective on Chinese Filial Piety in the Light of Christianity (Cong jidujiao kan Zhongguo de xiaodao)*, *Comprehensive Theology and Confucian Thinking (Rongguan shenxue yu rujiao sixiang)*, and *A Preliminary Discussion on Chinese Christian Comprehensive Theology (Zhonghua jidujiao ruxue chuyi)*. His basic argument is that Chinese theologians should encourage Christianity to absorb good elements from Confucianism while the faults of Chinese traditional culture should also be corrected with Christianity. In such a way the two strong, exclusive cultures can become complementary to each other, leading to the success of both. The Comprehensive Theology of He Shiming represents the general understanding of the Chinese Christian world.

In searching for a similarity between Christianity and Chinese culture, the Old Testament has usually been considered as similar to the Confucian Five Classics: the *Book of Changes (Yijing)*, the *Document of History (Shangshu)*, *Poems (Shijing)*, the *Record of Rites (Liji)*, and *Spring and Autumn (Chunqiu zuozhuan)*. And the New Testament has been considered as similar to the Confucian Four Books: *Analects (Lunyu)*, *Great Learning (Daxue)*, *The Mean (Zhongyong)*, and *Mencius (Mengzi)*.

In aspects of thought the following issues have been compared with one another: "the relationship between Heaven and people" and "the relationship between God and people"; "Heaven gave birth to human beings" and "God created human beings"; "Heaven loves the masses" and "God loves people"; "responding between Heaven and human beings" and "the exchange between God and human beings"; "offering sacrifices to Heaven" and "worshiping God"; "implementing the punishment of Heaven" and "the Last Judgment"; "the unification between Heaven and human beings" and "the unification between God and human beings"; "Confucian benevolence" and "Christian love"; "Confucian Five Ethics" (the relationships between father and son, between emperor and subjects, between husband and wife, between old and young, and between friends) and "Christian ethical morality"; and the "Confucian ideas of the mean (balance), forgiveness, and sympathy" and the "Christian spirit of humility, tolerance, and self-sacrifice." These comparisons range over issues of creation, humanity, wisdom, social order, self-cultivation, sanctification, etc.[1]

Of course, while people have been looking for similarities between Christianity and Chinese culture, they have also found differences between them. For example, after comparing the Bible and the Confucian Four Books and Five Classics, Rev. Chen Weizhong says, "In the light of Chinese culture, which is mainly represented by the Four Books and Five Classics, its conceptions of theology and God are comparatively difficult to understand. . . . However, the God hidden within the Four Books and Five Classics is the same as the God of the Bible, and this can be proven by the contents of these works." Chen further makes an analysis of the difference between them and says that the God in Chinese classics "is the mean, i.e., the Way of Heaven, earth, and human beings"; "the God in Chinese classics is neither isolated nor abstract, but is closely related with common life."

On the contrary, "the God in the Bible is direct and is easier to be understood," but just "because of this directness and easiness, Western theologians find it easy to make God plain. Now, Western theologians have either isolated God as a Wholly Other in the realm of heaven and spirit, or have isolated God as the one who serves only the earthly benefits. There are other people who consider God as only a God of individualism. All these have lost the mean feature of Heaven, earth, and human beings."[2] In order to keep and to stress the Chinese God's mean feature of Heaven, earth, and human beings, Rev. Chen has constructed "a mean systematic theology," and this is a Christian theology that is clearly different from Western theology and has strong Chinese Confucian features.[3]

Following such a way of thinking, Christianity has also had the experi-

---

1. Cf. Huai Renjin, *Tiandao gushuo: Huaxia xianxian yu shengjing xianzhe rushi shuo* (Beijing: Zhongguo wenshi chubanshe, 1999).

2. Chen Weizhong, *Gongtong de Shangdi*, p. 86.

3. Cf. Chen Weizhong, *Zhongyong xitong shenxue* (Shanghai: Zhongguo jidujiao xiehui, 2000).

ence of seeking the "mean" during its development in the context of Chinese culture, and this is an obvious feature when similarities are sought between Christianity and various Chinese religions. The attempts of Confucian Christians or Christian Confucians were a success in the Ming and Qing dynasties. In the recent time characterized by an interest in inculturation, there have also been Confucian Christians and Buddhist Christians in China. For example, Nie Yuntai and some other people have suggested that Christianity should adapt itself to Confucianism, while some missionaries, such as Ernst Faber, have suggested worshiping both Confucius and Jesus.

Others, like Zhang Chunyi, have suggested adapting Christianity into Buddhism. For example, the Christian Church of Baoguan Road in Shanghai has employed some Buddhist liturgies such as lighting incense and burning candles, and kneeling down while reading biblical texts and prayers. Karl L. Reichelt started a dialogue between Christianity and Buddhism in Jingfeng Mountain in Nanjing, which contributed to the formation of the Tao Fong Shan Ecumenical Centre in Hong Kong and continues to influence China today. In the beginning of 2002 there was a discussion about Pan Yue's comments on religions in mainland China, pointing to the potential of constructing a "mean" between Chinese mainstream ideology and the Christian spirit.

Through comparing Christianity with Chinese culture people start to find a place for Christianity in China. Among Christian scholars, Wu Leichuan, Wang Zhixin, Zhao Zichen, Xie Fuya, and Wu Jingxiong have spent much of their time delineating the relationship between Christianity and Chinese culture. Wu Leichuan thinks that Christianity should become a real Chinese religion by being an Eastern one in contrast to the Western tradition. This means that Chinese Christianity is "Eastern worldism" rather than "Western nationalism," "Eastern futurism" rather than "Western realism," "Eastern pacifism" rather than "Western competitionism," and "Eastern practicism" rather than "Western theoreticism." For Wu Leichuan this kind of Eastern Christianity can be combined with Chinese culture and can reach the essence of truth.

Wang Zhixin thinks that in order to have an exchange of Christianity with Chinese culture an approach of adjustment and acceptance should be followed, as connection, exchange, and adjustment can make differences become similarities or even the same thing. Adjustment includes three levels: life adjustment, moral adjustment, and spiritual adjustment. From adjustment, "a point of comprehending Christianity and Chinese culture can be found." Therefore, "adjustment" is the precondition of "accepting," and "accepting" is the final result of "adjustment." In the earlier history of politics the term "adjustment" was a negative word, but now in cultural exchange it has become a positive conception for finding a new way to solve problems.

Zhao Zichen is one of the most influential persons in considering exchanges of Christianity with Chinese culture. In order to construct a Chinese Christianity, he suggests employing an image of the exchange of the waters of a marsh.[4] There are two important features within this construction. One is to admit that there are "everlasting religious truths" within Christianity; another is to admit that there is "some spiritual inheritance and guidance" within Chinese culture. Therefore, he thinks, Chinese Christianity should do the following three things:

1. create a Chinese Christian terminology with Chinese language,
2. arrange a Chinese philosophy and ethics, and
3. write a kind of Christian historical philosophy using the Chinese historical-critical method of *yin-yang* order-disorder.

In addition, this Chinese Christian system should be an open religious system that can absorb new elements. In the literate sense, it uses beautiful language and absorbs essential good elements from Confucianism, Buddhism, and Taoism; in a philosophical sense it employs a theory of "entering the world to transcend the world, nature, and history" to complete the Chinese tradition of *Dao* that Heaven and human beings are united; in ethics the relationship between God and human beings should be added to Chinese ideas that the Under Sky is public for all, that all peoples within the Four Seas are brothers, with loyalty and filial piety, etc. This is the hope of Zhao Zichen's indigenous Christianity.

Xie Fuya has also made a critical analysis of the relationship between Christianity and Chinese culture. He admits frankly that Christianity has not yet comprehended Chinese culture, and the real situation now is that they have met each other but have not understood each other. Thus, many misunderstandings and conflicts have occurred. The result of such a situation is that Chinese culture does not grasp the real essence of Christianity, and Christianity is unable to influence Chinese culture. Therefore, he suggests the two sides

---

4. This means a deep exchange. See *Zhouyi, Dui* (Joy, Pleasure), p. 58: "It says in the Great Symbolism: [Two symbols representing] the waters of a marsh, one over another, from Dui. The superior man, in accordance with this, [encourages] the conversation of friends and [the stimulus of] their [common] practice."

should seek the similarities between them in order to create an atmosphere of understanding each other. Only in such a way can Christianity possibly be comprehended within Chinese culture. He points out that this "combination" is harmonious rather than "united" and "the same." He admits the regional and cultural differences within Christianity. He believes that unlike Western Christianity, Chinese Christianity contains a tolerance of critics, the mean of dynamics, and practical features, since "tolerance, mean, and practice" are the special features of Chinese culture. Only as Christianity and Chinese culture tolerate each other can they comprehend one another.

Wu Jingxiong has considered Christianity as a "treasure house," which includes everything in the comparison between Christianity and Chinese culture. He believes that the Eastern tradition can be found from Christianity and that Chinese wisdom can also be found from Christianity. Christianity can play a role in connecting East and West and can connect them and transcend them.

This kind of thought in seeking similarities has laid a foundation for Chinese comprehensive theology. In his books, He Shiming points out that the real root of Chinese culture remains neither in the political level of "loyalty to the emperor" nor in the ethical level of "filial piety to parents" but in the religious level of "faith in the ruling Heaven." It is in this level of faith that Christianity and Chinese culture can reach a kind of comprehension. Accepting Christianity cannot only correct the faults of Chinese culture but also can develop the good elements of Chinese culture, so that Chinese culture can participate actively in the development of the Christian system of faith.

It is clear that He Shiming considers Christianity as holding a dominant position in the comprehension between Christianity and Chinese culture, and they do not hold an absolutely equal position in the exchange. He Shiming further points out, "There are two approaches to comprehend Christianity with Chinese culture and to keep Christianity in the leading position. One is to let Chinese culture go into Christianity to act as a tool to interpret Christianity, and we call this Sinological theology. Another is to let Christianity come into Chinese culture to be corrected and reformed, and we call this theological Sinology. No matter whether it is Sinological theology or theological Sinology, the Dao of Christ should be a leading principle within it, and this is our proposed comprehensive theology."[5]

For He Shiming the main difference between Christianity and Chinese

---

5. He Shiming, *Rongguan shenxue yu rujia sixiang* (Beijing: Zongjiao wenhua chubanshe, 1999), p. 145.

culture is that God occupies a main position in the former and human be-ings occupy a main position in the latter; the former emphasizes transcen-dence and the latter immanence; the former knows both life and death and has a clear distinction between this and other worlds, but the latter knows only life and avoids facing the problems of death and the issues related to the other world. Because of this He Shiming stresses that Christianity enters ev-ery culture including Chinese culture. Therefore, the so-called Chinese com-prehensive theology "is to comprehend Chinese traditional cultural ideolo-gies into Christian faith and to lead the whole system with the Dao of Christ. Christian culture itself can both transcend and exist within every culture."[6] Such "entering" and "comprehending" are the practice of seeking similari-ties. Of course, for Chinese non-Christian intellectuals, the transcendence and universality of Christianity will appear as a relationship of "inequality"; thus, the chances of dialogue and of seeking similarities will probably be lost. This will also create difficulties for real dialogue and comprehension between Christianity and Chinese culture.

From the historical viewpoint, seeking similarities between Christianity and Chinese culture is the first step in their encounter and understanding each other. In the beginning of encounter, seeking similarity between differ-ent cultures is an essential and even the only approach to establishing ex-change and connection. Without "similarity" there will be neither common language with which to discuss nor the contact points of dialogue and the means of exchange. Although seeking similarity may lead to historical and epistemological mistakes, it helps the two different sides to start a dialogue and to coexist; thus, this is the first step toward real understanding and knowing each other. Generally starting with finding differences will lead to conflict or failure in cultural exchange. This can be indicated from the his-tory of Christianity in China.

Of course, from the viewpoints of cultural transmission and religious missiology, seeking similarity is not usually the final destination; it is only a preliminary stage of dialogue, exchange, and understanding each other, and the precondition and preparation for the good atmosphere of seeking new things and finding differences. Therefore, while seeking similarity can give people a good impression as an act of understanding, it only starts the cul-tural dialogue and exchange; the play of understanding human spirits has had only a starting point.

6. He Shiming, *Zhonghua jidujiao rongguan shenxue chuyi* (Beijing: Zongjiao wenhua chubanshe, 2002), p. 11.

In fact, there is still a long way to go from "seeking similarity" to "comprehension." In the attempts to combine Christianity with Chinese culture there seem to be many problems that are waiting to be resolved. Our above discussion of the comprehension of Chinese Christian thinkers offers mainly a platform for combining Christianity with Chinese traditional culture, especially the one dominated by Confucianism and assisted by Buddhism and Taoism.

The more important and urgent issue is how to comprehend Christianity within the new cultural system that is being formed in contemporary China and how to make Christianity contribute more actively and positively to this construction of the new Chinese cultural system. As to this issue, the younger generation of Chinese Christian theologians are constructing a new Chinese theology within the framework of the Chinese church, and they have explored areas such as the doctrine of God, the doctrine of Christ, and the doctrine of faith. As to comprehension, Chinese academic thinkers are also starting a more meaningful "academic theology" or "Christian academics." Of course, generally speaking, this comprehensive theology, which may possibly solve the relationship between Christianity and Chinese culture, is not yet a reality but an ideal, and it is still in the stage of exploration rather than a mature state. From this point of view we are still in the process and context of developing it. How we are going to start this process will decide its future.

A Response to Professor Zhuo Xinping

Notto R. Thelle

First I would like to thank Professor Zhuo for his paper, which I liked very much. It is balanced without losing dynamics, rounded without losing sharpness and edges. Perhaps it is "an expression of the ideal of the mean."

I like the point of departure where he characterizes both Christianity and Chinese cultures as "strong, exclusive cultures," along with the fact that these not only exist side by side in the same society, but coexist in people's lives. He describes Chinese Christians who hold double or dual identities as intellectuals deeply rooted in Chinese culture and at the same time committed Christians. In fact this is a phenomenon that is increasingly common where religious and cultural traditions meet, both in the East and in the West, and many of us experience similar things in our own lives or in the lives of people we know. So the paper is not only a case study of processes in the Chinese context, but an invitation to reflect upon processes that are familiar, in spite of all differences.

Since I only have an English translation that is probably not always an exact translation of the Chinese original, I would like to summarize my own reading of the paper in order to see whether it is correct.

I read the paper as a report on some characteristic examples of Chinese intellectuals who have tried to hold together two commitments — Christianity and Chinese culture — that are not necessarily in harmony, but are allowed to coexist in their tensions. The foremost example in the paper is He Shiming (Ho Sai Ming), who is introduced as representative of the attempt to formulate a "comprehensive theology." This implies a creative process of interaction where mutual learning and mutual criticism lead to a transformation of both

Christianity and Chinese culture, resulting in a new comprehension and integration. A few others are introduced, offering nuances in understanding and ways of thinking. But all seem to have a primary concern for the Christian faith and its potential for changing China, and a secondary concern for the way Christianity is changed by dialogue with Chinese traditions.

Professor Zhuo is somewhat critical of this tendency, referring to non-Christian intellectuals who find some "inequality" and one-sidedness in this way of "entering" Chinese culture, and warns that the real dialogue may be threatened. Instead he is advocating a dialogue that is primarily committed to searching for similarities on an equal level rather than a dialogue that involves cultural transmission or missionary concern. Anyway he regards most of the interactions as preliminary stages, a starting point for a process that is unpredictable. In particular the examples of "comprehensive theology" presented in the article are only to be understood as a preliminary platform for experimenting with integration between Christianity and the classical religious/philosophical traditions of China — Confucianism, Buddhism, and Taoism.

In one sense, I have a feeling that the paper ends where I would have liked to see a continuation, for only in the last paragraph does it suggest that the real issue is the question of how to relate Christianity to the actual realities in modern society and how to construct a new theology that contributes to a new cultural system.

If this is a fairly correct understanding of the paper, I would like to add a few questions and comments. These are not meant as criticism, but rather a follow-up of some themes suggested in the paper that invite further reflection about the complexities of interfaith and intercultural dialogue. I will limit myself to a few questions:

1. What is "China" or "Chinese"?
2. What is "Christianity" — essence or contextual manifestations?
3. Who is the subject of theological reflection? Who is speaking/writing and defining the terms of the dialogue with the others?
4. Principles may be important, but are the processes perhaps more interesting?

1. I think Professor Zhuo has already raised the first question: "What is China?" He has introduced various examples of theological reflection of Chinese Christians who have chosen classical culture (primarily Confucianism) as the preferred dialogue partner. He then suggests that perhaps other

contexts may be more relevant, vaguely characterized as "contemporary China," and that such dialogue may contribute to the construction of a new Chinese cultural system. This context is certainly another "China" than the classical culture.

One could easily add other "Chinas," for there are many "Chinas" and many types of "Chinese-ness": secular Chinas, political Chinas, post-ideological Chinas in need of new visions, the Chinas of the poor, landless, and homeless roaming toward the cities, China as a nation where half of the population are women. I think there is a need for many types of dialogues and many different attempts to search for a "Chinese" Christianity or for a China that is changed by the encounter with Christianity.

2. What is "Christianity"? In the same way that we tend to search for an essence of Chinese culture and Chinese-ness, we tend to search for a corresponding essence of Christianity, an ideal abstracted from the historical realities and concrete manifestations. I am not saying that this is meaningless or futile — many of us do that all the time when we engage in dialogue and want to share our conviction. I am just suggesting that we should not forget that Christian faith is always formed in a context — historical, geographical, cultural, social, etc. — and that we should be aware of that context. There are many "Christianities," not only because of the denominational traditions, but because of the various contexts. This should give us both humility and confidence. We share our faith from our own perspective with a conviction that this is a message to others, but are also open to learning from the other and being transformed by the other. Once we open our minds to insights and experiences formed in other contexts, things look differently. Christianity changes when we see it from the boundary where we meet other religions and cultures. Christianity is contextual, and real encounters are intercontextual.

3. Who is the subject? My emphasis on context is related to the question of who is the subject of theological reflection. Who is the speaker or writer who defines what Christianity is and has the power to decide the agenda? What does it mean, for example, that the theologians Professor Zhuo introduces are all male, intellectual, Chinese, Protestant, living in the twentieth century? Would their concerns and questions have been different, or would they have seen different things and told different stories if they had been women, or were poor, belonged to minorities, belonged to nonregistered Christian communities, were homosexuals, or had very different life experiences? I think so.

4. What about principles and processes? Professor Zhuo is somewhat concerned about principles, and seems to prefer the spirit of balanced reflec-

tion searching for a common platform and a common language rather than the ambition of some Christians to Christianize Chinese culture.

I see his point and know what sort of uneasiness it may create when people feel that they are targets for mission. On the other hand, I am not sure one should be so apprehensive about such motives and agendas, at least as far as they are not hidden. I have done quite a lot of research about interfaith cross-cultural relations in Japan, and to a certain extent in China, and have discovered that once there is an open encounter, principles and strategies often yield to the actual process of change. People may even start with an aggressive missionary motivation to transform China, but in the long run discover that they themselves are changed by the encounter.

Let me exemplify by referring to the process of change among the missionaries who came to China around 1900. Most of them came to conquer China for "Christ and civilization," making the Chinese "cleaner and happier and more Godlike." But for many of them the battlefield changed character, and they were themselves in some sense "conquered" by China. An American observer in 1919 described the "conversion" of these missionaries in the following terms: "He had gone out to change the East, and was returning, himself a changed man. . . . The conversion of the missionary by the Far East results in his being not only a missionary but an internationalist, an intermediary between the two great civilizations that inherit the earth."[1]

I could mention numerous other examples, but my only point is to suggest that in the long run, if one is really exposed to the other in dialogue or dialogical study, things will change, and the process of change is unpredictable. The encounter with Chinese culture may start with ideals of a balanced search for a common ground and a common language, or with strong missionary motives of transforming China. In both cases things seem to change, whether or not one has the "right" ideals and principles.

---

1. I have developed this theme in my essay "'The Conversion of the Missionary': Changes in Buddhist-Christian Relations in the Early Twentieth Century China," presented for the International Conference for Buddhist Christian Dialogue, at Xian University, November 2003.

10 The Contextualization of Chinese Christian Theology and Its Main Concerns

Yang Huilin

If the Christian faith and its dissemination are examined in a hermeneutic framework, the church will become a community of discourse in addition to being one of faith.[1] Discourse of this kind is not a "soliloquy," of course, but one expounding its value system in specific contexts and maintaining the alienating tension between earthly and ultimate reality. Viewed against this background, the proposition of "theology in the Chinese language" may be taken as a sign of major changes in the study of the contextualization of Christianity in China.

This means that theology must begin with transcendence over a specific cultural vehicle, and whatever approach a theologian may adopt (accommodation, inculturation,[2] interculturality,[3] or contextualization[4]), he must in practice shed the inertia of expounding a religion on the basis of its rituals and look at a religion such as the Christian faith and its dissemination as a process of internalization. In China, in the Tang dynasty (635-845) the Nestorians interpreted Christianity in terms of Buddhism and Taoism; in the late Ming (c. 1600) through the Qing, the faith was largely interpreted in

1. Francis S. Fiorenza, "Systematic Theology: Task and Methods," in *Systematic Theology: Roman Catholic Perspectives,* vol. 1, ed. Francis S. Fiorenza and John P. Galvin (Minneapolis: Fortress, 1991), p. 84.

2. Nicholas Standaert, *Inculturation,* trans. Chen Kuanwei (Taipei: Guangqi, 1993).

3. Gianni Criveller, *On Christianity in the Late Ming Dynasty* (Chengdu: Sichuan People's Press, 1999).

4. *Domestication of the Church: The 47th Series of Divine Thoughts,* ed. Wu Zhixun (Hong Kong: Siwei, 2000).

Confucian terms; and in the post–Cultural Revolution (1966-76) period, there has been a tendency to understand it in the framework of one's existential experience.[5] These efforts to understand the Christian church in China have opened up at least three areas for the study of theology in the Chinese language.

Linguistic Orientation

As theologies outside the traditionally Christian world in the West are usually defined by their awareness of specific phenomena and their geographic features, the term "theology in the Chinese language" will inevitably remind us of such theological studies as Liberation Theology, Minjung Theology (Theology of the Masses), and Grass-Roots Theology (C. S. Song). However, these terms should not be taken literally as to indicate their involvement in particular issues or the process of contextualization; they reflect the nature of theology in the Chinese language — a nature, though associated with its own concerns and circumstances, determined by its linguistic identity.

If "being that can be understood is language"[6] and if being means first of all words we share with others,[7] then the "dialogue" relationship of language is inevitably the prerequisite of any discourse. Dialogue is generally understood to take place between two different subjects, different texts, or between a subject and a text. Theology, being a kind of discourse, is not an exception. But its prerequisite is one of alterity, a more fundamental "the other" relationship, "the Wholly Other" relationship between the Word of God and the words of man, which transcends all forms of language. Chinese Christian theology, with its linguistic identity, therefore, should focus on the study of alterity as early Christian theologies in Latin and in Greek did. It should deal with the words of man and their limitations in expressing and interpreting the Word of God. In other words, when the Chinese language becomes one of the forms of Christian theology, we may recognize more clearly the fact that there cannot exist a total correspondence between theological significance and its language form. Such interlinguisticity, together

---

5. Yang Huilin, "Ethical Value of the Christian Church in the Chinese Language and the Ethical Value of Christianity," *Journal for the Study of Christian Culture* 2 (1999): 223-39.

6. Hans-Georg Gadamer, *Truth and Method*, trans. Garrett Barden and John Cumming (New York: Crossroad, 1975).

7. Raimondo Panikkar, *The Intra-religious Dialogue*, trans. Wang Zhicheng (Beijing: Religious Culture, 2001), p. 10.

with intersubjectivity and intertexuality of reading activities, has to be part of the pursuit of ultimate theological significance.

In the study of the interlinguisticity between the Word of God and the words of man, an interesting fact should merit our attention. The Bible is the book of the Christian faith, but it is not written in the mother tongue of Jesus Christ. This gives the unique advantage of translatability. Consequently, the Bible leaves its ultimate referential meaning open to interpretation in any language. That is to say, no language — Hebrew, Greek, or Latin — is able to give the Christian faith a perfect expression of the Word of God; for the Christian faith exists in alterity to any of its linguistic forms.

The above discussion on the linguistic features of the Christian faith will lead to the discovery that the essence of the Christian faith, its alterity and interlinguisticity, may be revealed more effectively in Chinese Christian theology than in any theologies of the West; this is so because there exists an alienating tension between the Chinese culture and the Christian faith, which is generally thought of as a part of the Western culture.

Nowadays, "meaning" is faced with the danger of being tyrannized by cultural exclusivism and blurred by cultural pluralism. It is pursued, interpreted, and argued about more and more on the basis of differences in linguistic form rather than on differences in faith, ideology, civilization, or theological significance.[8] Viewed against this cultural background, the awareness of interlinguisticity is essential in keeping "meaning" intact. And that is where the potential values and impact of Chinese Christian theology lie.

Extension into the Humanities Area

With its linguistic orientation as such, Chinese Christian theology, as the study of the Christian faith in the Chinese cultural context, naturally extends itself into the area of the humanities.

As we know, a religion cannot take root in the soil of a foreign culture unless it is adapted to it. For instance, it took Buddhism a long process of accommodation to become integrated with Chinese thought.[9] But Christian-

---

8. The linguistic conflict may be illustrated by the recent dispute over the war in Iraq between several English-speaking and non-English-speaking Christian countries, in which the U.S., Great Britain, and Australia called for war against Saddam, and France, Germany, and Russia (of the Orthodox faith) opposed a U.S.-led war.

9. Fang Litian, *The Essence of the Chinese Buddhist Philosophy*, 2 vols. (Beijing: Renmin University of China Press, 2003).

ity, in spite of its huge missionary efforts in China since the 1980s, has not established itself in the Chinese culture. This contrast reflects the fact that Chinese Christian theology has not yet fully revealed its potential power in the Chinese culture.

It is true that some academic achievements have been made in the mainland in the humanistic study of Christianity, such as the translation and introduction of Western Christian thought, the study of the contextualization of Christianity in China, the restoration of historical records of the development of Christianity in China, and the dialogue between Chinese culture and Christianity. But most of these achievements deal with religion or other humanities study rather than Chinese Christian theology. Although there are a large number of publications in Chinese on Christian theology outside the mainland, a large proportion of them, which record sermons, meditations, or biblical annotations, fall short of academic impact on humanities studies. There obviously exists a gap between the development of Chinese Christian theology and Chinese humanities.

Some influential figures of the Christian community in China have in recent years realized the importance of the development of Chinese Christian theology. For example, Bishop K. H. Ting has repeatedly called for efforts to institute a Chinese Christian theology by Chinese theologians. Bishop Ting's call, which has been endorsed by Chinese authorities in the mainland, may be expected to contribute to the closing of the above-mentioned gap and stimulate cooperation between the church and the secular in China, which is a prerequisite for the growth of Chinese Christian theology.

Chinese Christian theology, if it were to extend into the humanities area, would have to build itself on three disciplines.

First, theological hermeneutics. This discipline pursues absolute truth and knowledge in man's quest for the best understanding of "meaning" with his finite knowledge and limited power of reasoning.

Second, theological ethics. This branch of ethics tries to define goodness and righteousness. It aims to answer these questions: How can man, in his awareness of being incomplete, imperfect, and self-contradictory, fulfill the requirement for being morally good? How can man justify "moral correctness" with his faith in righteousness?

Third, theological aesthetics. This is the aesthetics that pushes values of beauty and artistic taste beyond the didactic and aesthetic points of art to meet man's aspiration for ultimate spiritual experience and salvation.

Chinese Christian theology, with these extensions, does not aim to set an ideological standard for the study of Chinese humanities, nor to become an established religion in China; it only tries to show the potential value of Christianity in the Chinese cultural context so that Christianity may gain recognition within the Chinese culture.

Empirical Research into the Present-Day Faith Practice in China

Apart from its extension in the humanities area, Chinese Christian theology, in its study of the modern contextualization of Christianity, needs empirical research into present-day faith practices in China in order to appreciate the Chinese Christian communities' contemporary interpretation of the Christian faith. Empirical research on the contextualization of the Christian faith in modern China is now a focus of religious study in the mainland, and its main concerns may include: the relationship between the Christian faith and its popularized practice in Chinese Christian communities, the impact of Chinese ideological systems on the modern contextualization of Christianity, the two types of faith practice prevailing in present-day Chinese Christian communities — secularization and charismaticization of the Christian faith — and their cultural bases.

It is generally known that the revival of Christianity and other religions in China since the 1980s has something to do not only with China's opening-up but also with changes in the earlier social structure as well. The Confucian ethic, a historically dominating ideology in China, had been under fierce attack since 1949 and was almost exterminated during the Cultural Revolution. Socialist ideology, the other ideological pillar, has been severely questioned since the end of the Cultural Revolution. The rapid economic development of the last two decades, instead of providing the new social structure with its spiritual basis, has revealed a potential danger of letting the power of the economy and the market determine the balance between social and spiritual as a negative result of globalization. This situation could further weaken the basis of the traditional ethic and ideological systems and lead to a significant malfunction of the existing social structure. As it happens, Christianity and other religions have been awarded the opportunity to grow vigorously in China, and some of them have become alternative or compensating beliefs within some social communities.

In some rural communities in China, it may well be said that the Christian faith has been so contextualized that it has become an alternative ethical system that maintains or at least helps to maintain their social function. Take a village in the Beijing suburbs. All the villagers, from the village head and the party secretary down, have been baptized. The village church is actually the cultural and power center where village leaders run daily business in consultation with the clergy. Such contextualization of the Christian faith may not need to rise above the interpretation of the Christian ethic as a guiding principle for daily conduct or pursue the spiritual significance of the Christian faith.[10]

Similar cases of contextualization are not rare in the young, highly educated Chinese Christian communities. The members of one such communion in Beijing, for example, say that when they meet in house congregations they experience the pleasant feeling of being "reunited with the home group." This feeling can be understood in the context of the current impotence of the two traditional beliefs discussed earlier. Similar cases are quite common among the socially marginalized population in China.[11]

One incident that occurred at my university early last May has further strengthened my belief that Christianity is becoming an alternative faith in China. Beijing was combating SARS. Twenty-eight students of the university were quarantined because an art student with whom they had had close contact was a suspected SARS case. For the first few days, these students were depressed. When they seemed to have lifted themselves from depression and begun to feel much better, the university authorities attributed the change of mood to what they had done to soothe them, such as bringing one of them a birthday cake on his birthday, and staging a concert for them in the square in front of the building where they were quarantined. However, in a conversation I had with them after the quarantine, I learned that it was the gospel they heard from two Christians among them during the quarantine that affected their mood. A few of them were even converted to the Christian faith.

While trying to fill the vacuum left by the disappearance of the traditional values, Christianity in China is not able to break free of its mundane concerns. This inability has given rise to at least two barriers to the establishment of Christianity in China as a faith in its own right: its tendency to

10. This village church has been a case study in a field survey of a project titled *The Cultural Function of Christianity in the Ongoing Chinese Social Reform,* undertaken by the Renmin University of China, a humanities study base of the Education Ministry. The initial surveys and analyses of the project show that Christianity has been playing an alternative role to the impotent social systems in the Chinese Christian communities in the last two decades, although what happens there may not for the present apply to Chinese society as a whole.

11. Li Pingye, "A Report on the Development of Christianity in China in the 1990s," *Journal for the Study of Christian Culture* 2 (1999): 318-28.

merge with ongoing modes of religious practice and the tendency to assimilate itself to the practice of folk religions. The first tendency as shown in its way of propagation and the activities of Christian fellowships is an easy reminder of what happened during the Cultural Revolution. In the 1970s some European scholars "misread" what was happening in China in their study of Mao Zedong. French scholars Guy Lardreau and Christian Jambert, for example, found many common elements in the teachings of Mao Zedong and the early Christian doctrines.[12] Another scholar, Hebblethwaite, called Mao "a Chinese sage." Like a modern Moses, he said, Mao led his people in their struggle to break free of the chains of tyranny, imperialism, feudalism, and capitalism. He compared the Long March to the trek to the Promised Land and drew a parallel between causes of the awakening of the Chinese people during the Long March and the revelatory Ten Commandments, calling Mao a sage with the power of God.[13]

To those who lived through the Cultural Revolution, the comparison is naturally inappropriate. But among the younger generation the legacy of the Cultural Revolution is very much alive, as this complex manifests itself when they get together and feel that they are "reunited with the home group," when they compare their experiences and reflect on their behavior in a purified atmosphere, and when they think they have closed the gap between those in the mainstream and those marginalized, and take credit for that achievement. However, this tendency to contextualize the Christian church in China spells danger for the faith, as it reflects the two types of "self-righteousness" that Reinhold Niebuhr repudiates.[14] And as the practices remind one of those prevalent during the Cultural Revolution, they may not remain effective for long. As we discovered in interviews, it is precisely those gatherings, concerning which a portion of the population is enthusiastic, that keep a larger part of the population at a distance from the Christian faith.

The effort to assimilate Christianity to the folk religions in China is mainly an effort to build charismatic power with the help of divine gifts. The

---

12. Peter Hebblethwaite, *The Christian-Marxist Dialogue* (London: Darton, Longman & Todd, 1977).

13. Hebblethwaite, *The Christian-Marxist Dialogue*, pp. 77-78.

14. The first type refers to the attempt to change the transcendental ideal of Christian ethics into an inner possibility in the historical process, the second to dependence on some historical miracles to realize an ideal social order. See Reinhold Niebuhr, *An Interpretation of Christian Ethics* (Taipei: Guiguan Books, 1995), pp. 6, 11-12; *The Nature and Destiny of Man* (Hong Kong: Christian Arts, 1989), pp. 186-87.

effort can be highly productive, but its impact on the growth of Christianity in China is only a brief one and cannot win the Christian faith the recognition it desires in China. What is more, this assimilation effort has produced a negative result in the form of many "faiths" that call themselves Christian.[15]

Toivo Koskikallio, a Finnish theologian who taught at Hong Kong Lutheran Theological Seminary, said that the fundamental difference between the Chinese and Western attitudes toward Christianity is that atheism is regarded as wicked in the Western Christian world, but in China it is considered only an expression of indifference.[16] His statement has set me thinking, as discussed above, just what the Christian church must do in the Chinese context to make it compelling so as to demand expression in speech. Consideration of this issue might perhaps be an important task in addition to Christianity's missionary work in China.

15. Li Pingye, "A Report on the Development of Christianity in China in the 1990s," pp. 318-28.

16. Kaisa Nikkilä, *Christian Faith and the Secret Wisdom of China* (Helsinki: Helsinki University Press, 2000).

A Response to Professor Yang Huilin:
Contextualizing Christian Theology in China

Thor Strandenaes

Professor Yang Huilin has delivered an articulate, clear, and constructive paper in which he proposes a path that the process of contextualizing Chinese Christian theology may follow. His suggestion to focus on three areas of study is both relevant and constructive.

Truly, theology needs to be expressed in the indigenous language of a culture in order to express itself adequately to the needs and challenges of its members. Since Christianity in China has to a large extent depended on translated theologies that have been embedded in Western cultures, the time has come for it to free itself from the cultural captivity of Christian theology. But — and I will return to this point later — contextualizing theology is a comprehensive process with several aspects, where there is always the risk of entering a new kind of captivity if one is not sufficiently aware of one's presuppositions. It is the experience of Christianity down the centuries that a contextual theology that isolates itself stands the risk not only of becoming parochial, but of isolating the local church from the rest of the worldwide community of Christians, or even leading the church to heresy. Keeping this in mind, I agree with Yang Huilin that through an indigenous theological pursuit "the essence of the Christian faith, its alterity and interlinguisticity, may be revealed more effectively in Chinese Christian theology than in any theologies of the West." I approve of his approach, provided it is done on the basis of the four following premises:

- One must have within one's perspective — and make use of — the Bible, the ecumenical creeds of the Christian church, and its rich theological heritage over the centuries.

- One must keep in mind and make use of past theological reflection in China and the rich theological traditions of the Chinese church.[1]
- One must have Chinese cultural and religious tradition as a reference.
- One must use an indigenous Chinese approach to reflecting religious and ethical ideas and the Chinese language as chief medium.

These and the interlinguistic focus are necessary if one wishes to develop a truly contextual Chinese theology.

Professor Yang Huilin observes that the development of a Chinese Christian theology has so far taken place in isolation from the Chinese humanities and therefore generously invites the theological process to extend into the academic humanities area. In this way one may bridge the existing gap. His suggestion that such cooperation might take place through three disciplines (theological hermeneutics, ethics, and aesthetics) seems both realistic and relevant. These disciplines may stimulate the church and provide valuable answers to the church as it tries to formulate its doctrine and ethical thinking relevantly for Chinese society today, and when it wishes to find adequate cultural expressions of Christian faith in worship and art that are useful and will serve Chinese believers in particular and society in general.

Third, Yang Huilin points out the need for positivist research into contemporary practices of faith in China. Such research is necessary in order to assess the lasting values of existing Christian practices, including spirituality and worship life, ethos, and catechetical material. But research will also serve the church by detecting practices of faith that are dehumanizing and otherwise in contradiction with the fundamental values of Christianity. Any truly contextual theology must be liberating and assist believers and society in overcoming practices, ideologies, and forces that are dehumanizing.

It may be useful to keep in mind the twofold role that theology has played in the church throughout its history. It is a servant of the church, but also its prophetic voice. If theology is not useful to the church in naming and overcoming its problems and challenges, it has not fulfilled its duty. There is also the prophetic task. This task is to question the traditional and contemporary attitudes and works of the church, challenge it to undergo self-criticism and reform, and suggest possible, realistic, relevant, and adequate

1. One may, for example, learn what kind of approach Chinese theology in the past has had to biblical interpretation; see Thor Strandenaes, "Biblical Interpretation in the Middle Kingdom: Focus on the Choice of Paradigm in Chinese New Testament Scholarship," in *Bible, Hermeneutics, Mission,* ed. Tord Fornberg (Uppsala: Swedish Institute for Missionary Research, 1995), pp. 85-111.

solutions to its contemporary problems. It is obvious that scholars in the Chinese humanities will be able to assist theology in fulfilling both its prophetic and servant roles if only the intellectuals and the church can find good means of cooperation.

The very attitude and approach of Yang Huilin represents an important contribution to the contextualizing or reconstruction of a Chinese theology. It also illustrates that academic scholars in Chinese universities have an important role to play in the effort of contextualizing theology in China. It demonstrates beyond doubt that the Christian church in China — be it Protestant, Catholic, or of other name — cannot fully accomplish its task of contextualization or reconstruction without the assistance of the scholars of humanities in the Chinese universities. Thus, when the promotion of the Reconstruction of Theological Thinking in the Protestant Church in China became a goal of the TSPM/CCC, as reported by Cao Shengjie,[2] it is an evident weakness that in this process the TSPM/CCC and its seminaries are included, but no reference whatsoever is made to the need for including also the relevant academics in the universities of China. With Yang Huilin's excellent contribution in mind, one can only marvel that the need for assistance from such scholars as him and his colleagues in other universities is not mentioned at all. If theology in the Chinese church is to be relevant to and constructively stimulate Chinese society and its members, then why has not the church solicited the assistance of those who have an in-depth understanding of the political, religious, and sociocultural processes and institutions in Chinese society as a whole?

Doing Contextual Theology with Grass-Root Christians

It is the experience of various Christian churches in the world that, in addition to academics and theologians, lay Christians must be involved in the process of contextualizing Christian faith, with regard to both theory and practice. This experience has grown out of the fact that it is only the common believers who are able to assess whether a specific contextual theology functions adequately in their lives and has relevance for their daily challenges, problems, and joys. Among many possible examples, I wish here to draw the attention to the process of contextualizing Bible reading and theol-

---

2. Cao Shengjie, "Put Down Roots and Build, Strengthen Ourselves, Move with the Times and Run the Church Well," *Chinese Theological Review* 16 (2002): 19.

ogy at large in South Africa.[3] It has become a bearing principle for these in-digenous theologies to insist that theology can only have relevance as long as it can be said to meet and match the experience and reflection of church members at large. So, when the reconstruction of Chinese theology is to be made, it cannot neglect Chinese Christians at large, their faith experience and hopes. Thus, the agenda of a Chinese theological reconstruction must not only pay attention to the views of academics and church theologians but also to those of the grass-root Christians.

This means that contextualizing Christian theology in China cannot succeed without a dialogue between Chinese academics, theologians, and common Christians. Without their joint involvement Chinese contextual theology may become a manifestation of the Chinese Christian leadership alone, or of academia, without relevant contact with daily life in Chinese society. Doing contextual theological reflection is not solely a task of trained theologians, the leaders of the church, and the academics. Unless grass-root Christians are involved in the process of doing theology, contextual theology will not be relevant for people at large and may fall short of adequately deal-ing with the pressing questions of life and death in the lives of people.

Four Perspectives When Doing Contextual Theology

Since a conscientiously developed contextual theology started to develop more than three decades ago, various theologians have undertaken to clas-sify different kinds of and approaches to contextual theology.[4] Past experi-ence from contextualizing Christian theology and church practices leads me to suggest that one must keep in mind the following four perspectives when doing Chinese contextual theology, that is, if one wishes to achieve an ade-quate result:[5]

3. Gerald O. West, *Contextual Bible Study* (Pietermaritzburg: Cluster Publications, 1993); Gerald O. West, *Biblical Hermeneutics of Liberation* (Pietermaritzburg: Cluster Publi-cations and Maryknoll: Orbis Books, 1995). Similar experience has been made in Latin America; see, e.g., Carlos Mesters, *Defenseless Flower: A New Reading of the Bible* (Mary-knoll: Orbis Books, 1989).

4. See, for example, Stephen B. Bevans, *Models of Contextual Theology* (Maryknoll: Orbis Books, 1992), pp. 23ff.; Tiina Ahonen, *Transformation through Compassionate Mission: David J. Bosch's Theology of Contextualization* (Helsinki: Luther-Agricola-Society, 2003), pp. 28-39.

5. These four perspectives have, for example, been pointed out as distinctive and neces-

- *The culture-affirming perspective.* Belief in the Creator implies that there is always something good, unselfish, and beneficial in human cultural activity, since men and women are considered co-workers of God. Contextual theology in China must search for these elements in Chinese culture and Christian tradition, name and define them, affirm their value, and include them.

- *The critical or counter-cultural perspective.* The fact that humankind in any cultural activity also includes evil, selfish, estranging, abusive, violent, and oppressive elements means that one task of theology is to identify, challenge, and reject them. This belongs to the transforming task of theology.

- *The cross-cultural perspective.* Belief in what the Apostolic Creed calls the "one, holy and Catholic church" implies that truth which is found in the church elsewhere in the world may not only correspond with the faith and experience of the Chinese church but also enrich and enhance its theology, and vice versa. Chinese theology should therefore feel free to adopt from other Christian cultures whatever is found to be acceptable and beneficial to Chinese Christians and corresponds to their own experience and hopes. A theology that isolates itself from the Christian community everywhere and throughout the ages, or neglects the common Christian heritage of faith, equally rejects the oneness in faith and the belief that the church has one Lord.

- *The transcultural perspective.* There are some nonnegotiable basic truths of Christianity that cannot be removed, altered, or tampered with in any church or theology without resulting in heresy. And, as heresy should be avoided and the common faith of the church universal — today and through the ages — should be recognized as normative, the transcultural truths of Christian faith must be recognized and respected.

It is evident that the process of contextualizing theology in the People's Republic of China should have China itself as its main focus. However, a true contextual theology cannot leave aside or neglect the church universal, and its experience and reflections in the ages when it developed elsewhere. The primary context for Chinese contextual theology may be China, but the

---

sary principles for contextualization of liturgy in the "Nairobi Statement on Worship and Culture: Contemporary Challenges and Opportunities," in *Christian Worship: Unity in Cultural Diversity*, ed. S. Anita Stauffer (Geneva: The Lutheran World Federation, LWF Studies, Jan. 1996), pp. 23-28.

wider context must certainly include also the sister churches all over the world. On the one hand their heritage of theological reflection since the birth of Christianity is a living resource for any church that wishes to develop a truly contextual theology. On the other hand Chinese Christian theology should not be surprised to find that its own methodology, reflection, and findings may be considered useful by other churches around the world in their struggle for providing liberating forces to society and believers. Based on the above assumptions of what may develop a truly Chinese Christian contextual theology, I welcome Professor Yang Huilin's constructive contribution and wish his project an early and successful completion.

How Do Social and Psychological Needs
Impact the Existence and Growth of Christianity
in Modern China?

Li Pingye

In addition to social, historical, and natural elements, the existence and growth of a religion is determined to a great extent by the cultural background and belief characteristics of a country or region. China is an old country that has a history of several thousand years. The richness of Chinese culture once led us to believe proudly that only in a context where no developed cultural tradition exists can Christianity be developed and that the ancient Chinese cultural tradition is self-sufficient for meeting China's spiritual, intellectual, moral, and social needs. Therefore, the Chinese cultural tradition left little space for the growth of Christianity in China. Christianity came to China during the Tang dynasty in the seventh century; afterward it was again introduced on several occasions, but Christianity has always been rejected. This history has usually been employed to support the hypothesis that Christianity cannot exist and grow in China. And this hypothesis has also been supported by the development of Protestant Christianity in China.

Deriving from a divergent civilization, Protestant Christianity has experienced difficulty in gaining acceptance by the Chinese people and in becoming one of China's main cultural streams since its introduction into China in 1807, when British missionary Robert Morrison came to China. Until the Opium War in 1840, the total number of Christians in China was less than one hundred. Even after the establishment of the unfair agreements following China's defeat in the Opium War, there were fewer than 700,000 Christians in China until 1949, when the Chinese Communist Party gained power. Thus, Christians are a very small part of the Chinese population, and it should not be forgotten that Protestant Christianity was closely related to

Western colonialism, and its mission in China has been characterized by cultural, political, and national conflicts.

After the establishment of the People's Republic of China in 1949, the Chinese people received atheistic education for over fifty years. Marxist historic dialectical materialism was sincerely accepted, and it became the Chinese people's worldview and value system. The number of Christians declined. As a foreign religion and a tool of imperialism, Protestant Christianity came to be looked down upon by many people in China. However, since the reform in 1978, various religions have again been able to grow in China, and Christianity has been especially successful. The number of Christians in China has increased by over one million almost each year. Seldom has a foreign religion been so welcomed by the Chinese people with such enthusiasm. This is not only a rare phenomenon in Chinese history but also in the history of world culture.

The recent development of Christianity in China has challenged our previous ways of thinking. The Three-Self Movement has rid Christianity of its image as "a foreign religion" to domesticate it in China; and this, of course, is one of the reasons contributing to Christianity's growth in China. However, it still cannot explain why so many people are converting to Christianity in the contemporary context, in which the Chinese economy, the living standard, and cultural education have all significantly improved. In addition, Chinese local religions such as Taoism and Buddhism seem to be developing more slowly than Christianity now. All these phenomena compel us to consider why Christianity has developed so rapidly in contemporary China from a viewpoint of the relationship between Chinese traditional customs and foreign culture. Can Chinese culture, which is dominated by Confucianism, offer space and social basis for foreign cultures to grow in China? What is the mode of relationship between the Chinese traditional culture and foreign culture? Will the development of Christianity in China again lead to new social or cultural conflicts? I will try to examine these questions in the present article.

Chinese Humanist Secularism

Chinese culture is characterized as humanist secularism. Ancient Chinese culture once possessed strong religious characteristics, and this has played an important role in the establishment and development of the Chinese nation. However, since the Period of Spring and Autumn (771 BCE), humanist culture has been established in China, and it has made Chinese culture different from other cultures in overlooking the future world and gods and spirits. On the one hand, Chinese humanist culture has opened a door for foreign religions to enter China easily and has made it possible for all religions to exist and grow in China; however, Chinese traditional culture has also dominated Chinese ideology and thereby limited the growth of all religions.

One feature of traditional Chinese humanist culture is its tolerance, which has given birth to a pluralist culture and faith in China. Chinese history over several thousand years has been full of conflicts among different ethnic groups, cultures, and religious faiths, and finally it has become a united pluralist culture. Theoretically each nation has its own culture, ways of thought, and value system; all religions have different gods and liturgical customs; and each one of them considers itself the only correct one and wishes to overcome others. In this sense, each culture has an exclusive feature. Once a religion is united with political power, this exclusive feature will bring religious wars and lead to persecution of people of other religious traditions.

In Chinese history, since the Period of Spring and Autumn (771 BCE), religion has always been separated from politics; no religion has ever occupied a dominant position in China, and almost all historical rulers have neither especially supported a local religion nor rejected a certain religion. This mode of politics and religion has left the Chinese people free to choose their faiths, and different religions can exist peacefully together. Thus, it is also normal for a certain person to belong to Buddhism, Taoism, and Confucianism at the same time, something that Europeans and Muslims can hardly imagine on the basis of their historical experience.

There were almost no religious persecutions or religious wars in Chinese history. In the Tang dynasty, some emperors tried to destroy Buddhism for political, economic, and personal as well as religious reasons; but this period of persecution was relatively short. The Chinese way of thought is to be concerned with the real world rather than a transcendental world, and there are many political disputations but very few religious disputations in China. Thus, one can find political heresies, but it is difficult to find religious heresies in Chinese history. This feature of tolerance enables foreign religions to enter China, and foreign cultures may become part of the Chinese cultural soil to grow in the Chinese pluralist culture. It was on the basis of the earlier experience of Buddhism, Taoism, Islam, and Catholicism in finding a place for themselves within Chinese culture that Protestant Christianity began to carve out a space for itself.

Any foreign culture and religion should respect Chinese traditional culture, folk customs, and Chinese authority if it wishes to exist and to grow in China. The Rites Controversy at the end of the Ming and beginning of the Qing dynasties indicated the typical strength and pride of Chinese traditional culture, and a challenge to this culture led to the failure of Roman Catholic Christianity. As to the anti-Christian movement since the 1920s and the slow development of Christianity in the eighteenth and nineteenth centuries, the main reason for these factors was the tension between imperialism and Chinese nationalism.

This-Worldly Confucianism

Although the Chinese system separated religion from politics and people had the freedom to choose their faith, religious adherents in China were only a very small part of the total population. On the other hand, atheists had never become a majority either. Between the two extremes are the people who hold folk beliefs, whose main features are ancestor worship and respect for ghosts and gods. This majority should not be forgotten by any research as far as Chinese culture is involved. In studying how Confucianism has influenced the Chinese people in choosing their faiths, we should investigate the folk beliefs in China; otherwise we cannot understand the Chinese religious phenomenon.

Since the Period of Spring and Autumn, humanism has influenced every aspect of Chinese social life, and it has also influenced people in choosing faith, lifestyle, and value system. Chinese traditional culture is dominated by Confucianism, but it is a pluralist system that also includes elements of Taoism, Legalism, the Yin-Yang school, and other folk beliefs. Early Confucianism focused on benevolent politics, humanism, and idealism; and it emphasized changing politics with morality, a concept that could not be accepted by a corrupt ruling class. Confucius, the founder of Confucianism, was rejected by most rulers then. However, as a political philosophy, Confucianism offered society and people a system of political ideology, moral principles, values, a philosophy of life, and a guide for people in dealing with other people. It offered the ruling class a knowledge system, legal system, and practical system.

Later, Confucius was honored as a great teacher and sage, especially through the cultural policy of appreciating Confucianism and rejecting others, which was introduced by Emperor Wu in the Han dynasty (206 BCE-220 CE). Confucianism thereby became the dominant and mainstream culture in

China, and finally it became the official ideology. In the process of becoming the official ideology, Confucianism lost much of its strength and power. Since then almost all Chinese officials have been Confucians. The National Examination System was established during the Tang dynasty (618-907), and Confucianism began to be closely related to politics. All people who wished to hold an official position were required to take Confucianism as their ideology.

Confucianism is not only the official ideology of China; it has also deeply influenced the common people, and its basic ethical principles has controlled Chinese values and faith. Confucianism is concerned with this world; it does not encourage people to talk about the abnormal, the strange, or gods, and it teaches people to respect ghosts and gods but to keep a distance from them. Consequently, it is characterized by secularism and utilitarianism. According to Confucianism, the *Dao* of Heaven is far away and the *Dao* of humanity is nearby, which means that the Heavenly *Dao* cannot be understood and grasped by human rationality, and in this respect Confucianism is not different from other religions. However, Christianity tells people to rely on faith because human rationality is finite and to depend on the *Dao*, which cannot be reached by human rationality. People should worship the Heavenly *Dao*, and for the sake of it Christianity teaches people that they may even sacrifice this-worldly benefits and themselves. Confucianism offers a different teaching.

Only after one understands certain issues can one believe in it; if one cannot understand something he will naturally keep a distance from it, and human beings should be led by rationality. The value and meaning of human life are found in finite life and this-worldly affairs, and a person is to do his duty and responsibility in practicing personal morality, taking care of his family, ruling the country, and controlling the world. Therefore, the following guidelines have become principles of human behavior: "If one cannot serve human beings, how can one serve ghosts?" "To perform one's own responsibility and to wait for the fate of Heaven." The Confucian feature of neglecting the future world and emphasizing this world is different from features of many other cultures.

The Confucian view of ghosts and gods has influenced Chinese intellectuals and the common people differently, and this is also an indication of a pluralist faith. On the one hand, people from different social positions, cultural levels, and ethnic groups have different faiths. On the other hand, a single religion can influence different people differently because of their social positions, cultural backgrounds, and the regions in which they live.

Among Chinese intellectuals Confucianism has occupied a dominant position, and Taoism has been in a secondary position. Confucianism offers an action principle and a basis for intellectuals to make society and their own personalities perfect. Taoism offers spiritual reliance when they fail in social and political life. Because Confucianism and Taoism do not have transcendence and mysticism, they cannot satisfy the religious needs of the common people in the context of unpredictable fate and an unjust world. The existence of religion is rooted in basic human psychological needs. In the pragmatic soil of Chinese culture, no transcendental or mystical religion can find space to exist and to grow. Buddhism has a concern with the future world after this life; thus, it was welcomed immediately by many people. However, different people have reacted to Buddhism differently. Intellectuals have found philosophical elements from Buddhism; the common people have found spiritual reliance and hope from it, but their worship of Buddha has become a style of folk religion. Taoism as a religion is welcomed by the common people, but intellectuals are interested in Taoism only from a philosophical perspective.

In summary, we may say that, among the common people, both Buddhism and Taoism occupy a dominant position, but behind them are the main folk beliefs such as worshiping ancestors and offering sacrifice to ghosts and gods. Since they lack strict organization, systematic classics, typical liturgy, and trained clergy, folk beliefs exist in the form of semi-religion. On the one hand, they cannot be compared with the systematic and high religions; on the other hand, their tendency toward theism becomes a resource in converting to higher religions. In China the stable religious adherents are always a small part, but the majority of common people, who believe in the ghosts and gods of folk religions or semi-religious faith, have become a potential group for conversion to Christianity and other religions as they do their missionary work in China.

Individual versus Collective Values

China has experienced many ideological difficulties, and this has offered a chance for Christianity and other religions to exist and to grow. Human beings are rational beings and are also feeling beings. Rationality and feeling are two important parts of human nature, and they are also the inner power that enables philosophy and religion to exist and grow. The essence of Chinese traditional culture is to unify rationality and feeling harmoniously so as to form a reasonable secular humanism. If feeling rejects rationality and the two forces become contrary to each other, human desire will be dominant; if rationality totally rejects feeling, it will lead to an irrational and anti-human situation. However, the Confucian emphasis on this world will naturally lead the Chinese people to appreciate rationalistic thinking. Especially among intellectuals rationality has occupied the highest position. Confucianism itself emphasizes benevolence, balance (or mean), and tolerance, but if it is developed to an extreme, it possibly leads to a split in human nature and even an irrational situation of "killing people in the name of principle."

Chinese secular rationalist culture has produced the ancient advanced civilization of China and many great thinkers, but its extreme manifestation has also prevented the development of society and human nature during modern times. Confucian emphasis on rationality has rejected almost all irrational elements in life. For example, Confucianism teaches: "Don't watch it if it does not fit ritual propriety, don't listen to it if it does not fit ritual propriety, don't speak it if it does not fit ritual propriety, and don't act on it if it does not fit ritual propriety"; therefore, "to keep Heavenly principle and to destroy human desire" has become the highest admonition of sages.

This kind of teaching limits human beings to a rational framework, and human individualism and personal ideas have lost the possibility for development. Confucianism has a strong idea of responsibility and participation; for example, it teaches people "to worry about [country] before all others in the world, and to enjoy [one's life] after all others in the world," and this teaching asks people to put personal benefit after community and country. However, if this emphasis is developed to an extreme, personal interest will be pressed and will come into conflict with the benefit of the community.

This kind of extreme emphasis has prevented the development of society, and has been criticized strongly since the beginning of the twentieth century. However, the critics of Confucianism in the May Fourth Movement of 1919 changed neither the essence of Chinese cultural secularism and utilitarianism nor the priority of community over individuals. This criticism has not led to change in the Chinese way of thinking, but it has shaken the Chinese power of criticism and principle of action and morality. Because of this criticism there has been a national nihilism in China. At the beginning of the twentieth century Marxism led the Chinese people to find a new way to the future.

Marxism was not in conflict with Chinese traditional culture, since rationality, participation, and the emphasis on community encouraged the Chinese people to actively join the revolution. On the other hand, the terrible conditions and corrupt government in old China forced the Chinese people to seek a new life. Therefore, the effectiveness of Marxism and the necessity of revolution contributed to the success of Marxism in China. The great progress shortly after liberation in 1949 also became an important reason for the decline of religions and the development of Marxism.

Since the 1950s there has been a series of criticisms of non-Marxist scholars such as Hu Shi, Yu Pingbo, Feng Youlan, and Liang Shumin. This criticism on the one hand strengthened the dominant position of Marxism (dialectical materialism and historical materialism) in Chinese ideology; on the other hand, it encouraged the style of emphasizing rationalism and pressing personal individualism. Therefore, if only one way of thinking is allowed, rationality will not be rationalist anymore. Dogmatism, extremism, and leftism have in this way been destroying Marxism.

The Cultural Revolution (1966-76) was a continuation of the cultural criticism of the 1950s. The whole nation became involved in a crazy movement, and the whole country became irrational. The aim of the "Gang of Four" was to gain ruling power in China, and they took advantage of the Chinese people's faith in Maoism and socialism and changed Marxism into a kind of religion. In fact, they played a game of "killing people in the name of principle." The Cultural Revolution finally became a crazy movement and badly damaged Marxism and Maoism. The worst damage of the Cultural Revolution was the damage to human minds (hearts), and people even forgot that their choices were a result of their rational thought. While it is probably not true to say that there is now a crisis of faith in China, some people indeed are in doubt, wandering and seeking.

Without Faith No Morality Is Possible

Since the reform and opening policy at the end of the 1970s, the discussion concerning the Standard of Truth has enabled people to liberate their thoughts, and personal individual thinking has become active in China. Many areas that were earlier forbidden have been explored, and many subjects formerly denied and criticized have been reconsidered. However, the development of economics has pushed social science to a side position, since people are more interested in how to make the country strong economically so as to become a great nation in the world.

In the following years, scientific research and economics developed rapidly, and the standard of living improved. However, many new social problems have also appeared. For example, the gap between Eastern and Western regions within China has become more and more problematic, and the gulf between poor and rich people has become greater and greater; social morality has been declining generally, the environment has suffered terrible degradation, human relationships have become colder, and corruption has become common. All these phenomena make people feel that society is losing its principles, and the evil of human nature becomes obvious in the face of material temptation. Chinese traditional values and ideology, action principles, and faith systems have been greatly challenged.

Again we must face the important issue concerning how to resolve the corruption of human nature and how to rebuild Chinese ritual propriety to be a good nation. In addition to feeling and rationality, morality should also be emphasized as a crucial element within human nature, since selfishness seems to be the source of every sin in the world. The Chinese are eager to rule the country with law and morality. The Chinese people have realized that not only the establishment of a legal system but also the building of morality and individual personality is necessary. The Chinese people have realized that without faith as its basis no morality can become really meaningful to people, no matter whether this faith is religious or secular. Chinese people have also realized that although Confucianism has not been destroyed during history, it needs new strength to help modern people become inwardly sages and to cleanse human nature and serve as a principle for the society.

In addition, the utilitarianism of Chinese culture can lead people to judge everything according to its contribution to success in this world, thus tempting them to denigrate morality and do anything necessary in order to reach their own goals. All these factors will lead to the decline of morality. Therefore, on the one hand, Chinese culture produces many heroes who sacrifice themselves for the nation; on the other hand, it also produces many "successful people" who are selfish but are good at the struggle for power and at deceit. We do not know whether such an extreme rationalism, lacking human concern, can help China achieve positive development, but we know that it can lead the whole nation into disaster. In a world of material desires, human beings need a power to transcend themselves and the material world.

It is a natural characteristic of human beings that they seek spiritual meaning and life value and seek to transcend themselves, and this characteristic distinguishes human beings from other animals. This feature and the limits of human beings themselves offer both a possibility and a need for religions to exist and to grow. Confucianism and other philosophies cannot resolve problems of human ultimate concern, human limitations, human identity, and the problem of death. In contemporary China we are facing a totally new environment that presents us with many challenges as we struggle to survive and cope with psychological pressures.

The Utilitarianism of Chinese Religious Life

Protestant Christianity has become the first choice for many Chinese religious people, and this phenomenon is closely related to the structure of adherents, the basic features of adherents, and the characteristics of Christianity.

The majority of contemporary Chinese religious adherents reside in the countryside. Most of them are aged, female, and illiterate. The secular, this-worldly focus and humanism of traditional Chinese culture have caused people's folk religions to develop in profoundly utilitarian and superstitious directions. These characteristics, in turn, have had an impact on other religions. For example, after its introduction into China, mystical Indian Buddhism took on a Chinese style that is quite different from the original Indian one. The Chinese-styled Buddhism, Taoism, folk religions, and even Protestant Christianity have been accepted by increasing numbers of people. In general, people are not exclusively loyal to any one of them, but on the other hand, these religions can satisfy their utilitarian needs.

Pragmatic utilitarianism has become a basic attitude of Chinese people to religions. Thus, Buddhism, Taoism, and Confucianism have coexisted peacefully in China, and they have absorbed elements from one another; very often it is difficult to ask a common person to identify himself or herself as belonging to a certain one of the three. It is quite common that a single person belongs to the three religions at the same time or today belongs to one and tomorrow belongs to another religion. For many Chinese people, the important question is which religion can satisfy their pragmatic utilitarian needs, regardless of which theology it affirms.

Survival needs constitute the basic reason for Chinese people to believe in a religion. Few people will ask questions such as "Who am I?" "Where am I from?" and "Where will I go?" since most of their concerns center on the realistic problems in their daily lives rather than on abstract philosophical or religious questions. Most Chinese Christians were not converted by rational argument. Christian doctrines such as the Trinity, the incarnation, the virgin birth, and original sin are in conflict with Chinese ways of thinking, but this does not bother Chinese Christians so much, since many people argue that "I believe in it just because it is irrational" (Tertullian's words). After knowing that Christianity can heal people, give them peace, and help their children behave well, and after coming to know the love of Christians, many Buddhists, Taoists, and folk religion adherents are very easily converted to Christianity. They accept Christianity in a characteristically utilitarian Chinese way.

Among the five official religions in China, Protestant Christianity is the only one that has developed with modern society. Although it has the same roots as Catholicism, it is simpler. The complexity of Catholicism has become one of the main obstacles to its acceptance by the Chinese people. The Reformation of Luther, Calvin, and Zwingli offered a new strength to Christianity in aspects such as theology, doctrine, liturgy, and religious rules, since it accords with the new developments in society. Protestants reject the control of the Roman Catholic pope and clergy over society, and Christians and have put the authority of salvation into the hands of common Christians.

This enables common people to enjoy greater freedom in choosing faith and in dealing with secular issues. Protestants appreciate a simple form, and this has made Christian development easier. The democratic administration of the church has also fit the development of society. Protestants especially oppose Catholic rejection of the value of secular life and have encouraged people to do their work well and to contribute to the development of society and regard this-worldly success as a mark of salvation. The Protestant Reformation made it possible for capitalism to flourish and became a spiritual power for the new inhabitants in North America. Consequently, Protestant Christianity finally became a worldly religion that developed quickly.

After the Open-Door Policy was applied in China, the Chinese people suddenly got a strong impression of the gap between China and the West. Chinese people noticed the advanced development of Western countries in science, technology, and education, and the contrary situation in China. This huge gap led the Chinese people to wish strongly to learn from the West so as to develop their own country. The Western way of development, its spiritual inheritance and cultural strength, have greatly interested the Chinese people. During the process of learning about the West, the Chinese people noticed the popular influence of Christianity in the Western world. Undoubtedly, if one wishes to understand the Western world, one must understand Christianity. We cannot simply regard Christianity as a tool of imperialism and superstition anymore. The Chinese Three-Self Movement has made Christianity a Chinese religion, and many misunderstandings regarding Christianity have already been eliminated. Some scholars, especially those who have studied abroad, have found a totally new spirit that is different from that of traditional Chinese culture. They propose that China respond to such a spirit, and consider this response a necessary process if China wishes to participate fully in the modern world. These factors constitute the background of the "Christianity fever" that swept over China shortly after adoption of the reform policy.

Of course, we should also admit that the destruction of Buddhism, Taoism, and other folk religions in the 1950s has also created space for Christianity to grow in China. Protestant Christianity has now become the most rapidly developing religion in China. Features of Protestant Christianity such as its concern with this world, its simplicity, and its adaptability have made it possible for Protestant Christianity to adapt easily to the utilitarianism of Chinese folk religions, and it has shown a superiority to Buddhism, Taoism, and Catholic Christianity in China in spite of the fact that these other religions have a longer history in China. Although each religion is established on the basis of rational thinking, common Chinese religious adherents do not usually think too much when they accept religions quickly, since utilitarianism is their primary concern. In fact, Buddhism, Christianity, and Islam all become mature in the process of social development and develop together with the development of society. Their classics are full of philosophical reasoning and are the result of human reason and human culture. The religious fever in China after the Cultural Revolution was not a result of the rational elements of these religions, and irrational feeling and mysticism are the main factors contributing to the growth of religions in contemporary China.

Christianity Attracts the Well-Educated

Christianity has different characteristics as it develops among different social classes. The faith of intellectuals in the cities is very different from that of common people in the countryside. Recently some highly educated people have been attracted to Christianity; and, although they constitute only a small part of the total Christian population, their influence is great and powerful. This group includes people who have received a good education abroad, white-collar workers in Sino-foreign joint ventures, teachers and students in universities, and others. Although they have different reasons for having become Christians, the features of their faith are similar.

The reason for their interest in Christianity may involve a spiritual search. Some are attracted through an academic interest in Western civilization, some are searching for values and the meaning of life, some are seeking consolation in their hearts, some come to Christianity because of doubts regarding their original faith, some come out of their environmental concerns, and some are responding to the difficulties and suffering they have experienced. Regardless of the reason for coming to Christianity, they all carry doubts and worries and hope to find answers from Christianity.

Their choice of faith is a result of rational thought. They are not influenced by the pragmatic utilitarianism that is so important to illiterate people. Furthermore, their faith is usually strong, and they are not easily persuaded to give up their faith regardless of what happens in the world around them. Their faith is more individual. For them faith is not only a personal issue but also an issue of the heart, and they can find satisfaction on their own. Thus they usually do not have close contact with local churches and pastors. They do not think that the local church can offer them what they are looking for. They often form their own groups to connect with people who have interests similar to their own.

There is also a deep distinction in the practice of faith among these people. Though deeply influenced by Chinese traditional culture, they do not strictly follow Christian liturgy or rules, and they are not so interested in worship, the sacraments, Bible study, or prayer either. They accept Christianity with the realistic spirit of Confucianism and the liberal spirit of Taoism. Outer form and rule are not so important for them; they are more interested in inner spirit. These people are usually open-minded, and they are open to dialogue with other scholars who study religions. They are also interested in academic exchange with foreign theologians all over the world. Others may be quite excellent specialists in their own scientific fields but may not know traditional Chinese culture well. Their faith in Christianity is usually traditional, conservative, dogmatic, and even fundamentalist. They emphasize worship and religious liturgy, and they are less open to academic exchange with international theologians.

Although the number of Christian intellectuals has increased recently, they are still a very small part of the entire group of Chinese Christians. Since intellectual Christians frequently do not identify with local churches, they are influenced very little by the Chinese church; for the same reason, they also have little influence on the Chinese church.

The Problems of the Growing Christian Religion in China

In the process of the Chinese economic structure becoming pluralist, Chinese ideology is also becoming pluralist. Marxism is the dominant ideology, but Confucianism remains deeply embedded in Chinese culture, and Protestant Christianity is the most rapidly developing religion. The three ideologies encounter one another, and together they are constructing the distinctive ideology of Chinese special socialism. Although the three ideologies are different from one another, because traditional Chinese culture is exceptionally tolerant, the three can finally coexist peacefully together in contemporary China. Of course, conflicts among them also frequently occur. Pluralism will be the feature of Chinese ideology for a quite long time into the future. What will happen in the future? Will Christianity, as a Western civilization, challenge Chinese Confucianism and socialist Marxism? Will this potential challenge lead to political struggle? These questions should be considered.

We will continue to take Marxism as the dominant ideology in China, since only Marxism can lead China to become sufficiently strong to survive in the world. However, Marxism is not only dogmatics; it is a living worldview and methodology. To apply Marxism with special Chinese characteristics has been a main task for Chinese leaders such as Mao Zedong and Deng Xiaoping. Marxism's ability to grow together with the time has given it a new living power in China, and it will coexist together with other ideologies. Our Communist Party has employed a religious policy to separate religion from politics and stresses that all people should be united together politically to contribute to the country and should respect one another in their faiths. This policy has guaranteed the implementation of religious freedom, and difference of faith is no longer a political issue. Thus, people with different religious faiths may live together peacefully under the leadership of the Chinese Communist Party and socialism. This policy has essentially resolved the tension between Marxism and other religions and ideologies.

Confucianism is one of the world's primary cultural traditions, and it has played a very important role in maintaining development in Chinese history continuously over several thousand years. The pluralism of Chinese traditional culture is dominated by Confucianism. It is a very special phenomenon in world history and has influenced China and the whole of East Asia for a very long time until, finally, a "circle of Confucian culture" has been formed. If Confucianism wishes to continue its contribution in the modern period, it needs to develop itself in order to fit the new requirements of the time. The fate of Confucianism and its future in China and the world depend on whether it can be modernized so as to fit the new developing situation of the world. Many resources within Confucianism should be able to face the challenges of modernity. For example, Confucian emphasis on the meaning of human life can act as a warning for contemporary people in their desire for material and money.

In contemporary China, because of the development of materialism and the emphasis on earthly success, individualism has been highly developed, but the spirit of sacrifice for the sake of community has been greatly ignored. Confucian traditional values of collectivism and ethics can offer great help for our reconstruction of the social spirit. In addition, Confucianism stresses harmony among human beings, the environment, and society; and this feature can also reduce the tensions and pressures that contemporary people face. Confucianism can act as an aid to Marxism in the areas of ethics and values, and the two can coexist together well. Today globalization has been becoming increasingly important; people who are tired of Western civilization are beginning to pay greater attention to Confucianism with a hope of finding insights to heal the corruptions of Western civilization. Confucianism should and can contribute to China and world civilization.

The development of Christianity in a non-Christian country shoul have two preconditions. One is to unite with local culture and to be accept by local people psychologically. Another is to modernize itself so as to fit requirements of the time.

Although Christianity has produced Western civilization and has d oped greatly in the contemporary China, it is a foreign culture for Ch people, and it does not have deep cultural roots in China. In order to and grow in China, Christianity should not only resolve the problem of ... tionship with Chinese traditional culture, but should also resolve the problem of relationship with Marxism. Additionally, it has to resolve its relationship with Buddhism, Taoism, Islam, and Chinese folk religions. Except for tension over the issue of theism and atheism, Christianity is not necessarily in conflict with Marxism; they are more similar than different, especially in aspects of ethics and value system. During recent history the conflict between Christianity and Marxism has been focused mainly on the aspect of politics. After the Opium War in the 1840s, nationalism became an element that created tension between Christianity and Chinese culture. In order for Christianity to coexist peacefully with Marxism, Chinese traditional culture, and other religions in China, the Chinese government should apply the policy of religious freedom and the separation of religion from politics; Christianity should employ ways to accommodate Chinese special socialism. Since the 1950s, Chinese Christianity has resolved the problem of authority by cutting relations with Western colonialism and by the Three-Self Patriotic Movement, and this has enabled Christianity to fit into Chinese society and to accept Chinese culture. However, it still has a long way to go if Christianity wishes to be united with Chinese culture and to resolve the problem of de-colonization and become as much a part of Chinese culture as Buddhism and Taoism are. This process will require a reform of liturgy, organization, and theological content.

The conservative nature of Protestant Christianity in contemporary China troubles many people. Although the number of Christians is becoming larger, the reason for conversion tends to be irrational rather than rational. Most Chinese Christians believe primarily in the fundamentalism and utilitarianism that were introduced into China by Western missionaries long ago and rejected by most mainstream Western Christian denominations. Although education has developed considerably in recent years, the educational situation in the countryside is, however, still far from satisfactory. Thus the irrational features of Chinese Christianity in the countryside remain very strong; feeling is valued more than reason, a situation that does not meet the requirements for social development.

This irrational feature often leads to conflicts between Christianity and society and other religions, and it sometimes leads to violence and craziness. Especially when some Christians follow heresies and break Chinese laws, not only Christianity itself is damaged but Chinese society and people are also damaged. In addition, this kind of anti-intellectual faith cannot interest Chinese intellectuals, and this situation isolates some Christian adherents from Chinese society and politics, leaving them unable to face challenges from inside and outside China. In this sense the influence of Christianity cannot be compared with that of Buddhism and Taoism in China.

The self-construction of Christian patriotic communities is also a big problem that should be resolved. Because of the Cultural Revolution, religious activities were greatly damaged, and China is now badly in need of patriotic clergy. The rapid development of Christianity in contemporary China makes the problem of lack of leaders especially obvious. Although recently many young patriotic clergy have taken positions in the church and Christian organizations, because of the immaturity of Christian communities, many problems such as corruption have occurred. Thus, in order to lead Chinese Christians to a patriotic way, in order for Christianity to maintain a place in Chinese society, in order to have healthy exchange with international society, in order to improve the relationship between Christianity and Marxism, Chinese society, and Chinese traditional culture and other religions, the church must be strengthened in its organization, thought, theology, principles and rules, and patriotic organizations. This will guarantee fulfillment of the above issues.

How Do Social and Psychological Needs Impact Christianity in China?

Although Protestant Christianity has rapidly developed in contemporary China, it cannot occupy a ruling position in Chinese ideology since no religious ideology has ever occupied such a position in Chinese history, and no religious group has held political ruling power. Christianity cannot be an exception among religions in China in this respect, as the exclusion of religions from ruling power is closely related to Chinese tradition and to the politics, economics, and cultural development of China. In Chinese history there has been no period when certain religious adherents constituted the majority of the population or a period of unification between politics and certain religions, and there will be no such period in the future. Since Marxism and Confucianism have strongly influenced the Chinese people, they will limit the development of other religions in China.

Chinese culture is great and possesses infinite potential to develop; it has produced a great history, it is producing a wonderful present, and it will also produce a good future. Today international exchange among different nations is becoming more common, and scientific development and world economic integration have produced ideological and cultural tensions in all nations. Both Confucianism and Christianity are influencing China today. This historical process will influence both China and the world. If China can resolve its various problems properly and, in the process, avoid the so-called "clash of civilizations," this will be a great contribution to the world.

A Russian Post-Soviet Response to Dr. Li Pingye

Vladimir Fedorov

It is only natural if someone, especially a Western European, suggests that the situations of the revival of religious life in post-Soviet Russia and the increasing influence of Christianity in today's China have much in common. In the consciousness of many Europeans, Russia is an Asiatic country; and besides, for many decades, the communist atheistic ideology similarly prevailed in both countries. However, in fact, the distinctions between these two countries are more essential than the similarities. A noticeable growth of Christianity in China was observed no earlier than the late nineteenth century, while the history of Christianity in Russia extends over more than a thousand years. In China, Christianity is the religion of a minority whereas the overwhelming majority of Russians in the nineteenth century were Christians (with considerable populations of Muslims and no negligible numbers of Buddhists in some areas). Nevertheless, there are common tendencies and common problems in the religious rebirth in both of our countries.

So, while Dr. Li Pingye says in her report that "Christians are a very small part of the Chinese population, and it should not be forgotten that Protestant Christianity has been closely related to Western colonialism, and its mission in China has been characterized by cultural, political, and national conflicts," we can assert with reference to Russia that dissemination of Christianity in Russia has never been related to Western colonialism.

As far as we can see, in Soviet Russia, Christianity was never viewed as a foreign religion, but connections of the church structures with Western ecclesiastical centers were treated as ideological and dangerous for the state. Slackening of open persecutions took place in the mid-1960s; and, since then, the communist atheistic ideology gradually became less aggressive. Real liberalization in religious affairs was only possible after 1988, the feast of the millennium of Christianity in Russia.

Noteworthy is the statement that "Chinese culture is characterized as humanist secularism." We in Russia cannot say that pre-Christian culture paved the way for humanism. To the contrary, it was Christianity that undoubtedly served as the ground for the seeds of humanism and specifically of Christian humanism, as can be seen today. As far back as the late nineteenth and early twentieth centuries, Russian religious and philosophical thought took the path of Christian humanism that has only recently become a major force within the Roman Catholic Church. An attempt at overcoming secular humanism failed in Russia but was successful with the Russian emigration in Western Europe from the 1920s to the 1960s.

The thesis according to which "ancient Chinese culture once possessed strong religious characteristics, and this has played an important role in the establishment and development of the Chinese nation" also requires comment. Such an approach to the issue is very close to the reflections on culture of many Orthodox theologians, e.g., the discourse of the priest Pavel Florenski: "The majority of cultures, in keeping with etymology (i.e., that which develops from *cultus*) were precisely the germination of a grain of religion, a mustard tree which grew out of a seed of faith."[1]

Such an interpretation helps to emphasize the reality and necessity of religious pluralism and calls for respect for every traditional culture because all are recognized as having a religious basis, a system of absolute values. It is obvious that both Greek and Slavonic paganism were stages of religious growth of the peoples that were not monotheistic, and overcoming paganism was not only its denial but also, to a certain degree, its inculturation, as well. Interesting too is the following statement: "One feature of traditional Chinese humanist culture is its tolerance, which has given birth to a pluralist culture and faith in China." Is this feature peculiar to Chinese culture, or is it typical of the entire Asiatic region? Generally known, for example, is the pluralism of ancient Indian religious and philosophical thought.

Another historical fact cited by Dr. Li Pingye deserves our attention: "In Chinese history, since the Period of Spring and Autumn (771 BCE), religion has always been separated from politics; no religion has ever occupied a dominant position in China, and almost all historical rulers have neither es-

---

1. Pavel A. Florenski, "Christianisme et culture," *Revue semestrielle publiée par la Bibliothèque slave de Paris* 21 (1989): 71.

pecially supported a local religion nor rejected a certain religion. This mode of politics and religion has left the Chinese people free to choose their faiths and enabled different religions to exist peacefully together." Comparing this situation with that in Russia, we have to admit that in Russia, quite to the contrary, there was always either the state religion or the totalitarian atheistic regime, and it is only for the last twelve years that an attempt at establishing a democratic society with observance of the principles of the liberty of conscience has been made. Christianity in its Orthodox tradition is predominant, a fact not related to any legal factors but, rather, to the people's culture being rooted in that tradition.

Another principal difference between the two countries lies in the fact that in Chinese culture "it is also normal for a person to belong to Buddhism, Taoism, and Confucianism at the same time," and in the fact that "it is difficult to find religious heresies in Chinese history." On the contrary, in European culture and Russian history in particular, the medieval zest for attacking and eradicating heresies became a part of communist ideology, since in Russia the latter was a kind of a parody of Christian church culture. The very term "Orthodox" (as signifying a firmness in one's convictions and not deviating to heresy) was coined in the secular Russian language despite its Greek ecclesiastical origin.

While examples of tolerance can be found in Chinese history, it is a new notion for Russia, although based on Christian values (love, peace, liberty of conscience). Dr. Li Pingye says that "this feature of tolerance enables foreign religions to enter China, and foreign cultures may become part of the Chinese cultural soil to grow in the Chinese pluralist culture. It was on the basis of the earlier experience of Buddhism, Taoism, Islam, and Catholicism in finding a place for themselves within Chinese culture that Protestant Christianity began to carve out a space for itself."

As to assessment of the level of religiousness of the majority — I mean Li's observation that "between the two extremes are the people who hold folk beliefs, whose main features are ancestor worship and respect for ghosts and gods" — it seems appropriate to suggest that in Russia, too, the intermediate attitude (between the two extremes, i.e., deep devotion to religious principles and active rejection of religion) prevails: faithfulness to the customs and traditions (in the case of Russia, partly Christian, partly pagan, partly superstitious). No wonder that after the crash of communist ideology, the secularized society of convinced atheists made up such a huge clientele for all sorts of fortune-tellers, "prophets," wizards, etc. who have come to be an integral part of everyday life and whose ads fill all sorts of newspapers.

Dr. Li observes that "since there is a lack of strict organization, systematic classics, and typical liturgy and trained clergy, folk beliefs have existed in the form of semi-religion. On the one hand, they cannot be compared with those systematic and high religions; on the other hand, their tendency of theism becomes a resource in converting to higher religions. In China the stable religious adherents are always a small part, but the majority of common people, who believe in ghosts and gods of the folk religions or semi-religious faith, have become a potential group for conversion to Christianity and other religions as these do their missionary work in China." People of such religious mentality need a special missionary approach that should essentially differ from the approach to a consistent materialist and atheist. True, after seventy years of atheism predominating in Russia, consistent materialists are surprisingly few. It is also true, though, that religiously literate practicing Christians are in the minority.

Dr. Li says that "since the Period of Spring and Autumn, humanism has influenced every aspect of Chinese social life, and it has also influenced people in choosing faith, lifestyle, and values. Chinese traditional culture is dominated by Confucianism, but it also includes Taoism, Legalism, the Yin-Yang school and other folk beliefs, and it is a pluralist system. . . . Later, Confucius was honored as a great teacher and sage, especially through the cultural policy of appreciating Confucianism and rejecting others, which was introduced by Emperor Wu in the Han dynasty (206 BCE-220 CE). Confucianism thereby became the dominant and mainstream culture in China, and finally it became the official ideology. In the process of becoming the official ideology, Confucianism lost much of its strength and power. Since then almost all Chinese officials have been Confucians." Confucianism has never been familiar to Russians, with the natural exception of specialists. Still, it is an object of interest to some Russian intellectuals who are keen on reading Russian translations of ancient Chinese philosophy that were published some twenty years ago. At present, of 21,000 registered religious communities in Russia, none are Confucianist, only one is Taoist, and 218 are Buddhist.

It is interesting to learn that "Confucianism has a strong idea of responsibility and participation; for example, it teaches people 'to worry about [country] before all others in the world, and to enjoy [one's life] after all others in the world,' and this teaching asks people to put personal benefit after community and country." Patriotic and national values can also be involved in religious education in Christianity. It is noteworthy that the first step toward tolerance of Christianity in the time of socialism in Soviet Russia was the realization that without a patriotic attitude there was no chance of winning the Great Patriotic War against fascism (World War II). In 1943 a special loosening of persecution was permitted by Stalin, and the Russian Orthodox Church began to grow.

The topic "ideology and religion" is very important. "China has experienced many ideological difficulties, and this has offered a chance for Christianity and other religions to exist and to grow." We need to analyze the concept of ideology and the conflict between faith and ideology. For Russia it is a big temptation to understand Orthodox belief as ideology. But we need time for this discussion.

"Marxism was not in conflict with Chinese traditional culture, since rationality, participation, and emphasizing community encouraged the Chinese people to actively join the revolution. On the other hand, the terrible conditions and corrupt government in old China forced the Chinese people to seek a new life. Therefore, the effectiveness of Marxism and the necessity of revolution contributed to the success of Marxism in China. The great progress shortly after liberation in 1949 also became an important reason for the decline of religions and the development of Marxism. . . . they changed Marxism into a kind of religion, and they, in fact, played a game of 'killing people in the name of principle.' The Cultural Revolution finally became a crazy movement and badly damaged Marxism and Maoism."

As to the positive understanding of Marxism in China and understanding it as a kind of religion, we can find many issues in common, and perhaps common understanding. This is a very deep and important topic. It is also interesting to analyze changes in today's communist mentality in Russia in relation to religion and especially to Orthodoxy.

A comparison between the Chinese and Russian economies leads us Russians to suppose that the Chinese one has developed far more efficiently and that, consequently, social problems are not so prominent in China. However, when I read that "the gulf between poor and rich people has become greater and greater; social morality has been declining generally, the environment has suffered terrible degradation, human relationships have become colder, and corruption has become common. All these phenomena make people feel that society is losing its principles, and the evil of human nature becomes obvious in the face of material temptation," I see that we are facing the same problems, and that not only the "Chinese traditional values and ideology, action principles, and faith systems have been greatly challenged," but also traditional Russian Orthodoxy.

"In order to exist and grow in China, Christianity should not only resolve the problem of relationship with Chinese traditional culture, but should also resolve the problem of relationship with Marxism. Additionally, it has to resolve its relationship with Buddhism, Taoism, Islam, and Chinese folk religions. Except for tension over the issue of theism and atheism, Christianity is not necessarily in conflict with Marxism; they are more similar than different, especially in aspects of ethics and value system."

I find some sentences on Christian fundamentalism to be very important: "Most Chinese Christians believe primarily in the fundamentalism and utilitarianism that were introduced into China by Western missionaries long ago and rejected by most mainstream Western Christian denominations. Although education has developed considerably in recent years, the educational situation in the countryside is, however, still far from satisfactory. Thus the irrational features of Chinese Christianity in the countryside remain very strong; feeling is valued more than reason, a situation that does not meet the requirements for social development. This irrational feature often leads to conflicts between Christianity and society and other religions, and it sometimes leads to violence and craziness. . . ."

We need to discuss the meaning of "fundamentalism," but there is a point in that discussion. There is a phenomenon of religious life that we meet in each religion and in each religious confession. The word "fundamentalism" is not adequate and not correct for describing the phenomenon, but it is difficult to find another good word. Terms such as "extremism," "integrationism," "extreme conservatism," and many others may be weak and incorrect. I can describe this complex with some characteristics. Among these characteristics will be radical anti-ecumenism, lack of tolerance, piety with violence, ideology instead of faith, the ignoring of social activity because of faith in the power of prayer, and many others. For a country experiencing religious rebirth, this phenomenon is a real danger. We have had this experience in Russia.

12 Eliminating Five Misunderstandings about Christianity in Chinese Academic Circles

Wang Xiaochao

Christianity is a worldwide religion with a long history. In the process of its development in different countries and areas, many conflicts and misunderstandings have appeared between it and various cultures. This is also the case in its relationship to China. The conflicts and mistakes have, on the one hand, resulted from Christianity and, on the other, from the Chinese side.

Since 1949, when the People's Republic of China was established, Christianity has become one of the official religions recognized by the Chinese government. During the period of the Cultural Revolution (1966-76), like other religions, Christianity was damaged, but it has not disappeared in China. After the Cultural Revolution, the government restored the policy of the freedom of religious faith, and Christianity again became one of the religions that may be chosen by people. The religious life of Christianity in China has been generally normalized. However, there is still a need to deepen the mutual understanding between Christianity and China in order to normalize fully the relationship between Christianity and China. In this sense, it is necessary to eliminate the misunderstandings of Chinese society.

During the thirty years since 1949, when the People's Republic of China was established, to 1978, when the Third Conference of the Eleventh Committee of Chinese Communist Party was held, many political movements swept the country and academic practice in China was abnormal. During

---

In the present work "Christianity" refers to the Catholic, Protestant, and Orthodox forms of Christianity.

this period a number of works and translations on Christianity were published. The viewpoints of some of them are extreme, but they have had great influence and have become obstacles for Chinese people's understanding of Christianity and its history. Through the efforts of Chinese scholars over the past twenty years, many results have been achieved in Chinese researches on Christianity, and one result of this success is that the misunderstandings of Christianity have been lessened to a certain extent. However, although some of the extreme viewpoints have been corrected, their influence has not been totally eliminated. In this sense, we may still say that it is necessary to eliminate the misunderstandings of Christianity within Chinese academic circles.

Academic works (or the branches of learning) are instruments of cultural heritage to be passed to future generations. They are also a bridge to connect different national cultures. This paper lists several misunderstandings of Christianity by Chinese academic critics. The purpose is not to criticize the authors of these one-sided and inaccurate viewpoints, for, in the particularly abnormal period of Chinese society in which they were shaped, such mistakes were inevitable. I have come in recent years to fear that when misunderstandings appear in academic materials, it is very hard to correct them even if you apply great effort to the task. Such materials not only influence a period but also last longer, even if scholars of religious studies have already changed their opinion. Since 1982, many viewpoints about Christianity have already changed in the Chinese fields of religious studies, but scholars in other branches of learning, the majority of them, still hold wrong viewpoints and impressions about Christianity. Many more such misconceptions are held by the common people. It is thus the responsibility of all Chinese scholars who study Christianity to change this situation. This paper will examine five major historical misunderstandings.

The Misunderstanding of the Origin of Christianity and Its Founder Jesus

For quite a long time, Chinese scholars held the viewpoint that "Christianity is a mystical kingdom, whose establishment closely relates to the legend of Jesus."[1] Concerning the origin of Christianity and its founder Jesus, some of the viewpoints of the nineteenth-century German Young Hegelians had a

---

1. Zhang Wenjian, *The History of Religions* (Changchun: Jilin Publishing House, 1981), p. 86.

strong influence in China academic circles. The book *The Life of Jesus Critically Examined,* written by David Friedrich Strauss (1808-74), the representative of this school, was not translated and published in China until 1981,[2] but its influence can be found in some later Chinese scholars' works. For example, that work posed the question:

> Whether Jesus Christ was a historical figure or a religious imagination? In the 1830-40s German Young Hegelian scholars such as David Strauss and Bruno Bauer (1809-82) criticized the stories in the Gospels; in fact, they challenged Christian belief in miracles. Strauss thought that the miracle stories in the Gospels were not historical truth but that they are the result of the transmission and development of ideas of a savior in the early Christian communities. This was a man-made concept, but it was not a deliberate fabrication by the authors of the Gospels.[3]

The British Mythology school also had a great influence within Chinese academic circles. Archibald Robertson's *The Origins of Christianity* was translated into Chinese and published quite early. The author's basic opinion concerning Jesus, the founder of Christianity, is as follows: "It is better to say that Christianity has created a Jesus than Jesus has established Christianity, since this fits historical truth."[4] Influenced by the British Mythology school, Japanese scholar Saidoku Akimitsu (1871-1911) wrote a book, *Who Is Jesus? The Obliteration of Christ,* which was translated into Chinese. He listed many cases of conflict in the Gospel narratives so as to point out that the record of Jesus can only be considered as "mythological fiction" rather than "historical truth." He concluded: "Jesus Christ was not a historical figure, and he was an idol without life, which was compounded from various matters and fragments of ancient mythologies."[5]

Many Chinese scholars' works on Christianity that were published shortly after the Cultural Revolution held opinions similar to those of the

---

2. D. F. Strauss, *Biography of Jesus,* trans. Wu Yongquan (Beijing: Commercial Press, 1981).

3. Lu Daji, *The General Introduction of the Science of Religion* (Beijing: China Social Sciences Press, 1989), p. 201.

4. Archibald Robertson, *The Origin of Christianity,* trans. Song Guihuan (Beijing: Sanlian Press, 1958), p. 29. The English version was published in 1953 (London: Lawrence & Wishart).

5. Saidoku Akimitsu, *Who Is Jesus? The Obliteration of Christ,* trans. Ma Cai (Beijing: Commercial Press, 1986), p. 85.

above scholars. For example, the book *Three Great World Religions,* which was edited by Huang Xinchuan and Dai Kangsheng, says:

> The earliest preliminary Christianity was not from heaven, but the result of class struggles in the slave system of the Roman empire. . . . In fact, no historical evidence can be found concerning Jesus who was mentioned by Christianity; none of his contemporaries had claimed to have seen him, either. All legends concerning Jesus Christ were fabricated by the church after the preliminary establishment of Christianity. History indicates that it is not like the Christian church claims that Jesus established Christianity; on the contrary, it was the Christian church which created Jesus, the image of savior.[6]

Mr. Yang Zhen's *The Outline of the History of Christianity* says also: "Christianity was not established by any single hero, but was the result of historical ages"; "There is no historical evidence faithful enough to prove the existence of a historical figure Jesus. On this point, even capitalist scholars do not deny it either. As to the Savior Jesus, who was described by the later Christian church, he is simply a representative of the slave, who fits the need of the slave-lord."[7]

Translations of Russian scholars' works since the 1980s have deepened such an opinion. For example, Klevilev's *History of Religions* advances a mythological viewpoint and claims that "Jesus was a mythological figure."[8] As academic research develops, Chinese scholars have gradually started to analyze Christianity from other perspectives. Hu Yutang, a scholar from Hangzhou University, stated quite early:

> One opinion holds that Jesus was a true historical figure, and there indeed existed such a person Jesus. There are three evidences for such an opinion: 1. The Jewish historian Josephus from the first century mentioned Jesus and said that "He was Christ." This sentence was probably rewritten by later people, but that fact cannot act as evidence to prove that Jesus did not exist as a historical figure. 2. Roman historians have mentioned that Christianity was established by a person who was called "Christ," and for Christians it was the special title of Jesus. 3. The sources of the Gospels are

6. Huang Xinchuan and Dai Kangsheng, *The Three World Religions* (Beijing: Sanlian Press, 1979), p. 18.

7. Yang Zhen, *The Outline of the Christian History* (Beijing: Sanlian Press, 1979), p. 1.

8. Klevilev, *The History of Religions,* trans. Wang Xianrui (Beijing: China Social Sciences Press, 1984), p. 137.

from those of Jesus' lifetime to the time when the Gospels were completed; various legends and records have a certain degree of authenticity. Based on these three evidences, it can be argued that Jesus was a historical figure and that he was probably the leader of a people's movement; after the failure of their movement, he was remembered by people as the Savior.[9]

At the end of the 1980s Professor Yu Ke wrote: "I think that, before new historical materials will be discovered, in the light of historical science, it is difficult to say clearly whether Jesus existed or not. But according to the present signs and Christian legends, I agree that it is more difficult to prove that Jesus did not exist than to prove that Jesus existed. The final solution to this issue will be found in reliance on new historical materials."[10] Mr. Guo Shengming wrote: "We are not able to prove whether Jesus existed in history, but one thing is certain: the historical Jesus is definitely different from Jesus Christ in mythology."[11]

Since the 1990s the major trend in Chinese academic circles is to affirm that Jesus did exist as a historical figure. Mr. Tang Yi says:

> Jesus of Nazareth was a historical figure who really existed. This Nazarene opposed the corrupt lives of the Jewish elite priests, proposed reform, gathered a group of followers, and established a small religious school: the Nazareth School. Later, because of the needs of faith or sincerity, based on the prophecy concerning a Messiah in the Jewish prophetic tradition, his disciples considered him the Messiah; thus they described him as a mythological figure, and finally he became the object, Jesus Christ, whom people worship.[12]

Two other translations, which were published at the end of the 1990s, have deepened the opinion of Tang Yi. In 1997 the translation of American scholar John Dominic Crossan's book about Jesus was published in China. The orientation of this book is cultural-anthropological, historical- and textual-critical rather than apologetic and theological. It is concerned only

9. Hu Yutang, "Jesus in History," *Journal of History Research* 2 (1981).

10. Yu Ke, "An Evaluation to the Studies of Christianity in the Recent Decade in China," *Journal of World History Research* 7 (1989).

11. Guo Shengming, *The Outline of World Civilization* (Shanghai: Shanghai Translation Press, 1989), p. 426.

12. *The History of Christianity*, ed. Tang Yi (Beijing: China Social Sciences Press, 1993), p. 25.

with the historical Jesus rather than Jesus as the object of faith; it is concerned only with the human Jesus rather than the Christ, who is God. This book has offered Chinese scholars new information concerning Western theological research on the origin of Christianity and the life of Jesus.[13] Over fifty years ago, Professor Liang Gong had translated Ernest Renan's book on the *Life of Jesus* in which the author affirmed the historical existence of Jesus and denied the divine. This work continues to have a strong influence in Chinese academic circles.[14]

China is a country where Marxism occupies the dominant ideological position. Since the 1950s there has been a process of development in opinions concerning Jesus: from totally denying to partially affirming, from total disbelief to partial belief in the records in the Gospels, from confusing history and faith to separating history from faith. This process still has a long way to go for Chinese scholars to accept the unity of historical Jesus and Christ which is the basis of religious faith.

The Misunderstanding of the Relationship between Christianity and the Roman Empire

The birth of Christianity was almost simultaneous with the establishment of the Roman Empire. "The Graeco-Roman world was the soil where Christianity was planted; the growth of seeds not only relied on the life of the seeds themselves but also relied on the soil."[15] The correct understanding of the relationship between Christianity and the Roman Empire is essential for grasping the history and tradition of Christianity. Chinese academic circles have been deeply influenced by the British historian Edward Gibbon (1737-94), who examined the reason for the fall of the Roman Empire.

Gibbon's *The Decline and Fall of the Roman Empire* (an abridgment by D. W. Low, London: Chatto & Windus, 1986) was translated into Chinese by Huang Yisi and Huang Yushi with a foreword by Qi Guojin and published by Shangwu Publishing House in 1997. The translators' preface introduced the author's biography, the background and aim of the book, and Gibbon's main ideas. With respect to Christianity, Qi Guojin wrote: "The author

---

13. John D. Crossan, *Biography of Jesus,* trans. Gao Shining and Duan Qi (Beijing: China Social Sciences Press, 1998).

14. Ernest Renan, *The Life of Jesus,* trans. Liang Gong (Beijing: Commercial Press, 1999).

15. S. Angus, *The Religious Quests of the Graeco-Roman World: A Study in the Historical Background of Early Christianity* (London: John Murray, 1929), p. 9.

[Gibbon] continually stresses that the fall of the Roman Empire was, in fact, the victory of barbarians and Christianity."[16]

This foreword has given Chinese readers the strong impression that Gibbon believed that Christianity was responsible for the fall of Roman Empire. The foreword in the Chinese translation has confused two things: one is the viewpoint of Gibbon concerning the relationship between Christianity and the fall of the Roman Empire; another is the criticism of Gibbon from British Christian churches. Qi Guojin, the author of the foreword, wrote:

> In China the original version of *The Decline and Fall of the Roman Empire* has been available for quite a long time; recently there have been some introductions to and remarks on Gibbon and his great book, and these may be represented by Professor Wu Yujin's article "Gibbon's Historical Criticism and the Rationalist Trend" (in the *Journal of Social Sciences Frontier*, no. 1, 1982). The common opinion of these works is that "The historical critical spirit of Gibbon is in accordance with the rationalism of the Enlightenment tradition, and the obvious feature of that tradition is a critical attitude to the traditional doctrines, creeds and rules of Christianity. Without doubt, these are the best parts of Gibbon's book."[17]

In fact, in his abridgment Low pointed out that "Gibbon has never attacked 'the simple and pure ideas of the Gospel,' nor has he criticized the moral ideas of Christianity as some later agnostics did. He always respected the attitude of seeking ideals sincerely and bravely."[18]

Clearly there are different emphases between English and Chinese editors of the book, and the author of the Chinese foreword and many other historians in China have misinterpreted the opinion of Gibbon himself. Through a careful reading of the original version of Gibbon's book, we may find that Gibbon "has always believed that the transmission of the Gospel and the growth of churches have been closely related to the fall of the Roman Empire; thus he has emphasized the reason and influence of such a change and has distinguished the writings and apologies of Christians themselves and those of pagans' just or unjust attitudes to Christianity."[19] However, Gibbon neither claimed Christianity as the reason for the fall of the Roman

---

16. Edward Gibbon, *The Decline and Fall of the Roman Empire* (Beijing: Commercial Press, 1997), p. 10.

17. Gibbon, *The Decline and Fall*, p. 13.

18. Gibbon, *The Decline and Fall*, p. 5.

19. Gibbon, *The Decline and Fall*, p. 11.

Empire nor denied Christianity totally. What he did was to analyze rationally the relationship between Christianity and the Roman Empire. That relationship was not a simple one of the rise of Christianity as cause and the fall of empire as effect but rather a relationship of mutuality.

Some other translated publications published in China since the end of the 1970s have also mentioned reasons for the fall of the Roman Empire, but no one has had as great an influence as Gibbon's book.[20] Some of Gibbon's opinions, which have been wrongly interpreted by Chinese scholars, have produced fear among Chinese people that a new religion can probably make an empire fall. Thus, it is natural that Chinese people are on guard against Christianity. In recent years in my works I have expressed the opinion that the origin of any empire's fall exists within the empire itself; no external elements should be claimed as the reason for an empire's fall. The Roman Empire had a close relationship with the rise of Christian culture. It does not fit the historical facts and is also too narrow-minded to say that Christianity was the reason for the Roman Empire's fall.[21]

The Misunderstanding of the Relationship between Christianity and Western Classical Philosophy

As a theistic culture that originated in the Middle East, the essence of Christianity is different from the polytheistic Western classical culture. Thus, the rise and development of Christianity resulted in conflict with the Roman-Greek classical culture. After Christianity became the state religion, the beautiful classical images of the pagan religions were destroyed; the literatures and scientific activities that were related to idol worship were forbidden. Christians obliterated the earlier texts inscribed on sheepskins and wrote Christian Scriptures on them, and the pagan temples were changed into Christian churches. Especially after the fall of the Western Roman Empire, Western culture experienced a wave of decline. Therefore, many people believe that Christianity was a causal factor in the decline of Western European cultures before the Middle Ages. Greek and Roman philosophies were

20. Edward Zeller, *The Outline of the History of Greek Philosophy,* trans. Won Shaojun (Jinan: Shangdong People's Publishing House, 1992), p. 222; George Foot Moor, *History of Religions,* vol. 2, *Christianity* (Beijing: Commercial Press, 1981), p. 143; Bertrand Russell, *A History of Western Philosophy,* trans. He Zhaowu (Beijing: Commercial Press, 1981), p. 342.

21. Wang Xiaochao, *On the Argument between Hellenization and Christianization* (Hangzhou: Zhejiang Social Sciences Press, 1997).

important parts and representatives of the Western classical culture. Classical Greek philosophy also faced decline while the Roman Empire collapsed. Thus, the relationship between Christianity and Western classical philosophy has naturally been noticed by Chinese scholars.

Regarding this issue, Chinese scholars have been accustomed to reflecting upon it from the standpoint of philosophy. Mr. Ye Xiushan has pointed out as follows:

> It has long been attempted to meld Christianity, which has been rooted in Europeans' hearts, together with European philosophy, which was based on the Greek tradition; to make Christianity a necessary part of the philosophical system rather than external to philosophy; to absorb Christianity into philosophy; to consider and to offer philosophical explanations and apologies for Christian doctrines. This attempt was made by many philosophers, thinkers such as the medieval Sts. Augustine, Thomas and Anselm, especially by the later Descartes, Spinoza, and Leibniz, and especially Kant, the most important synthesizer.[22]

However, the relationship between Christianity and Western classical philosophies should not only be examined from the context of philosophy but should also be analyzed in the concrete cultural context.

When Christianity began, Greek philosophy had already existed for several hundred years. The systems of Democritus, Plato, and Aristotle had shown their glories during the greatest age of Greek philosophy, and they had been appreciated by many people. The later Greek philosophical schools were not as powerful as the earlier ones were, and strong pragmatic, ethical, and religious tendencies had been appearing; but they were still a spiritual power that was opposed to Eastern religions. After the establishment of the Roman Empire, the tradition of appreciating Greek culture resulted in a revival of the Greek culture and philosophy all over the empire. It seems that Greek culture had developed very well. A variety of original Greek philosophical schools had been able to continue and develop. In the process of urbanization, philosophical classrooms had become a common phenomenon in cities. Philosophy had been included in the education program for elite youths. Philosophers had the opportunity to enter into royal courts and to participate in political activities. Seneca, the court adviser of Nero, and the Roman emperor Marcus Aurelius were important representatives of the Aristotelian school. Plato's ideal of philosopher king became almost a reality in the Roman Empire.

22. Ye Xiushan, "How Philosophy Destructed Religion," *Journal of Philosophy* 7 (1997): 20.

After its rise, Christianity spread and sought to capture the spirit of the Mediterranean area. Because of the conversion of many intellectuals who knew Greek culture and philosophy, Christianity quickly changed its primary mystical features and finally developed its own theology and philosophy. From the second century, Christian church fathers started to criticize the various polytheistic religions of the Roman Empire. The Greek philosophies, which became gradually ethical and religious, also received criticism from them. Because of political developments, Christianity finally occupied the position of the state religion. In 529 the Eastern Roman emperor Justinian ordered all the philosophical schools in Athens closed, and the development of Greek philosophy was arrested.

If we examine the above history of thought objectively rather than only in the light of philosophical development, it is not difficult to realize that the relationship between Christianity and Western philosophy was mainly expressed in the process by which Christian intellectuals selectively chose various Greek philosophies, rather than in intellectuals accepting Christianity in light of Greek philosophies. Of course, such a claim does not deny that Greek philosophers also absorbed certain elements from Christianity. For example, Gnostic philosophers absorbed and changed some Christian doctrines. Nor does it deny certain commonalities between Christianity and Greek philosophies, for example, the rationalism of Greek philosophy and monotheism of Christianity. Some scholars argue that "Christian intellectuals absorbed Greek philosophical understanding and forms of argument to develop an apology for the Christian faith." In fact, absorption is selective acceptance. Concerning the relationship between Plato and Christianity, Karl Marx wrote: "It is more correct to say that in Christianity there are Platonic elements than to say that in Plato there are Christian elements."[23]

Similarly, the main issue in understanding the relationship between Christianity and Western philosophy is not the question as to whether some ideas of one were absorbed by the other; the main issue is in what light these absorptions took place — that is to say, in what orientation the absorptions were made. Christian intellectuals such as Augustine, Anselm, and Thomas absorbed many elements from Greek philosophies, but they never left their Christian positions; their absorption had a clear purpose of creating an apology for the Christian faith. This fact is undoubted. It is not factual to say that they deconstructed religion through philosophy, since such a claim presupposes that

---

23. Karl Marx, *Collected Works*, vol. 40 (London: Lawrence & Wishart, 1983), p. 141.

Christianity does not have its own philosophy. "Deconstruct" is the key word of contemporary deconstructionism, which is represented by Derrida.

It is not the best choice to employ such a term to summarize the relationship between Christianity and Western philosophies. If one has to employ this term in the light of the final result of the encounter between Christianity and Western philosophies, it was Christianity that deconstructed Greek philosophies rather than Greek philosophies that deconstructed Christianity. Employing a common symbol used by a Western scholar, it was the sword of the Holy Spirit, i.e., Christianity, that deconstructed Greek philosophies and culture.[24] In my opinion, correctly understanding the relationship between early Christianity and Greco-Roman philosophies cannot only help us understand the development of Christianity but also help us understand the essential position of Christianity in the whole of Western culture.

The Misunderstanding of the Relationship between Christianity and the Western Middle Ages

The understanding of the relationship between Christianity and the Western Middle Ages within Western academic circles has passed through a process of development.

> One century ago, almost everyone felt pity for the Middle Ages: the period from AD 500 to AD 1500 had been considered as a long period without aim in which the poverty, superstition and darkness of the 1000 years had separated the Old Golden Period of the Roman Empire and the New Golden Period of Italian Renaissance. A 19th century scholar wrote that, during this 1000 years, human consciousness was in a situation of half-waking and half-sleeping: nothing great happened, no individual great opinion was expressed, and the whole society was controlled by the benighted priests of the Christian church. Another 19th century scholar said that this was the period which had not taken a shower for 1000 years. For most people the Middle Ages was a dark period. Not until the 15th century was the dark curtain removed; only then did it have a chance to take a shower and to start reflecting and reforming. Passing through this long middle gap, human kind once again went forward.[25]

24. Wang Xiaochao, *On the Argument between Hellenization and Christianization.*
25. Helisite, *Xiyang zhonggu shi,* p. 1.

Such an opinion has deeply influenced Chinese academic circles; not only Chinese historians but also philosophers hold the same viewpoint. This influence is very deep and is not easily overcome. Let's see more examples. *The Brief History of European Philosophy,* which was edited by Beijing University at the end of the 1970s, reads:

> In the Roman Empire, as the state religion, Christianity had served the system of slavery and strongly advocated the slavery system. However, after the overthrow of the Roman Empire and the destruction of the slave system, it [Christianity] again served the need of the New Feudal ruling class and was united with the feudal lords so as to serve feudalism and to offer a foundation of holy color to the Middle Ages' feudalistic rule. . . . In 476 when the revolutionary people destroyed the Western Roman Empire, Christianity, which had once served the slave system, was suppressed by the Germanic people as were the slave-lords. The iron brush had destroyed Christianity, which was once very powerful.[26]

The Textbook of the History of Western Philosophy, which was edited by Fudan University, reads:

> After the fall of the Roman Empire, Christianity had changed from the religion of slave-lords into that of feudal lords, and it had become the tool for protecting the feudal system. In Western European feudal society, the Christian church did not only control the areas of thought and culture, but was also a strong political and economic power. . . . The church exploited farmers through their possession of land, took a one-tenth tax from inhabitants, robbed people through various superstitious activities, and permitted priests of churches to have very luxurious and corrupt lives. . . . Politics, law, philosophy, and literature were only sub-subjects under theology, and all thoughts which were not in accordance with the traditional doctrines of theology were forbidden and persecuted as heresies. In one word, Christianity gave every aspect of the Western feudalistic society a religious color.[27]

The History of European Philosophy, which was edited by Wuhan University, reads:

26. *A Brief History of European Philosophy,* ed. Zhu Desheng and Li Zhen (Beijing: People's Publishing House, 1979), p. 60.

27. Quan Zenggu, *The History of Western Philosophy* (Shanghai: Shanghai People's Publishing House, 1983), p. 273.

The process of Western European feudalism was not preliminarily completed until the 9th century and was completed totally at the end of the 11th century. Before the 9th century, the productive forces developed very slowly, natural economics occupied an absolutely dominant position. Society was divided politically, it was undeveloped and ignorant culturally, and it was in the primary and wild situation. . . . In the later several hundred years, even individual philosophers and philosophical activities almost disappeared. The priests were the only people who had received education. In order to protect the Christian rule, they had mercilessly destroyed the ancient philosophies and were satisfied with employing very crude religious ideas, i.e., the Biblical stories and the creeds, which were regulated by Church Fathers, to fill their own and other people's minds. There was no need of philosophical activities at all.[28]

It is understandable that the above works contain such opinions, since they were published shortly after the end of the Cultural Revolution. However, some recently published books hold similar viewpoints. For example, Zhang Chuanyou says:

Christian philosophy was formed in the ancient Roman period when Europe was in the slave period. It developed in the European Middle Ages; and, as the ideology of the ruling class, Christianity served the slave-lords first and then had no difficulty becoming the tool that was employed by the feudalistic class to control people's thoughts. With regard to spirituality, the European Middle Ages belonged to Christianity. Since it had become the legal religion and the state religion of the ruling class, Christianity not only controlled European politics and economics but also controlled the social, spiritual, and cultural lives of common people.

As a rational force that was considered the opposite to the power of religion, philosophy was suppressed by religious theology. If Christianity had insisted upon its [original] way of thinking and its mystical features, there would not have been any Christian philosophy. Because Christianity had absorbed the form of philosophical argument and Greek philosophical thought, in the process of Christianity becoming the universal religion a Christian philosophy appeared with philosophical argument as its form and religious doctrines as its content. Religion put on philosophical clothes, phi-

---

28. Chen Xiuzhai and Yang Zutao, *The History of European Philosophy* (Wuhan: Hubei People's Publishing House, 1983), p. 99.

losophy found its master, and under the control of its master philosophy developed with difficultly as the servant [of theology]. This was a pity in the development of philosophy, it was the shame of human rationality, but it was also the historical result. The Middle Ages was the purgatory of philosophy, but philosophy is like the phoenix, which will rise from the ashes with new life and development after the baptism of fire.[29]

To get rid of the traditional idea that the Middle Ages were a totally dark period so as to better understand the period is the necessary precondition for understanding the relationship between Christianity and the Western Middle Ages. We admit that the Middle Ages was a period when Christian faith had a dominant position; it was a period when Westerners viewed everything in the light of God; and it was a period when religion and politics were closely united. As long as these features developed to their extremes, their opposites would be denied. For example, to stress the importance of faith too much will result in suppression of rationality, to stress God too much will result in suppression of humanity, and theistic-politics may very easily become autocratic. In this sense, later humanism was to a certain extent correct in rejecting the Middle Ages and its corruption and intolerant attitudes and activities directed toward other religions; these were also historical facts. However, the later humanism criticized the Middle Ages to the extreme, and it seems that the Middle Ages was totally rejected. Thus, we need to recorrect the extremes of humanism.

It is necessary for Chinese scholars to have a transformation of worldview in order to correctly grasp the relationship between Christianity and the Western Middle Ages. It is necessary to get rid of the ideological standard and to insist upon the academic principle of seeking truth from facts. Since the early twentieth century, Western academic circles have made great progress in the study of the Middle Ages. They have investigated the experience and thought of the Middle Ages and have found that this period was a bright time for literature, arts, religion, and philosophy. For example, they have studied these topics from aspects such as Catholic reconstruction of European society, the Carolingian cultural revival, the twelfth-century cultural revival, the birth of European universities, the experimental science of the Middle Ages, and the vigor of Scholastic philosophy in the thirteenth century.[30] They consider that

29. Zhang Chuanyou, *The Origin and Trend of Western Philosophy* (Wuhan: Wuhan University Press, 1999), p. 105.

30. Cf. E. Gilson, *Medieval Philosophy,* trans. Shen Qingsong (Taipei: Taiwan Commercial Press, 2000) p. vi.

the Middle Ages, when Catholicism was in the dominant position, was an important stage in Western historical development; it maintained the ancient Greco-Roman culture and led to the late-modern Western culture, thus playing an important role in the process of world history that cannot be denied.

Recently two academic books published in China have played important roles in correcting earlier misunderstandings. One is *The Contributions of Christianity in Medieval Europe,* written by Mr. Yang Changdong.[31] Another is *Faith and Rationality: The Revival and Decline of Christian Culture in the Middle Ages,* written by Professor Tian Wei.[32] I believe Chinese scholars, especially those who study the history of Western philosophy, will change their original viewpoints after reading these two books; and, through a further study on Christian philosophy, will realize that the relationship between religion and science is not simply one of opposites and enemies.

The Misunderstanding of the Relationship between Christianity and Modern Humanism

In the Chinese context, once humanism is mentioned people consider it a social ideological trend with its source in the European Renaissance. The authoritative Chinese encyclopedia says:

> In the time of the Renaissance, the Western capitalist productive relationship started to be formed within the feudal system. The new capitalist intellectuals despised the feudal culture which was dominated by Christian theology; they were eager to discover the cultural heritages of ancient Greek and Roman societies, to study the ancient languages, literatures, natural sciences, and philosophies. . . . In the period of the Renaissance, humanism affirmed and emphasized the human and humanity and sought to liberate the human and humanity from religious theological limits in every area.[33]

In the above quotation, medieval Christianity was considered the opposite of humanism. First, the quotation opposes the theology of the Middle Ages because of its viewpoint of elevating God and suppressing the human;

---

31. Beijing: China Social Sciences Press, first published in 1936, reprinted in 2000.

32. Baoding: Hebei University Press, 2001.

33. *Chinese Encyclopedia,* the volume of *Philosophy* (Beijing: Chinese Encyclopedia Press, 1987), p. 711.

it affirms human values and stresses the glory of the human. Second, it opposes asceticism and the medieval idea of a future life and advocates human happiness and valuing of the present life. Third, it opposes the religious limitations and the idea of feudal classes in the Middle Ages and asks for the liberation, freedom, and equality of individuals. Fourth, it opposes Scholastic philosophy and the obscurantism of the Middle Ages, and appreciates human experience and rationality and proposes investigation of nature to bring benefit to human beings. Over fifty years, in all Chinese universities and schools, all history books considering the relationship between Christianity and humanism — no matter whether they are histories of thought, politics, literature, arts, or philosophy, no matter whether they are academic or general books — all have taken the above viewpoint. Even today, this is still the case.

Modern Western humanism, which developed since the Renaissance, holds a paradoxical position in China's modern history of thought. Whenever capitalism is criticized in the light of politics, humanism is taken as the object of criticism. Whenever religion is criticized, the Western Renaissance and humanism are taken as evidence to prove the reactionary character of religions.

This approach appeared in China even before the establishment of the People's Republic. China's modern enlightenment movement commenced with the May Fourth Movement in 1919; democracy and science became its two primary goals; and the slogan of democracy includes humanist elements such as freedom, equality, and human rights. Chen Duxiu proposed the free and independent personality, Lu Xun criticized the ritual propriety of "eating" human beings, Ba Jin appealed for the freedom of marriage, Zhou Zuoren suggested a human literature, and Hu Shi propagandized for liberalism. All these propositions are humanistic in nature, and they reflect criticism of and reflections upon Chinese reality under the influence of the Enlightenment tradition.

However, from 1942, when Mao Zedong published his famous Speech in the Conference on Literature and Arts in Yanan, some writers in Yanan were criticized by Mao because of their speeches concerning humanism and love of humankind. Mao said: "Is there such a thing as human nature? Of course, there is. However, there is only concrete human nature, and there is no abstract human nature. In the society of classes there is only human nature which possesses class nature, and there is no human nature which is beyond class nature." This statement later became the standard for all critics concerning human nature, humanity, humanism, etc. in China.

After the establishment of the PRC, as early as in the 1950s, some writers affirmed the general nature of human beings beyond classes. Wang Renshu (also called Ba Ren) and Qian Gurong are two representatives of those writers. In January 1957 Wang published an article titled "On Human Nature" ("Lun renxing") and a book, *On Literature (Wenxue lungao)*. Wang insisted that, in addition to their class identity, human beings also have a common nature and ideas and that writers should take this into account when a fictional figure is described. The common characteristics of people constitute human nature. He criticized the contemporary situation by saying, "The thing, which is most lacking in our literatures is human nature, i.e., humanism, which derives from original human nature."

He traced this phenomenon to the mechanical understanding of the class nature of human beings. Wang declared that, according to Marxism, the class nature of human beings is "self-alienation." Therefore, "class struggle is also the struggle to liberate human nature."[34] In February 1957 Qian Gurong published a long article titled "On 'Literature Is the Study of the Human Being'" ("Lun wenxue shi renxue"). He wrote: "Not only should literature take human beings as the center of literature's description, but literary criticism should also take the description and treatment of human beings as its highest standard." "The writer's opinion of human beings and the writer's aesthetic ideals and humanist spirit constitute the essential element in their work." Therefore, "We should do our best to uncover the anti-humanist nature of capitalism and to protect the true humanism."[35]

Both writers considered themselves members of the proletariat in accordance with Marxism. Qian referred to Gorki's literature as the study of human beings, and Ba Ren referred to the holy family of Marx and Engels. Their opinions were not criticized too much in the "anti-rightist struggle" in 1957, but they were criticized in 1959 in the light of the political situation in the whole of China, and that criticism lasted over one year.

In 1961, after the criticism of humanism, there were some signs of relaxation in the area of arts and literature. Some movies with a humanist coloration such as *Daji and Her Father* were welcomed by people but also led to disputes. Prime Minister Zhou Enlai declared that proletarian human nature, friendship, and humanism should be affirmed, and it is not good for the prosperity of literature if everything is classified by its theory of human

34. Ba Ren, "On Human Nature," *Xingang* (Jan. 1957).
35. Qian Gurong, "Literature Is the Study of the Human Being," *Literature Weekly* (May 1957).

nature.[36] In 1963 the Chinese Communist Party officially began to criticize the Soviet Union's revisionism, and its representative Khrushchev and the capitalist theory of human nature became once again the focus of critics. During the several years prior to the Cultural Revolution, there were many critical movements in the area of arts and literature. Critics insisted that humanist stories expressing a longing for personal happiness and the expression of human nature cannot hold a position in "proletarian arts and literature." There was thus no theoretical development concerning human nature at that time. In the period of the Cultural Revolution, individualism (modern theism) and ruthless struggle (animalism) were popular.

Since the end of the Cultural Revolution humanism has experienced a revival in China. First, the Scar Literature emerged, which was provoked by the Cultural Revolution. Then there was discussion about "common beauty" and "the nature of people," and this was followed by a great discussion about humanism. In the 1980s Chinese intellectuals reflected on the meaning of life, values, aims, and the universal nature of human beings. Since these ideas have a certain distance from the official ideology, they later became objects for elimination by political movements advocating the elimination of spiritual pollutions.

Shortly after the end of the Cultural Revolution, European humanism was criticized by the following argument:

> The ideological trend of humanism played a progressive role in history. In the period of the Renaissance and the Enlightenment movements, in one word, in the historical stage when capitalism opposed feudalism, this trend challenged the superiority of the feudalistic class; it attacked the Christian church and theology, which were the spiritual pillars; and it had shown the anti-feudalistic spirit of new capitalism. However, after capitalists gained ruling power and established their own ruling system, humanism lost its progressive revolutionary features. Humanism had gradually become a sweet supplement for the capitalists to suppress the proletariat, and it had played a role which bare violent suppression alone could not achieve. Humanism became one of the spiritual pillars for the capitalists to strengthen their ruling, as medieval theology had served the feudalistic system.[37]

---

36. See Zhou Enlai, *The Selected Works of Zhou Enlai* (Beijing: People's Publishing House, 1984), pp. 326, 339.

37. Xing Bensi, *Humanism in the History of European Philosophy* (Shanghai: Shanghai People's Publishing House, 1979), p. 7.

By theoretical analysis, it can be found that humanism was in conflict with official ideology before the policy of reformation in China. On the one hand, the universal nature of humanism was in conflict with the official ideological emphasis on "class struggle" and "authority coming from guns." On the other hand, humanist elements such as freedom, equality, human rights, liberation of human nature, and individualism were in conflict with then official ideological emphasis on "the proletarian dictatorship" and "collectivism." During the 1990s, in the development of socialism with Chinese characteristics, this dominant ideology went through a process of change. Those theorists who were against humanism in the 1980s had disappeared from the political platform. Chinese Marxist study of humanism has gradually replaced the previous "orthodoxy." Many Marxist philosophers have changed their attitudes toward humanism, and they have started to study Marxist humanism.

The Dongfang Publishing House (i.e., the People's Publishing House) published a series of works based on research in humanism in 1996. The foreword of this series declared:

> Humanism is the excellent part of human traditional thought and is also the great ideal of human beings. From ancient times to today, society has been through many changes, but humanist thought has always been continuing and developing. Now it has become an academic theory that has rich content, deep meaning, and is closely related to human lives. Although there are different schools in the theory of humanism, the basic content of humanism has become the common property of all human beings. Marxism has inherited and developed the excellent parts of humanism in history and has melded humanism into its communist theory. Thus, Marxism has become the highest level of humanism in the contemporary world. The great Chinese reformation needs to enlarge the spirit of humanism; the building of a socialist market economy needs the principles of humanism; and the new culture, which is in the process of rebuilding, also needs the spirit of humanism. The process of development in contemporary Chinese society cannot be separated from humanism.[38]

The above quotation may seem ridiculous to foreign scholars since for them Marxism has nothing to do with humanism and the two appear to be opposites, but this passage indicates the real development of Chinese Marx-

38. Paul Kurts, *The Defense of Secular Humanism,* trans. Yu Lingling et al. (Beijing: Dongfang Press, 1996), Preface.

ist epistemology with respect to humanism. Chinese Marxists have realized that the essence of humanism does not belong only to capitalism but to all human beings; thus Marxism, which is the dominant ideology in China, should also absorb or include humanism. We may say that Western late-modern humanism, which has been criticized many times, has now been treated comparatively justly in China. However, almost every time humanism is evaluated, Christianity is used as a foil to raise it. Even today, Christianity is still regarded as a foil to the progress of humanism in China. What kind of relationship actually exists between Christianity and late-modern humanism? Answering such a question not only requires further scientific research but also requires a greater understanding of Christianity on the part of Chinese intellectuals.

A Response to Professor Wang Xiaochao

Choong Chee Pang

I wish to thank the Conference for giving me the honor of responding to Professor Wang's instructive and insightful paper. Christianity in China has had a relatively long history that could be traced back to the first arrival of Nestorianism in Changan (now Xian), the capital of the Tang dynasty, in 635 CE. The other two most significant periods would be the late Ming–early Qing period when the Catholics, especially the Jesuits led by Matteo Ricci, were most active, and the beginning of the Protestant missions with the arrival of Robert Morrison of the London Missionary Society in 1807. However, Professor Wang has chosen the modern period, from around 1949 to 2003, as the historical context for his inquiry.

Misunderstandings about Christianity in Chinese academic circles are obviously many. Professor Wang has only singled out five, which I also believe to be among the most important and common ones. He begins by acknowledging the changing attitude of Chinese academics toward Christianity, especially those who are engaged in religious studies. This is largely due to the reform and Open-Door Policy that was inaugurated in 1978. However, some serious misunderstandings are still rather prevalent in other academic disciplines and among people in general.

I am particularly gratified to hear that it is the "social responsibility" of those who are involved in Christian studies in China, scholars such as Professor Wang himself, to eliminate those misunderstandings. For the sake of clarity I will now proceed to comment on the "five misunderstandings" according to the original order.

254

Misunderstanding the Origin of Christianity and Its Founder

This was clearly not an issue raised by Chinese academics themselves. They have simply (and unfortunately!) picked up some of the pieces left behind by Western scholars' "quest of the historical Jesus" and their attempts to "de-mythologize" what they arbitrarily considered "myths" or "legends" in the Gospels. Chinese academics' misunderstanding on the issue is often a reflection of their lack of grasp of an issue that requires substantial biblical and theological background knowledge, which the Western scholars generally possessed. As such, the Chinese should not be expected to have anything original or creative to contribute to this old issue. In fact, very few serious scholars in the West today would want to pursue the matter much further. The only comforting thought, according to Professor Wang, is that most serious Chinese academics have now come to acknowledge Jesus as a true historical figure. However, he is also right in thinking that it will take a very long time for Chinese academics to consider the "Jesus of history" and the "Christ of faith" as one integrated entity.

Misunderstanding the Relationship between Christianity and the Roman Empire

Professor Wang uses Edward Gibbon's famous work, *The Decline and Fall of the Roman Empire,* to show how some Chinese academics have grossly misunderstood and misinterpreted Gibbon's real intent, and consequently put the blame on Christianity for the fall of the Roman Empire. This most unfortunate blunder made by the Chinese, in Professor Wang's opinion, has very serious sociopolitical implications and repercussions that are not difficult to understand in the current Chinese context: If Christianity as a new and vibrant religion indeed caused the collapse of the great Roman Empire, will history not repeat itself in modern China?

Erroneous and unwarranted fear is thus generated. In the long history of China, quite a few revolutions, rebellions, etc. were closely associated with popular religious movements. The Chinese government's attitude toward Falun Gong must also be viewed partly from this perspective. I agree with Professor Wang fully that the Chinese view on the relationship between Christianity and the Roman Empire is not only incorrect historically, but also far too simplistic and narrow as a way of handling such a delicate and complex issue.

Wang Xiaochao

Misunderstanding the Relationship between Christianity and Western Classical Philosophy

Chinese academics are quite right in recognizing the inevitable clash between Christianity and classical Greco-Roman thought, both religiously and intellectually. But again, it is far too simplistic, as some Chinese academics have done, to make Christianity responsible for the decline of Western classical philosophy. Great Christian thinkers such as Augustine, Thomas Aquinas, Anselm, and others had in fact selectively and skillfully used certain thought forms in classical tradition in the rationalization of the Christian faith and apologetics. They did not always perceive the relationship between Christianity and classical thinking in antithetical and confrontational terms. May I add that one should always remember Anselm's famous dictum: *fides quaerens intellectum.* For Anselm as well as for many other Christian intellectuals, it is always "faith seeking understanding." Professor Wang is also wise in his suggestion that when Christianity met with Western classical philosophy, the concern was not narrowly confined to the question of *who* is absorbing *what* from the other party, but more fundamentally, from what *position* is the encounter handled. Augustine, Thomas Aquinas, Anselm, and the rest had in fact never departed from their firm Christian position in their encounter and dialogue with classical philosophy. So in the end it was Christianity that "deconstructed" classical philosophy and not the other way around, as Professor Wang has clearly noted.

Misunderstanding the Relationship between Christianity and the Middle Ages of the West

In Professor Wang's paper several modern examples have been cited to show how the relationship between Christianity and the Middle Ages has often been seriously misinterpreted by Chinese academics, so that in the end the whole medieval era is characterized in terms of complete darkness and pessimism. Again, Christianity is identified as the culprit. Professor Wang is correct again in thinking that class struggles and conflicts between religion and philosophy in the Middle Ages have been highly exaggerated and become unnecessarily ideological. This is a very complex issue, which must be handled realistically and objectively according to stringent academic principles.

Misunderstanding the Relationship between Christianity and Modern Humanism

In modern Chinese intellectual history, humanism occupies a rather ambivalent and uncomfortable position. Besides being put antithetically in relation to Christianity, especially from the perspective of the European Renaissance (which is positively perceived by the Chinese), modern humanism is often being exploited at the dictates of sociopolitical agendas in modern China. Humanism can either be portrayed as a bright angel by the liberal/progressive or as an ugly demon by the leftist/conservative. Modern humanism, with its emphasis on the universality of human nature, freedom and equality, human rights, and the respect for personal autonomy, was often regarded as essentially incompatible with China's state ideology until quite recently. The spirit of humanism is now quite generally recognized as a shared human heritage that has a significant role to play in China's long march toward full modernization as well as active participation in the world community.

However, even this apparently encouraging line of thinking is still far from having explained the delicate and complex relationship between Christianity and modern humanism. Its satisfactory explanation will depend on an in-depth understanding of Christianity itself on the part of the Chinese, as Professor Wang has suggested. But in-depth understanding of "Christianity itself" is an enormous task for Chinese academics, and I have a lot of sympathy for them in this respect. The problem is not difficult to understand. For about fifty years until most recently, Chinese academics had very little or no contacts with the church. As such, they cannot be expected to have good instruction about "Christianity itself" from the Chinese church or from Christians. Most, if not all of them, have managed to acquire certain knowledge *about* Christianity through reading, and more recently, through courses on Christianity that are offered by some universities and academic institutions.

Moreover, most, if not nearly all of those who are currently engaged in Christian studies in Chinese universities and academic institutions are not members of the church, and their academic background is predominantly social sciences and humanities, especially philosophy. As such, it is only natural that they tend to read, study, interpret, and perceive Christianity from those perspectives. Not many are able to handle biblical texts as their colleagues in other disciplines do, with regards, for example, to Taoist and Confucian classics or the Buddhist texts. Not having the opportunities to acquire a working knowledge of the biblical languages, Hebrew and Greek, is also an obvious handicap academically speaking. Given these and other possible factors, it is therefore not surprising that very few serious works have been produced by Chinese scholars in the areas of biblical exegesis and biblical theology.

On the other hand, writings and publications (including translation) on nonbiblical subjects, such as philosophical theology, the works of great theologians, Christian ethics, church history, etc., have been quite impressive. They include scholars who are present in this conference. Professor Zhao Dunhua's *1500 Years of Christian Philosophy,* for example, has already run several reprints since its publication. In my humble opinion, unless one has a relatively firm biblical foundation it is very difficult to understand "Christianity itself" in depth. This is also true with other world religions. The understanding of the basic texts or scriptures of a particular religion is most essential. In the case of Christianity, even the controversial "human rights" issue requires some basic understanding of biblical creation, biblical anthropology (including the concept of *imago Dei*), and biblical ethics.

The picture I have just sketched may appear rather gloomy in the eyes of our Chinese academics. However, I am optimistic that given the necessary conditions and time, Chinese academics will eventually be able to understand "Christianity itself" more clearly and fully. When that happens, those "misunderstandings" highlighted by Professor Wang as well as the rest will stand a better chance of being eliminated. But as it is, our "responsibility is heavy and our journey long" *(ren zhong er dao yuan).*

13 The Faith of Chinese Urban Christians: A Case Study of Beijing

Gao Shining

In the spring of 2002, I started to do fieldwork in Beijing on our research project "Faith and Life," which is being conducted by the Institute of World Religions in the Chinese Academy of Social Sciences. Thus far, with the help of each member of our project, we have interviewed fifty-four Christians,[1] we have participated in various church meetings, and we have come to know many Christian friends. In our fieldwork, we distributed over 400 question and answer sheets.[2] The present article aims to offer an analysis of urban Chinese Christian faith based on our fieldwork.

Main Changes of Urban Christianity

As is generally known, Chinese Christianity has developed very quickly since the 1980s, and the number of Chinese Christians is now thirty to forty times that of 1949. In fact, there are two distinct groups of Christians in China. One is in the countryside; the other is in urban areas. These two do not have much to do with each other, and this has become one of the main features of Chinese Christianity's development. The revival of urban Christianity began

1. The people we initially interviewed were mainly those Christians who have a high education. Later, a change was made, and many common Christians were also interviewed freely. It should be noted that although Catholic Christianity was also included in our study, the Christians we interviewed were all Protestants.

2. We planned to distribute 1000 sheets, but this plan was interrupted by SARS in China. Until now we have received only partial answers, of which 128 are valuable.

in 1979, when the urban churches were reopened. During the past twenty years of development, the main changes can be seen in three areas.

The Church Is Pluralistic

At the beginning of 1949 there were around 5,000 Christians and seventy-two churches in Beijing. Until 1958 there were sixty-four churches, and after 1958 there were only four churches. During the Cultural Revolution there was only one church left. Since 1979 there have been eight churches, all of them opening gradually. Statistically there are about 40,000 Christians in Beijing; but there are still only eight churches (five in the downtown and three in other urban areas of Beijing). If we do not consider the relationship between politics and religions but rather consider only the need, these eight churches are inadequate to satisfy the needs of Christians in Beijing. Therefore, it is natural that with the growth in the number of Christians in Beijing, many meeting points have been appearing.

There are many kinds of meeting points. In addition to those meeting points that are attended by Christians who do not agree with or are not satisfied with the official church and Christians who dislike the so-called Trans-Denominational Church that emerged in the 1950s, more and more practical meeting points, which have nothing to do with the above two reasons, have been appearing in recent years.[3] According to our investigation and analysis, these meeting points have the following features: (1) They are based on professions, for example, the Businessmen's Fellowship, Medical Fellowship, and Artists' Fellowship, etc. (2) They are based on group demographic features, for example, Old People's Fellowship, Housewives' Fellowship, Couples' Fellowship, University Students' Fellowship, Blind People's Fellowship, etc. (3) They are based on a working unit, and this kind of meeting point appears usually in a place where the leaders of the unit are Christians. (4) They have developed on the basis of family and friendship groups.

The Christians participating in these kinds of meeting points can usually employ biblical teaching to solve their own problems according to

3. In his book *Gaige kaifang yilai de nongcun jiaohui* (Chinese Countryside Church since the Reform) (Hong Kong: Jiandao shenxueyuan, 1999), Liang Jialing has made an analysis of the so-called house churches, which were established for political and denominational reasons. In the present article, I am borrowing the term "practical independence" to describe those meeting points that were not established for political or denominational reasons.

their own features. For example, the Businessmen's Fellowship emphasizes that "God does not ask us to struggle in the line of survival." For them to earn money is their duty, success in business is a gift from God, and failure is a test from God. If they follow biblical teaching, they will be able both to earn money and to be in harmony with their faith. And the meetings arranged by the Couple's Fellowship require both husbands and wives to participate. A topic related to family life is usually discussed at each meeting, and they aim mainly to show that the family, composed of husband and wife, is the primary social unit of relationship. Thus, based on biblical teachings on the features of male and female, they stress that the marriage relationship between husband and wife should be built on the basis of worshiping God. These features make Christians happy to participate in such activities.[4]

The Structure of Christianity Has Been Changed

Several years ago, research into Chinese Christianity usually mentioned the phenomenon of three majorities, i.e., among the Chinese Christians, the majority were old, female, and illiterate. This was the true situation at the beginning of Christianity's development in China, and even today this situation is still true in the countryside. However, the structure of Christianity in urban areas has greatly changed during the past twenty years. For example, in Gangwashi Church, there were almost no young people in Sunday services at the beginning of the 1980s; however, 35 percent of the baptized members were younger than 35 in 1995, and in 1999 this percentage was 39 percent. In addition, the educational level of Christians has also increased dramatically, and there are now more and more Christians who have more than three years of college education. From 1995 to 1999, among Sunday service participants, the percentage of baptized with more than a three-year college education were respectively 15.6, 27.7, 31.8, 31, and 31.1 percent.[5] Although we do not yet have reliable statistics concerning the recent three years (2000-2003), based on our observation and research of the last several months in the Gangwashi

---

4. I have personally witnessed a very receptive incident in the Businessmen's Fellowship; at one of the meetings three people claimed immediate conversion to Christianity. I have also experienced how the Couples' Fellowship has saved quite a few marriages that were in crisis.

5. See the unpublished manuscript of Wang Xiaonan, *Dangdai jidujiaohui gean fenxi* (An Analysis of Individual Cases of Contemporary Chinese Christian Church).

Church, the percentages of young people and people with a higher education level have again risen significantly.[6]

According to our observation and investigation among meeting points, the change in the Three Majorities is even larger there, and this is to say, there have been more and more young people, more highly educated people, and more males. Among the fifty-four Christians we have interviewed, thirty-seven are younger than 40 years of age, forty-two have more education than the three-year college, four have high school diplomas, two have two-year college educations, and six have completed middle school education. Among the 138 useful answers we have received, 64.8 percent are younger than 40 years of age, and 52.7 percent have received higher education. As to sex, females are slightly more numerous than males.[7]

Church Activities Become Rich

We again take the Gangwashi Church as the example. Each Sunday there are four services, and each of them has more than 1,000 participants. The first service is scheduled from 7 to 8 a.m., and the participants are mainly older people, who usually get up early in the morning. The second and third services start respectively at 8:30 and 10:30. The evening service lasts from 7:00 to 8:00 p.m., and this service can fit the needs of those who have to work on Sundays and others who cannot join the daytime services. In addition to Sunday and Saturday services, there are other regular activities such as Bible study meetings, prayer meetings, youth meetings, and women's meetings. There are also irregular activities such as visiting and conversations, Lord's Supper (once a month), and baptisms, etc.

Compared with the official church, many meeting points have richer and livelier activities. Since the regular participants are fewer than thirty people, they usually sing, preach, read the Bible, and pray. Testimony and in-

---

6. Over 85 percent of participants in the four services each Sunday in the Gangwashi Church are young people.

7. Note by the editors: The Chinese educational system is as follows: six years of primary school and three years of middle school. Students who have completed primary and middle school can continue to a two-year college education or three years of high school. The students who have completed primary, middle, and high school can continue to a three-year college program or a four-year college baccalaureate program. Master's degrees are normally awarded for an additional three years of study, and doctorates for three years of study beyond the master's degree.

tercessory prayer are two main activities. In addition, among Christians there are many discussions concerning topics from faith to concrete life problems; sermons are usually closely related to Christians' concerns, many lay Christians participate in the services, and love among them has been clearly shown. Many meeting points also arrange activities such as spring and autumn short trips, lunches or suppers, inviting specialists to give theological lectures, and entertainment activities during important festivals, etc. Such activities cannot usually be arranged by the official church.

These obvious changes in urban Christianity reveal the development of Chinese urban Christianity, not only in the increase in the number of Christians but also in the rising levels of education and understanding.

Elements of the Formation of Urban Christian Faith

It is an issue worth studying as to why Christianity has attracted Chinese people so rapidly recently. An exploration of elements in the formation of Chinese Christians' faith will be helpful in answering this question. In fact, there is a great difference between the faith processes of countryside and urban Christians. In the Chinese countryside, miracles, especially those miracles that heal people from illness, are the main factor in converting people to religious faith. If a person has been healed because of the Christian faith, such miracles usually bring a whole family, a whole village, or even a whole area to believe in Jesus Christ.[8]

This kind of phenomenon cannot, of course, be separated from the special situation of life and medical care in the Chinese countryside. However, for many people who live in cities, miracle is not the main reason for their conversion to religious faith. Although reasons for people converting to Christianity are various and individual, in most cases there are multiple reasons. However, there are still some common elements that influence almost every urban Christian.

---

8. Cf. Deng Zhaoming, *Chengshou yu chishou* (Hong Kong: Xianggang jidujiao Zhongguo wenhua yanjiusuo, 1998). Between the autumn and winter of 2000 I listened to Mr. Deng's lecture; he concluded that as long as miracles appear, Chinese farmers will convert to Christianity.

Family Influence

Our investigation has shown that some Christians believe in Jesus Christ naturally, since they were either brought up in Christian families or their close relatives or friends are Christians. They have been influenced by Christian faith since they were very young. This kind of Christian is usually a little bit older than 40 years; however, there are not many such Christians. The formation of this situation is closely related to the special political environment of China. Before the 1980s religion was suppressed as a superstition and a reactionary worldview. Therefore, because of fear some Christians did not dare to speak publicly of their faith, some even gave up their faith, and they usually opposed their children becoming Christians. In such a situation, family religious influence had been suppressed and reduced. Therefore, in regard to family influence, there is a gap between different ages. On the other hand, we have also noted that the young generation of Christians who were almost all converted since the 1990s have been paying much attention to the faith of their young children. They almost all take their children to church every weekend and sincerely hope that they too will become Christians.

In fact, although many children are still young (usually younger than 11-12 years), they have already accepted the Christian faith. This indicates that when religious life is in a normal condition, the family influences children's faith normally. However, our investigation has also shown that, generally speaking, family influence is being reduced. We have interviewed many Christians whose parents are Buddhists, atheists, or Communists, but their families have not influenced them so much in their faith. Even when their faith is different from that of their parents, very few families have opposed their children's choice of Christian faith. From a sociological viewpoint this has indicated the relationship between social openness and family influence upon children. The more a society is traditional and closed, and social culture is more homogeneous, the more important and stronger family influence is in the growth of children. To the contrary, the more open a society is, and the more pluralist the ideology, the less the family will influence their children. This conclusion can properly fit Chinese contemporary society and its religious situation.

Suffering, Unhappiness, and Difficulties in Life

For many people religion is related to suffering. Communist leader Lenin said, "Where there is suffering, there are religions." Although these are not the words of a religious believer, they are totally correct. Even today, this fits the religious situation. However, in Chinese cities, the content of suffering, unhappiness, and difficulty has changed, and such experiences usually are not the result of material lack but rather derive from complicated human relationships and unpredicted individual fate, even though individuals are living without any material lack.

Among the fifty-four Christians we have interviewed, one family (three people) was converted to Christianity because the son in the family had been suffering form a terrible sickness and Christianity offered an explanation for their suffering. Nine people became Christians because of life's difficulties; some of them had experienced financial decline from wealth to poverty and thus had run into an end; some of them had broken families because of trying to go abroad to study, and life in foreign countries had disappointed them; some of them had been addicted to bad habits such as drug use, and thus they felt they had lost life's meaning. These represented 22 percent of the Christians we interviewed. Among the 128 respondents, 24.8 percent of the people converted to Christianity because of suffering, unhappiness, and difficulty. This indicates that suffering, unhappiness, and difficulty are no longer deciding elements in religious faith.

Other People's Influence

In modern society, every individual is a member of a reference community that influences other people, and every member is also influenced by other people to a certain extent. Our investigation has proven the importance of "other people" in influencing people's religious faith. Twenty-eight percent of our interviewed people were baptized because of the direct or indirect influence of other Christians' good examples in their lives; 50 percent of the 128 answer sheets say that their own Christian faith has been extremely influenced by other Christians, and 23 percent say that they have been greatly influenced by other Christians.

The importance of this element is related to the contemporary social background: China is in the process of transformation, traditional values are declining, society is losing its order, and good examples for other people are becoming fewer; the crisis of trust between human beings is increasing, and corruption is becoming more apparent. However, within such a society Christians love others and act as salt and light, and their deeds are obviously different from the general trend of seeking selfish benefits, money, and power in contemporary China. Therefore, Christians have become a good example for the people around them, and Christianity is finally becoming a serious choice that attracts other people. Thus, although Christians are only a small part of Chinese society, their power of influence is great.

Spiritual Seeking

Chinese urban inhabitants, especially young people, have been experiencing the following stages in the development of spiritual lives during the past twenty years, a period when China has been applying an open policy with regard to economics: (1) Between the end of the 1970s and the beginning of the 1980s, there was a crisis in faith and trust because of disappointment with the failure to fulfill the original ideals. People were commonly experiencing disappointments, wandering, and seeking. (2) Between the middle and end of the 1980s, people criticized the past on the one hand and looked forward to the ideals of truth, goodness, and beauty on the other hand; and some people even tried to revive the spirit of holiness and lofty idealism. (3) Since the 1990s economic development has become the main trend of society; "all look forward to money" has become popular. On the one hand, people have become very rich financially; on the other hand, people have become very poor, since they have nothing except money. (4) Since the end of the 1990s China has entered into a "self-centered" period.

Especially the young generation, who are usually the only children in their families, often care only for themselves, with a focus on self-feeling, self-need, and self-benefit. The aims of their lives become more practical and secular. Living for a long time in an environment without spiritual seeking causes people to become upset, although the contemporary main trend of social life is not different from that at the end of the 1990s. However, we have also noticed that more and more people, especially the younger generation, who have received a good higher education, are walking out of the circle that has only concern for material life, and are starting to seek some kind of spiritual lives. Spiritual seeking is the main reason that has converted 29 percent of our interviewed Christians; and 38.7 percent of the 128 answer sheets say that they have been converted to Christianity because of spiritual seeking. In this seeking of spirituality, the raising of individual spirits is closely related to their worries concerning their nation. Many contemporary intellectuals have opinions such as: "China cannot be reformed only in politics. The root of democracy is a Christian spirit. Only God can save the Chinese people." And this opinion has become a main feature of Chinese urban Christians.

In addition to the above common reasons, there are also some other elements that have converted individuals to Christianity, for example, seeking friendship and receiving a special calling from God. Of course, these factors concern only a small portion of Christians. One element that needs to be noticed is "the hope to enter heaven after death." Twenty-seven percent of the 128 answer sheets considered this as the main reason for their conversion, and this percentage is higher than the elements of suffering, unhappiness, and difficulty.[9] Although this element influences mainly those people who have received only primary and middle school educations (nine years), 30 percent of the people who have higher than three-year college education also consider this an important reason. This is one of the religious elements that have not been given up because of scientific development, since science can neither prove it true nor prove it false.

The Faith and Identity of Urban Christians

American religious sociologist Clifford Geertz says that no one lives exclusively in a world that is built with religious symbols, even if he is a sage. Most people live only sometimes in this world.[10] I think, by this "sometimes," Geertz means probably those moments when a Christian participates in church activities, when he or she reads the Bible or prays. However, during our fieldwork we have found that, to a certain extent, the scope of "sometimes" has been enlarged by urban Chinese Christians. Once a person who was responsible for arranging services said: "I have been a Sunday Christian for over ten years. Then I thought that eating and sleeping are a life-related, working and earning money are a job-related, and going to church is a faith-related reality. Thus, my faith had been only a custom in my life, and it had not played any role in my life. However, now I understand that faith is all of our lives."

Her speech was accepted by her audience and welcomed with applause. Now, for more and more people, faith is not only an individual seeking of the heart, a hope, a looking forward to God, or to a spiritual life, but the all

9. I have not listed this element as a common reason to convert people to Christianity, since all fifty-four of the Christians we interviewed have not mentioned this issue.

10. Clifford Geertz, "Religion as a Cultural System," in *Anthropological Approaches to the Study of Religion*, ed. M. Banton (London: Tavistock, 1966).

of their lives. Most of the Christians we interviewed told us that faith is very important in their lives. In the answer sheet, to the question about "the position of faith in your life," 74.2 percent answered "very important," 22.6 percent answered "important," only 2.3 percent said "not very important," and no one answered "does not matter." Related to this answer is the concrete expression of "very important" (of faith in life). Among the ninety-five Christians who said faith is very important in their lives, seventy-five often participate in church activities, read the Bible, and pray every day.

In making friends, it is very important that they have the same faith; in bringing up children, it is very important that their nurturing be based on biblical principles; and in dealing with human relationships and their benefits, respondents said that the Christian faith has played a very important role. In other words, they have also realized that they are Christians in their daily lives. The enlargement of their religious world and the extending of religious influence beyond "sometimes" made Christian faith not only a faith but also a source of identity for urban Christians.

When faith has become a source of identity of a Christian, we have found the following phenomena. (1) More and more Christians publicly declare that they are Christians. Eighty-two percent of Christians would like to let others know they are Christians, 10.9 percent consider that it does not matter, and only 6.2 percent would not like to let others know they are Christians. This is not only an indication of the normality of Chinese religious life but also an indication of the openness of Chinese society.[11] (2) There are special features in their speech. Concerning this Geertz says: "If they are religious adherents, their daily language will be influenced by their religious faith."[12]

The speech of contemporary Chinese Christians has such features, and their speech is usually related to Bible texts and church life, and the meaning and usage of their speech is very different from popular usage in contemporary China. For example, for common people, the word *baoshou* means conservative and unwilling to accept new ideas and things. For Christians this word means God's love to them, and it has replaced the word for "protect" and "bless." (3) Christians think that all successes result from the grace and goodwill of God, and all failures and difficulties are considered a result of

11. At the end of the 1990s a statistic indicated that only 45 percent of Christians would like to let others know they are Christians. During the Cultural Revolution period most Christians tried their best to avoid telling others they were Christians.

12. Clifford Geertz, *Islam Observed: Religious Development in Morocco and Indonesia* (New Haven: Yale University Press, 1968).

their disobeying God's will. Thus, to pray and to ask the will of God when facing everything is very important for most Christians. (4) Compared with common people, Christians seem to be peaceful and happy psychologically and emotionally. This feature is normal for all the Christians we have interviewed. (5) Christians' deeds and behavior are special.

We have asked in the question-answer sheet: Compared with non-Christians, do you think Christians should be "much better" or "at least a little bit better" or "no different" morally? Ninety-nine percent of the Christians who answered chose one of the first two answers, and more than half said that Christians should be much better than non-Christians morally. In our discussion we have also noticed that many Christians believe they should prove Christians' morality is much better by their deeds. A Christian said: "I have not told others publicly that I have been baptized, but other people around me do not often understand my behavior and they only guess that 'She must be a Christian.' I consider this as the highest compliment to me."

Faith becoming the identity of a Christian shows not only the importance of faith in Christians' lives but also their strong self-realization of the faith. Of course, this kind of strong faith makes Christians feel happy together with other Christians. When they meet non-Christians, they have a very strong intention to "preach" their faith and would like to defend their faith, and their missiological intention is very strong. This situation is closely related to the position of Christianity in China. Compared with other religions, Christianity is not only a minority but also a foreigner in China, and during its long history it has been persecuted. This history has shaped these features of Chinese Christians both in the countryside and in cities, and these features are also common in Chinese minority communities.

Urban Christians Who Are Living in Tension

In John 18:36 Jesus said to Pilate, who judged him, "My kingdom is not of this world." According to biblical teaching, "Christians live in this world but do not belong to this world." Here the term "this world" has three meanings: the natural material world, human society or the country, and fallen human nature, which has disobeyed God and truth.[13] Like all other people, on the

---

13. David F. Wells, *God in the Westland: The Reality of Truth in a World of Fading Dreams* (Grand Rapids: Eerdmans, 1994). Cited in Dong Jiangyang, "Lun jidutu zai shehui zhong 'zuoyan zuoguang' de geren yingxiang celue."

one hand, Christians have to live in today's material world; on the other hand, Christians should be beyond the material world. Such Christian teaching offers both an identity with this world and an identity with the kingdom of heaven. They are two totally different kingdoms, and there is a tension between them. The heavenly kingdom is filled with love, and the secular kingdom is filled with evil; the former is absolute justice, and the latter has injustice; the former requires only loyalty to God, but the latter requires people to obey all kinds of human authorities. Because of participation in both kingdoms, Christians have to keep a balance between these two worlds. On the one hand, they have to be good servants in this world; on the other hand, they have to hold a clear criticism of this world. Thus, Christians are living in tension between the two worlds.

In contemporary China, while modernization is occurring, many people have become opportunistic, human rationality has weakened, trust among people has been shaken, much corruption has appeared, people are losing their traditional moral values, ethical standards are becoming more relative, the relationship between human beings is becoming worse, and materialism and the worship of money have become popular. In summary, in today's China, Christians are experiencing many strong tensions, and some of these have forced Christians to make difficult decisions that deeply influence their lives. In our discussions we have paid special attention to how Christians deal with tensions in value choices and ethics.

We have found that those Christians who have a strong faith can resist all kinds of temptations in contemporary society and can maintain their high values. Because they have faith, they focus on matters of ultimate concern. Thus, they can choose a life that is not always determined on the basis of individual material benefit and loss. In today's society, which has pluralist values, their faith has supported them in making different choices from common people, and they have been able to follow a moral example that is based on their values. I am here giving two cases. Ms. L is responsible for propaganda in a government office. Because of her good work, she was promoted and became a preparatory member of the Communist Party. However, during the period when she was preparing for Communist Party membership, she accepted Christianity. Because of her faith, she noticed that almost all her successes in her work were based on lies that she had advanced in pleasing her leaders. She became very upset about this. Through a period of suffering struggle with herself, she finally decided to quit the Communist Party, since she could not work in a manner contrary to her Christian faith. The result of her decision was that she had to quit her job. To lose her job was a big issue not only for herself but also for her whole family. She had doubts; her family and friends opposed it. However, she still gave up her "wonderful future" in her career and became a Christian.

Mr. Z had experienced a totally different situation. After he lost his job, through the introduction of a friend he got a part-time job working two days a week, and his monthly salary was 800 yuan. This benefited his whole family. However, Mr. Z experienced great pressure on the first day of work, since his duty was to make false bookkeeping entries for his boss. Mr. Z and his whole family are Christians, although they needed money to pay their living costs: his son had to pay tuition fees in school, and his parents were sick and needed money to pay for medical care. However, the whole family decided that they could not earn money in this way. They said, "We cannot accept this even if the pay were 8,000 yuan per month." Today Mr. Z is still jobless, but he feels peaceful in his heart. Loyalty to their faith has enabled many Christians to overcome material temptation when tension appeared. They would rather remain poor than give up their faith. Their deeds come from their hearts and are natural choices for them. Thus they have experienced peace even though they have sometimes had to bear the burden of poverty.

Of course, not all Christians are the same. Even though they have a strong faith, under pressure some will follow the general way that is most popular in their environment. However, such compromise usually leads to spiritual suffering and to tension between the concrete benefit and spiritual faith. I have interviewed two Christian lawyers who experience similar pressures but whose feelings in their hearts are different. Lawyer W says he feels that his heart has become abnormal when he has to defend people who have committed crimes and he feels a heavy burden when he has to defend innocent people. However, many things are not decided by him; he suffers and has no alternative. He would like to flee and feels that someday he will give up this job as a lawyer. Lawyer Y has a custom of praying every morning and confessing every evening before God, since he sometimes has to do things he considers contrary to his faith. In his prayer, he tells everything he is faced with, and, in his confession, he asks forgiveness from God. Such practices have reduced the tension in his life.[14]

Those Christians who do not have strong faith are easily influenced by the environment and secular pressure. Such influences will shake their faith.

---

14. Lawyer Y was one of the earliest lawyers I interviewed; he has now given up his job as a lawyer.

Observation has shown that every Christian has to experience three stages after accepting Christianity. One Christian we have interviewed has described these stages as "from belief to trust and finally to obedience." Only after passing through these stages can Christians actively serve the role of salt and light.

Although most urban Christians have experienced tensions between two identities and worlds to a certain extent, the majority of them have felt that faith has offered them peace and happiness. Tension and suffering can be resolved in faith, and this has become a kind of reward. Of course, in addition to Christians' individual devotion, church, fellowship, and love and support among Christians have also helped in resolving these tensions and sufferings. This again strengthens the influence of church and fellowship.

Today, many urban Chinese Christians think that if a lamp is only under a bowl or if salt is only kept within a vessel, they will not be able to play the roles they should play. They believe that Christians should keep their special identities as Christians in facing the tensions between two identities and worlds. Christians should keep their faith, values, standards, and lifestyle; otherwise, they will be like salt that has lost its taste and will be thrown out. Although criticism of Chinese society by individual Christians is limited, as a community Chinese Christianity has already become an important power in the reconstruction of Chinese ethical morality.

A Response to Professor Gao Shining

Zhang Minghui

Almost a quarter century after the end of the Cultural Revolution and the normalization of church activities, the rapid conversion of Chinese people to Christianity has attracted attention in church and academic circles throughout the world. Professor Gao Shining from the Chinese Academy of Social Sciences has made many valuable observations in her study of Chinese conversion to Christianity focusing on the urban area. Because this conversion is urban in particular, it ties in with the question of modernization and urbanization, and leads to the further question of whether Christianity is an element of Westernization.

As Professor Gao notes, there are only eight Protestant church buildings in Beijing,[1] which is completely inadequate for the number of believers. As a result, many "meeting points" have developed, consisting of people who often have a similar professional background and common interests. Although the underground church has attracted big publicity abroad, and is based on disagreement with the official church, it is increasingly the case that "meeting points" exist due to lack of space rather than any objection to the Three-Self Principle.

It is unclear from Gao's study whether the participants at the meeting points also attend official congregations. It is also unclear whether Three-Self pastors lead these meeting points. If not, then some tension could arise between the two forms of congregation. This could pose a challenge for the

---

1. An editorial note: this was the situation in 2003; thereafter, three new Protestant church buildings have been opened in the city of Beijing.

Three-Self Patriotic Movement in the future: at the moment, there is no difference in doctrine between many of these meeting points and the official church, but this may not always be the case. We can speculate as to what would happen if Pentecostalism or the charismatic movement, for instance, came to dominate the meeting points. Then there could be the possibility of a split between the meeting points and the official church.

Since the official church has not received government permission to build the required number of churches, it is likely that meeting points are going to multiply. By not responding adequately to the need for new church buildings for expanding congregations, government policy is weakening the official church and thus diminishing its influence over Christians. At the moment, the government can afford to ignore the meeting points because most Christians are not involved in politics and do not have strong links abroad; nor do they create problems. But that may not always be the case.

The rise in the number of young educated Christians is particularly strong at meeting points, and females and males are roughly equal in number, in contrast to the old image of the public church as a place for the sick, the illiterate, and old women. Throughout the world, few young men attend the older denominations but go to Pentecostal or Evangelical churches instead. So, similarly young Chinese educated men go to meeting points rather than official congregations. I would like to add that the preaching in the public church is not always of high quality, which could explain the preference of young educated people for the meeting points.

Professor Gao writes that the more pluralist the ideology, the smaller the influence of the family. Chinese culture is now becoming less collective and more individualistic. This is partly caused by the economic reform policy promoting individual initiative, and partly by a popular reaction to the excessive collectivism of the Cultural Revolution. Today many young urban people have a good salary and their own apartment, so they can make their own decisions. In the past, young educated people benefited greatly from joining the Communist Party, so being active in the church was unwise in career terms, but now most people of this type work in the private sector or for foreign companies, where membership in the party is not important.

Professor Gao notes that the phenomenon of religious miracles is an important factor in conversion in the countryside, partly because of the lack of medical care. However, there is a sociological observation to be made here: in the countryside, the collective culture of a village means that when a person is healed everyone hears about it and considers it a blessing for the community. In a city, on the contrary, a healed person has fewer contacts in society, and since the collective factor is less important, miracles are less influential for the conversion of others.

Professor Gao mentions that unhappiness is not the key determinant in conversion, and it is interesting that young educated people who are the most successful section of the population are embracing Christianity. Christianity can serve as an ethic for the new urban middle class: it gives a sense of respectability, plus it has an empowering capacity in that a person who is able to change his or her private life feels able to cope with the challenges of a changing society. Christianity also promotes the ethic of moderation; money is not wasted on gambling or drinking. Furthermore, a strict Christian lifestyle brings good health and appearance, and promotes hard work and good manners, all of which are an advantage in professional life. If we look at the meeting points designed for business people or married couples, we see that they serve a practical, problem-solving role.

Professor Gao has noticed that Christianity has become the identity of believers rather than just an element of their life. She points to similarities with American conservative evangelical Protestantism, in which some of the key elements are: (a) the importance of giving a Christian witness, (b) following a high moral code, and (c) feeling separate from the unbelieving society. These Christians feel responsible for the good image of Christianity. Confucianism was commonly counted by Western scholars as a religion, but the Chinese tend to view it more as an ethical system, the ritual elements of which are seen as part of folk religion. So, following this line of interpretation, religion for urban Chinese people can be understood as something that is very important for their ethics and behavior. I suggest that in the popular understanding, Christianity has been put into the place that was left empty by the decline of Confucianism.

Professor Gao correctly notes the tension between Christian values and the real world. As we saw earlier, Christianity can act as a practical help for believers in their working lives. But there is another side: employers do not always want strictly honest employees. Employers value results rather than honesty. The business environment causes problems of conscience for believers who are asked to lie or be dishonest in their work. Since Chinese Christianity values morality very highly, Christians feel that they cannot behave in a dishonest way, because it will look bad to nonbelievers.

It is important to note that this current expansion of Christianity in China is taking place without much input by foreign missionaries. It is based on the initiative of individual Chinese Christians who want to spread the gospel.

14 The Position of Religion in Chinese Society

Li Qiuling

The birth and development of a new religion, and the coming and acceptance of a foreign religion, are not only determined by the content of the religion and its relationship with the cultural context in which it finds itself but also, to a great extent, by the basic attitude of the society to religions. Because of their historical and cultural differences, China and the West have very different attitudes toward religions. I will not draw a complete contrast between them in this regard but will take Western society as a reference point to explore Chinese social attitudes to religions. I will examine this topic from three perspectives: the basic attitude of the Chinese common people, the attitude of the Chinese dominant ideology, and the attitude of Chinese authority to religions, so that the basic position of religions in Chinese society will be clarified.

The Basic Attitude of the Chinese Common People to Religions

We first examine the basic attitude of Chinese common people to religions, because common people are the main adherents of religions, and their attitudes significantly influence the other two factors (the dominant ideology and the attitude of authority). To a certain extent, the attitude of the common people can be considered as the underlying factor in the development of the dominant ideology and the reaction of Chinese authority to religions.

In China, religious adherents are a minor part of the whole population; and, among these adherents, many are minorities whose whole nations belong to some religion (e.g., Islam). Strictly speaking, these latter groups are not the object we are going to explore in the present article. In addition to various major religions, there are also folk religions, especially in the countryside. They are probably not true religions, but they have influenced many common people and their attitudes to religions.

Generally speaking, Chinese folk religions have the following three characteristics:

1. Utilitarianism

Chinese folk religions derive from ancient nature worship, the worship of gods and spirits, and shamanism. They have continuously influenced Chinese people for several thousand years, and they have very strong support among common people. These folk religions have a very strong utilitarian feature. The reason that people worship gods and spirits is in order to receive blessings and to prevent disaster. In fact, people usually have a very concrete purpose when they engage in these folk religions. In other words, only when people need to ask for something do they come to communicate with the religious objects of the folk religions. This fact has influenced their attitudes to religions in general, especially to Buddhism and Taoism. It is not because of piety that people come to worship gods and Buddha; their purpose is to receive blessings and protection. This utilitarian feature is especially indicated in the various promises that people give to the various gods and spirits.

In this situation, in order to exist and to develop, religions have also employed measures to satisfy the psychological needs of the common people. Taoism asks for gods and expels devils, and Buddhism releases souls from purgatory. Although these are not the essence of these religions, they are welcomed by common people since they can satisfy their psychological needs. In many Buddhist and Taoist temples, there are many promise-bearing slogans such as "You can get anything you ask" or "Magic arts are infinite," and they indicate the utilitarian needs of common people. Even Christianity, after it was transmitted into China, was also influenced by such utilitarian features. Investigations conducted several years ago indicated that, among Chinese Christians, the majority are illiterate, aged, female, and sick. This fact is offered as evidence to support the theory that people look for utilitarian benefits. The structure of the Chinese Christian community has changed recently; however, the basic psychological feature of Chinese religious adherents has not yet changed.

2. Nonpious Faith

One result of the utilitarian characteristic is that Chinese people believe in religions but are not pious. The relationship between people and the objects of their worship is one of asking and giving, sacrificing and promising, and it is like a commercial relationship of exchange. Although gods and spirits have great magic power, they do not have the characteristic of holiness; they are only partners in an exchange relationship. Since people's requests are usually very concrete, once their hopes cannot be satisfied, the relationship between gods and people generally faces a crisis. In China, there is not the sincerity of Job in the Old Testament who did not lose his faith in God even though he experienced much suffering. In Chinese literature there are many examples of people destroying the images of Buddha and gods when their requests have not been answered as they hoped. Many people change their adherence to different religions after they are disappointed with the original object of their faith.

3. Pluralist Faith

Utilitarianism and nonpious faith have led to a pluralist faith. Since the purpose of faith is to attain utilitarian benefits, since each god or spirit has some kind of magic powers, people think that the more gods and spirits one believes in, the better it will be. Claims of great magic power and effectiveness are the main reasons that people are attracted to religions, but other gods and spirits, which do not belong to the objects of their faith, should not be offended. Yanwang (the King of the Yin world in charge of death) is indeed terrible, but small devils are also difficult to deal with. Even though some gods and spirits seem to have nothing to do with a person's life, it does not bring harm if he worships them. In fact, perhaps someday these gods and spirits will remember these experiences of someone's respecting them and offer that person help.

Except in certain minority areas, this pluralist attitude to religious gods and spirits pervades China. A person may believe in one religion today and another tomorrow; and it is also very possible that he believes in different religions at the same time and worships different gods and spirits at home. The Chinese traditional religions of Taoism and Buddhism themselves are, in fact, polytheistic; and it can be said that they have satisfied such needs in China. In addition, such a polytheistic religion has produced an inclusive feature in the attitude toward different religions. Although there have been conflicts and attacks among different religions in China, there have not been real religious wars in Chinese history. The fate of each religion in China has mainly depended on its own magic power. Even a person who believes in only one religion usually holds a tolerant and inclusive attitude to other religions. In China, there has never been a truly exclusive religion that rejects other religions.

The Basic Attitude of Chinese Dominant Ideology to Religions

The basic attitude of Chinese dominant ideology to religions has played a deciding role in establishing the position of religions in Chinese society. In a country like China, there is a continuous tradition of culture, and this feature should be especially emphasized.

There should be no doubt that the Chinese dominant ideology is Confucianism. It is difficult to say whether the periods of Xia, Shang, and Zhou had a real ideology. Until the periods of Spring and Autumn and the Warring States period, hundreds of schools emerged, among which Confucianism and Moism became strong. In the Han dynasty, Dong Zhongshu proposed that all other schools should be forbidden and only Confucianism should be respected; and this established a basis for Confucianism to become the dominant ideology in China. Later, although Confucianism, Taoism, and Buddhism became mixed together, the dominant position of Confucianism never changed.

Confucius, the founder of Confucianism, established a basis for the attitude to religions. Although Confucius believed in the Heavenly mandate, it was regarded as only a need that could neither be understood nor resisted. Confucius says:

What has Heaven said?
The four seasons proceed and the myriad things are born.
What has Heaven said? *(Lunyu, Yanghuo)*

Such a Heavenly mandate should be respected but should not be worshiped, and it is also useless to pray for it, since

If one receives punishment from the Heaven,
there is no use to pray. *(Lunyu, Baxiu)*

As to devils and gods, Confucius had a suspicious attitude:

> The subjects on which the Master did not take were —
> extraordinary things, feats of strength, disorder, and spiritual beings.
> *(Lunyu, Shuer)*

Confucius did not deny their existence but did not talk about them. Although he did not know whether they exist or what kind of use they might be, he believed it is better not to talk about them. It is interesting that, although Confucius held a suspicious attitude to the faith objects of religions, he held an affirmative attitude to religion itself. Confucius was originally a literate officer who took "ritual property" as his profession, and "sacrifice" was, in fact, an important part of "ritual property." The purpose of "sacrifice" was to educate society:

> Let there be a careful attention to perform the funeral rites to parents, and let them be followed when long gone with the ceremonies of sacrifice; then the virtue of the people will resume its proper excellence. *(Lunyu, Xueer)*

If the object of sacrifice does not exist, the ceremony of sacrifice itself will lose its basis of existence. Thus, Confucius suggested that

> he sacrificed to the dead, as if they were present.
> He sacrificed to the spirits as if the spirits were present. *(Lunyu, Bayi)*

The term "as if" is, in fact, a hypothesis. Although it is not clear whether they exist or not, if they exist they can be helpful to educate people. This is perhaps not necessary for gentlemen, but it is essential for "mean men," since

> the mean man does not know the ordinances of Heaven, and consequently does not stand in awe of them. He is disrespectful to great men. He makes sport of the words of sages. *(Lunyu, Jishi)*

This is quite similar to the French Enlightenment philosopher Voltaire's assertion that "even if there is no God, it would be necessary to invent one," and it is similar to the German philosopher Kant's hypothesis of God's existence grounded in practical rationality. Confucius's plan to educate people through sacrifices to devils and spirits has been summarized as "laying down instruction with the spirit-like way" in the *Yijing*, which reads:

When we contemplate the spirit-like way of Heaven, we see how the four seasons proceed without error. The sages, in accordance with (this) spirit-like way, laid down their instructions, and all under Heaven yield submission to them. *(Yijing, Guan)*

This idea was developed by Xunzi. He believed that "Heaven has its normal principle in proceeding." He even suggested "to control the Mandate of Heaven so as to use it" (Xunzi, *Tianlun),* and he denied the existence of devils and spirits; however, he paid attention to the function of sacrifice. He said:

Sacrifice is the feeling of expressing and thinking; is the pinnacle of loyalty, faith, love and respect; and is the prosperity of rites and culture. If one is not a sage, he cannot know it. Sages know it clearly, officials and gentlemen follow it peacefully, officers take it as a protection, and the mass consider it as secular. For the gentlemen it is considered as the human way, and for the mass it is considered as serving devils. (Xunzi, *Lilun)*

Only sages can understand the mystery of religion; for other people, religions play their role in the form of following, protecting, and secularity. However, Xunzi was also cautious about the tendency of religions to become absolute. He warned that the activities such as sacrifice and shamanism are

accomplishments for the gentlemen, and are spirits for the mass. It would be fortunate if it is considered as accomplishment, and it would be disaster if it is considered as spirit. (Xunzi, *Tianlun)*

In such a sense the highest summary of the Confucian understanding of religion is found in the words of Confucius himself:

To give oneself earnestly to the duties due to men, and, while respecting spiritual beings, to keep aloof from them. *(Lunyu, Yonge)*

Religions are closely related to rites. Religion itself is not the purpose but the mean, and the essence of education is built on the basis of the patriarchal clan system of monarchy, which is again based on filial piety. Therefore, although the basis of religion is the spirit-like way, its purpose is totally for the sake of human beings. Confucianism admits and even stresses the great social function of religions, and it also supports those religions that are in accordance with the purpose of official education. However, it has never allowed religions as such to go beyond the status of acting as a tool of education. To the religions or those religious elements that are contrary to the official educational purpose, Confucianism holds an attitude of rejection and even employs political measures to forbid their existence and development.

However, Confucianism is not an organization that has strict rules, and its ideology is not always systematic. Different religions also have various forms of expression in their history of development. Thus it is necessary to make a concrete analysis of the relationship between Confucianism and religions. Generally speaking, Confucianism has a source similar to Chinese official religions. "Worshiping Heaven and ancestors and emphasizing the importance of the nation" are the common content of both Confucianism and Chinese official religions. The Confucian view of religion is an affirmation of the existing official religions, and it also offers support to them theoretically and practically.

Local Chinese Taoism is also in accordance with Confucianism in assisting and rectifying the monarchical system. Therefore, although Confucianism sometimes criticizes Taoism because of its elements of celestial being and magic power, generally speaking Confucianism and Taoism live in peace with each other. When Buddhism was transmitted into China, it was welcomed by some Chinese Confucians. However, because of the difference in doctrines between them, Buddhism has been criticized by most Confucians. In history there have been occasions when Buddhism was forbidden in China, and this decision was, of course, made by Chinese officials; but Confucians also played an important role in encouraging such rejection of Buddhism.

Because of the special status of Confucianism in Chinese society, various religions in China have employed a cooperative and even compromising attitude to work with Confucianism. Taoism and Confucianism have the same root in Chinese ancient worship of Heaven and ancestors. Later in the process of development, they became mixed together to a great extent so that a complementary relationship was formed, since the former emphasizes the ultimate concern and the latter stresses this-worldly concerns. In the beginning stage when Buddhism was transmitted into China, it employed a measure of "reaching Buddhism through Confucianism and Taoism." It actively employed Confucian and Taoist terminologies and ideas to defend Buddhism, it made compromises with Confucianism in the aspects of loyalty, filial piety, and rites, and it even put forward the theory that the Three Religions (Confucianism, Taoism, and Buddhism) are in accordance with one another. The famous Buddhist monk Zong Mi in the Tang dynasty said in his *Huayan yuanren lun*:

Confucius, Laozi, and Buddha are all sages. They laid down religions through different ways in reaction to the times and situations, and they considered from both inside and outside in order to benefit the mass.

Therefore, a kind of Chinese Buddhism was formed. Between the Ming and Qing dynasties, Christianity was transmitted into China through Jesuit missionaries' work. Matteo Ricci and his colleagues put forward the policy of "rejecting Buddhism and complementing Confucianism." They tried their best to interpret Christian doctrines with the terminologies found in the Chinese classics, and they made compromises with Chinese rites such as worshiping Heaven, ancestors, and Confucius. Consequently, they achieved success.

It should be pointed out that, since the May Fourth Movement in 1919, Confucianism has lost its dominant status in Chinese ideology, especially its role of partnership in ruling the country. It is interesting that the Confucian attitude to religions has been retained in the minds of Chinese intellectuals. Since the 1980s, religions have been increasingly studied in Chinese academic circles. More and more academic journals and research institutes have appeared, more and more universities have begun to have courses in religions, and more and more publications have appeared in the area of religious research. However, what people usually care about is not religions themselves but the social function of religions. In other words, the social function of religions enables people to understand religions themselves. In summary, "while respecting spiritual beings, to keep aloof from them" is still the basic attitude of Chinese intellectuals to religions.

The Basic Attitude of Chinese Authority to Religions

Chinese authorities have always paid considerable attention to the issue of religion. Because of the influence of Confucianism and the stability of society, the attitude of Chinese authorities to religions has the following features.

1. Chinese authorities emphasize, use, and even support the educational function of religions, and especially stress the spiritual ruling function of religions.

According to historical documents, as early as the end of Primary Society, King Shu ordered Qi to distribute Five Educations in the Four Directions (*Shiji, Wudi benji*). Though "education" here does not refer to religion, it indicates that Chinese authorities emphasized education. Chinese traditional religions of the patriarchal clan system have always been the means through which the authorities proposed loyalty and filial piety and justified kingship rule in the country. Even the birth of Chinese religions such as Taoism and the transmission into China of foreign religions such as Buddhism and Christianity were welcomed by Chinese authorities of the time. During many historical stages in China, when the religious status of the patriarchal clan system was guaranteed, many authorities actively supported development of religion, as was the case with Buddhism during the South and North dynasties and Taoism in the Tang dynasty. The main reason was that these religions were helpful for the rule of Chinese authorities in those times.

2. Chinese authorities are very cautious about the possibility that religions harm kingship, ruling secretly.
Religions take gods and spirits as the objects of worship and the Other Shore as the ideal, and they stand aloof from worldly affairs. These features of religions differentiate their concerns from those of secular authorities, and thus, religions may possibly harm the rule of authorities in the country. In addition to using the unified function of religions in attracting people to the official ideology so as to strengthen the position of their rule, Chinese authorities have also been careful about the negative influence of religions and have never allowed religions to harm their rule. When it was considered necessary, Chinese authorities employed strict and brutal measures to forbid the transmission of certain religions. For example, Buddhism has been destroyed several times in Chinese history.

Two primary reasons explain these attacks. On the one hand, Buddhist temples and monks competed with Chinese authorities in gaining material and human resources. On the other hand, Buddhist ideas of standing aloof from worldly affairs conflict with Confucian ideas of expressing filial piety to parents and being loyal to the authorities. In some of the most dramatic cases, religions, mainly branches of Buddhism or Taoism, united with rebelling powers to overthrow the rule of Chinese authorities. Chinese authorities have always been very hostile toward such movements and have sought to destroy them.

3. Chinese authorities strictly control religions and have never allowed religions to override political power.
According to a legend, a religious reformation called "cutting off the connection between Heaven and Earth" emerged at the end of Primary Society

in China. The essence of this reform was to deny the right of common people to sacrifice to Heaven and the gods, and finally to extend this right only to rulers. Thereafter, the primary worship of Heaven and the gods became the State religion, serving the rulers with emperors and kings as high priests in a patriarchal clan system of religion. Chinese authorities have always strictly controlled folk and foreign religions such as Taoism, Buddhism, and Christianity. In various dynasties in Chinese history religious leaders were frequently treated as "State Masters."

On the one hand, this indicated the emphasis that authorities placed on religions; on the other hand, this was also a measure adopted by authorities to control and use religions. Though certain individual emperors in Chinese history appreciated certain religions, no religion has ever gained the position of "State Religion" so as to control the whole country. In the Chinese cultural tradition, religion cannot exist as an independent power separated from politics. In the eyes of authorities, religion is always a tool for fulfilling their rule in the country. Only when a religion is helpful or at least is not harmful to their rule will it be permitted to exist and develop in the country.

This attitude of Chinese authorities to religions has compelled various religions to adjust their relationship with Chinese authorities and frequently to rely on the favor of the authorities. When Taoism was first established, it encouraged opposition to Chinese authorities and, as a result, was brutally suppressed by those authorities. From the reform in the South and North dynasties, Taoism began to absorb and to emphasize elements that were in accordance with Confucianism and the patriarchal clan system. Thus, Taoism gained support and welcome from Chinese authorities. The famous Taoist leader Kou Qianzhi clearly established obeying and following authority as the first rule of Taoism. He asked that Taoists "neither rebel against the emperors nor harm the country." A famous Buddhist monk, Dao An, clearly expressed this sentiment: "If it does not rely on the Lord of the country, Buddhism cannot exist."

The reason that led to Christianity's success between the Ming and Qing dynasties was to a great extent that the Jesuits had actively gained support from authorities. Otherwise, if a religion seeks to be against the state and to override the authorities, it will usually experience disaster. In the Qing dynasty, a controversy over rites developed between the Roman pope and the Chinese emperor. Finally, as a result, Christianity was forbidden in China. In addition to differences in culture and theological understanding, the major reason for the exclusion of Christianity lay in the pope's attempt to override the position of the Chinese emperor Kangxi and to compel Chinese Christians to give up traditional rituals.

Now we are in the twenty-first century, and China is a socialist country led by the Chinese Communist Party. However, the relationship between Chinese authority and religions has not changed. Jiang Zemin, China's former president, put forward a principle "to actively lead religions to adjust to socialist society," and this can be considered as the basic state policy of China in dealing with religious issues.

A Response to Professor Li Qiuling

Fredrik Fällman

Professor Li analyzes the position of religion in Chinese society and the attitudes toward it from the three aspects of common people, dominant ideology in society, and ruling authority. The latter two are most likely closely related and connected since a ruler would try to promote his own ideology or even adopt the dominating ideology.

Believers of organized religion are a minority in China, but they are quite a large minority, consisting of over 100 million people. They could have a profound influence and exert considerable power if they united, even if only uniting within their own groups. The recent example of Falun Gong shows how such a situation can suddenly develop and how the authorities and society react in response. Folk religions are usually not counted within the numbers mentioned above but constitute a large group if taken all together. They are even the fastest-growing religious group in contemporary China, along with Christianity in its various forms. Professor Li claims that folk religions "are probably not real religions" — but what then are "real religions"? Religions with scriptures, structures, and temples? Since Li Qiuling bases his analysis of religion on folk religions this needs further clarification.

Officially, religion in China has often been considered as a matter of private and personal concern, in both imperial and republican times. As long as religious belief is kept on the individual level it has been tolerated by both government and dominating ideology. It poses no real threat to their authority. This attitude can also be connected to the utilitarian aspect that Professor Li points out. The purpose of religion is only for individual needs and need not interfere with, and cannot do anything in, matters of state or other affairs beyond the realm of the family.

Confucius had "an affirmative attitude to religion itself" according to Li but "held a suspicious attitude to the faith objects of religions." Li categorizes Confucianism as agnostic. To me this inclines to a certain *deistic* approach, not only from Confucius but Confucianism in general. The Confucian attitude is summed up in the following quotation from Confucius, "while respecting spiritual beings, to keep aloof from them." This implies a distant Creator power that can neither interfere with individual lives nor be reached by man.

As has been said earlier, Confucianism has sometimes been somewhat carelessly applied to all Chinese, so as to represent "the Chinese," when this today is certainly not the case. Confucian thought is an indispensable part of Chinese culture but not all encompassing, and not of great importance in contemporary society, despite the work of "neo-Confucians." Supposedly the attitude of many intellectuals today is still of a Confucian kind, and the main interest and focus in the developing religious studies in China is in the social function of religion.

Here one can make an interesting connection to the issue of "Cultural Christians" that has developed in recent years. Some criticism pointed at these intellectuals with interest in Christianity is that they are using Christian ethics to modernize and "save China," thus having a utilitarian approach. Some of them are also openly critical of Confucianism and Taoism, which may explain part of the criticism directed toward them. Many of the scholars doing research about Christianity also have a great interest in the very basic issues of faith and reason. Others focus on the idea of "true faith" and how to achieve it and why it is so important, both for the individual and for society.

The *deistic* aspect of Confucianism could be of some importance when analyzing why the issues of salvation, sin, and guilt have been differently interpreted and not so easily communicated in the Chinese context. When "God" is at best a distant Creator that one cannot influence and who certainly cannot punish, then such concepts are not central.

There are also mainland intellectuals who reject the idea that merely social ethics and aesthetics form the base for Chinese culture. Some claim that *Tian*, usually translated as Heaven, originally was a name for a supreme power similar to the Christian God. The concepts of *Tian* and *Shangdi* existed already during the Xia and Shang periods and represented a spirit or God with free will, the root of all things, both good and evil. This Godlike notion of *Tian* should have gradually disappeared from the Zhou period and onward, supported by the learned men advocating the Confucian system of thought. The fact that Chinese culture once possessed a notion of a transcendent God under the name of *Tian* would then show that it is not unique to Western culture and may even develop again in China. The problem with this argument is the difficulty in interpreting texts from the early periods and that any interpretation fits its proponents perhaps too well and also runs the risk of making assumptions — wrongly or not — about the origins of Chinese culture.

In Professor Li's analysis one can see the rather common division between "the common people" and the intellectual elite. The masses worship folk deities for utilitarian purposes, and the intellectuals stick to the Confucian ideal of "keeping aloof" from the spirits while acknowledging the existence of a supreme force. This is again an analysis from within and for the ruling elite and the intellectuals. Folk religion and common people have not had a voice to portray their beliefs in the same way.

Drawing further consequences from Li's analysis, another issue comes to light. Any devout Chinese Christian or any other believer who is pious and has no or at least less utilitarian motives would be very "un-Chinese," and as such not be considered a true Chinese. He or she could come under suspicion of harboring thoughts against the state, against (Chinese) culture, and so on. This question of identity is not to be underestimated since it also encompasses an issue of loyalty — loyalty first to faith or to the ruler. Any ruler is afraid of a true believer since he puts loyalty to his faith before loyalty to the ruler. The slogan among patriotic religious organizations in contemporary China, *aiguo aijiao* (love the country, love religion), puts loyalty to country first, not religion or faith. This slogan is a prerequisite for the existence of such patriotic organizations and is a direct interference in both matters of faith and of religious organization. Accordingly, the place for religion is supposed to be patriotic and supportive of the present ruler.

Commenting on the situation in contemporary Chinese society Li quotes the statement by former president Jiang Zemin from 1993 about "religions adapting to socialist society" *(zongjiao yu shehuizhuyi shehui xiang shiying)*. I agree with Professor Li that this is indeed the "basic state policy of China in dealing with religious issues." This principle, and comments made about it by certain cadres, can give the impression that also the state or the party should "adapt" in one or the other way for the benefit of religion. However, openly accessible educational material for cadres[1] quite bluntly

---

1. Gong Xuezeng, *Zongjiao wenti ganbu duben* (Beijing: Zhonggong zhongyang dangxiao chubanshe, 2000), p. 210.

states that this is not at all the case. Religions should merely adapt to socialist society and further its development. Trying to control the doctrines of various religions and thus the content of faith itself, the present government of China goes a step further than many predecessors, which focused on religious structure and the possible political and economic power of religions. The officially atheist government even defines various religious groups as "sects," sometimes on good grounds, sometimes not.

As Professor Li points out, many rulers in China have actively supported religions occasionally because they could be of use to them and their politics. Persecution of religions has also mostly been based on a perceived or real political or economic threat. Professor Li Qiuling argued that today intellectuals no longer become officials to influence, but they still work within the state framework, although not embracing the prescribed Marxist ideology. Very few venture outside the system, and some even claim that they do want to work and change the system from the inside.

The theme for Professor Li's paper is "The Position of Religion in Chinese Society" and one can see the title and the whole approach as an example of the lingering Confucian attitude to religion among Chinese intellectuals that Li mentions himself. However, to deal with contextualization and issues of the true impact of religious belief one has to investigate how *faith* is experienced and lived out among these groups. What does faith mean to "common people"? How is it viewed by dominant ideologies and by rulers? "The Position of Faith in Chinese Society" could perhaps be the theme for a whole conference, and not only a single paper.

Faith would also survive without the religious structure and even seek new loose organizational form under oppression. Christianity has shown several times that faith survives and even flourishes under pressure from governments or other oppressors. China is no exception, with the Cultural Revolution as a fairly recent example.

The place for religion in Chinese society stills seems to be that of a supportive function to the government, if it is allowed at all. Seen from a different perspective it may also be a resource for constructing a new worldview for Chinese society. This implies that a study and analysis of religious structure and outer form is not enough in the Chinese context. One should investigate faith and its individual and societal implications. In modern society the relation between God and the individual is also becoming increasingly important and may even be "the modern form" of belief, outside systematized religion, e.g., a church.

A Response to Professor Li Quiling

Birger Nygaard

Professor Li Qiuling outlines distinctions in the Chinese understanding of the place of religion in society that are fundamental to an intelligent conversation between the Chinese and the Western world. If we were not told, none of us in the West would know of the three distinctive segments with vastly different attitudes to and expectations from religion. These distinctions certainly complicate the quest for developing a well-founded Christian theology in the Chinese setting. In my response I will take Professor Li's paper as a point of departure for a couple of reflections on how to respond to the situation outlined in the paper. What methods of inquiry and action could be employed in order to move on from the traditional position in Chinese society?

A Need to Go outside the Box

It seems that Christian theology is easily taken captive by one of the three groups:

(1) Zealous missionary groups responsible for much of the growth of Christianity among common people in the countryside — without realizing how the results of their missionary efforts might be akin to and drawing on mere traditional folk religion.
(2) Intellectuals who may tend to see Christianity as a philosophical addition to an already well-developed Confucian or some other philosophical tradition.

(3) Authorities — reducing Christian religion to a tool in their governance system.

None of these options allow for an unfolding of the full nature of the Christian faith. Christian faith does not want to be domesticated by any of these, but Christian faith can provide hope, wholeness, meaning, and service to all three. But is there any way that these three groups can start working together in a constructive way? Could the development of religious studies in the academy be the beginning of such a development? Any attempts to get a proper meaning out of Christian theology without some kind of holism will in fact be deficient.

When — from a traditional Christian perspective — we seek to compare the traditional Chinese and Christian view on the place of religion in society, it seems fundamental that Christian tradition does not really allow for such a split between the three layers (1) common people, (2) dominant ideology, and (3) authorities. It is a basic Christian premise that all people are created equal by God.

Chinese tradition	Christian beliefs
1. **Common people** (the masses) Utilitarian relationship to the spirit world Nonpious = a-ethical Pluralist faith	Transcendent God (faith-meaning-worship) $\updownarrow$
2. **Dominant ideology** (intellectuals) Social functions of religion (ethics) Focus on life here and now Spirit world: is there — but keep aloof	Spirit world (utilitarian-power- healing-protection) $\updownarrow$
3. **Chinese authorities** (ruling class) Utilitarian pragmatic use of religion in order to strengthen governance Ranked below government Suppressed if conflicting with ruling class	Ordinary life (one family under God ethics: building society)

The transcendent God in heaven is the one to be worshiped, and all human beings are called to take part in his ongoing creative initiative and mission in the world. This God is not believed to be a philosophical abstraction, but in reflection on the ultimate meaning, in ordinary life matters, and in dealing with the spirit world, he is very much present in incarnational reality by the Holy Spirit.

Dealing with the Spirit World

It may be very scary in the Chinese setting that Christianity also deals with the spirit world, as this in the Chinese view relegates Christianity to the realm of superstition. This is also the case in modern Western Christianity, where theologically we are very uncertain and uncomfortable with this dimension, although it is so real to many ordinary people. Our Enlightenment worldview — which still dominates theological education in the West — does not have categories for this. But the phenomenological evidence that emerges in the new climate of a postmodern culture forces us in the West to start reading the Bible and church history once again in order to look for and integrate a proper theology of the spirit world that resonates with the real-life experiences of ordinary people. If Christian theologians are not faithful in this task, they do indeed abandon the masses to become victims of all kinds of superstitions. Instead, a proper biblical theology will in fact be able to engage the spirit world and liberate common people from its powers without denying its existence. Wherever Christianity is growing in the southern hemisphere, such a theology is an important feature.

It seems to be an urgent task in the Chinese setting to provide the kind of theological reasoning and ecclesiastical praxis that can bridge the gap between the intellectuals and the common people. Is it not the task of the well-formulated Christian elite — in both church and university settings — to do this, and at the same time demonstrate to the authorities that Christianity is not a religion subject to the spirit world, but indeed a religion that — by its spiritual powers — encounters and disarms the spirit world and leads on toward an ethical lifestyle for the benefit of people and society? The ethical reflection among the elite needs to be the salt among common people.

What Changes Are Ahead?

Now you may say that this is only wishful thinking. Can it ever happen in a society that for thousands of years has had the traditional divisions? I do not know. But I will tell a parallel story from my own setting. Twenty-five years ago the church and questions of faith and religion in our northern European setting were utterly removed from public space and relegated to the private world. Religion was not really talked about anywhere, especially not among intellectuals. Today religion has become very visible in the public sphere: in the mass media, in everyday conversations among common people and the intellectual elite. But over these last years an entire religious transformation seems to have taken place — away from the standard dogmatic faith systems to late-modern self-composed noninstitutional belief systems, which we in the church really do not know how to relate and respond to. None of this was planned. No ideological groups have promoted this. But it has happened as an unexpected result of a multitude of influences in the globalized world in which we live today.

Can similar changes that will eventually change old ways take place in Chinese society? Or is this for the rest of the world only? In preparing for this response I went to the library and found an anthropological book from 1973 on the place of religion in Chinese society. Nearly all case studies were from Hong Kong and Taiwan, as it was not possible to get access to China. Today we are gathered here openly discussing Christianity and Chinese culture. This seems not like thirty years of development, but light years of change. With the Open-Door Policy, World Trade Organization, mass media, mobile phones, the Internet, etc., China has opened itself to the same globalizing forces that have heavily changed belief systems in the West over the last generation. What does that mean to the future place of religion in Chinese society?

In the light of this, is it possible to supplement the research on the past with research on emergent trends in the cultural centers of contemporary China? Professor Diane Obenchain describes what she senses among her students: a quest "among Chinese students for guidance that will offer them a consistent and reliable way (a) to experience healing of the individual, family, and the larger social whole, (b) to give meaning to life, (c) to cultivate care and concern for others along with a sense of conscience, (d) to bring fairness to economic practice, and (e) to bring political safeguards that allow for, encourage, and protect these processes."[1]

These questions seem quite similar to the questions of students in the West. Christianity would have important contributions to offer to a new generation of young Chinese that may be more dominated by the anomie and uncertainties of their new globalized realities than by the traditional divisions of the past.

---

1. Diane Obenchain, "Nourishing the Spirit in China Today," *China Church Quarterly* (Spring 2001).

PART III

Challenges to the Contemporary Chinese Protestant Church

15 The Basis for the Reconstruction of Chinese Theological Thinking

Deng Fucun

At the Second Plenary Session of the Sixth Chinese Christian Council Conference, held in November 1998, a resolution was adopted on the Strengthening of the Reconstruction of Theological Thinking. Over the past five years, the Chinese church has been rethinking its theology, and this has been noticed by churches in other countries. After discussion, some other churches understand and support Chinese theological rethinking. Some do not understand and are doubtful about it because of the fear that it may weaken Christian faith or that it is not biblically grounded. I would therefore like to offer clarification.

A Historical Review

In 635 CE, the emperor Taizong of the Tang dynasty sent Fang Xuanling, his prime minister, to welcome Alopen, the Nestorian missionary, to Changan (the capital of the Tang dynasty) with great honor. Christianity was called Nestorianism *(Jingjiao)* at the time, and it was the forerunner of all later Christianity in China. Nestorianism had considerable success in China at that time. It reached ten provinces and established its churches in over one hundred cities. However, it did not adapt its theology to Chinese traditional culture. When it articulated its doctrines, it adopted too many Buddhist terms that were familiar to the local people. That caused the misunderstanding that it was a branch of Buddhism from the West. Therefore, when the emperor Wuzong of the Tang dynasty converted to Taoism and started suppressing Buddhism, all the Nestorian missionaries were expelled, and all the Nestorian churches were remodeled into Taoist temples.

When the Mongolians ruled China, Nestorian Christianity was brought into China again. The Mongolian term for Christianity was Arkhun, which means the religion of the Cross. Since it was only popular among the Mongolian rulers, it was swept out as a foreign religion when Zhu Yuanzhang, the first emperor of the Ming dynasty, overthrew the Mongolian domination.

During the later period of the Ming dynasty, the Roman Catholic missionary Matteo Ricci arrived in China. With awareness of the unsuccessful experience of the Nestorian church in China, he studied Confucianism and dressed like a Confucian. He also introduced Western astronomy and mathematics into China. His efforts and those of his colleagues were appreciated by emperors in the Ming and Qing dynasties. His evangelism was authorized, and he was also appointed as the director of the astronomical observatory. By the time of the Kangxi emperor, the Catholic believers in Beijing and its surrounding areas numbered one hundred thousand. Suddenly, however, the Rites Controversy (by nature, it is a theological debate) broke out. Because the pope could not accept the emperor's position, Christianity was forbidden in China for two hundred years. The records of this history argue that it is impossible to imagine that Christianity will be able to take root and develop in China without identifying itself with the culture and the context of its mission object.

In the early nineteenth century, Protestantism entered China again from the West. Missionary theology was generally a conservative Protestant one that stressed the sinfulness of the world and the fact that humanity had no future without conversion to Christianity. It held a negative attitude toward social achievements. Some missionaries also maintained some weird theological notions equating the red dragon and the red horse in the book of Revelation with communism, and therefore begged God to drown the People's Liberation Army in the Yangtze River as he had drowned the Pharaoh's charioteers in the Red Sea. The colonial theology also claimed Japheth the ancestor of Caucasians, Shem the ancestor of the yellow race, and Ham the ancestor of the blacks. Consequently the Caucasians could live in the tent of the yellow people, and the blacks should serve the Caucasians. Since the establishment of new China, the Three-Self Patriotic Movement of the Chinese church has been stressing "self-evangelism." This not only means that Chinese Christians should carry on the mission of evangelism by themselves, but also means they should adapt the content of mission to the development of the new era.

In the 1950s, *Tian Feng,* the publication of the Chinese church, provided an open forum for a general discussion of issues arising with adaptation to our new society, such as the opposition between believers and nonbelievers, and the question of whether participation in the construction of a socialist society was in conflict with Christian faith. The discussions received positive results. However, discussion and adaptation were not able to go further because of the change of the situation.

After the Cultural Revolution, our churches were busy in restoring church activities. Most of our pastoral personnel and seminary teachers taught the conservative theological concepts inherited from the past. Some of them had started to open their minds in the 1950s. After the Cultural Revolution, their way of thinking returned to the old days. In the 1980s, the Three-Self Movement placed one-sided emphasis on "unity" but failed in providing adequate and necessary guidance of theological thinking. Some churches outside of China purposely tried to sneak their narrow theological understanding into the Chinese church. All of these factors made the theological understanding of some Chinese pastors and especially young people even narrower.

The fifty years' endeavor by the Three-Self Movement proves that Christian theology can be adapted to a socialist society. It is shown in the following aspects:

1. The emphasis on the necessity that Christian faith must be in accordance with the Bible, and it must oppose any heresy.
2. The emphasis on personal spiritual formation and gaining inner peace and strength of life through faith enables believers to establish a psychological balance that will benefit the society.
3. Under the guidance of Christian ethics and "being the light and salt, and glorifying God and benefiting people," many Christians are admirable citizens and make contributions to the construction of our socialist country.

However, conservative theological thinking can have results that are not compatible with our socialist country. The major examples are as follows:

1. The negation of this world. It holds that even though the world is rich in resources and technological progress is apparent, human nature is becoming more and more corrupt, and this must result in extermination. It holds that earthquakes, famines, and wars are the signs of the immediate coming of doomsday.

2. It draws a clear line between believers and nonbelievers, and regards all Christian believers as of one family, but does not extend this sense of community to nonbelievers and may even encourage confrontation with them.

3. It places the church above the country and emphasizes that Christians' love for the church must be prior to that for the country. It advocates that to love the church is to love the country and that Christians should be apolitical, listening to God but not to men.

4. It claims that to join with the Three-Self Patriotic Movement is to "submit the church to government control," to cater to worldly authority, and thereby to damage the spiritual position of Christ as head of the church.

5. It stresses "being spiritual" but negates rational thinking. This attitude encourages fanaticism. There are also other negative results caused by conservative theological thinking. Churches in rural areas tend to be superstitious, and churches in cities tend to be utilitarian. Some of the churches emphasize the exclusiveness of Christian faith, and are not in line with the society. As a result, Christianity can only attract the ill-educated and those who are not satisfied by society. Such a church is unable to adapt to our socialist society, and its future will not be bright.

In their pastoral work, some pastoral personnel lack a consciousness of loving the country and abiding by the law. If the Three-Self Movement does not have a sufficient theological basis, its orientation will not be well rooted. It will not be able to resist the penetration of ideas introduced by overseas churches using theological language. The call of such groups for an "evangelized China" puzzles many people. It leads many Chinese Christians to perplexity as to why they cannot love the country and love the church.

Many overseas church circles believe that the Chinese church has no theology. Some people even say that "Besides 'Thanks to Jesus,' Chinese Christians have no other words to communicate with other Christians." The Chinese church will never waver in its adherence to the principles of self-independence and self-management of the church. The above-mentioned issues, however, have some negative impacts on our agenda of running our church well. What is worth noticing is that some pastoral personnel are satisfied by the current numerical growth of church members without realizing the significance of guiding praxis by theological thinking. If we do not carry through the Reconstruction of Theological Thinking betimes, the future of the Chinese church will be a failure.

The Identification and Adaptation of Theological Thinking

If theology is the knowledge of God and the relation between God and human beings, theological thinking is then the reflection of human beings upon the issues in the theological sphere. For a religion, theology is responsible for articulating its doctrines and defending its fundamental faith. For Christianity, the Bible is its most original theological dissertation, explaining the fundamental Christian faith. In addition to presenting the four Gospels, it reveals the life of the early church clearly to us. In order to assure that its mission objectives were identified with Jesus Christ and adaptable, the early church continually adjusted its theological thinking.

When the apostles initiated their mission among the Jews, they used all the prophetic sayings about the Messiah for the purpose of making it easier for Jews to receive Jesus as the Savior. When the early church brought its mission into the Greek world, the "incarnated Jesus" was easier to be understood and accepted by the people living in the Hellenistic culture along the Mediterranean seacoast. "I have become all things to all people" became the rule that Paul observed to "share the blessings." Circumcision, which Jews observed as the sign of the chosen people, became a burden for gentile Christians and hindered the work of the Holy Spirit. "Proclaim the good news to the whole creation."

The Process of Launching the Reconstruction of Theological Thinking

First of all, I shall explain why our two organizations initiated the resolution for strengthening the Reconstruction of Theological Thinking at the all-members' committee in Jinan in 1998. Some of our colleagues attending the meeting felt that the resolution was brought forward rather abruptly. They were not ready for it. Yet Bishop K. H. Ting had raised the issue of the Reconstruction of Theological Thinking rather early. In 1993, leaders from all five Chinese religions met in Hainan. The meeting discussed the issue of how to guide religions to be adaptable to the socialist society. In that meeting, leaders from each religion discussed the issue. At that time, all religious leaders expressed their support for the idea. But the method of adapting religions to the socialist society was still uncertain. In that meeting, Bishop Ting mentioned that the most important adaptation was the adaptation of thinking. He was concerned with changing concepts.

After the meeting, when Bishop Ting exchanged ideas with colleagues from our two organizations, he emphasized the adaptation of thinking which, for Christianity, implies the adjustment of our theology. Then some of our colleagues said that the term "adjustment" generally refers to correcting something that is wrong and therefore in need of adjustment. Therefore, they feared that the word "adjustment" might very easily be misunderstood. It might be better to put this issue forward from an obverse side. When Y. T. Wu initiated "the three-self innovation movement," many of our colleagues did not appreciate the expression, for they were afraid that innovation might "innovate" faith into nothing. Many worried about this matter. On the basis of that experience, Bishop Ting phrased the matter as an adaptation of thinking and insisted that it is very necessary for Christianity in China to carry through the Reconstruction of Theological Thinking.

In August 1996, when religious leaders talked about this issue, Bishop Ting articulated it more concretely. In Chinese church theology, there are many elements that are not compatible with our contemporary context or with our socialist society. What we shall do right now is to make our Christian theology in China compatible with our context and our socialist society. When we drafted the work report for the Sixth National Assembly of the Chinese Church, the phrase "Reconstruction of Theological Thinking" appeared for the first time. In 1998, at a conference with religious leaders from all religions, Bishop Ting spoke about the innovation of religious concepts not only within Christianity but also within all religions. He said that religious concepts must be renovated in order to make religions compatible with our socialist society. He mentioned many concrete examples from Christianity and other religions.

Bishop Ting recalled his experience as the principal of Nanjing (Jingling) Union Theological Seminary. Originally he expected the seminary to lead other seminaries in understanding the Three-Self Principle, training pastoral personnel, and promoting theological thinking. As a matter of fact, the seminary has been behind others. For instance, when there was a terrible flood in China, some people there considered the flood as God's punishment of the Chinese people. After this speech of Bishop Ting was later published in *Renmin zhenxie bao,* some staff members from the seminary said that Bishop Ting had blackened the name of the Nanjing Seminary in a public meeting, resulting in loss of face for the seminary. Some people said that the actual situation in Nanjing was not as the bishop described it. Thus, there was a disputation concerning Ting's employment of such an example. In such a situation, the Chinese Christian Council and the Three-Self Patriotic Movement committee have responsibilities to lead Christians in the correct direction.

The Common Understanding of Promoting the Reconstruction of Theological Thinking

Through discussion of the topic of the Reconstruction of Theological Thinking at the conference in Jinan, we reached some common opinions on the issue. Later on, the common understandings played a positive role in guiding and encouraging people in promoting seminars on this issue at different levels. These understandings are as follows:

1. Basic faith is unchangeable, but theological thought can be adjusted.

Christian fundamental faith is summed up in the Apostles' Creed and the Nicene Creed, which have been accepted universally by the church and are the standard for distinguishing orthodoxy and heresy. No faith belief or church rules should go beyond the statements in the two creeds. Neither systematic theology nor doctrinal theology should contradict them. The fundamental faith offers a forum for theological studies, and theology interprets the fundamental faith with understandable language, ideas, and expressions. Theological thought has a close relationship with the fundamental faith, but it is not the fundamental faith. It can by no means replace the fundamental faith. To properly distinguish theological thought from basic faith, the former should be integrated with various local cultures and social backgrounds in such a way that the basic faith will be contextualized and will be easy for people of different cultural backgrounds to accept.

2. Free discussion and rational thinking are encouraged.

Theological thinking belongs to the sphere of thinking. Only through exchanges of ideas and free discussion can theological issues be pondered deeply. Free discussion needs an atmosphere of mutual respect and the willingness to hear the views of others rather than forcing others to accept one's own opinions. We should keep searching for new light and give up the old concepts. In the process of theological discussion, the discovery of each new light will challenge old concepts that do not fit the situation of the age anymore. This is, in fact, in accordance with the biblical teaching that new wine cannot be put into an old wineskin.

3. Exploring new light must be done on the basis of the Bible.

It was necessary for the Protestant church to be grounded on the authority of the Bible in order to challenge the authority of the pope. We are rooted in the Bible because it is the utmost revelation of our God and the basis of our faith. However, we should have a correct understanding of the Bible and the revelation of God. God's revelation to us is gradual, and our knowledge of God also grows gradually. If we rely only on a literal interpretation in reading the Bible, we will not be able to discover new light from it. We should continually enlarge our horizon and follow the guidance of the Holy Spirit; otherwise we cannot receive new revelation from our God. In the vision at Joppa, if Peter insisted in not eating those foods that he had never eaten earlier, he would not have heard the voice from heaven that "you should not consider them as dirty while God has already cleaned them."

4. Opposing disputes over denominations and avoiding monopoly are encouraged.

If one wishes to make a study of theology, one must dare to reflect and to enlarge one's reflection. If one limits oneself within certain concepts or a certain traditional understanding that does not fit the situation of the age, one will not be able to develop one's thinking. It is natural that different opinions appear in the process of the development of thinking. We should respect different opinions and learn to respect each other. We should not put labels on others or fall into denominational struggles.

5. The Reconstruction of Theological Thinking means the deepening of the Three-Self Patriotic principle.

The Three-Self Patriotic Movement needs theological support. The Chinese church exists in a socialist society, and there it has had many experiences affirming its Three-Self Patriotic principles. These experiences need to be studied and analyzed theologically, and they need to be considered in the development of an effective ecclesiology.

6. The Reconstruction of Theological Thinking should be integrated with Chinese culture.

The essence of Christianity was integrated into Greek society through the Word, and we should also integrate it into Chinese society through Chinese culture as its carrier. Western theology is based on Greek dualist culture that considers the material part of humanity as evil and therefore tries to separate flesh and spirit from one another. The Chinese cultural tradition is very different from that, since Chinese culture emphasizes the unity between Heaven and human beings and the harmony between human beings and nature. It is a natural choice to construct Chinese theology from our own Chinese cultural resources.

The Issues That Are Being Discussed in the Reconstruction of Theological Thinking

Theological construction is a systematic project that cannot be accomplished in a short period. Many issues should be discussed, and they touch many aspects. Some of them are difficult theoretical issues, and they seem far away from congregational lives and do not attract people to investigate them. Earlier in the present paper I mentioned some negative influences of Western conservative theology in China, and they are the issues that urgently need to be studied in the present time.

1. The status of human beings in the creation of God:
After our human ancestors fell into sin, what is the situation of human beings now in the plan of God? Is human nature evil and unrighteous? Are human beings only five-chi insects?

2. The relationship between God's creation and the atonement:
What is the relationship between God's creation and the atonement? Has the failure of human ancestors led God's creation into failure as well? Why does God grant atonement? What is the relationship between creation and atonement?

3. The relationship between believers and nonbelievers:
Who are the objects of God's love? Is the relationship between believers and nonbelievers one of confrontation or of neighborly love? Is it one of cooperation or separation? What is holiness? What is sanctification? What is the relationship between faith and deeds? Is it permissible to have faith only without deeds?

4. The relationship of churches and Christians with the state:
Are the principles of loving the country and of loving the church contradictory? Is supporting the communist authority opposing faith? Is it true that believers and nonbelievers can only be separated rather than unified, that

separation is holy but unity is sinful? Is it true that Christians are citizens of the heavenly kingdom and therefore should listen only to God rather than human beings? Is it true that the church belongs to the Holy Spirit and therefore is not under the supervision of an earthly authority? Is it true that neither Christian individuals nor churches should obey government or accept the administration of the state?

5. The Holy Spirit and the works of the Holy Spirit:

What are the major works of the Holy Spirit? If an individual does not have the ability to perform faith healing, speak in tongues, dance in the spirit, or sing spiritual songs, does this mean that the person has not received the Holy Spirit? Does this mean that the church does not have a living testimony?

6. The meaning of faith and the evidences of theological thought in the Three-Self Patriotic Movement:

What is the relationship between the church's universality and locality? What is the relationship between a body and its elements? Should Christians be apolitical? Is it true that loving one's country and loving one's church at the same time mean serving both Mammon and God?

7. Eschatology:

Is it true that the eschatology of Christianity is concerned only with the end of heaven and the earth? Is the whole world under the hand of Satan? Does the world belong to Satan? Does the end of the world mean destruction?

8. Rationality and other issues:

Can issues concerning God and loving God only be understood through the Spirit rather than through rational thinking as well? Is it true that human thinking, rationality, and knowledge cannot help people know and follow God rather than make people know God even less, resist God more, and depart more from God? Is it true that God has completed his revelation once and for all, and that revelation has ceased? Is it true that gradual revelation does not exist and that it contradicts the biblical teaching?

The Popular Issues

At a conference in Beijing, Bishop K. H. Ting talked about the issue of "soft-toning the doctrine of justification by faith." During and after the conference many people said that they could not understand what the term "soft-toning" means. Does this mean that the doctrine of justification by faith will be eliminated from our church doctrines? I would like to employ a young colleague's interpretation to answer this question.

When we had breakfast together with Bishop Ting, he asked our opinions concerning the soft-toning of justification by faith. A young colleague said: "It is not impossible to soft-tone it, since that means neither elimination nor cutting off. The opposite of soft-toning is emphasizing, and if it is not emphasized, it is soft-toned." He gave an example by saying, "According to Marxism, 'Religion is spiritual opium,' and this was emphasized very much in the past whenever religion was mentioned. Recently this has been soft-toned. However, this does not mean that this statement has been eliminated from the classics of Marx and Lenin. Since it has not been eliminated, this is a kind of soft-toning. The purpose of such a soft-toning is to unite religious people better."

Why do I employ such an example to answer this question? The purpose of our soft-toning of a certain doctrine that was emphasized very much in the past is to make the gospel more readily acceptable to people in the context of our lives. You cannot on the one hand emphasize how terrible nonbelievers are and on the other hand ask them to become believers. Can they accept such a gospel? Furthermore, the doctrine of justification by faith is not included in the two creeds we mentioned earlier, and it is only a doctrine. In fact, it is a principle of the Protestant Reformation. Of course, it is a very important statement of Christianity, but we do not emphasize it, and that is soft-toning. Soft-toning does not mean elimination, and it is by no means equal to changing doctrines. The purpose of soft-toning is to unite people more effectively. In the modern Chinese version of the Bible, "justification by faith" (*yin xin cheng yi*) has been translated as "to have proper relationship with God by faith" (*yin xin yu shen you heyi de guanxi*). Ephesians 2:8 says: "For by grace you have been saved through faith, and this is not your own doing; it is the gift of God. . . ." Thus, God's grace is prior, and faith is secondary.

In the conference, some of our colleagues asked why we have to be adaptable to our socialist society. Why cannot a socialist society be adaptable to us? At least, adaptation should be mutual in that we are adaptable to you and you are adaptable to us. Mutual respect may make sense only when the adaptation is understood in such a way. Their opinion seems to make sense. This reminds me of what a communist leader and an official of the religious affairs bureau in Shanghai, Mr. Wang Liping, chairman of the People's Political Consultative Conference, once said. At a religious conference, Mr. Wang stated:

Who said that only religious people should adjust? Communist Party members also need to adjust. In socialist society, especially in the present stage of our society, there are many things that require Communist Party members to adjust. For example, now we have a socialist market system; many old Communist Party members still stick to ideas of the planned economy. They cannot fit themselves into the socialist market system. We often mention the reformation of ideology and the need of adjusting socialist development, and these ideas are spoken to Communist Party members. Even the officers like us, who are responsible for political education, should also have ideological reformation in the new situation. Therefore, the issue of adjustment is not spoken especially to any side (Communist Party or religious people); everyone who does not fit our socialist development, should adjust.

I think such a speech is serious and sincere. Times are changing, and society is developing, and that does not depend upon anyone's subjective hope. The wheel of social progress and historical development is moving forward. Anyone who does not follow it will be cast away. Human thought and ideas should change with time to accommodate time's progress.

A Response to Rev. Deng Fucun

Chen Xun

Rev. Deng's paper clearly tells us the story of building and developing Chinese theology in modern China. He also gives us many examples to illustrate the history of the theological development of the Chinese church, the necessity for reconstructing theological thinking, and the current challenges to Chinese Christianity. Rev. Deng's paper concentrates on the background of this theological renewal from a practical perspective. As for myself, his paper benefits me a great deal, and what he says is reasonable and convincing. Hence, my response will focus on the following three things that relate to the process of developing theology within the Chinese context.

First, the Reconstruction of Theological Thinking can be considered as a form of theological contextualization. On the one hand, Chinese Christians may freely understand and interpret Holy Scripture according to their own context, which includes political background, cultural tradition, and social conditions as well as the church's self-development needs.

On the other hand, Chinese theological reconstruction should be concerned about the relationship between the theological traditions of universal Christianity (such as the ecumenical creeds and some fundamental doctrines) and Chinese cultural tradition. In this context, the dialogue between Western dogmatic theology and Chinese mainline culture is still an important task. From the viewpoint of theological thinking, it is not good for Chinese theologians to copy mechanically from Western theology. If so, Chinese theology would just be like a potted flower or a borrowed landscape. Therefore, it is necessary to deal with two relationships in this process, namely, between "national and international" and between "independent and interdependent."

From the point of view of classical theology, we cannot simply say that Western theology is based upon a presumption according to which "nature is evil." On the contrary, that kind of view was rejected by the early church as the heresy of Manicheanism. For example, Augustine is sure that God is absolutely good; human nature is created by God according to his own image and likeness, and is therefore good. In other words, Augustine strongly teaches that "human nature is good." Chinese Christianity needs to emphasize a positive doctrine of creation, including positive theological anthropology, eschatology, and Christian ethics. At the same time, it is necessary to distinguish between the concept of "Western theology" and understanding of the nineteenth-century Western missiology. Many Chinese Christians have been influenced by some negative Western missiological ideas, deriving from very conservative Western missionaries. They had their own denominational aims; they did not represent the whole positive spectrum of Western theology.

Second, we may look upon theological reconstruction as a process of continuing the construction of the indigenous church in China. The indigenous church means that the church must be deeply rooted in the Chinese context. It must become Chinese Christianity in substance. The indigenous church must be based upon contextual theology. In other words, theological theory and church practice are closely connected and cooperate with each other. In this respect, Chinese Christianity in particular should be more focused on the practical task of "running well" the local churches.

Third, theological reconstruction is regarded as a logical continuation of the Three-Self Patriotic Movement. From the viewpoint of political sensibility, we see theological reconstruction being in harmony with the ideals of the Three-Self. It is impossible that the existence of Christianity in any nation could be entirely isolated from its national political context. The political function of Christianity is unavoidable and absolutely natural. Likewise, in its own context, Chinese Christianity has its own political role to perform. And from the viewpoint of the history of Chinese Christianity, the historical meaning of theological reconstruction is linked with its modern mission — seeking a more positive theological interpretation in understanding the role of the Chinese church in the modern society of China.

On the basis of the above discussion, as a part of Chinese society, Chinese Christianity has a responsibility to take part in developing the society. Hence, it is very necessary and important for Chinese Christians to adapt to the development and changes in Chinese society. According to Bishop K. H. Ting, "theology means the church in the act of thinking." Indeed, the Chinese church needs to consider many problems in the modern Chinese context, such as the church's political function, theological reconstruction, theological education, its practical role in the community, etc.

Surely, theological renewal is a part of the nature of any lively church. Here, I just have one question about theological reconstruction: How could we precisely and practically, step by step, carry out this process of theological reconstruction in modern China? More and more Chinese people should know and understand what Chinese Christians are doing. I know that the program of the Reconstruction of Theological Thinking is welcomed by a great number of Chinese Christians by now, and I believe that it will be more and more understood and supported by other churches in the world. I hope that foreign theologians and Christians will no longer think that "there is no Chinese theology"; instead, they might say, "Look, these theologies are 'made in China.'" Meanwhile, I really believe that God has done great things in China and he is still working, creating, loving, and blessing us now.

A Response to Rev. Deng Fucun

Gerald H. Anderson

In her report to the Seventh National Christian Assembly in Beijing in May 2002, Rev. Dr. Cao Shengjie — the president of the China Christian Council — said, "The Reconstruction of Theological Thinking has become the central task of our church today in its being rooted and built up in Christ, and it will play a guiding role in the overall building up of Christianity. We expect that the fruits of theological reconstruction will raise the quality of faith of Christian believers in general, and enable Chinese Christianity to increase not only in 'years' but in 'wisdom.'"[1]

In his paper, Rev. Deng gives a helpful background to some of the issues and concerns that are the basis for this task. The Chinese character for "reconstruction" can also be translated "construction" or "renewal." Bishop K. H. Ting prefers "reconstruction" because, he says, it stresses using the best theological thinking from the past and making it relevant for the new context of the Chinese church. Bishop Ting is chair of the Commission on Promoting the Reconstruction of Theological Thinking, appointed by the China Christian Council.

Already in 1999, Zhuo Xinping, director of the Institute for Christian Studies and of the Institute of World Religions in Beijing, noted in the first issue of the new journal he edits, *Studies in Christianity,* that "the movement for theological reconstruction in Chinese Christianity has attracted

---

1. Cao Shengjie, "Put Down Roots and Build, Strengthen Ourselves, Move with the Times and Run the Church Well: Work Report of the Seventh National Christian Conference," *Chinese Theological Review* 16 (2002): 15.

the attention of scholars in China and abroad."[2] This is evidence of the interest and importance attached to the project, both inside and outside the church, at home and abroad. There is also an urgency about it, because — as Wang Aiming observes — it "concerns the future and fate of the Chinese church."[3] Thus both the China Christian Council (CCC) and the National Committee of the Three-Self Patriotic Movement of Protestant Churches in China (TSPM) revised their constitutions in 2002 to include within their "Scope of Duties" a statement "to actively promote theological reconstruction."[4]

The motivation and aim of theological reconstruction, as described by Bishop K. H. Ting and other leaders, is to adapt, revise, and renew the church's theology for the benefit of more effective Christian ministry in the context of China's socialist society in the twenty-first century. It is the task of theological updating and rethinking that faces the church in every society in every generation. It is more momentous in China, however, in light of the significant stages of upheaval that China has undergone over the last several decades, and also in light of the history of Protestant churches in China.

Two points are emphasized in this process. First, as Rev. Deng points out, in the process of reconstruction the church must maintain the essentials of the faith, as set forth in the Apostles' Creed and the Nicene Creed. It is theological thought and reflection about the faith that are open to adaptation and reconstruction. God does not change, but our understanding of God does change, under the inspiration of the Holy Spirit and the guidance of Scripture. Cao Shengjie made the following distinction: "In the course of promoting theological reconstruction, we have come to see that we must separate basic faith from theology where appropriate. The Reconstruction of Theological Thinking in no way changes the basic faith; rather its role is to protect and guarantee our basic faith."[5]

Second, there is a commitment in this process to uphold the Three-Self Principle while promoting theological reconstruction. They are linked to such an extent that Wang Aiming says, "Whether the Chinese Church can follow the path of upholding three-self and running the church well in the century just begun hinges on the success or failure of the Reconstruction of Theologi-

---

2. Wang Aiming, "The Nature and Purpose of Theological Reconstruction in the Chinese Church," *Chinese Theological Review* 15 (2001): 21.

3. Both are found in *Chinese Theological Review* 16 (2002): 26, 35.

4. Wang Aiming, "The Nature and Purpose of Theological Reconstruction," p. 20.

5. Cao Shengjie, "Put Down Roots and Build," p. 15.

cal Thinking."[6] Self-governing, self-supporting, and self-propagating are significant features in the selfhood of the church in China.

Rev. Cao Shengjie summarized the factors to be followed in the promotion of theological reconstruction: "that it be founded upon the Bible; that it is part of the continuity of the historical traditions of our basic faith; that we begin from our church's experience of following the three-self path; that we seek to unite with the special characteristics of progressive Chinese culture. We must study our forebears' theological knowledge and fruits, but we cannot be constrained by any particular theological system; nor can we imitate the ancient or Western views. We want only thinking which is in line with biblical truth, of benefit to running the church well according to the Three-Self Principle and able to help Chinese Christianity adapt to socialist society." She added that "theological viewpoints which are tinged with colonial consciousness, which offend our national essence, which are not appropriate to the development of the times, will naturally be scrutinized and adjusted."

At what stage is the process of theological reconstruction at present, and what are some of the issues that are believed will have a substantive effect on the work of the church? The Rev. Wang Aiming, vice-principal and dean of Nanjing Theological Seminary, has given fifteen propositions which, he says, "are basic to the work of the Reconstruction of Theological Thinking in the Chinese Church" and which summarize the many issues that are under consideration among church leaders. They are:

1. God is love, and all God's attributes, such as justice or compassion, are rooted in love, God's paramount divine attribute.
2. Christ is cosmic in his nature; or, we might also say the nature of his Lordship over all creation is cosmic.
3. God's revelation is gradual and progressive, as is human understanding of God.
4. God's work of creation is ongoing.
5. Seek a proper understanding of "justification by grace through faith" that does not lead to the nullification of good deeds or morality.
6. Affirm that Truth, Goodness, and Beauty created by God exist not only in the visible church (the Chinese church), but also outside it.
7. Human beings are a work-in-progress in God's creation. Martin Luther says we are all in an unfinished state.

---

6. Wang Aiming, "Understanding Theological Reconstruction in the Chinese Church: A Hermeneutical Approach," *Chinese Theological Review* 16 (2002): 145-46.

8. To establish a correct understanding of the Bible requires us to anchor ourselves in the supreme authority of the Scriptures and in the two basic creeds of the Christian church (Apostles' Creed and Nicene Creed), and to study and to preach the Word of God in response to the context of Chinese society. In other words, the most important ministry of the Chinese church and the most important study of the gospel ministry in China is how to establish a proper view of the Bible.

9. At China's current stage of social development, it is imperative that the moral aspect of Christianity be amplified to its greatest extent.

10. It is insufficient to expound the Three-Self Principle merely in light of the historical background of imperialism and the corresponding Western missionary movement. Our understanding of the Three-Self Principle shall be grounded in biblical and doctrinal evidences, with reference to its profound meaning in the history of Christian faith as a whole.

11. The positive contributions of many Western missionaries to China should not be denied. It is unacceptable to brand all Western missionaries as imperialists and dismiss their contributions.

12. Efforts shall be made to adjust religious viewpoints and actively bring about the adaptation of Christian faith with socialist Chinese society. The aim is to bring the church in China out of its marginal position and into that of a moving force contributing to Chinese social development.

13. In administration, the direction should be toward a democratically run church. The church is seriously concerned with avoiding the patriarchal and autocratic models prevalent in the church and is determined to change this situation to bring about healthy development.

14. Theological reconstruction in China is founded on the following principle: the fundamentals of our faith are unchangeable, but theological thinking can be adjusted.

15. Theological reconstruction in China shall follow three basic principles: (a) upholding the Bible and its supreme authority, and a better understanding of the fundamentals of our faith; (b) prevention of factionalism in the Chinese church — no one shall be permitted to use theological reconstruction to belittle those who hold different views; and (c) effective mobilization of the work of evangelism in China.

In the 1950s, D. T. Niles of Sri Lanka said that the gospel had been transported to Asia, but not transplanted; it was a potted plant that had not reached the rice-roots level of Asian culture and society; it was still viewed as a Western religion, influenced by Western concepts and interests. Much has changed since then, but the desire for theological reconstruction in China is part of the ongoing process for the "Asianization" of the church in Asia by Asians. Obviously, in this case, it has to be by Chinese for the church in China. Therefore, as a North American, my first obligation is to listen and learn, because there is much about the circumstances of the church in China that I do not fully comprehend. As a Western church scholar — despite having lived in Asia for a decade — I have much to learn, and I am eager to do that, because I see exciting developments and prospects for the churches in China. And there should be lessons here for the benefit of the church in other parts of the *oikoumene* as well.

At the same time, the church in China is open to dialogue about what they are doing, and it is in response to this openness that we are invited to engage in discussion with them.

In Southeast Asia there has been a somewhat similar initiative to pursue the Asianization of theology through the Association for Theological Education in South East Asia (ATESEA) and the South East Asia Graduate School of Theology (SEAGST). In the 1970s they adopted what was called the "Critical Asian Principle" for the advancement of contextual theological scholarship in the region. This phrase "seeks to identify what is distinctively Asian, and use this distinctiveness as a critical principle of judgment on matters dealing with the life and mission of the Christian community, theology, and theological education, in Asia."[7] They identified seven features that are characteristic of the region:

First, plurality and diversity of races, peoples, cultures, social institutions, religions, ideologies, etc.
Second, most of the countries in this region have had a colonial experience.
Third, most of the countries in the region are now in the process of nation building, development, and modernization, using science and technology, to achieve economic growth, social justice, and self-reliance.
Fourth, the people of this region want to achieve authentic self-identity and cultural integrity in the context of the modern world.

---

7. From the *Handbook* of the Association for Theological Education in South East Asia and the South East Asia Graduate School of Theology, 2000-2001, compiled by Yeow Choo Lak (Quezon City, Philippines), pp. 68-71. I have relied on this source for the discussion about the "Critical Asian Principle," and have condensed and adapted it for this presentation.

Fifth, Asia is the home of some of the world's major living and renascent religions, and these religions have shaped both the culture and consciousness of the vast majority of Asians. They represent alternative ways of life and experience of reality.

Sixth, Asian peoples are in search for a form of social order beyond the current alternatives. In some countries there is a resort to authoritarian forms of government as an emergency measure. There are efforts to revise and reformulate alternative forms of socioeconomic systems and adapt them to the Asian context. All of this is an indication that the human issues in Asia today are of such a magnitude that none of the current ideological systems seem adequate for dealing with them. And so, like the rest of the peoples of the world, Asians are looking for a form of social order that would enable them and humankind to live together in dignity in our planetary world.

Seventh, and finally, the Christian community is a minority in the vast Asian complex.

Next, they have taken these distinctive characteristics of their situation in Asia and used them as a frame of reference in making critical judgments and decisions on matters that have to do with the tasks of doing theology, of Christian formation for leadership and ministry, and of helping the Christian community in Asia to assume its responsibility for witness and service.

As a frame of reference, they have used the critical Asian principle in at least four ways:

1. As a situational principle, by which they seek to locate where they are and thereby indicate their area of responsibility and concern, namely, the varieties and dynamics of Asian realities.

2. As a hermeneutical principle, whereby they will approach and interpret the gospel and its traditions in relation to the needs and issues peculiar to the Asian situation. Alternatively, they will approach and understand Asian realities in the light of the gospel and its traditions.

3. As a missiological principle, which aims at the responsibility of equipping people with a missionary commitment that is informed by a missionary theology capable not only of illuminating Asian realities with the light of the gospel, but also of helping manage and direct the changes now taking place in the region along lines more consonant with the gospel and its vision for human life.

4. As an educational principle, which should give shape, content, direc-

tion, and criteria to the educational task in the member schools and in the South East Asia Graduate School of Theology.

Thus, in the judgment of ATESEA/SEAGST, the critical Asian principle is a way of doing theological contextualization. They see it as a method, and a method is judged by how well it works. As recently as November 2001, at the quadrennial general assembly of ATESEA, they reaffirmed and discussed means for the advancement of contextual theological scholarship, using the "Critical Asian Principle," first adopted in 1972. For instance, from the outset it was determined that "the distinctly Asian orientation is to be the critical principle of the whole doctoral studies program" in the SEAGST. And it has been reported that "subsequent developments showed that the phrase is critically significant not only for graduate theological education in the region but also for the task of theology and the mission of the church."

In the discussion of the Reconstruction of Theological Thinking in the Chinese Protestant Church, is the "Critical Asian Principle," as developed in southeast Asia, helpful? Are there significant points of convergence with the experience of the church in China? Is it already implied, for instance, in some of the fifteen propositions set forth by Wang Aiming? Is there a comparable "Critical Chinese Principle" for doing theological reconstruction? Is it contained in the factors described by Cao Shengjie?

Finally, as we discern how the triune God is at work in China today, and how the church is witnessing to the faith, we pray that the Holy Spirit will guide those who are engaged in theological reconstruction, that they may "be ready to make [their] defense to anyone who demands from [them] an accounting for the hope that is in [them]" (1 Peter 3:15).

16 Call for Dialogue and Cooperation: Reflections on *Jianshe* or the Reconstruction of Theological Thinking

Zhu Xiaohong

"When talking about 'believing or not believing,' people in the Chinese Church always connect it to heaven and hell; the believer will be in heaven, no matter how sinful his behavior is, while the non-believer will be in hell, no matter how respectable his morality is. It seems only a problem related to the faith, but it also could be regarded as a political problem. The believer goes up to heaven, so Chiang Kai-shek might have eternal life, while Chairman Mao, Liu Shaoqi, Deng Xiaoping, Zhou Enlai and Leifeng who are non-believers would be in hell. Of course, such a faith relates to one's political attitude . . . in this sense, so far in China, about one billion people would go down to hell. I suggest that we should dilute 'justification by faith,' so that the Chinese outside the church can be attracted to know Christ, . . . and know the charm of Christianity."[1]

The above is quoted from the works of Bishop K. H. Ting, the former leader of the National Committee of the Chinese Christian Council (CCC) and the Three-Self Patriotic Movement (TSPM) and the promoter of the project of the Reconstruction of Theological Thinking (RTT), which began at the end of 1998 in the Chinese Protestant churches. However, RTT is such a contro-

1. K. H. Ting, "Building a Correct View of Scripture," in *Symposium on the View of Scripture* (Shanghai: TSPM/CCC, 2001), p. 4.

As there has been some confusion about translating *Jianshe* into English, I prefer to use the Chinese original term "Shenxue sixiang jianshi" alongside the English translation. *Jianshi* can mean both construction and reconstruction.

versial issue that some people in the Chinese Protestant churches are skeptical and hesitant to applaud and participate in it.[2] Far more severe criticism was received from the Chinese Christians overseas, who accused the promoter of the RTT of being an "unbeliever" and a "whore of Evil," and accused the project of being a faith reform campaign.[3] Meanwhile, the Chinese academy is indifferent to this important religious phenomenon.

Starting from this situation, this paper examines the standpoints of both the promoter and the opponent, indicates the promoter's commitments to the church in context examining some CCC/TSPM documents, and looks at the misunderstanding through papers written by opponents and published on the Internet. By introducing David Tracy's revisionist model of theology, the paper calls for dialogue and cooperation among the academy and the two sides in the Chinese church.

The materials used in this paper are taken mostly from publications of CCC/TSPM, the journal *China Religion* of the State Administration for Religious Affairs (SARA), and materials downloaded from the Internet, including *Christian Life Quarterly,* which is published by overseas Chinese Christians, and a declaration from the Chinese house church website.

The Context

The first issue is the sociopolitical setting. During the process of building a Chinese indigenized socialist country, the theory of "accommodation" has generally replaced the theory of religion being the "opium" of the people. The third-generation political leader Jiang Zemin has mentioned many times that religion has three characteristics: mass engagement, complexity, and longevity. He says that the main religious policies for the Chinese government are to protect freedom of religious belief, to supervise religious affairs by law, and to initiate the adaptation of religions to the socialist society. The traditional Marxist view of religion, which claims that religions would

2. Cf. K. H. Ting, "The Future of the Christian Church in China," in *Chinese Religion* 1 (2003). The number of subscriptions to the leading Chinese Protestant magazine *Tian Feng* declined from 100,000 to 70,000 after the RTT was launched. See "The Report of the *Tian Feng* Editing Committee," in *The Seventh National Conference of the Chinese Protestant Church* (Shanghai: TSPM/CCC, 2002), p. 207.

3. Such criticism expresses the opinion of many Chinese Christians in the mainland church. See, for instance, "An Example of a Non-believer," *Christian Life Quarterly* 10 & 14-17 (2003).

die out before the classes expire, has been succeeded by the notion that religions would last even longer than classes and nations. In light of such a new viewpoint, it is necessary to induce religions to accommodate to the society.

In order to adapt well to Chinese society, Chinese religions accept values such as patriotism, being law-abiding, adhering to the Communist Party of China and its socialist system, advocating the reunion of the nation, and interpreting religious doctrines in accordance with the needs of social progress. It should be a commitment not just for a government or party but also for religious groups to introduce such an accommodation. The five officially recognized Chinese religions have been adjusting their own doctrines or doing social work to adapt to the society, actions that have been encouraged and affirmed by the government in recent years.

RTT in the Protestant church takes place in such circumstances. Bishop Ting once claimed, ". . . [the church] should avail itself of the advantage of the political situation to promote the reformation of the religious concept. The reformation should not be just a political attitude but should also dilute those elements which do not conform to socialist society, and enforce those which are."[4] So in some sense, RTT is the way to accommodate to socialist society and find the theoretical elements for this accommodation. Some high-ranking officials praised RTT highly and thought it would deeply influence the Chinese churches.[5]

The second situation is that of the church itself. Neither the Catholic nor the Protestant church in China has developed its own inculturated and contextualized systematic theology. The Chinese Protestant church is really young and weak; and, for many reasons, the indigenizing movement launched in the 1920s hasn't been continued. In the CCC/TSPM opinion, the church is in its third phase of development since liberation. The three phases began from the "Three-Self" (self-administration, self-support, and self-propagation) Patriotic Movement, R 21; the second phase is "three-goodness" (administer well, support well, and propagate well), and the third one, the latest, is RTT.[6] The aim of the RTT is to found a contextualized theology guided by the Three-Self Principle, through dialogue between theolo-

---

4. K. H. Ting, *Renmin zhengxie bao* (Sept. 4, 1988).

5. One of them was Wang Zhaoguo, the former director of the National United Front. See his "Speech at the 50th Anniversary of the TSPM," www.chinaCatholic.org/LAW/Law012.htm.

6. The first phase started in the 1950s and the second phase in the 1980s. Cf. K. H. Ting, "Go Forward with the Time," in *Thinking and Praxis* (Shanghai: TSPM/CCC), p. 11.

gians and believers, dialogue between native and international theologians, and dialogue between faith and culture, science, or philosophy.[7]

Since the new working principle of three-goodness *(san hao)* carried out in 1980s, marvelous growth has taken place in the Protestant churches. However, fundamentalism, which holds a dichotomy between "the world" and "the spiritual," has a wide influence in China. Preachers in the rural areas have poor theological training and give a simplified message of punishment for nonbelievers and reward for believers, while the urban youth and the intellectuals cannot be attracted by this method of preaching, which is so out-of-date and dull.[8] In order to make church growth balanced between quality and quantity, CCC/TSPM thinks it is necessary to carry out RTT and claims that RTT is so crucial that it should be the center of all the other missions in the church.[9] RTT can be regarded as a church's response to its reality, a guarantee of quality improvement.

Procedure, Principles, and Some Achievements

It has been four years since the resolution on "Strengthening the Reconstruction of Theological Thinking" initiated in the Jinan national committee meeting, and it has made some progress. Under the guidance of the "team to accelerate theological thinking" headed by Bishop Ting, the national CCC/TSMP has organized several conferences, e.g., "The symposium on anthology of K. H. Ting" (July 1999), "The Symposium on the view of Scripture" (September 2000), "Workshop on accelerating Chinese Christian thinking" (2001), etc. The national CCC/TSMP has also published a collection of five books by Bishop Ting, including *On the Reconstruction of Theological Thinking, On Scripture, On God,* and so on, and the series of books on *Chinese Christian Reconstruction of Theological Thinking* (numbers 1 and 2). Two key journals, *Tian Feng* and *Nanjing Theological Review,* have created columns to discuss theological thinking. The local offices of the CCC/TSMP have also held many activities related to theological thinking and published some books.

The procedure for RTT was supposed to follow this pattern. First, semi-

---

7. See K. H. Ting, "The Preface of the Chinese Theological Annual," in *On the Reconstruction of Theological Thinking* (Shanghai: TSMP/CCC, 2000), p. 23.

8. Cao Shengjie, "On the Indispensableness and Content of the Reconstruction of Theological Thinking," in *Thinking and Praxis* (Shanghai: TSMP/CCC, 2002), p. 25.

9. Cao Shengjie's speech, in *The Seventh National Conference of the Chinese Protestant Church* (Shanghai: TSMP/CCC, 2002), p. 22.

nars would be held by local churches to study selected materials or questions. Second, further research would be done by those well trained in theology. Third, results would be shared and popularized. These three procedures are complementary and are designed to reconstruct theology generally from top to bottom in the church and from the superficial to the profound.[10]

There are several main principles for church people to bear in mind when starting RTT. First of all, theological thinking and fundamentals of faith should be separated appropriately. It is said that the fundamentals of the faith are the essentials and should not be changed, while theological thinking must be adjusted. The aim of the modification of theological thinking is to vindicate the fundamentals of the faith.

Second, RTT must uphold the Scripture and its supreme authority, respect the tradition or the creeds of the historical church, integrate the experience of the Three-Self Movement, and adapt to the native advanced culture. Finally, conflicts among different theological streams should be avoided. Solidarity and discussion in harmony should be encouraged.[11]

It is necessary to emphasize the principle of distinguishing the fundamentals of the faith from theological thinking, because this seems to be the most central and innovative idea in the RTT. RTT is to develop/enrich/re-adjust/induce generally, but not to change or alter totally the content and way of theological thinking.[12] There are two dimensions to such development or adjustment, namely, general adjustment and special adjustment.[13] It has been said by many RTT papers that general adjustment is very common in church history and in the biblical narrative, and has happened in many places and at many times.[14]

Special adjustment is especially necessary for that passive and conservative thinking that grew up within special historical circumstances. For example, one should not exaggerate the gap between the Christian and non-Christian by citing the biblical passage "do not be mismatched with nonbelievers," disparaging works by faith, emphasizing the evil in human

---

10. Cao Shengjie, "On the Indispensableness and Content of the Reconstruction of Theological Thinking," pp. 32, 108.

11. Cao Shengjie, "On the Indispensableness and Content of the Reconstruction of Theological Thinking," p. 30.

12. K. H. Ting, "The Necessity to Adjust Theological Thinking," in *On the Reconstruction of Theological Thinking* (Shanghai: TSPM/CCC, 2001), p. 30.

13. Ji Jianhong, "The Indispensableness of the Reconstruction of Theological Thinking," in *Thinking and Praxis* (Shanghai: TSMP/CCC, 2002), p. 45.

14. K. H. Ting, "The Necessity to Adjust Theological Thinking," p. 32.

nature, cutting off the relationship between creation and salvation, neglecting the gradual unfolding of revelation. All these theological ways of thinking in the church should be led in the right way in the light of the fundamentals of the faith. Bishop Ting and many other leaders in the CCC/TSMP have declared many times that such a distinction is essential for RTT. The doctrines of the Trinity, the Incarnation, and the Resurrection are unchangeable, but theological thinking is ever changing to help believers keep the faith in an advancing society: "The adjustment in theological thinking is to keep or protect the faith."[15]

What then are the main achievements in this process of adjustment? Some important propositions have already been established and will be the guideline for later RTT as follows: God is Love is primary, and the other attributes such as righteousness and benevolence are secondary. Jesus is the cosmic Christ; the revelation of God is unfolding, and God's creation is still evolving. The human being is semi-finished in the creation; the doctrine of justification by faith should be watered down; beauty, goodness, and truth may also be found outside the church; etc.[16]

The Resistance to RTT on Different Levels

As a controversial project, RTT has not received strong support in the Protestant church in China. In the Three-Self system, there are many difficulties in pushing this project forward. Because of the weakness of the institution and professionals, many local churches do not know how to make theological-thinking construction relevant to their own lives. Because of the influence of different denominational backgrounds,[17] some people would like to charge the dissenters in the church with theological or other political errors, and this makes many believers reluctant to become involved in RTT.

Most of the resistance and hostility to RTT comes from some of the household churches and overseas Chinese churches. RTT is regarded as a faith reform campaign similar to the one in the 1950s, which had too many political motivations.[18] The sharpest criticism of the RTT is of its intention

15. K. H. Ting, "The Necessity to Adjust Theological Thinking," p. 33.

16. Wang Aiming, "Understanding the Reconstruction of Theological Thinking from the Perspective of Theological Hermeneutics," www.21sz.org/sxzsz/xzz1/21jzgjh.htm.

17. Before the unification of the Protestant churches in the 1950s, there were over a hundred Protestant denominations in China.

18. K. H. Ting, "The Necessity to Adjust Theological Thinking," p. 32.

and implied political elements. One paper on the house church website, titled "On the Anthology of K. H. Ting: A Political Theology for the Three-Self Church," makes the criticism that political skills had been borrowed to launch RTT:

> Recently Mr. Ting gathered public speeches and articles and published them in his anthology, while the official media in mainland China held some press releases to introduce and advocate his book. It was said that Ting has been making addresses everywhere in support of the government to hawk his "theological thoughts." The theological seminaries and local CCC/TSPM committees call on Christians to study "Ting's selected works," which awakens reminiscences of people studying "Mao's selected works" during the days of the Cultural Revolution, and try to launch a campaign in support of the RTT, which also somehow makes us take it as a religious revolution.[19]

Moreover, because of its many political elements, RTT is undoubtedly a manifestation of the church's politicization. On the same website, there is a seminarian's announcement of the reasons why he dropped out of the Nanjing Union Theological Seminary where Ting was president. The announcement says that President Ting, the spokesman and the representative of the TSMP, is leading "the orientation of theology" in the TSPM. In this manner, his thoughts are the thoughts for the TSMP church, the main characteristic of which is political orientation. The student critic maintained that RTT adapts to the mainstream ideology, cooperates with the political and compromises its own principles, so that the principle of self-government, self-support, and self-propagation becomes an empty slogan. What the "Three-Self" church has done in past decades doesn't help but destroys the Chinese church in the name of loving the church.[20]

Christian Life Quarterly is one of the journals that speak with a voice different from CCC/TSMP. It is edited by overseas Chinese Christians as one channel to express the opinion of the household church. Since June 1999, it has published a series paper titled "An Example of a Non-Believer" and written by Mr. Li Xinyuan, in which the writer condemns RTT, "which keeps so close a relationship to the modern Chinese modern political regime, . . . is

19. Qiu Yan, "On the Anthology of K. H. Ting: In the Perspective of the Political Theology of the Three-Self Church," www.chinahousechurch.org/chinese2/threeself.htm.

20. Liu Yuchun et al., "Why Do We Leave School?" www.chinahousechurch.org/Chinese/give%20up.htm.

destroying the church rather than constructing."[21] RTT has been regarded as a political movement by these dissenters.

Another criticism thrown at RTT's theological orientation is mainly an objection to Bishop Ting's theology. These critics think that Ting's theology is so liberal that it will confuse common believers' faith. "Since its departure point is liberal theology, RTT changes the Gospel and confuses the truth."[22] The following points against RTT come from a series of articles by Li Xinyuan in the journal *Christian Life Quarterly*.

As to the concept of God, the critics think that love without justice and holiness will present an unbalanced concept of God. God is Love is an important topic in RTT, to which Li's objection is that "Love without Justice would be a kind of emotion."[23] Love couldn't be the first attribute of God if it is without Justice, Holiness, Mercy, Faithfulness, Truth, and Goodness. Commenting on the concept of a gradually unfolding revelation, Li indicates that Ting's proposition of "unfolding revelation" is doubtful, because Ting thinks that "God reveals himself according to the sequence of the books in Bible, namely, from the early book to the latest book, from few to full,"[24] then finally denies the doctrine of the Bible as a sacred revelation.

In relation to Christology, Li thinks that the concept of the "cosmic Christ," which introduces the third attribute of Jesus besides his humanity and deity, is a springboard to "Universalism." "K. H. Ting's 'cosmic Christ' is a universal Savior who saves everybody. Between the lines in the books of Ting, the so-called 'theological thinking' just implies this message (of a Universalist)."[25] It is impossible for most Christians to accept such a theology, which tries to interpret Communism in a reasonable way. From this kind of theology, Li insists that one can see how political society shapes RTT.[26]

Questions of humanity and soteriology are the most controversial topics. The human being is defined as "a semi-finished product" by Bishop

21. Li Xinyuan, "An Example of a Non-believer: Reflections on Ting's Works," *Christian Life Quarterly* 10 (1999).

22. Liu Yuchun et al., "Why Do We Leave School?"

23. Li Xinyuan, "An Example of a Non-believer: The First Reflection on Ting's Works," *Christian Life Quarterly* 14 (1999).

24. Li Xinyuan, "An Example of a Non-believer: The Second Reflection on Ting's Works," *Christian Life Quarterly* 15 (1999).

25. Li Xinyuan, "An Example of a Non-believer: The Third Reflection on Ting's Works," *Christian Life Quarterly* 16 (1999).

26. Li Xinyuan, "An Example of a Non-believer: The Third Reflection on Ting's Works."

Ting, and later on this became the proposition of the RTT. Since the distinction between "believing or not believing" becomes the most obvious obstacle to theological thinking's accommodation to socialism, Bishop Ting has repeatedly asked church people to think about this question: how to accept the idea for most Chinese that morally respectable persons such as Chairman Mao, Liu Shaoqi, Deng Xiaoping, Zhou Enlai, and Lei Feng who are nonbelievers would go to hell. So the human being is defined as semifinished in order to avoid magnifying or debasing human beings,[27] and to help people understand the pluralist situation in a particular society. Moreover, RTT dilutes "justification by faith, so that the Chinese outside the church can be attracted to know Christ, . . . and to know the charm of Christianity."[28]

However, Li argues against this concept of humanity, which "denies the universality and authenticity of sin" and "denies the perfection of creation and the result of sin."[29] The "dilution" of justification by faith couldn't shorten the distance between believers and nonbelievers;[30] on the contrary, Li infers that "it intentionally sublate [sic] the doctrine of justification, forsakes the freely given Grace of God,"[31] and bends the orthodox position toward the concept that humans can be saved by their morality and works.

The third accusation against RTT is in regard to its principle of the appropriate separation between theological thinking and the fundamentals of the faith. Some other critics comment that this distinction might become a confused work, deciding "whether accepting salvation is theological thinking, while the atonement in Jesus Christ is the fundamental of the faith."[32] The critic Li even indicates that the separation is impossible because theological thinking definitely mirrors and interprets its faith, "what they call 'the appropriate separation' is no more than to deny and destroy the fundamentals of the faith in Chinese churches."[33]

---

27. K. H. Ting's Interview, *Tian Feng* (June 1999).

28. K. H. Ting, "Building a Correct View of Scripture," p. 4.

29. Li Xinyuan, "An Example of a Non-believer: The Fourth Reflection on Ting's Works," *Christian Life Quarterly* 17 (1999).

30. K. H. Ting, "Context and Theology," in *On the Reconstruction of Theological Thinking* (Shanghai: TSPM/CCC, 2001), p. 77.

31. Li Xinyuan, "An Example of a Non-believer: The Fourth Reflection on Ting's Works."

32. Xu Wuhao, "'Yin xing fei xin' and 'yin xin fei xing,'" in *China Journal* (Christian Communication of Canada, 2002), www.ccican.org/chbm_feature_article.htm.

33. Li Xinyuan, "An Example of a Non-believer: Reflections on Ting's Works."

Zhu Xiaohong

Reflections on the Resistance

Concerning the first criticism of RTT's dissenters, the premise is that "the relation between *zheng* (politics) and *jiao* (religion) should be widely divided."[34] In the Chinese character, there are many levels for the interaction of *zheng* and *jiao*, for instance, the relation between state and religions, state and church, politics and church, politics and religions. On the last two levels, the church or religions might have some political elements, namely, they might involve political rights or activities; and thus the Christian or church might not be totally separated from politics. As for the first two levels, the political regime determines the relationship between state and church or religions.

Given the totalitarian state framework, religious freedom and church-state separation in China are limited compared to the situation in Western countries, but they have been improving. From viewing religions as "opium of the people" to the theory of "religions' accommodation to the socialist society" and other phenomena, the policy of the Chinese authorities now grants the surviving church a better living space after many years of struggle. Changing its image of "a foreign religion" to win the understanding of people outside the churches, using "easy words for people living in modern industrial society"[35] to explain the fundamentals of the faith, the church's efforts and motivation are honorable and understandable.

In the Chinese Protestant church there have been controversies over the church's political involvement and the relationship between the political party and religion for many decades. Since the 1920s, conservative church leaders such as Watchman Nee and Wang Mingdao insisted that the church and the political arena should be widely separated, while modernist church leaders such as T. C. Chao (Zhao Zichen) and Wu Leichuan claimed that political involvement should be a part of social evangelization.[36]

The theological foundation of those accusations against RTT, according to which this world is totally fallen or manipulated by the devil, so that Christians must separate from this world, and *zheng* should be widely separated from *jiao*, are not far different from those conservatives some eighty years ago. Moreover, most church leaders today are members of the national or local Chinese People's Political Consultative Conference, i.e., they are pol-

34. Liu Yuchun et al., "Why Do We Leave School?"
35. K. H. Ting's Interview, *Tian Feng* (June 1999).
36. Lam Wing-hung, *Half a Century of Chinese Theology 1900-1949* (Hong Kong: China Alliance Press, 1998), pp. 257-77.

iticians who are involved in political issues and granted some privileges. It might be easy for the dissenters to find excuses to accuse them.

However, neither context should be ignored; nor should people bury their heads in the sand. The spirit of the martyrs is respectable, but prudent realism is also commendatory. From "Three-Self" to "three-goodness," leaders of the CCC/TSPM have tried to be more ecclesiastical to overcome the politicization of the churches. A Western scholar, Philip L. Wickeri, has a very insightful comment on this matter:

> Chinese Christianity is so powerless that it could not have real equality as a dialogue partner with the state. Leadership in the church should not bash its head against a brick wall. It should however lead and support the people in a responsible way. On the other hand, the CCC in China is also very weak. The leaders or theologians in the church should better not be in such a hurry to introduce the initiatives. Restriction in this situation is an expression of weakness but also a resource of strength.[37]

Although it is very meaningful when we talk about context and accommodation, we should notice that accommodation to the state or politics is just a small part of the RTT. Context is not only the sociopolitical background in localization but also the science-economic background in globalization. Contextual theology is a way of doing theology, a response to the issues in either local or global contexts. However, both the promoter (CCC/TSPM) and the critics (some house churches and overseas Chinese churches) of the RTT like to make comments from a political perspective and use some language conveying strong political emotions. For example, many people in the CCC/TSPM like to link conservative theological thinking to imperialism and colonialism and evaluate spiritual life by patriotism and political involvement while paying less attention to the silence and impotence of the church on moral or other social issues. Similarly, they tend to compare those conservatives to the "laggard,"[38] while neglecting other "lag-

---

37. The quotation is translated from Chinese from Philip L. Wickeri, "A Theologian to Promote the Uniting Church," *Tian Feng ganyu* (Nanjing: Nanjing University Press, 2001), p. 100.

38. Slogans such as "Chinese theology falls behind" or Chinese theology "is laggard" are common when the TSPM/CCC theologians speak about accommodation. For instance: "Many notions and ideas existing in the church are inconsistent with socialist society. Compared with the nation's thought, theological thinking has fallen behind the socialist reality. We are really laggard." Chen Zemin, "How Will Chinese Christianity Get into the 21st Century?" in a speech at the Jinan meeting (Nov. 1998).

gard" phenomena such as weak and dull preaching or doing nothing with the individual in secular society.

Can Theological Thinking and the Fundamentals of the Faith Be Separated?

Concerning the controversy regarding the appropriate separation between theological thinking and the fundamentals of the faith, we need to bring up three points. First, divergence between different sects or branches has been a major characteristic of the Chinese Protestant church. Before unification of worship in the 1950s, there were over a hundred denominational groups, including the churches created by overseas missionaries and by native missionaries. All the different church groups had their own traditions, doctrines, and institutions. After great effort for over half a century, the divergences and confrontations, especially between the so-called modernists and conservatives, have not been removed. Even Bishop Ting admitted that conflicts between the different church groups remain: "There are always some people who are likely to pick out the conflicts between the modernists and fundamentalists. . . ."[39]

However, Bishop Ting claimed that adjustments in theological thinking, which doesn't mean giving up the fundamentals of the faith, are necessary for both sides. He insisted that an appropriate separation between theological thinking and the fundamentals of the faith is the precondition for the adjustment or construction of theological thinking. From Bishop Ting's perspective, it wouldn't be necessary to bring forth conflicts between the different parts of the Chinese church if all the people held to their fundamentals of faith during their adjustment. Nevertheless, such adjustments are taking place in various parts of the Chinese church, and conflict comes into being whenever progressives attempt to "help" or "push" those regarded as "laggard."

Second, many articles for RTT and Chinese church observers point out that there are some extreme conservative theological inclinations that limit the notion of evangelism to saving of souls for the kingdom of God and care less about work in the world, history, and society. Distortion is unavoidable in any institution of faith or religion at any time, so adjustment is necessary. RTT is such an adjustment in the Chinese church. Dr. Ying Fuk-tsang, an ex-

---

39. K. H. Ting, "The Necessity to Adjust Theological Thinking," p. 32.

pert in the history of the modern Chinese church, once indicated that yes, an extreme conservative theological inclination really exists in the Chinese church. It is from such a spiritual tradition that denies life in this world, and follows strictly the dichotomy of body and soul. These believers narrow the gospel mission to spreading the message and saving the souls of nonbelievers, and they condemn social service or involvement as "not belonging to the spiritual" or as "social evangelism." So it is positive for modern theological thinking to accuse advocates of such views of rigid exclusivism and a narrow vision of spirituality.[40]

Even though adjustment is indispensable for the church to become a relevant institution, there are other essential relevant questions, such as how to solidify the majority parts in the church, how to establish goals for the Reconstruction of Theological Thinking, how to assimilate those existing or historical theological resources, how to use a better phraseology during RTT. In my opinion, pluralism is one of the conditions we should accept in our lives; from it we learn tolerance for thinking different from our own. The differences and divergences between the promoter and the critics of the RTT call for dialogue and cooperation. Both sides need more channels and space to speak out their opinions. In this sense, pluralism is not a weakness but a gift for the Chinese church.

Third, how can theological thinking and the fundamentals of the faith be clearly separated? As the critics point out, theological thinking must be the explanation of or reflection on the fundamentals of the faith, and it would be hard to divide them. May we find other similar terms that are popularly understood to express this principle? For instance, can we use "central doctrines" and "peripheral doctrines" in the hierarchy of truth in correspondence with "the fundamentals of the faith" and "theological thinking"? When the paradigms of theological understanding shift, those doctrines on the edge must change while the fundamental or central doctrines remain the same.

This reminds me of another similar dispute about the glossary for RTT, which concerns the "Reconstruction of Theological Thinking" itself. It was said that the earliest term for this project, "Theological Construction," raised many questions. Then the "Reconstruction of Theological Thinking" was adopted to replace the former term. Later on, there was another minor discussion on its English translation, i.e., whether "construction" or "recon-

---

40. Ying Fuk-tsang, *Church-State Relations in Contemporary China* (Hong Kong: Alliance Bible Seminary, 1999), p. 178.

struction" should be used to refer to the *Jianshe*, because in *Putonghua* (Mandarin Chinese), *Shenxue sixiang jianshe* corresponds to the characters in the "Construction of Theological Thinking," while someone claimed that "reconstruction" might be a more appropriate translation for the essence of the project. In case there are any misunderstandings of this word, I would suggest a use of a combination term, "Theological Thinking *Jianshe*."

Owing to the limitations of theological resources and experience in the Chinese church, it should be emphasized that RTT has a long way to go and that many additional issues and questions will be uncovered. One of the leaders of the CCC frankly admitted: "It has not yet constructed and put forward a systematic and comprehensive theology so far. We have just begun to start from the context, to combine the Christian faith with the traditional culture and national peculiarity. Anyway, our 'contextualized theology' is impossible to be built as a systematic theology, because the context of China is still experiencing a drastic social change, which began with the reformation and the open-door policy."[41]

Response and a Vision

Here I would like to borrow David Tracy's "revisionist model of theology" in response. In his books, theology is divided into three branches, namely, fundamental theology, systematic theology, and practical theology, which have a mutually critical correlation both in their content and method. And through reason, faith, and praxis, the three branches correspond respectively to three communities or spaces, viz. academy, church, and society, which also have a mutually critical correlation.[42] Each branch of theology should be responsible for its own space by interpreting and finding its own criterion. In a word, the mission of theology is to find the truth and interpret meaning within secular society and Christian tradition through mutually critical correlation. Then what kinds of insights does this model contribute to our reflection on RTT? I would like to emphasize two aspects.

41. Chen Zemin, "The Preface," in *Anthology of K. H. Ting* (Nanjing: Yilin Press, 1998), p. 5.

42. David Tracy, *The Analogical Imagination: Christian Theology and the Culture of Pluralism* (New York: Crossroad, 2002). See also Philip Shen, "Theological Pluralism: A Response to David Tracy from an Asian Perspective," in *Si*, 29 (Hong Kong: Hong Kong Christian Association, 1994), p. 12.

1. Theology for Church and Society

The revisionist model of theology appeals to the publicness of theology, which is expressed in the scientific concept, principle, and method. Theology is not an individual activity, no matter in which space it is located. In the *ekklesia*, theology is the self-expression and commitment of the community in the same faith, but this fact is not an argument for the subjection of theology to the church. As a reflection and expression on the Christian faith, theology can also challenge and criticize ecclesiastical reality. Similarly, the faith community, the church, will also modify and define theology. We can see this balance in RTT in the Chinese Protestant church. Moreover, the mutually critical correlation between the church and theology also encourages us to think about the relationship between the thought of church leaders and the theological thinking of the community. Any intention to manipulate this would result in the loss of independence of theological thinking.

The same correlation exists between theology and society. A true Christian neither totally identifies with nor completely discards society; a true theology neither compromises with nor separates from the context. This tension between theology and context, Christian and society, is brought about by the tension between the transcendent faith and the finite human being. On the one hand, sociopolitical and cultural contexts become the background for theological reflection; they push "laggard" theological thinking forward.

On the other hand, a theologian or Christian should often ask himself how to retain the uniqueness of the Christian faith in secularization, what is the particularity of the church, and "whether the church might so closely come to terms with the world as to lose the possibility of making any progress."[43] Theology should engage society with a prophetic and critical character; religions live by resisting.[44] Obviously, the prophetic and critical character is the fundamental condition for retaining the uniqueness of the faith. It is really a sensitive and puzzling task for Chinese churches to keep this character.

---

43. K. H. Ting, "A Chinese Christian's View of the Atheist," in *Anthology of K. H. Ting* (Nanjing: Yilin Press, 1998), p. 144.

44. David Tracy, *Plurality and Ambiguity: Hermeneutics, Religion, and Hope* (London: SCM Press, 1988), p. 84.

2. Theology for Church and Academy

The revisionist model is shaped in the Western context in which Christianity is the main traditional religion, in which theology is not only for the church but also an important faculty in universities. The high status of theology is unimaginable for the Chinese academy, and the division between academy and church is a solid reality. On the one hand, the church has been deprived of educational and medical institutions and has had little to do with the national culture since the 1950s; nor, in recent decades, has the church played as important a role as the intellectuals. The intellectuals are sick of boring sermons and the anti-intellectual attitude, and they will not stay in the church even if they are baptized.[45] On the other hand, tired of atheist ideology and worried about the moral vacuum in the rising market economy, more and more scholars have turned to the study of Christianity since 1980. But these scholars maintain a distance and show an indifference to ecclesiastical life.

This situation reminds me of the controversy regarding the so-called Cultural Christians in 1995.[46] Faced with censure from Christian scholars in Hong Kong, the Cultural Christians in mainland China had to vindicate their identity and put the question something like this: Should theoretical theology and practical theology, human theology and ecclesiastical theology, necessarily be separate? It should be taken into consideration that the Cultural Christians were wooed by Bishop K. H. Ting, who tried to express "a friendly welcome" to these scholars.[47] Speaking about the urgency of the RTT, Ting later said: "Christians should adapt to the advanced culture, shorten the distance between themselves and the academy. We Christians should not stay in such a low position in the dialogue with the intellectuals. Otherwise our Christianity will be like Falun Gong and other evil cults. RTT should not only accommodate to socialist society but also adapt to developing knowledge. Otherwise the intellectuals will look down upon us and be reluctant to dialogue with us; then, we Christians will be left far behind."[48]

Is it only because RTT has been completed that the dialogue and cooperation between the church and the academy will take place? I hope the con-

---

45. Chao Shengjie, "On the Indispensableness and Content of the Reconstruction of Theological Thinking," p. 25.

46. For details, see *Cultural Christians: Phenomenon and Argument* (Hong Kong: Institute of Sino-Christian Studies, 1997).

47. Chen Zemin, "The Preface," p. 7.

48. K. H. Ting, "Context and Theology," p. 80.

tact will be strengthened immediately. We already have some positive evidence: Christians in the church and intellectuals of the academy worked together in the 1980s when fighting against the ideological slogan "religion is the opiate of the people."

A Response to Professor Zhu Xiaohong

Sun Yi

I appreciate Professor Zhu Xiaohong's presentation very much, and I am honored to have this chance to respond to it. In her paper, Zhu shows us objectively some controversial issues concerning the project of the Reconstruction of Theological Thinking (RTT), which began at the end of 1998 in the Chinese Protestant churches under the leadership of the Three-Self Patriotic Movement (TSPM) and the China Christian Council (CCC). She expresses her own views on these issues from the perspective of a scholar; and finally, Professor Zhu responds by using David Tracy's "revisionist model of theology," calling for dialogue and cooperation. I have learned a lot from her presentation. Now I will try to respond only to two questions raised in her presentation.

First, Professor Zhu describes objectively some controversial issues concerning the project of RTT and expresses her own views prudently from an academic perspective. She thinks it is a necessity for Chinese theologians to adjust their theological thinking: "RTT is such an adjustment in Chinese churches." I agree with Ms. Zhu completely at this point. I think the Chinese churches need to adjust or establish their own theology, and RTT is an important effort in this direction. In the process of developing their own theology, inevitably all kinds of controversial issues will arise in different churches, as we see here in the case of RTT. In this situation, Professor Zhu's call for dialogue and cooperation between the Three-Self-led churches, nonregistered or house churches, and overseas Chinese churches is a very significant point. But there is a deeper question: How could all sides enter into a constructive dialogue and fully understand each other?

Professor Zhu points out very precisely that, so far, there is still not a constructive dialogue between the registered churches, nonregistered churches, and overseas Chinese churches. On the contrary, there is only negative criticism from a political perspective. "Both the promoter (TSPM/CCC) and the critics (some house churches and overseas Chinese churches) of the RTT like to make comments from a political perspective and use a language with strong political emotions."

In fact, as we could see in Professor Zhu's paper, "accommodation to the state or politics is just a small part of the RTT" — or it should be a small part of RTT if one of RTT's aims is to found a contextualized theology. The new generation in both sides may find that, apart from the relation with politics, there are still many areas where they may exchange their opinions and have a good dialogue; one example of common interest is the threat of heresies among Chinese churches. So, in order to push the project of the RTT forward, to help the Chinese churches face their present reality, it is very important to develop a positive and constructive dialogue between all kinds of Chinese churches.

But how could such a constructive dialogue promoting mutual understanding become possible? The premise of such a dialogue is, I think, to grant equal positions for all sides taking part in the dialogue, so that each side may express their ideas freely. Equality is especially important; each side must have enough legal channels and space to speak out their opinions. Otherwise it is impossible to develop a constructive dialogue between these sides.

This premise presupposes a more primary premise: that various modes of thinking and concepts concerning Chinese theology should be accepted. In other words, to an extent, a healthy pluralism in theological thinking should be accepted as a premise. For this premise, Professor Zhu also points out: "Pluralism is one of the conditions we should accept in our lives; from it we learn tolerance for thinking different from our own. The differences and divergences between the promoter and the critics of the RTT call for dialogue and cooperation. . . . In this sense, pluralism is not a split but a gift for the Chinese church." While "pluralism" is used in Professor Zhu's paper to mean the different opinions concerning RTT, I use it to signify the different theological thinking concerning Chinese theology.

My second comment concerns "the revisionist model of theology." In the last section of her presentation, Ms. Zhu borrows David Tracy's "revisionist model of theology" to respond to RTT issues, presuming that this model may contribute to the reflection on RTT. So far I have paid attention to how Zhu analyzes varying opinions of the Chinese churches on RTT. Now I will pay some attention to how she tries to respond to the controversial

RTT issues in a wider context — not only in the church community (*ekklesia*), but in three communities that are mutually critical: academy, church, and society. I think this response is quite thought-provoking and raises the reflection on RTT to a higher level.

When discussing the relation of theology with church and society, on the one hand, Professor Zhu emphasizes the publicity and openness of theological thinking. But, on the other hand, she also stresses its independence, which is manifested in its critical correlation both with *ekklesia* and with society. In the case of the church, Zhu points out that "any intention to manipulate would lose the independence of theological thinking." In regard to society she says that, "Obviously, the prophetic and critical character is the fundamental condition for retaining the uniqueness of the faith."

Here our question is: How could the independence of theology be guaranteed? It seems that Professor Zhu's presentation does not deal with this question. But when introducing the revisionist model of theology, she borrows from David Tracy something from which we may find a clue for answering this question. In the context of the revisionist model of theology, we may say that the independence of theology comes from mutually critical correlation of the three branches, namely, fundamental theology, systematic theology, and practical theology. These correspond respectively to three communities: academy, church, and society. So to some extent, the correlation may contribute to the independence of theology.

But this model of correlation was formed in the Western world, where Christianity takes a dominating place. The Chinese context is quite different. For example, we are not clear which community in Chinese society may correspond to the community in Tracy's model. Furthermore, there has never been any relation between academy and church in China as in the West. In this sense, Tracy's revisionist model of theology seems not so relevant to the Chinese situation.

However, it is meaningful trying to respond to the issues raised by Professor Zhu's use of a revisionist model of theology. Indeed, Chinese academy, church, and society really need more critical correlation, especially between academy and church. I think this conference is a very good beginning for Chinese scholars and leaders of Chinese churches to understand each other. In fact, there should be more opportunities and ways to encourage the dialogue and mutual understanding for Chinese scholars and the leaders of the churches, so that their dialogue may contribute to the independence of theology. Zhu Xiaohong's paper represents a scholar's effort to promote this kind of a dialogue between *akademia* and *ekklesia*.

17 Christ and Culture: A Reflection by a Chinese Christian

Chen Yongtao

Once, in the region of Caesarea Philippi, Jesus asked his disciples two very important questions. The first was: "Who do people say that the Son of Man is?" Another was: "Who do you say that I am?" To the first question, the disciples answered: "Some say John the Baptist, but others Elijah, and still others Jeremiah or one of the prophets." To the second question, Simon Peter answered: "You are the Messiah, the Son of the living God" (Matt. 16:13-16; cf. Mark 8:27-30 and Luke 9:18-20). These two questions pose the issues of faith and theology that people cannot avoid. The answers to the two questions also involve the relationship between Christ and culture. This is to say, human understanding of Christ is always related to culture, and it cannot be separated from the cultural context of those who understand.

As H. Richard Niebuhr says, the question of Christ and culture is an eternal issue. Jesus Christ is pure God and is also a pure human being. As a human being he lived in a particular cultural context; "he was born as a Jew and he also died as a Jew." When the Logos became flesh to be a Jew, Jesus had to face Jewish culture. When he faced Jewish culture in the world, the encounter between Christ and culture began. Klausner, a Jewish scholar, considers the rejection of Jesus by the Pharisees and Sadducees as an issue of culture.

> The reason that the Pharisees and Sadducees rejected Jesus of Nazareth was that Jesus threatened Jewish civilization. . . . Jesus was the result of Jewish culture; thus, in the Gospels nothing of what he said concerning

ethics and religious persuasion, etc., is contradictory to Jewish clas-sics.[1]

It is not only that Jesus had much to do with Jewish culture but also that human understandings of Christ cannot be separated from culture either, since God's revelation in Christ is not separated from culture as the medium. Without culture we will not be able to understand and accept God's revelation; nor would Jesus Christ would be able to connect with our lives.

Because of this, the question for Christians concerning Christ and culture is also an issue that cannot be avoided. Since Christ cannot be separated from culture and we have to talk about and preach about Christ within cultures, this issue cannot be avoided. On the other hand, because of human cultural characteristics, i.e., human beings are cultural beings, when we talk about Christ with others such an issue cannot be avoided. Our understanding is a kind of cultural understanding, bearing deep cultural marks.

First, we are human beings who live within cultures. When we talk about Christ, we cannot manage without culture as the medium. Second, the listeners and receivers are also human beings living within cultures, and when they understand and receive the speech they cannot separate it from their living cultural context either. It can be said that understanding and speaking concerning Christ always take place in cultures; where there is speech about Christ, there is culture.

Christ and Culture: Some Shortcomings

As to the relation between Christ and culture, I wish to point to some of the shortcomings of Niebuhr's classification. The relationship between Christ and culture is very complicated. On the one hand, Christ turns to God and leads people to leave the cultural present with its secular and multiple characteristics. On the other hand, Christ himself also belongs to a particular cultural tradition, and his sending of disciples to preach the gospel was accomplished through cultural activities. Therefore, the relationship between culture and Christ is developed through stages such as affirmation and rejection, reconstruction and compromise, and new rejection.

---

1. H. Richard Niebuhr, *Christ and Culture* in Chinese: *Jidu yu wenhua* (Hong Kong: Dongnanya shenxue jiaoyu xiehui chubanshe, 1992), p. 2.

For the past two thousand years, the relationship between Christ and culture has always been a disputed question. Niebuhr's largest contribution is his description of the five modes of relationship between Christ and culture in his classic work *Christ and Culture*.[2] His classification has proved convenient for discussion of the relationship of Christ and culture. The problem, however, is that Niebuhr's classification is too simple and it addresses only theological concerns while ignoring other historical issues. Therefore, his classification is highly theoretical. No individual believer or the whole community of believers in history can simply belong to any one of his modes. Therefore, many scholars have tried their best to revise Niebuhr's classification; here I introduce the work of two people.

The evangelical scholar Charles H. Kraft follows Niebuhr's classification but has made some revisions to it. Professor Chen Zemin of the Nanjing Union Theological Seminary has introduced his classification as well.[3] For Kraft, God transforms cultures and becomes immanent within cultures. "Although God is totally outside cultures, human beings are totally inside cultures, and God has chosen the cultural context, where human beings live, as the place where he has fellowship with people."[4] "God is absolute and infinite, but he has freely chosen and used human cultures, and in his fellowship with human beings and in certain particular important times, he has even limited himself so that human culture can accept him."[5]

Professor George Marsden of the University of Chicago thinks that if the classification is not based on abstract theological principles but on the practical lives of Christians, a new classification of the relationship between

---

2. They are: (1) Christ-against-culture: exclusivism; (2) Christ-in-culture: inclusivism; (3) Christ-transforming-culture: synthesism; (4) the paradoxical relationship between Christ and culture: dualism; this mode affirms the tension between the authority of Christ and that of culture, and holds that Christians are under the control of both; and (5) Christ is the transformer or reformer of culture; according to this mode Christ is the reformer, who lives within cultures and societies. Such a reform is never separated from culture and society.

3. Charles H. Kraft introduced a different classification from that of Niebuhr in his *Christianity in Culture: A Study in Dynamic Biblical Theologizing in Cross-cultural Perspective* (Maryknoll: Orbis, 1979); Chen Zemin introduced his own classification in the article "Christ and Culture in China: A Dialogue between America and China," which was first presented in a conference "Christ and Culture" at Columbia University in October 1992 and published in *Jinling shenxue zhi* 17 (1992).

4. Kraft, *Christianity in Culture*, p. 114.

5. Kraft, *Christianity in Culture*, p. 115.

Christ and culture will appear. He suggests dividing the mode of Christ-against-culture into two types: church-outside-culture and church-in-conflict-with-culture. He suggests also combining the third and fourth of Niebuhr's modes into the type of church-adapting-to-culture, since the two modes are based on different theological principles but are the same in practice. He also suggests changing the Christ-reforming-culture mode to a church-influencing-culture mode. In addition, he suggests two new modes: church-deciding-culture and culture-deciding-church.[6]

When Niebuhr discusses Christ and culture, culture is considered as something opposite to revelation and covering the whole process of human activities. Culture is the "human reproduced context," which was added to nature by human beings, and it includes language, habits, ideology, faith, customs, social organizations, results of civilization, technological processes, values, etc. Based on such a broad sense of culture, Niebuhr mentions several features of culture: (1) Culture cannot be separated from society and its social functions. (2) Culture is the achievement of human beings. (3) The cultural world is the world of values, and it is concerned with human benefits. (4) Culture concerns the realization of all values in the present world. (5) Culture is also multiple, and the values that culture seeks to realize are complicated.[7]

Although Niebuhr's definition of culture has been criticized by many,[8] theologically his theory — which treats Christ and culture, grace and natural action, as corresponding (rather than contradictory) categories — is a practical one. Without question, both grace and culture are requisites for the lives of Christians. Without culture we will not be able to understand nature; and, as human beings cannot be separated from nature, human beings cannot be separated from culture either; since pure natural human beings do not exist, all people live in different cultural contexts.

---

6. George Marsden, "Christianity and Culture: Transforming Niebuhr's Categories," *Insights* (Autumn 1999): 13.

7. Niebuhr, *Christ and Culture*, pp. 29-34.

8. The main criticism of his use of the term "culture" is offered by John H. Yoder, who believes that Niebuhr's use of the term "culture" is often confusing. See John H. Yoder, "How H. Richard Niebuhr Reasoned: A Critique of *Christ and Culture*," in *Authentic Transformation: A New Vision of Christ and Culture*, ed. Glen H. Stassen, D. M. Yeager, and John H. Yoder (Nashville: Abingdon, 1996).

Christ and Culture: The Symbolic Interpretation of Several Biblical Passages

Both understanding and misunderstanding Christ have much to do with culture. Let us first return to the Bible. I will interpret three biblical passages symbolically, and we will find out that the question of the relationship between Christ and culture cannot be avoided and is rather complicated.

The first passage is Matthew 5:17-20. This is a part of Jesus' Sermon on the Mount, where he says: "Do not think that I have come to abolish the law or the prophets; I have not come to abolish but to fulfill." The law and prophets represent Jewish culture, and Jesus did not come to abolish but to fulfill them. This indicates the essential meaning of the relationship between Christ and culture: Christ became flesh in a particular culture, and his work cannot be separated from culture. This is to say, Christ's gospel neither has nothing to do with culture nor is it in conflict with culture, but is related to culture. Christ is the fulfiller of Jewish culture rather than its destroyer. To other cultures, Christ is also a fulfiller rather than a destroyer. Therefore, it is possible and meaningful for the Chinese Christians to talk about the relationship between Christianity and Chinese culture.

The second passage is Luke 9:51-56. In this passage we can see that before his crucifixion, Jesus decided to go to Jerusalem. When he and his disciples passed through a Samaritan village, the people there did not welcome him. Why? The Bible tells us that the reason was his heading for Jerusalem. Jerusalem here represents a culture; thus, the Samaritans did not reject Jesus because he is Christ or because of the gospel; what they rejected was the culture in which Jesus the Jew lived.

The third passage is Luke 15:11-32. The Parable of the Prodigal Son has a spiritual meaning, which refers to the repentance of a sinner and the grace of God. However, some people also interpret the parable as a story about the captivity and revival of the whole of Israel. In the time of Jesus, many Jews believed that the captivity was still continuing since, although Jews had returned from Babylon to the land of Israel, the great restoration of Israel had not yet occurred.

They believed that Israel would be saved, sins would be forgiven, and the covenant between God and the Jews would continue. What God had done for them in the Exodus from Egypt was the background of Jewish hope. For the Jewish people this wish was coming true, since the real return (including from death) was happening in the mission of Jesus. All those who did not welcome the return belonged to the group that did not experience the captivity and opposed the return and repentance of others; the Elder Brother in the parable was one such person.[9] In this sense the parable here has its meaning in the relationship between gospel and culture, since accepting the gospel refers to cultural adjustment and regeneration.

This parable shows that Israel was at a point of change, and such a change was happening in the mission of Jesus. This parable affirms the continuation of the tradition concerning the relationship between God and Israel and the regeneration of the relationship between God and the church. From this parable we can see both a continuation of the Jewish tradition and a break, which understands the tradition differently. It makes us realize that everything has both its continuation and its break, and it also offers some knowledge about the Jewish background. Human understanding of Christianity can neither be separated from tradition nor limited to tradition; this is to say, the Christian can separate neither from the tradition of faith nor from the cultural tradition and context. Therefore, every understanding of Christ has its own value, since each can touch some aspects of the truth but none of them can comprehend the whole truth. Christ can only become flesh within culture, and culture can be the medium through which Christ comes to us.

Christ and Culture: The Perspective of Hermeneutics

The cultural categories employed by the anthropologist Clifford Geertz belong to the field of semiotics. Like Max Weber, Geertz believes that human beings are within a semiotic network knitted by themselves. He considers culture as a network that he seeks to interpret. For him cultural analysis is not a science of experiment that intends to find principles; rather, it is a science of interpretation. Human beings are semiotic beings. All cultural activities are social events since they are, in fact, the construction, understanding, and employing of semiotic forms.

The relationship between Christ and culture is, in fact, the issue of semiotics. When Christ meets cultures or when cultures meet Christ, there will be tension between them. These tensions are a process of two-way interpretation. Christ is one, but cultures are many. The same Christ may conflict with many different cultures, and in different cultures the same Christ may be interpreted differently. Every cultural interpretation of Christ is an inter-

9. See N. T. Wright, *Jesus and the Victory of God* (Minneapolis: Fortress, 1997), ch. 4.

pretation of the truth, but none of them is the truth itself — just as the moon shines upon many rivers, but the image in every river is not the moon itself. The cultural understanding of Christ is also like this; all cultures interpret the same Christ, but they only point to Christ and they are not Christ himself.

Christ is alive; thus Christian understandings of Christ should also be alive, dynamic, and developing. If we hold negatively to some doctrines, the Jesus we know will only be a dead Jesus rather than a living Jesus; and we will have only a dead Christianity rather than a living faith. Such a Jesus and Christianity can rarely speak to us in the contemporary context of our lives. In this sense, we should keep in mind that when we believe our understanding of Christ is correct, this should not mean that other interpretations are wrong. Such an understanding may bring tolerance in faith and richness in theology rather than dictatorial faith and hegemony of theology.

Here is the problem of the interpretative angle, since different perspectives usually lead to different conclusions. When I was in San Francisco, a Spanish professor told a story about a Mexican boy's understanding of the creation of human beings by God. He says that God created human beings in a way similar to the way a baker bakes bread. Some of them were baked too long a time so as to become black, some were baked too short a time so as to become white, some were baked a little bit longer so as to become yellow, and some were baked a little bit shorter so as to become brown like Mexicans, who are the best. This is an interesting story, but note: the angle of interpretation decides the conclusion. If the interpreter were not a Mexican boy but a Chinese boy, he would probably consider yellow the best color; an African boy would consider black the best, and a European boy would consider white the best. When we talk about the relationship between Christ and culture, there is the question of cultural identification.

Facing the same text, different people will have different interpretations. The same text will have different interpretations and answers in different cultures. Christianity is the religion of revelation. As Christians, we accept God's revelation; however, we Christians cannot fully understand the revealed truth of God. Every Christian in each cultural context can only understand and comprehend a part of Christian truth, like the proverbial blind men touching the elephant.

As the Bible says, God's revelation has come many times and from many perspectives; God always reveals himself through the medium of different cultures and uses different methods with people in different cultural contexts. Thus, in a certain sense, we may say that without culture God cannot reveal himself to people. This does not mean that God's self-revelation is limited by culture, but it means that human beings, as the receivers of God's revelation, are limited by cultures.

Christ is the self-revelation of God, and in this sense, he transfers cultures. On the other hand, in order to establish relationships with people, Christ always becomes flesh in different cultures. Thus, he is again immanent in culture. Jesus Christ, who became flesh in a manger, is closely related with cultures, since the manger has its theological and cultural symbols. When Christ encounters different cultures, every culture may become a manger to receive Jesus Christ.

The New Testament also shows this feature. Different authors in the New Testament testified to the same Jesus Christ, but they may have had different understandings and witnesses. Since every author had his own cultural background and different readers, every book in the New Testament has its own purpose and perspective. They indicate the multiple features of the first generation of Christians in the experience of faith and the understanding of theology. However, there are many differences among them in their understandings of Christ. Within the New Testament we find many different understandings of Christ because of the different readers and different cultural contexts, but each of these understandings and witnesses is valid.

On the other hand, in the relationship between Christ and culture, Christ is not only a text that is passively read by people. For Christ, culture is also a text. Culture should also be interpreted through the group of believers. Thus, the relationship between Christ and culture is mutually influenced and mutually interpreted. Through such a mutual interpretation, different groups of believers may establish their own local theology that has both Christian and local cultural marks. For Chinese Christians the real Chinese theology is the interpretation of the Christian gospel in the context of Chinese culture. As Bishop K. H. Ting says, there are two "C's" — Christ and China — that concern Chinese theology.

According to K. H. Ting, theology is "faith seeking understanding," and "the church in the process of thinking." On the one hand, theology should answer Christians' questions and offer them help, and on the other hand, theology should face the challenges arising from the cultural and social context where Christians live. Thus, theology should have a two-way interpretation of Christ and culture and should through such two-way interpretation reconstruct its Christian faith in its own cultural context. It is in this respect that Christ is closely related to culture. Thus, the main task of Christianity is not to rationalize and to defend universal doctrines, but is to make Christians open our minds to God's different ways of working. God works with different ways in different places, generations, and nations.[10]

The cultures of people are the resource of Christian theology. The most important thing in constructing an Asian theology is to have a theological insight into its culture. Within people's culture we touch the hearts of human beings, we are filled with the Holy Spirit, we receive power, we promote the development of history, and we change the direction of history.[11]

Theological thought cannot be separated from culture, and Chinese theology should be both Christian and Chinese. It should be the thinking and the answers of the Chinese church and of real Chinese Christians to the questions faced in their own cultural and social contexts.

Christ and Culture in China

An Asian theologian thinks that the essence of theology concerns human beings rather than God. In theology, speech about human beings must be more emphasized than speech about God. If we overlook the real situation of human beings, we will not be able to see the existence of God. The real situation of human beings is the reality of God.[12] What this theologian says, in fact, is the essence of Chinese culture rather than that of Christian theology, since Chinese culture focuses on humanism. It is quite different from Western Christian culture, which takes God as its basis. Thus, how to face Chinese culture becomes a necessary question when the encounter between Christianity and Chinese culture is discussed.

Christianity is a kind of faith in God and Jesus Christ, and it is also a kind of culture with divine and transcendental features. Christianity cannot be separated from culture. If Christianity is to be transmitted in China, it must encounter and be integrated with Chinese culture so that the two cultures may complement each other.

Historically we may say that the history of Christian mission in China is

---

10. Guo Peilan, *Shangdi zai Yazhou renmin zhi zhong* (Hong Kong: Jidujiao wenyi chubanshe), p. 25.

11. Guo Peilan, *Shangdi zai Yazhou renmin zhi zhong*, p. 31.

12. Guo Peilan, *Shangdi zai Yazhou renmin zhi zhong*, p. 26.

a history of conflicts and misunderstandings. If we look at the history of the Chinese church, during the past 1,400 years[13] Christianity has experienced several developments and difficulties. First, because of persecution in the eighth century, Nestorianism disappeared from the center of China, and later, with the retreat of the Mongolian rulers of the Yuan dynasty, Christianity again disappeared. During the late Ming and early Qing dynasties, because of the contribution of the Jesuit missionary Matteo Ricci, Christianity succeeded very well in China, but the later Rites Controversy during the Qing dynasty led to the forbidding of Christianity in China.

Later Christianity got another chance to develop together with the Opium War and imperialism, but it met strong opposition from the Chinese people. However, Christianity has now become an important religion in China, especially since the liberation of China in 1949, with the help of the Three-Self Patriotic Movement of the Chinese Christian church. Christianity has been increasingly accepted by the Chinese people. Although we have not yet established a real Chinese Christianity, the Chinese church has awakened; she is no longer a mission field of foreign churches but a Three-Self Chinese church.

If Christianity wishes to become a real Chinese Christianity, it has to take root in Chinese soil. However, when we try to integrate Christianity into Chinese culture, several errors should be avoided. For example: (1) A nihilist tendency, which considers Chinese culture as nonsense and believes that Chinese culture should be abolished and be replaced by Christianity. (2) A blind optimism that considers Chinese culture as perfect and needing no exchange with other cultures, and holding that Christianity does not have any place in Chinese culture. (3) A cultural relativism that considers every culture as a perfect system and believes that no cultural exchange is needed and that Christian mission is a cultural invasion. All three of these errors should be noted and avoided.[14]

Chinese culture has its good aspects and its shortcomings; but, as an old culture with a long history, it can become soil for the benefit of Christian development. As Jesus Christ did not come to abolish Jewish culture, he will

13. This is counted from the arrival of Nestorianism to China in 635 CE, but some people disagree with this and argue that Christianity entered China earlier, during the Eastern Han dynasty (25-220 CE); cf. Wei Juxian, *Zhongguo gushi zhong de shangdi guan* (Hong Kong: Jidujiao wenyi chubanshe, 1971), and Ake Mur, *Chinese Christianity Before 1550* (Beijing: Zhonghua shuju, 1984).

14. I have published an article concerning this issue, "Cong wenhua chuanbo de jiaodu qiantan jidujiao yu Zhonguo wenhua de guanxi," *Jinling shenxue zhi* 14-15 (1991).

not abolish Chinese culture but fulfill it. Christianity can complement the shortcomings of Chinese culture, and the latter can become soil for the development of the former.

Although Christianity and Chinese culture are very different, conflict between them is not inevitable. Most elements of Chinese culture are neutral, and the truly good and beautiful parts of Chinese culture are not contradictory with Christianity. The relationship between them is that between a part and the whole, between a shadow and an actual body. The apostle Paul says,

> Ever since the creation of the world his eternal power and divine nature, invisible though they are, have been understood and seen through the things he has made. So they are without excuse. (Rom. 1:20)

Christianity has a special revelation from God, and Chinese culture also includes revelation of God, but it is his universal revelation to human beings. This universal revelation is a good part of Chinese culture and an organic part of the whole human truth, goodness, and beauty. This is the contact point between Christianity and Chinese culture, and it is the rich soil in which Christianity may take root in China.

In his article "Zhongguo renwen zhuyi he jidujiao lingxing," Wu Jingxiong says:

> If the East does not find the West in Christ, it will never meet and admire the West. If the West does not find the East in Christ, it will never meet and admire the East. If the East becomes Westernized, it will be worse than the West. If the West become Easternized, it will be worse than the East. If the East marries the West outside Christ, their marriage will not last for long, since it will be only a momentary emotion, which only gives birth to strange things. Only when they are united in the embrace of Christ can they love each other with the love of Christ and can their union give birth to new people.[15]

Instead of this parable of marriage, Chinese theologian Wang Zhixin employed John 12:24 to discuss the relationship between Christianity and Chinese culture. He says that Christianity is like a seed that can be planted anywhere, but two things should be noticed. First, the seed should be put

---

15. Cited from Lei Libo, *Lun Jidu de da yu xiao* (Beijing: Zhongguo shehui kexue chubanshe, 1998), p. 226.

into a soil so as to absorb nutrition, i.e., Christianity should be rooted in a local culture. Second, the seed must die so as to give birth to a new life to bear much fruit.[16]

What is Chinese culture? This is a vague concept that is difficult to define. Usually when Chinese culture is mentioned some features are listed. In my limited understanding, it has the following main features:

1. It is human-centered rather than theo-centered; although the unification between Heaven and human beings is often mentioned in China, a feeling of reverence is lacking.
2. It is inclusive rather than exclusive. Among the three traditional Chinese religions, Confucianism, Taoism, and Buddhism, there has always been the tendency of connection and integration. Buddhism was not Chinese in its origin, but through integrating with Chinese culture it has become a part of Chinese culture. In Chinese history, there have been debates concerning religious affairs but there have been no religious wars. Religious inclusivism and syncretism have been an important tendency in China.
3. It is ethical rather than metaphysical. In Chinese culture morality rather than mysticism is emphasized, present life rather than future life. There is a concept of immortality in Chinese culture, but it is still within the present life: morality, speech, and merit have been considered as three immortals.
4. It is united rather than dualist or contradictory in its way of thinking. In Chinese culture, Heaven and earth, Divinity and human beings, *yin* and *yang*, light and darkness, the five elements (metal, wood, water, fire, and earth) are all united beyond conflicts rather than dualistically divided by absolute conflict.
5. It is collectivistic rather than individualistic. In Confucianist ethics, human relationships are emphasized. Human relationships are like a network; without this network human beings cannot exist. The real "individual" does not exist in China.
6. It is balanced (mean) rather than radical.
7. As to the quality of human nature, it is optimistic rather than pessimistic; the nature of human beings is believed to be good rather than evil.

16. Wang Zhixin, "Zhongguo bense jiaohui de taolun," in *Bense zhi tan: 20 shijie Zhongguo jidujiao wenhua xueshu lunji,* ed. Zhang Xiping and Zhuo Xinping (Beijing: Zhongguo guangbo dianshi chubanshe, 1999), p. 236.

8. It is educational rather than soteriological. When Mencius was seeking a relaxed heart or a Buddha-like realization, all relied on education rather than salvation provided by an external power.

Through these features we may find how Christianity and Chinese culture are different.[17]

Some Problems Faced by Contemporary Chinese Christians

Chinese Christians do not live in a vacuum but in a cultural tradition that has a long history and a strong life. We are compelled to ask ourselves: How can we talk about Christ in such a cultural context? As a Chinese Christian, how should I treat the relationship between Christianity and Chinese culture? Is Christianity going to be Sinicized? Or is Chinese culture going to be Christianized? Or are Christianity and Chinese culture going to be conformed?

Like many other Asian countries, China has a polyreligious tradition; Confucianism, Taoism, and Buddhism all influence Chinese people very strongly. As a religion with an exclusive color, how can Christianity coexist with other religions in China? How can it become a socially stable and developing power together with other religions?

Today's China is a country that has been liberated and is developing quickly under the leadership of the Chinese Communist Party. How can Christianity be integrated into this society? How can it be adapted to the Chinese socialist society? How can it become a positive and progressive power?

Chinese Christians live in a context dominated by atheism. Although the Chinese Three-Self Patriotic Movement has helped Christianity to become accepted by local Chinese people, and Christianity itself has developed extensively during the past years, Christianity is still a subculture in China. Protestant Christians are a small minority and occupy only a little more than 3 percent of the population. How can Christianity enlarge its living space? How can it influence the society where it lives? How can Christians give witness in such a society?

In addition to great material development, the Chinese social reformation has also brought democratic and legal improvement; social and spiri-

---

17. See also Chen Zemin, "Christ and Culture in China," pp. 126-28.

tual life has been lifted to a higher level. However, many negative elements have also been brought in during the process of change; for example, the gap between the rich and the poor, pornography and drugs, etc. How can Christianity help the government improve social morality? How can it contribute to the construction of spirituality?

All these questions should be asked by theologians, church leaders, and anyone who cares about the encounter between Christianity and Chinese culture. As a subculture in China, Christianity should open itself to enlarge its living space rather than close itself off from the rest of Chinese society.

Chinese Folk Christianity

Although folk Christianity is a vague concept that is difficult to define, it indeed exists in China and has many followers. It has the following main features:

1. It is charismatic; it seeks phenomena such as visions, dreams, speaking in tongues, and mystical experiences.

2. It is pragmatic; it pays more attention to the present life, and many people come to church in order to seek health, a good job, a happy marriage, and even wealth. Many testimonies related to such success have been heard; in this respect the Chinese Confucian pragmatic tradition plays an important role in folk Christianity.

3. Ethical and moral teaching is emphasized. For instance, many people consider being a Christian as a matter of being a "good person," being a good citizen, since good deeds will lead to a reward and evil deeds will lead to punishment.

4. Superstitions are common. If the organized churches are considered as orthodox churches in China, many of the unorganized churches may be considered as non-orthodox ones. Non-orthodox does not mean heresy, but it usually means heretical and superstitious elements. By the term "superstition" I mean the kind of blindness and ignorance in the life of faith that expresses itself against orthodox Christianity and against society; it may have feudalist, heretical, and antinomian characteristics. Therefore, many heresies have a close relationship with folk Christianity.

5. Lay Christian leaders of the unorganized churches are usually not well educated; organization is usually loose, and individual Christian leaders sometimes acquire too eminent a position, etc.

6. Folk Christianity is influenced by folk religion and culture, and its understanding of Jesus Christ is mainly from the viewpoint of ethics and pragmatism. For example, Jesus Christ is seen as a healer: Jesus can heal people, and they often come to Christ in order to be healed. Another important image is that of a protector: Jesus can offer peace to people, and they come to Christ in order to get peace for themselves and their families.

Moreover, Jesus tends to be seen in terms of the following images:

- An educator: Jesus can teach people, and they come to Christ in order to become better persons and to have a better personal relationship with others;
- A blesser: Jesus blesses people, and they come to Christ not only for the future life but also for the present life;
- A provider: Jesus can offer all that people need, and they come to Christ in order to get material needs;
- A consoler: Jesus gives comfort and help for people who are facing difficulties.

In some areas, folk Christianity has been mixed together with folk religions, and for some people Jesus Christ can do all that folk religion's gods do. Thus, Christ has replaced folk-religious gods. Others believe that, like folk-religious gods, Jesus can help them when they are in need. Thus, God is not very different from the folk-religious gods. We should notice that some elements of Chinese folk religions are good, but some clearly are not. In order to have a good church, we must take advantage of Chinese folk religions in a wise manner. Some questions rising from the relationship between Christ and culture should also be discussed. What I am doing here is only pointing out some phenomena; the reasons behind them have not yet been studied.

Conclusion

For Chinese Christians facing the relationship between Christ and culture, it is necessary to maintain our own special identity. We are Christians who have our own faith, and we believe that Jesus Christ is our Savior and Lord not only for the sake of being saved and being blessed, but also for the sake of sharing the grace of Christ with others and bearing witness to him. On the other hand, we are Chinese, who live in a particular cultural context. How to testify to Christ within such a cultural medium is a question that should be asked by every Chinese Christian. It is not easy to find an answer.

What we are going to witness and preach is Christ rather than doctrine; the latter is speech *about* Christ rather than Christ himself. Interpreting doctrine is a theological activity, and it is related to culture. Our culture is developing and is full of living strength. Although Christ is eternal and the truth of the gospel is eternal, human understandings of the truth are also in process of development. The Reconstruction of Theological Thinking in the contemporary Chinese church aims at a better testimony to Christ and a better preaching of the gospel in the Chinese cultural context.

18 A Chinese Christian's Reading of Two Ethical Themes of *Zhuangzi*

Lin Manhong

Zhuangzi, an early Taoist writer who wrote at least the inner chapters of *Zhuangzi,* was a prominent Chinese thinker during the fourth century BCE. Lin Yutang, well known in both China and the West as a modern Chinese writer and translator of classic Chinese texts, considers Zhuangzi "the greatest prose master of Classical China" and "the greatest and most profound philosopher China has produced."[1] According to Wing-tsit Chan, a renowned neo-Confucian scholar, Zhuangzi's philosophy had tremendous impact on Chinese Buddhism and neo-Confucianism, as well as on Chinese landscape painting and poetry. Nevertheless, regarding ethics, the general consensus in both the Chinese tradition and among Western Sinologists is that *Zhuangzi* has little to offer.

Chan writes that even the leading neo-Confucian Zhu Xi, whose philosophy was deeply influenced by Zhuangzi, complained that "Lao Tzu still wanted to do something, but Chuang Tzu (Zhuangzi) did not want to do anything at all. He even said that he knew what to do but just did not want to do it."[2] In his article, Eske Møllgaard also names several modern Western scholars seeing in Zhuangzi an ethical relativist or amoralist, among whom Robert Eno and Chad Hansen are recent examples. Eno argues that Zhuangzi regards butchering people and butchering oxen as the same exercise in which spiri-

---

1. Lin Yutang, *From Pagan to Christian* (Cleveland and New York: World Publishing Company, 1959), pp. 129-30.

2. See *A Source Book in Chinese Philosophy,* trans. and ed. Wing-tsit Chan (Princeton: Princeton University Press, 1963), pp. 178-79.

tual spontaneity could be achieved. Chad Hansen says that Zhuangzi is unable to censure even the worst atrocities beyond saying "it happened."[3]

In agreement with Møllgaard's argument that Zhuangzi does indeed have a moral imperative and unique religious ethics,[4] this paper endeavors to first examine that ethical insight based on a scholarly understanding of two themes in *Zhuangzi*: the perfected person and the idea of equality in human relations. After examining these themes, a Chinese Christian reading of these two ethical themes will be presented in order to contribute to the ethical discussion in the Protestant church in China.

The Perfected Person

According to scholar Huang Jinhong, the ethical ideal state for Zhuangzi is to be with the *Dao* or the Way; one's ultimate ethical goal is to be the Perfected Person or the True Man.[5] A main characteristic of the Perfected Person, as portrayed by Zhuangzi in *The Great and Venerable Teacher*, is to be with the *Dao* by "fasting of the mind" and "self-forgetting." We will follow Zhuangzi to see how one is able to reach such an ethical state.

For Zhuangzi, just as fasting from food is to abstain from certain kinds of food, or even any food, in order to empty the stomach, "fasting of the mind" is to set the mind in the realm of emptiness where the Way "gathers" alone. Zhuangzi explains "fasting of the mind" in this way:

> Make your will one. Do not listen with your ears, listen with your mind. No, do not listen with your mind, but listen with your spirit. Listening stops with the ears, the mind stops with recognition, but spirit is empty and waits on all things. The Way gathers in emptiness alone. Emptiness is the fasting of the mind.[6]

Here, Zhuangzi spells out the steps leading to the "fasting of the mind." One should first banish all the distracting thoughts from one's mind and be

---

3. Eske Møllgaard, "Zhuangzi's Religious Ethics," *Journal of the American Academy of Religion* 71, no. 2 (June 2003): 347-48.

4. See Møllgaard, "Zhuangzi's Religious Ethics," pp. 347-70.

5. Huang Jinhong, "Zhuangzi," in *Zhongguo lidai sixiangjia*, ed. Wang Shounan (Taipei: Taiwan Shangwu Yinshuguan, 1978), p. 435.

6. *The Complete Works of Chuang Tzu*, trans. Burton Watson (New York and London: Columbia University Press, 1968), p. 58.

single-minded, and then concentrate on listening. One should listen with the mind rather than with the ears, because what comes to the ears, so often, is gibberish rather than true words. Furthermore, listening with the mind alone is still not adequate, because what comes to the mind, sometimes, is only the recognition of the appearance of things instead of the essence of things. Only the spirit is able to encounter with the *Dao,* the essence of all things. To be with the *Dao,* the spirit has to reach a state of emptiness, because the *Dao* resides in the realm of emptiness alone.

"Fasting of the mind" will lead to "self-forgetting," which means that one is no longer conscious of self after getting to the realm of emptiness, as indicated by Yen Hui in the fourth chapter of *Zhuangzi.*[7] According to Huang Jinhong, though "self-forgetting" and "fasting of the mind" will jointly lead one to reach one's ethical goal, they carry different meanings and have their own focuses. While "fasting of the mind" is something that occurs within one's self, "self-forgetting" deals with the relationship between the self and the outer world, according to Heaven's patterns and processes.[8]

For Zhuangzi, despite all the differences among people and things in the world, there is a perfect unity bringing all things together to the wholeness of the *Dao.* Self-forgetting helps one live in accord with the wholeness of the *Dao.* It can be said that such a state is like the harmony between a part of the body and the body. The part of the body listens to and goes with the will of the body without any opposition to the body. As a result, it forgets its own self and is in total accord with the body. If the part of the body is self-centered instead of self-forgetting, it is in opposition to the body. An example is pain, in which a part of the body insists on itself and puts itself in opposition to the whole body. If a person is like a part of the body that is contrary to the body, this person is in separation from the *Dao.* Hence, self-forgetting is crucial for a person to be in accord with the *Dao* and to move toward the ethical ideal state of being a Perfected Person.

The Perfected Person has many attributes, which are depicted in *The Great and Venerable Teacher.* Without looking at those descriptions in detail, it could be argued that the Perfected Person is the one with a perfected mind. Lee Yearley suggests that two particular images: "the hinge in a socket" and

---

7. "Yen Hui said, 'Before I heard this (the fasting of the mind), I was certain that I was Hui. But now that I have heard it, there is no more Hui. Can this be called emptiness? That's all there is to it'" (*The Complete Works of Chuang Tzu*).

8. Huang Jinhong, "Zhuangzi," p. 436.

"a mirror" in *Zhuangzi* are helpful in deciphering the perfected mind.[9] The first image is described by Zhuangzi, thus:

> Everything has its "that," everything has its "this." I say, "that" comes out of "this" and "this" depends on "that." . . . The sage recognizes a "this," but a "this" which is also "that," a "that" which is also "this." His "that" has both a right and a wrong in it; his "this" too has both a right and a wrong in it. . . . A state in which "this" and "that" no longer find their opposites is called the hinge of the Way. When the hinge is fitted into the socket, it can respond endlessly.[10]

The key idea of this image of "the hinge in a socket" or "the axis in the center of a circle" in an alternative translation,[11] according to Lee Yearley, is that of the centered responsiveness. The hinge moves smoothly in its socket; it does not stand for "this" or against "that"; it only responds from a center to whatever occurs. Yearley argues that such an image has provided an alternative for our normal patterns of thought. Our thoughts, attitudes, and actions are formed by the oppositions that we are taught: we should respect this and disregard that; we should be this and should not be that; we should pursue this and avoid that. Zhuangzi replaces our normal notions of oppositions in our judgments and actions with this image, with something that moves continuously, with something that responds constantly yet is centered.[12]

The second image for describing the perfected mind is that of a mirror, as found in the following text:

> Do not be an embodier of fame; do not be a storehouse of schemes; do not be an undertaker of projects; do not be a proprietor of wisdom. . . . Be empty, that is all. The Perfect Man uses his mind like a mirror — going after nothing, welcoming nothing, responding but not restoring. Therefore he can win out over things and not hurt himself.[13]

Yearley provides a good description of the "attitude" that a mirror has. He writes that a mirror accepts whatever is presented to it without interpre-

---

9. Lee Yearley, "The Perfected Person in the Radical Chuang-tzu," in *Experimental Essays on Chuang-tzu*, ed. Victor H. Mair (Honolulu: University of Hawaii Press, 1983), p. 131.

10. *The Complete Works of Chuang Tzu*, p. 40.

11. *Chuang-tzu: The Seven Inner Chapters and Other Writings from the Book Chuang-tzu*, trans. A. C. Graham (London and Boston: Allen & Unwin, 1981), p. 53.

12. Yearley, "The Perfected Person in the Radical Chuang-tzu," p. 132.

13. *The Complete Works of Chuang Tzu*, p. 97.

tation, judgment, or desire. It simply reflects any new image put before it without further interpretation; it impartially reflects whatever happens in front of it without making judgment on rightness or wrongness. A mirror possesses no desire to pursue or to grasp what passes before it; it just lets desirable objects come before it and then pass away. Mirrors accept; they do not evaluate or cling to or seek.[14]

With the help of these two images, we posit that a perfected person with a perfected mind has constant adaptive appreciation of whatever happens without any bias, just like a hinge moving freely in a socket. The perfected person applies no interpretation, makes no judgment, and grasps no desire. His mind is like a mirror, only reflecting the way things are. "That mind maintains peace within strife, tranquility within disturbance; it sends off and welcomes whatever occurs."[15]

This state of peace and tranquility is the state of "fasting of the mind" and "self-forgetting," the state of being with the *Dao*, and the ideal ethical state of Zhuangzi. Møllgaard addresses the perfected person as a "person of Heaven" looking at things from the Heavenly perspective and considering all things equal and that none could be said to be better than the other. The perfected person is not entirely inscribed in the realm of Heaven, however, because this person is situated between the realms of "Heaven" and "man," and is free to be in either of the realms. The perfected person is sometimes "of Heaven's party" and sometimes "of man's party," and of which neither one is better than the other.[16] This attitude of the perfected person will help us understand Zhuangzi's idea of equality in human relations.

The Idea of Equality in Human Relations

According to Philip J. Ivanhoe, Zhuangzi uses the Heavenly perspective as a therapy to free one from the confines of one's cramped and narrow perspective and to enable one to appreciate one's true place in the world. For Zhuangzi, viewing things from the Heavenly perspective means that, while believing that all things are equal, one still deems some ways to live as better and some as worse. People have particular roles to play in the world according to their different natures and circumstances, but they should play their

---

14. Yearley, "The Perfected Person in the Radical Chuang-tzu," p. 133.
15. Yearley, "The Perfected Person in the Radical Chuang-tzu," p. 135.
16. Møllgaard, "Zhuangzi's Religious Ethics," p. 365.

roles within the scheme of Heaven. There are certain ways of living or acting that are either in accord with or contradictory to the way of nature.[17] In terms of human relations, instead of following the maxim of the Silver Rule of Confucianism, Zhuangzi suggests a maxim of "friendship," which is expressed in the following story of three friends:

> Master Sang-hu, Meng-tzu Fan, and Master Ch'in-chang, three friends, said to each other, "Who can join with others without joining with others? Who can do with others without doing with others? Who can climb up to Heaven and wander in the midst, roam the infinite, and forget life forever and forever?" The three men looked at each other and smiled. There was no disagreement in their hearts and so they became friends.[18]

The human relationship based on Zhuangzi's understanding of friendship differs from that guided by the Silver Rule. The Silver Rule — do not impose upon others what you do not desire yourself[19] — though key to moral evolution, according to Heiner Roetz, has its ethical deficiency.[20] Møllgaard summarizes Roetz's argument saying that first, the equality implied in the Silver Rule can easily decline into the hierarchical reciprocity characteristic of ancient societies, due to their hierarchical social and political order. Second, the Rule could become a simple device of prudence. Third, the Silver Rule presupposes a prior concept of the good. Consequently, what is needed for the Silver Rule to be a genuine principle is above all the self-cultivation of the moral subject who is to apply the Rule. Hence, the Silver Rule is unable to immediately guide the will, the mark of moral law.[21]

Møllgaard continues his argument that Zhuangzi's maxim — "do with

17. Philip J. Ivanhoe, "Was Zhuangzi a Relativist?" in *Essays on Skepticism, Relativism, and Ethics in the Zhuangzi*, ed. Paul Kjellbery and Philip J. Ivanhoe (New York: State University of New York Press, 1996), p. 201.

18. *The Complete Works of Chuang Tzu*, p. 86.

19. *Lun Yu* (Analects of Confucius) (Beijing: Sinolingua, 1994), p. 296 (15/24).

20. Heiner Roetz argues that the Silver Rule is found in particular political contexts that highlighted the hierarchical social and political order. It is more individually based than group based. It is also dependent on a preceding concept of the good, the attempt at self-cultivation. Possibilities of reading strategically the Silver Rule exist due to its lack of discussion on human motives. See Heiner Roetz, *Confucian Ethics of Axial Age: A Reconstruction under the Aspect of the Breakthrough toward Postconventional Thinking* (Albany: State University of New York Press, 1993), pp. 133-48.

21. Møllgaard, "Zhuangzi's Religious Ethics," p. 362.

others without doing with others" — suspends all reciprocal relations, let alone hierarchical reciprocity. As a form of nonaction, it transcends all technical action, and therefore, it cannot fall into merely strategic action. Zhuangzi's maxim also does not presuppose the concept of the good, for nothing is imposed on the other. Furthermore, Zhuangzi's maxim makes no reference to a will or desire for a presupposed good. This lack of will sets one free to will or not will, and free for the moral law.[22]

In other words, friendship is a relation of equality, a relation not based on hierarchical relation — a fundamental inequality. It opens up the possibility of being influenced by the other, and therefore, it helps one obtain a genuine ethical consciousness. On the contrary, within human relations guided by the Silver Rule, moral influence goes from one direction only, from the cultivated noblemen to the common people: "The virtue of the noblemen is like the wind, the virtue of the common people is like the grass. When the wind blows on the grass, it must bend" (*Analects* 12/19).

Zhuangzi's idea of equality in human relations also broadens the early Chinese view of what is worthy of respect and admiration, according to Ivanhoe. Zhuangzi believes that one does not need to be a good Confucian to be worthy of respect and admiration; the person in harmony with the world is, in fact, the one who has things right. Zhuangzi ventures even beyond this broad view of human dignity to see genuine value in the things of the world; the equality of all things is part of nature, part of the great *Dao*.[23]

A Chinese Christian Reading of *Zhuangzi's* Ethical Themes

Zhuangzi's ethical discourse may be applied to Christian life. This is not to say that *Zhuangzi* is Christian-like, that *Zhuangzi's* understanding of the *Dao* is similar to the Christian understanding of God, or that *Zhuangzi's* religious ethics has a particularly Christian implication. These notions would be a violation of *Zhuangzi's* true context, even though "that which is called the Christian religion existed among the ancients and even existed from the beginning of the human race until Christ came in the flesh."[24] To relate *Zhuangzi's* ethical insight to Christian beliefs is an attempt to enrich the vi-

---

22. Møllgaard, "Zhuangzi's Religious Ethics," pp. 364-65.

23. Ivanhoe, "Was Zhuangzi a Relativist?" pp. 206-7.

24. Augustine, *De vera religione* 10; quoted in Thomas Merton, *The Way of Chuang Tzu* (New York: New Directions, 1965), p. 10.

sion of Chinese Christians in interpreting and understanding our Christian faith by using a given cultural resource as a reference.

As indicated previously, "fasting of the mind" and "self-forgetting" are both ways leading a person to be with the *Dao*, Zhuangzi's ideal ethical state, and to be a perfected person, the ultimate ethical goal for a person. "Fasting of the mind" is to expel all distracting thoughts in the mind and be single-minded. One does this in order to listen with the spirit so as to reach the "emptiness" where the *Dao* resides. The notion of "fasting of the mind" echoes a Christian understanding of the beatitude: "Blessed are the pure in heart, for they will see God" (Matt. 5:8).

According to Augustine's interpretation, it is impossible or even foolish for a person to seek God with the bodily eyes, because God is only seen with the heart. Not just in heart can one seek God, but in the singleness of heart, because a pure heart is a single heart.[25] For Zhuangzi, the mind cannot be attentive if one listens with the ears. Only in being single-minded can one grasp the spirit and reach the realm of the *Dao*.

The "heart" and "mind" have different connotations in Western thinking, but in Chinese understanding, they are interchangeable. Literally in the Chinese language, "fasting of the mind" is read as "fasting of the heart." Zhuangzi's "fasting of the heart" and Jesus' "purity in heart" are not alien to each other in a Chinese understanding. In fact, they carry the same message: if a person wants to transcend his or her own limitation and to have a profound self-transformation, he or she has to begin with the heart or the mind. Moreover, both of these notions are seen as a means of leading a person to a higher spiritual realm: to be with the *Dao* or to be with God.

Zhuangzi's "self-forgetting" is to eliminate the self that is in opposition to the *Dao*, so that the self can be at one with the wholeness of the *Dao*. This also echoes what it is written in Scripture: "If any want to become my followers, let them deny themselves and take up their cross and follow me" (Matt. 16:24). It is in following Jesus' example of self-denial in taking up the cross as he emptied and humbled himself (Phil. 2:7-8) that Christians can properly be called Jesus' disciples or God's children. Similarly, in dealing with the outer world, if a person is not willing to give up that which is required for the cost of discipleship, he or she will not be part of the kingdom of God.

Zhuangzi understands that the one who is able to fast the mind and forget the self is a perfected person with a perfected mind. The perfected mind

---

25. Augustine, *The Preaching of Augustine: "Our Lord's Sermon on the Mount,"* ed. Jaroslav Pelikan (Philadelphia: Fortress, 1973), p. 28.

is like a mirror that only reflects without applying its own interpretations, making its own judgments, or possessing its own desires. If a mirror tries to do something other than reflecting, it is no longer a correct mirror that reflects things impartially. What about the mind of a person if it does something contrary to its nature?

While interpreting the beatitudes, Augustine relates them to both the gifts of the Holy Spirit and the petitions in the Lord's Prayer. Thus, the sixth beatitude, "Blessed are the pure in heart, for they will see God," is in relation with the prayer "do not bring us to the time of trial" (Matt. 6:13). Augustine writes, "If understanding is that by which the pure of heart are blessed, since they will see God, let us not be led into temptation, lest we have a double heart from not seeking after the single good to which we refer everything we do and from pursuing temporal and eternal things at the same time."[26] For Augustine, temptation is what can draw people to have a double heart or to seek after more than a single good. Indeed, Adam and Eve, making their own interpretations and judgments with their own desires, fell into such a temptation. After that, they were no longer as God created when "God saw that it was very good" (Gen. 1:31).

As Zhuangzi describes, the perfected mind is also like a hinge fitted into a socket. The hinge moves smoothly in its socket; it does not stand for "this" or against "that"; it only responds from a center without any bias or prejudice. With such an attitude, a person is able to see things equally as well as to apply equality in human relations, in which friendship is regarded as the model.

Although as scholars have pointed out, the moral role of friendship is seldom mentioned in Christian ethics and receives scarce attention in theological, biblical, or liturgical reflection,[27] the concept of friendship does appear in the Bible. Jesus said, "This is my commandment, that you love one another as I have loved you. . . . You are my friends if you do what I command you" (John 15:12, 14). While acknowledging the fact that God and human beings can never be equal, we should also realize that the friendship announced by Jesus does bridge a hierarchical gap and leads human beings to a closer relationship to God through the incarnated Divinity. As Jesus said, "I do not call you servants any longer, because the servant does not know what the master is doing; but I have called you friends, because I have made

---

26. Augustine, *The Preaching of Augustine*, p. 131.

27. Joseph Kotva, *The Christian Case for Virtue Ethics* (Washington, DC: Georgetown University Press, 1996), p. 172. See also Elizabeth A. Johnson, *She Who Is: The Mystery of God in Feminist Theological Discourse* (New York: Crossroad, 2003), p. 145.

known to you everything that I have heard from my Father" (John 15:15). To acquire such a wonderful friendship, we need to follow the commandment of loving one another as Jesus has loved us. The love that Jesus loves or the love that Christians should learn to know is an equal love, a love that "does not stand for this or against that," and a love that not only loves our neighbor, but also loves our enemy. With this kind of love, we can be called children of our Father in heaven, and "become participants of the divine nature" (2 Peter 1:4).

Not all Christians in China are familiar with Zhuangzi's ethics, philosophy, or even the figure of Zhuangzi, especially those in the rural areas who constitute the majority of Chinese churches. The biblical teachings, however, such as the beatitudes, the Lord's Prayer, the story of Adam and Eve, and the texts about Jesus humbling himself, are well known among Chinese Christians, for these passages are often preached from the pulpit. Knowledge of biblical passages is a good thing and important to Christian life, but the application of these passages to our daily life is not always easy. Nevertheless, applying the biblical teachings to our real life is an imperative for Christians. Zhuangzi's ethical viewpoints may offer us some insights in fulfilling our Christian task.

What it means to be a Christian and how to live a Christian life are questions often asked and discussed among Chinese Christians. Many would agree that the ideal Christian person is to "Be perfect, therefore, as your heavenly Father is perfect" (Matt. 5:48). As mentioned previously, for Zhuangzi, to be a perfected person is to banish all disruptive thoughts so as to grasp the essence of things, and to overcome the selfish nature in order to be in accord with the *Dao*, the authentic nature. Since the perfected person is able to seize the essence of things and to become authentic, he or she is without partiality and can reflect things as they are without subjectivity. Following Zhuangzi, to remove the impediments in Chinese Christians' understanding of the essence of Christian faith, we need to first outline some of the distracting thoughts that they may have.

According to the Christian historian Ryan Dunch, many Chinese Protestants, especially in rural areas, understand their Christian faith in a way similar to Chinese folk religions: Jesus is treated as a Chinese deity, a source from which to seek healing for illness and other supernatural help.[28] Many

---

28. Ryan Dunch, "Protestant Christianity in China Today: Fragile, Fragmented, Flourishing," in *China and Christianity: Burdened Past and Hopeful Future*, ed. Stephen Uhalley, Jr., and Xiaoxin Wu (Armonk: M. E. Sharpe, 2001), p. 203.

Christians in the cities also believe that going to church on Sundays, or having a family member as a seminary student, will win God's pleasure and bring health and well-being to the whole family.[29] We cannot say that these Christians are absolutely wrong, but their understanding of the Christian faith does not reach the essence of Christianity. The authentic meaning of being Christian is to follow Jesus' commandants of loving God with all our heart, all our soul, and all our mind, and loving our neighbors as ourselves. Seeking only what we can get from God, the church or church people act in contradiction to Jesus' commandments, even though God is always willing to give.

To be Christian is to follow Jesus' example of serving people instead of being served, of taking up the cross, and of self-humbling and self-emptying. While being aware of the difficulties in such a Christian task, we should remind ourselves more often of the importance of responding to this particular call of Jesus and go to great efforts to put it into practice in our daily life. Unfortunately, some of us often forget this. This has resulted in conflicts among Christians, among church workers, and even among church leaders at various levels. The conflicts are often caused due to "this" or "that" group's being judgmental, "this" or "that" person's being self-seeking, or "this" or "that" party's prejudice against the other. Conflicts induce oppositions and division. When there is division among Christians, we have lost unity, the unity in Jesus Christ who is our center, the "axis in a circle." As a result, there is no harmonious relationship among fellow Christians.

For Zhuangzi, the ideal human relationship is based on the model of friendship, embodying the spirit of equality. In general, the Chinese church appreciates the idea of equality in human relations, but there is still a minority who do not welcome it. Some of us prefer hierarchy to equality, because the hierarchical relationship enables us to grab more power, be more privileged, enjoy more benefits, and get more opportunities. It could be that we forget that we are supposed to be servants as Jesus served, that the church is a place for the people of God gathered in service to the world, not a place for career development.

Although there is not much inequality in the relationships among the common Christians in China, some Christians like to draw a line between believers and nonbelievers. Some think that Christians are the chosen ones, and that there is no significant common ground for us to associate with the

---

29. K. H. Ting, "One Chinese Christian's View of God," in *Love Never Ends: Papers by K. H. Ting*, ed. Janice Wickeri (Nanjing: Yilin Press, 2000), p. 434.

rest of the people. Some of us tend to belittle the true, the good, and the beautiful outside the church. In fact, we may forget that God is a cosmic lover[30] who loves the whole world, not only Christians; God "makes the sun rise on the evil and on the good" and "sends rain on the righteous and on the unrighteous" (Matt. 5:45). It is as if we forget that it is God who has the final word on what is good or evil, or who is righteous or unrighteous. Zhuangzi's teaching on equality may broaden our horizons if we are humble enough to listen to it.

Zhuangzi's ethical insights not only are relevant to Chinese Christians but can also be helpful in Chinese society, especially in the enhancement of its social morality. If more people in society followed Zhuangzi's teachings of "fasting the mind" and "self-forgetting" and learned to reduce their selfish desires and appreciate what has been achieved in their life, there would be less corruption, bribery, embezzlement, production and/or sale of fake products, or illegal activities driven by unrestrained avarice. If society applies more the idea of equality in human relations, it will decrease the gap between officials and nonofficials, between the wealthy and the poor, between the urban and the rural. All people have their unique roles to play in society, according to their abilities and opportunities, despite their social status. For each of them contributes to society's prosperity, as Zhuangzi teaches that all things are equal, and each person is part of Heaven and needs to fulfill a particular role in the scheme of the greater natural pattern.

With such a vision, in building up a harmonious society, everyone is able to "use his knowledge of what he knows to help out the knowledge of what he doesn't know, and lives out the years that Heaven gave him without being cut off midway."[31] Zhuangzi's own words tell us that he is neither an amoralist nor a relativist. As Wing-tsit Chan writes, Zhuangzi "seems to transcend the mundane world, yet he is always in the very depth of daily life. He is a quietist, yet for him life moves on like a galloping horse. He is mystical, but at the same time he follows reason as the leading light."[32]

---

30. K. H. Ting addresses God as the cosmic Lover, or Creator-Lover, who is revealed through Jesus Christ, both the lover of men and women and in whom all things are created. See "One Chinese Christian's View of God," p. 434.

31. *The Complete Works of Chuang Tzu*, p. 77.

32. *A Source Book in Chinese Philosophy*, p. 177.

19 A Flourishing Discipline: Reflections on the Study of Christianity in Academic Institutions in China Today

Wu Xiaoxin

The history of Christianity in China reflects complex and sometimes tumultuous social, political, economic, and cultural encounters and exchanges between China and the West. Similarly, the study of Christianity in China and its relationship with the study of other religions in China reflects equal amounts of tension and complexity from the stage of its infancy to its current status of development in China today.

It is generally recognized that, chronologically, religious studies as an academic discipline[1] in China have gone through three stages of development during the past one hundred years. In his article summarizing this development, Professor Zhuo Xinping confirms the three-period analogy by saying that the first period was from the beginning of the twentieth century to 1949, the second from 1949 to 1978, and the third from 1978 to the end of the twentieth century.[2]

Each period, rather than being viewed in chronological isolation, is shaped and influenced by the social and political atmosphere in which religious studies evolved. New social and political changes in each successive pe-

1. As a matter of convenience, the phrase "religious studies" in this essay mainly refers to the study of Christianity unless otherwise specified.

2. Zhuo Xinping, "The Hundred Year Chronology of Religious Studies in China," *China Study Journal* 16, no. 1 (2001): 27-29.

This essay is based on an earlier survey commissioned by the Henry Luce Foundation. I wish to express my gratitude to Dr. Terrill Lautz for his encouragement to share my report with others.

riod provide conditions that influence religious studies as they assume their new forms. This was, is, and will continue to be an important factor for any future development of religious studies in China.

Looking back, it is not hard to realize that it is the third period, the years between 1979 and the present, that has witnessed a new birth in religious studies. The reasons behind this change, of course, are multifaceted. While the official explanation may attribute the blooming phenomenon to the openness of the social and political policies that the government has been vigorously implementing since 1979, scholars, both Chinese and Western, view such a change not only as a revival of an academic subject that had been politically dismissed for half a century, but also as a direct academic response in the wake of the surging interest among ordinary people in search of a vital spiritual life under the new social and economic environment that China is currently embracing.[3]

The focus of religious studies, the study of Christianity in particular, has also undergone remarkable changes in the last twenty years. Generally, it has developed from the more traditional data collections and text annotations and analyses, translation of classics, historical and missiological accounts of events, to multilevel and interdisciplinary studies involving an increasing number of scholars with an unprecedented number of publications. As Nicolas Standaert has emphasized, "In the past twenty-five years an important paradigm shift took place in the study of Christianity in China. In general, this shift can be described as a change from a mainly missiological and Eurocentric to a Sinological and Sino-centric approach."[4]

Parallel to the speed of economic development in China, changes have been taking place in religious studies at an overwhelming pace, with rich substance. This paper therefore is set against such a background. It is intended to reflect on the following questions: What is the landscape for religious studies in China today?[5] What are the issues, as observed, that may affect future development in this field?

---

3. Gianni Criveller, "Christian Studies in Mainland China," *Tripod* 21, no. 122 (Summer 2001): 22-27.

4. Nicolas Standaert, "New Trends in the Historiography of Christianity in China," *The Catholic Historical Review* 83, no. 4 (1997): 573-74.

5. Statistics used in this report are by no means completely thorough and inclusive. Based on selected publications and informal research, they are used to illustrate general trends in religious studies rather than a comprehensive and statistical analysis of particular areas.

The Landscape: Development of Religious Studies in China Today

The reform and more open policies of the Chinese government in the late 1970s brought tremendous changes to the country. "What is more important," as Zhang Kaiyuan points out, "is that the increasingly frequent exchanges between China and foreign countries have enhanced research on the history of Chinese-foreign cultural communications."[6] Academic research in both science and humanities began to revive after decades at a standstill. Religious studies also gradually began to receive increasing attention from scholars.

With the gradual disappearance of the politically charged notion of religion as "superstition" and "spiritual opium," it began to be viewed, even by the government, as a cultural phenomenon with deep roots in history and tradition, a social reality that continues to play an important role in almost every aspect of human life.

One unique development in the 1980s is that, in addition to the traditional focus on the late Ming and early Qing exchanges through Catholic missionaries (mid-sixteenth to the early nineteenth centuries), scholars began to explore the interactions between China and the West through Protestant missionaries. Zhang Kaiyuan credits it to Gu Changsheng, who authored two well-accepted books in 1981 and 1986, respectively, on Protestant missions in China. "Though the historical conditions cited contained a few biased or false points," Zhang comments, "they could still be regarded as works that initiated the current trends."[7]

But more significant is the start of research work in the late 1980s at the Central China Normal University on the history of Christian universities and colleges in China. This project-based initiative sparked new opportunities. It was the beginning of a community of scholars from different parts of the country with the same interests. Such a phenomenon may be taken for granted in Western countries, but it is truly remarkable given the history of China. Moreover, with a new emphasis on the study of original sources, the first completely open archives were established on the premises of the school, which still provides regular public service today.

Third, although small in number in the 1980s, there was a growing inter-

---

6. Zhang Kaiyuan, "Chinese Perspective — A Brief Review of the Historical Research on Christianity in China," in *China and Christianity*, ed. Stephen Uhalley and Wu Xiaoxin (New York: Sharpe, 2000), p. 33.

7. Zhang Kaiyuan, "Chinese Perspective," p. 35.

est among the younger generation of professors and their students in religious theories and systems.[8] To meet the demands and fill in the gap for the shortage of trained professionals, lecture series at higher educational institutions became a popular format for learning. For example, foreign scholars were invited during this period to offer such lectures on the Bible, John's Gospel, religious studies in the United States, etc., at both Beijing University and Fudan University in Shanghai. The lecture series model inspired many young people for their scholarly interest and still remains popular at schools today.

The Growth of Religious Studies since the 1990s

The development of religious studies in the 1990s is marked by the establishment of an increasing number of new institutions and programs, advancement in credentials of a growing number of younger scholars, and expansion of diversified subjects in the field as indicated by publications and conferences.

New Institutions and Programs

Institutionalization of religious studies in China is not a "post–Cultural Revolution" phenomenon. In fact, the well-known Institute of World Religions of the Chinese Academy of Social Sciences was established as early as 1964. Similar institutions have been in existence for many years.[9] However, because these government institutions were either attached to an academy or under the supervision of the local religious affairs bureau, their functions were mostly limited to theoretical research or were considered as secondary reference sources by the government for religious policies. This by and large continued into the early 1990s.

---

8. Theology courses are not, and will not be in the foreseeable future, permitted in higher educational institutions in China. However, religious theories and systems have been gradually accepted as the basis for classes in religious studies departments at universities.

9. Some of these institutes are the Institute of Islamic Studies at the Academy of Social Sciences in Ningxia Autonomous Region, the Institute of Minority Studies of Gansu Province, the Research Development of the Chinese Society of Taoism, the Chinese Institute of Buddhist Studies, and the Chinese Institute of Islamic Studies. See *Guonei zongjiao yanjiu jiaoxue jigou* (Religious Research and Teaching Institutions within China), ed. Cao Zhongjian, pp. 385-426.

The last decade in the twentieth century witnessed rapid development in religious studies in China, especially in the study of Christianity. First, over a dozen new institutes, centers, and departments of religious studies were established throughout China in academies and universities. Presently, they not only exist in such internationally known universities as Beijing University, Renmin University (also known as People's University), Fudan University, Tsinghua University, Nanjing University, Nankai University (Tianjin), and Central China Normal University (Wuhan), but also have taken root in less-known schools such as the Central University for Nationalities (Beijing), Fujian Normal University, Wuhan University, Zhejiang University, Sichuan University, and Shaanxi Normal University.

Moreover, in the year 2000, as part of a national endeavor to promote academic research, two institutions, the Institute for the Study of Buddhism and Theories of Religious Studies at Renmin University in Beijing and the Institute for the Study of Taoism and Religious Culture at Sichuan University, have been selected with ninety-eight other institutions as "established educational and research bases" in humanities under the State Educational Commission. Although these names may appear to be awkward, reflecting political considerations intended to promote the "Chinese religions" of Buddhism and Taoism against the "foreign religions" of Protestantism and Catholicism, to include religious studies in the government's "key" research agenda is an encouraging sign. Such a prestigious status not only offers additional and unprecedented government financial support and priority for qualified personnel needs and equipment, but also has more administrative freedom, such as an approval by the home university to sponsor international conferences.[10] The scholarly impact of such establishments, of course, remains to be seen in the years to come.

It should be pointed out that many of the new institutions regularly enroll Ph.D. students. Some schools, such as Beijing University, Fudan University, and Wuhan University, have also established religious studies departments in conjunction with philosophy departments. Although they may appear to be relatively slow in coming, it signifies that this particular field is being recognized by the government today as an established discipline in the academic curriculum of universities.

10. Normally, any international conference within a higher educational institution has to be approved by both the university and the Educational Commission of the central government.

More Scholars with Advanced Credentials

Along with the establishment of new institutions, scholars in the field have been growing in number and are better equipped with advanced credentials. In the mid-1980s, as Chinese scholars were beginning to display renewed interest in religious studies, few received advanced academic training. A decade later, the landscape changed completely. An annual conference hosted for several years by the Institute of World Religions of the Chinese Academy of Social Sciences regularly attracts more than a hundred participants from all over the country. Most of these scholars are in their forties and fifties, and many publish regularly in this field. Some were educated abroad, but many received their advanced degrees in China in the 1990s. The number will continue to increase as more candidates graduate from the institutions in religious studies in the coming years.

What is more encouraging is the even more rapid growth of the younger generation of scholars. In 2002, the Center for the Study of Religion and Chinese Society of Chung Chi College, the University of Hong Kong, and the Ricci Institute for Chinese-Western Cultural History at the University of San Francisco co-sponsored a symposium for young Chinese scholars. Titled "Christianity and Chinese Culture and Society," this symposium was attended by thirty-two young Chinese Ph.D. and M.A. candidates from over thirteen universities in China. Further, at the time this paper was written, the second symposium, scheduled to take place in December 2004, had attracted approximately one hundred applicants.

These trends suggest that in China today this field is staffed by people with both enthusiasm and academic experience. Moreover, they indicate that the field will be even more vibrant in the near future.

Expansion of Research Subjects

A significant advancement in religious studies can be seen through the quality of scholarly meetings that have been taking place during the past two decades. On a national level, between 1981 and 1996 there were approximately twenty national and international conferences with religion as the general theme. These meetings were sponsored by government institutions — the Academy of Social Sciences, the Ministry of United Front, the Religious Affairs Bureau, or an academic society. In the 1980s, the theme was exclusively on religious policies. In the first six years of the 1990s, general themes of the meetings began to expand and involvement of higher educational institutions in sponsorship became more apparent. Some of the subjects included the meaning and contents of religious studies, religion and culture, religion and economic development, Chinese religious culture in the context of world culture, the Boxer rebellion and anti-Christian movements, the history of Christian universities and colleges, Sino-Western exchanges in the late Ming and early Qing eras, religion and philosophy, religion as a cross-cultural exchange phenomenon, etc.[11]

Between 1999 and 2001, however, over twenty-five national and international conferences were held in China. Not only do people see more collaboration between academies and universities, it is also obvious that such meetings have been held more frequently in collaboration with foreign organizations, such as those in France, Germany, Italy, Japan, and the United States. The subject matter during this period continued to expand to include Islamic culture and Chinese nationality, Christianity and science, religious experience and cultural values, religion and peace, religion and civilization at the threshold of the new millennium, dialogues among religions, research concepts and methodology in religious studies, Buddhism and modern civilization, religion and humanities, etc.[12]

Besides conferences, the most extraordinary development in recent years in religious studies in China is reflected in publications. The entire field of religious studies is blossoming, with a record number of publications that touch upon many subjects in unprecedented magnitude. A bibliography compiled in 1998 indicates that from 1950 to 1980, there were barely 150 or so articles in China on Christianity in China. Almost all of these appeared exclusively in official newspapers with a monologue style of condemnation of Western imperialism. The number of publications soared to about 2,300 in total from 1980 to 1997, and their appearance can be found in almost every province of the country, and in newspapers and journals of all kinds.[13] An informal survey in preparation for this paper reveals that between 1998 and the early part of 2001, over 350 articles, excluding books and monograph

---

11. Yu Guang, "Summary of the Scholarly Conferences in Religious Studies in China, 1979-1996," in *Zhongguo Zongjiao Nianjian,* ed. Cao Zhongjian (Beijing: Zhongguo shehui kexue chubanshe, 1996), pp. 337-44.

12. The data is based on an informal bibliographical search by a Chinese scholar. I am indeed grateful for his assistance.

13. Bian Xiaoli et al., "Bibliography of Research Articles on the History of Christianity in China: 1949-1997," in *Jidu Zongjiao Yanjiu* (Study of Christianity), ed. Zhuo Xinping and Xu Zhuwei (Beijing: Zhongguo shehui kexue chubanshe, 1999), pp. 245-401.

series, were published in journals and magazines in China. "Not a single field of specialty in China," observed a Chinese scholar, "has experienced such a drastic change in its nature, depth, and breadth in the past fifty years."

A quick examination of the kind of publications may also offer useful content information in religious studies to which Chinese scholars in the past decade have devoted their efforts. First, study of the Sino-Western exchanges in the late Ming to mid-Qing dynasties remains very popular. Described by Zhang Kaiyuan as having an "inherent advantage" derived from earlier academic traditions in China,[14] this "research paradigm has been to a great extent both refined and broadened" in the past two decades.[15] Published articles on the early Jesuit mission, on missions of other Catholic societies, as well as on individual missionaries are abundant, and topics range from document studies to exchanges in art, science, religion and philosophy, societies, and civilizations.

Surveying publications relating to the late nineteenth through the mid-twentieth centuries, one quickly realizes that there are other predominant themes. History remains the strongest discipline, and it is expanding into the history of local church development, both Catholic and Protestant, and other mission-supported endeavors. Studies on Christian schools, mainly at the higher educational level, have developed rather extensively. Over a hundred individual papers appeared in different academic journals and as chapters in books during this time. Moreover, studies in this area have developed from general history to "the sharpest intellectual debates that revolve around the question of the precise roles played by mission schools, and the significance of their influence at local, regional, and national levels,"[16] creating a more in-depth base for future discussions.

Another significant advancement is the recognition by Chinese scholars of Chinese Protestantism. Publications appear with higher frequency on this subject as time passes by. Many of these studies seem to have "bypassed" the phase of condemnation of Christian missionaries. In this area, serious scholarly publications tend to focus on activities of individual denominations, such as the Methodist, Baptist, or Presbyterian churches, and in national minority-concentrated provinces, such as Yunnan and Sichuan. It should also be noted that scholars are becoming more aware of the presence of

14. Zhang Kaiyuan, "Chinese Perspective," p. 33.

15. Eugenio Menegon, a book review in *China Review International* 8, no. 1 (2001): 118.

16. Shen Dingping and Zhu Weifang, "Western Missionary Influence on the People's Republic of China: A Survey of Chinese Scholarly Opinions Between 1980 and 1990," *International Bulletin of Missionary Research* 22, no. 4 (1998): 156.

Christianity locally and have been producing research papers on related subjects as well. Such a move signifies the realization by many people that Christianity in China is gradually being recognized as an integral part of Chinese society and culture.

One notices that publications gradually become more scholarly in focus and less politically charged. Take the study of the anti-Christian movements — for example, over 200 articles were produced between 1980 and 1997 in newspapers and journals. Most center on anti-Christian incidents during the Boxer movement. Many articles are obviously written with the preconceived notion that these incidents were "anti-foreign imperialistic invasions." However, between 1998 and 2001, there were only a dozen or so such papers published in academic journals, signifying an attitude change toward this episode in China's history.[17]

In recent years, two subject areas that have begun to attract great attention are comparative religion (between Christianity and Buddhism, Taoism, Confucianism, or Islam) and comparative culture studies. Approximately one hundred out of 350 papers published between 1998 and April 2001 deal with these subjects. Publications introducing theological theories from the West, the issue of "Chinese theology," indigenization of the church, exploration of religious concepts, and discussion on the Bible are also apparent. Also visible are the number of recent translations of the works of contemporary Western theologians and philosophers.

Some efforts among institutions and scholars have been devoted to publication of archival materials or catalogues. The much-appreciated collection of archival catalogues relating to Christian universities and colleges edited by Peter Ng in Hong Kong in 1998 includes the holdings of two archives and three universities in China. In October 2003, a collection of facsimiles of over 1,300 Qing documents on Western missionary activities was published by the First Historical Archives in Beijing.

And finally, it is important to be aware that almost none of the newly established institutions in religious studies produce regular magazines, partly due to the complexity of the approval procedures. Instead, three of those institutions, namely, the Institute of World Religions of the Chinese Academy of Social Sciences, the Institute of Christian Culture Studies of Renmin Uni-

---

17. Although the canonization incident between China and the Vatican in October 2000 drew a wave of condemnations in the press and publications in the Chinese press, scholars I interviewed for this survey regarded such a move as political rather than scholarly, thus with little, if any, academic value.

versity, and the Christianity Research Center of Zhejiang University, publish regular monograph/journal series with a similar signature theme, "religion and culture." They have gradually become important and regular publications that scholars look for as an important reference and information source in religious studies today.

Observations for Institutional Growth

The landscape of religious studies in China today is constantly changing with new departments, institutes, and centers being proposed and established each year. Institutionalization of religious studies both as an academic discipline and as research focus guarantees a promising future for this subject. Therefore, it is important to discuss some of the unique aspects of some institutions in regard to the future development of religious studies in China. As Zhuo Xinping points out, there are four kinds of institutions in China today that are engaged in religious studies: government departments, research institutes under the Academy of Social Sciences, departments, centers, and institutes under the university system, and seminaries of both Catholic and Protestant churches.[18] My discussion is limited to the second and third kinds of institutions as identified by Zhuo, namely, academic institutions.

Many similarities and differences exist among institutions and programs in religious studies in China today. Through many encounters and visits I have had in recent years, I am intrigued that most of the institutions are headed by energetic, open-minded, well-accomplished, and relatively young scholars. Obviously, some institutions are more advanced than others in terms of mission and long-term plans, curriculum development, scholarly achievements as an institution, collaborations with other institutions at home and abroad, financial resources, and personnel support. Among these institutes, detailed "dream plans" differ, the amount of available funding varies, and participation of colleagues within an institution depends on particular circumstances.

It will be almost impossible to list all departments and centers within a limited space. To begin with, the Philosophy/Religious Studies Department of Beijing University is perhaps the oldest to offer undergraduate education in religious studies since the 1980s. Tsinghua University, Beijing, which tra-

18. Zhuo Xinping, "The Study of Christianity in China Today," *Chinese Theological Review* 15 (2001): 1-3.

ditionally specialized in science and technology, also established a Center for the Study of Religion and Ethics in 2001. The Christianity Research Center at Zhejiang University, Hangzhou, is among the earliest research centers in universities that produce regular monograph publications on the study of Christian religions. Even in the Central University for Nationalities, Beijing, which focuses on academic programs on studies of ethnic nationalities in China, there are professors who devote their research to and offer courses on the study of Christianity in China. This indicates how rapidly this special field has been expanding institutionally. Therefore, by introducing a few specific institutions below, I hope to offer a glimpse of how institutions in religious studies in China have evolved, and what unique contributions they have made in this field.

1. A Service-Oriented Center: Research Center for History of Chinese Christian Colleges at the Central China Normal University, Hubei Province

Officially established in 1992, this center is a research institution that devotes its attention to the historical and cultural exchanges through mission studies, with an emphasis on the history of Christian colleges and universities. The center has proven itself, through its own achievements, to be an innovative leader in the field by not only regularly sponsoring unique scholarly meetings and producing publications, but more important, consistently collecting primary source materials.

In addition to all archival materials on the history of Central China Normal University, which was evolved from a Christian school, the center also holds a unique collection of microfilms, including "Archives of United Board for Christian Higher Education in China," "Church Mission Society," "China through Western Eyes: Manuscript Records of Missionaries and Diplomats (1792-1942)," "Methodist Missionary Society Archives (China part, 1791-1948)," "Methodist Episcopal Church (Board of Foreign Missions, China part)," "Presbyterian Church of England Foreign Missions Archives (China part)," and "American Board of Commissioners for Foreign Mission (China part)," just to name a few. What is more important, and unprecedented in China, is that all of these materials are open unconditionally to researchers and students. While many institutes and departments have "reference rooms" of their own with limited public access, and individual researchers and professors may have a small personal library that may be off-limits to others, this center provides the unconditional service that is crucial and basic for anyone interested in the subject. For this, it is indeed another pioneer in China.

2. A True Facilitator: Institute of World Religions at the Academy of Social Sciences, Beijing

This is one of the early institutions established for religious studies in China. Traditionally, its key social function was to serve the government in its capacity as a "think-tank" for policymaking decisions. It has a few dozen regular full-time and well-established researchers specialized in all the main religions in China. In recent years, however, it is being challenged by a growing number of institutions in the higher educational sector with much more innovative initiatives, creativity, and flexibility. In a more practical sense, due to the still rather rigid salary and benefits system within the government, it also faces competition from higher educational institutions with higher salaries, better housing accommodations, and even more academic freedom.

Nevertheless, the institute has "reinvented" itself in recent years. Taking advantage of its status as a government institution, it has been playing a new and unique role in the wake of increasing interests in religious studies in China. In the past few years, it has organized in collaboration with both academic as well as church-based organizations home and abroad a number of groundbreaking international conferences. For the first time since the founding of the People's Republic, government officials, scholars, and clergy from different denominations and religions from China and foreign countries have had the opportunity to sit together and discuss the role of religions on an equal basis at these meetings. This is a remarkable accomplishment that institutions in higher education have difficulty achieving, because of their own limitations.

By positing itself as a facilitator and collaborator rather than a competitor, the institute has also successfully organized a series of annual *shenxian hui* ("all saints meetings") among Chinese scholars in the field since 1998.[19]

19. Similar to an old Taoist fable that saints *(shenxian)* of different kinds would meet *(hui)* periodically about matters of common interests, the name "all saints meeting" is given to those meetings. Presenters from different disciplines are often loosely grouped together according to their proposed subjects, and programs for the meetings are less structured.

Although the atmosphere at those meetings is informal and the quality of scholarship varies, they are a positive measure of encouragement for scholars and a treasured occasion for association and networking. As a result, the institute itself is gradually proving to be a vital force in promoting religious studies in China in light of global changes.

3. An Innovative Department: Department of Philosophy/Religious Studies at Fudan University, Shanghai

One common characteristic among the programs that offer degrees in religious studies in China is that all of them are linked to a philosophy department. This is certainly true for the Department of Philosophy/Religious Studies at Fudan University in Shanghai. Although it shares faculty members with other departments, and operates without its own independent budget and administrative personnel, the program nevertheless consists of a comprehensive and well-developed curriculum for an undergraduate major in religious studies. In addition to courses that can be found in other schools, its curriculum also includes as required classes religious psychology, religion and science, religion and national minorities, and religion and literature. Religious studies majors also have to choose Latin, Greek, Hebrew, or Sanskrit as a second foreign language.

It should also be pointed out that the Philosophy Department of Fudan University has been entrusted many times by the Religious Affairs Bureau of the central government to offer training courses for religious affairs officials. The credibility the department has gained from the government certainly will play a positive role in the years to come. One concrete example is a new initiative by the department. Approved by the government, in collaboration with the local "Three-Self Movement," the department in 2003 developed a new cohort-based M.A. program for over thirty Protestant clergy. This two-year program consists of many classes that are otherwise unavailable in seminaries, whose degrees are not recognized by the Ministry of Education. It will only be a matter of time until a similar program will be offered in collaboration with the Catholic organizations. It is a special niche that this department has developed on the basis of its curriculum development experience. Such an innovative approach is yet another way to promote education among the clergy and create a bridge between religious and academic institutions. Undoubtedly, its educational and social impact will be profound in the years to come.

4. An Institute within an Institute: Institute of Christian Culture Studies at Renmin University, Beijing

The Department of Philosophy of Renmin University offers degrees and a variety of courses in religious studies, including Christianity. Moreover, a special Institute of Christian Culture Studies operates within the Institute for the Study of Buddhism and Theories of Religious Studies, one of the two centers approved in 2000 as research bases in religious studies under the higher educational system. Although the rationale for such an obscure administrative arrangement may be hard to understand for outsiders, it does not prevent the institute itself from conducting unique projects and producing remarkable research results. Traditionally, Renmin University was best known for its efforts to train qualified administrators of the government and Communist Party. The new status certainly offers this institute within an institute more opportunities for the immediate future.

For the past years, the institute has consistently devoted great effort to its key academic product, a biannual publication called *Jidujiao Wenhua Xuekan* (Journal of Christian Culture). It is one of the few regularly published journals in religious studies in China today. In addition to many unique features in this publication, the institute has been practicing a national peer and anonymous review system for all of its articles to be published. In the midst of rapid development in religious studies, it addresses the increasing concern for quality scholarship among researchers in this field.

Recently, on the basis of a nationwide project, "The Cultural Role of Religion in a Period of Social Transformation in China Today," which is part of a major research program in humanities sponsored by the Ministry of Education, the institute has engaged itself in a new initiative to promote exploration of research methodology in religious studies today. In October 2003, a seminar on this subject, apparently the first of its kind in China, was held between eighteen Chinese and American scholars in philosophy, sociology, anthropology, theology, psychology, and education. In 2004, a summer workshop was held in Beijing for empirical research methodology and religious studies by the institute and by Purdue University in the U.S.

A Few Reflections

The above discussion offers a stimulating picture of religious studies in China today. Instead of treading timidly in a long-forbidden area of historical and cultural controversies, social sensitivities, and even political "land-mines," Chinese scholars are gradually establishing religious studies as a new, rich, multidimensional, and Chinese discipline. Given time, the efforts by institutions and individual scholars will produce profound educational, scholarly, social, and even theological impact in China in the near future.

Certainly, these developments suggest grounds for optimism. On the other hand, it is important to note that "these optimistic developments for religious studies in China have to be seen in the perspective of the enormous investment that is being made generally in higher education, and in the light of the strong secular and materialistic tide that characterizes life in China to-day and dominates the many changes that are taking place in society, despite some curiosity about religion and spirituality on the periphery."[20]

The refreshing reality also poses new challenges to all of us who have been witnessing the changes and working internationally with scholars, institutions, and also church organizations to promote education, scholarships, and other forms of exchanges with full sincerity and diligence. The following three points are some of my reflections on this new development.

1. Government Policies and Religious Studies

In a country where rapid economic and social changes have taken place while an authoritarian system remains at the helm, it is inevitable for people to be concerned about policies that are in place and about any possible change in the future. This is just as important to foreign scholars and institutions that are seeking to make meaningful contributions in the academy as it is to Chinese scholars and institutions.

The general consensus among Chinese scholars is that the decade of the 1990s was probably the most academically "relaxed" period in the history of the People's Republic. Although anything related to religion may still be perceived as sensitive by the government, one should realize that there are significant differences between policies toward churches or particular religions, which sometimes are considered rather strict especially by outsiders with less understanding of the complexity of Chinese society, and those toward religious studies. In the latter case, government control is not so much in what one can study or not study, or how to study (with the exception that one cannot preach inside a classroom), but more so on what one will produce pub-

20. Stephen Uhalley, Jr., personal correspondence with me, 2002.

licly in the form of scholarly meetings and even more so publications. In regard to approval procedures to hold conferences, especially in collaboration with foreign scholars and institutions, and censorship for publications, the power of the government is still paramount. In either case, the approval procedures can be administratively tedious and politically unpredictable.

Having pointed out the above, it is also evident that as China becomes more involved as an active member in the global community, the government has been demonstrating stronger interest in the role of religions in China's future development. In addition, positive changes are bound to take place as those in charge of government are now younger, better educated, and more prepared for the changing world.

2. Institutions with Strong Leadership Will Continue Playing a Leading Role

As discussed above, one of the most significant developments in religious studies is the number of institutions recognized by both individual scholars and government to offer educational programs and conduct scholarly research. Organizationally, many institutions bear much resemblance. Although each institution has its own strengths and weaknesses, and most scholars affiliated with those institutions are remarkable people with outstanding achievements as individuals, the potential for future success of an institution depends on many factors. Some of these factors about a well-developed institution include:

- whether it has regularly worked on particular areas of strength, with an established track record as an institution, rather than with sporadic projects that reflect a collection of individual interests;
- whether it has been steadily building up a good organizational structure that will sustain itself regardless of personnel changes;
- whether it has been continuously building a resource base that is "public-access" oriented instead of "internal use only," or as a personal collection of references;
- whether it has gradually developed a self-sustaining system with its own administrative personnel and funding, which includes both funds from the government and other sources, rather than a "one-man's shop" with few financial resources other than the salary of the director, which often comes from another department;

- whether it has been regularly promoting collaborative relationships with other institutions and individuals both from home and abroad, with recognized results; and
- whether it has been systematically developing plans that involve increasing participation by younger scholars rather than always maintaining a system of seniority for any opportunities.

Certainly, some of the institutions are more advanced than others in China today. With an institutional history of ten years or less, many institutions are still headed by the founding members. It becomes their responsibility to realize that there are basic criteria for them to achieve if they are to grow. As the field of religious studies in China deepens and becomes more competitive for stronger leadership, better scholarship, and stronger financial foundation, it is the uniqueness, not the duplication, of any given institution that will contribute most to the growth of this field.

3. Curriculum and Methodology Are Just as Important as Content Development

The progress in the landscape of religious studies in China described above provides the opportunity to reexamine the subject and new potentials in scholarship that will be of interest to both Chinese and foreign scholars. Evidently, there are many new areas that have evolved as the result of the rapid development in recent years, and each will contribute concretely and extensively to the future development of religious studies.

In an educational environment, curriculum and faculty development are the keys for future success. These two factors complement each other. Proper selection and adaptation of readily available pedagogical textbooks from abroad may be important, but it is even more important to systematically develop materials from within. Shortage of well-trained faculty members will remain a problem for the time being. The fact that most of the Chinese faculty members who teach religious studies course do not have much religious experience will also pose a special challenge. However, the demographic changes in recent years, encouraging exchanges and collaboration among scholars within a university and between universities, and that between Chinese and foreign scholars, seem to produce better results than offering scholarship money for lengthy doctoral training abroad.

As the field continues to develop, it is inevitable for more and more Chinese scholars to examine the relationship between religion and other disciplines, such as art, science, literature, "Chinese theology," archival research, oral history, etc. More important, the growing attention and desire in the past few years among scholars for interdisciplinary studies, either from the historical point of view or from the contemporary point of view, should be taken seriously. The nature of such an approach demands not only knowledge of a given subject but also awareness of as well as respect for other approaches. Therefore, it may even take time and creativity just to explore possible opportunities. Such interdisciplinary studies reflect the reality of the encounters between and among people through religion, and will enrich our knowledge in history and our experience in contemporary life.

Therefore, just as important as the contents of educational programs or research projects are the formats and methodologies employed for the above initiatives. Recognizing that many of the works produced in the past decade are the result of independent efforts by individual scholars, there is an urgent need for scholars, both Chinese and foreign, to exchange information and learn from each other about the basic methodology they have used to conduct research or to develop programs of mutual interest.

Conclusion

The field of religious studies in China is still developing. In this paper, I hoped to illustrate that this is a multilayered and multidimensional situation as the result of the historical, social, political, and even scholarly development in the country for the past two decades. Such an imbalance offers both risks and opportunities, a reality that Chinese scholars, together with their colleagues from abroad, are encountering. Eventually they will be able to find and define the new contents and, more significantly, the new or renewed meaning of this important field that has occupied the mind and touched the heart of so many of us for so long. We will all feel grateful and blessed for whatever we are able to contribute in the years to come.